This new edition of R. A. Hudson's widely acclaimed textbook *Sociolinguistics* will be welcomed by students and teachers alike. To reflect changes in the field since publication of the first edition in 1980, the author has added new sections on politeness, accommodation and prototypes; and he has expanded discussion of sex differences in language use, and the relationship between language and thought. Over a third of the second edition is completely new, and there is one entirely new chapter, but ample coverage of classic topics such as varieties of language, speech as social interaction, the quantitative study of speech and linguistic and social inequality, remains. Like the first, the second edition of *Sociolinguistics* is an exceptionally clear and helpful overview of the relationship of language and society.

CAMBRIDGE TEXTBOOKS IN LINGUISTICS

General editors: S. R. ANDERSON, J. BRESNAN, B. COMRIE,
W. DRESSLER, C. EWEN, R. HUDDLESTON, R. LASS, D. LIGHTFOOT,
J. LYONS, P. H. MATTHEWS, R. POSNER, S. ROMAINE, N. V. SMITH,
N. VINCENT

SOCIOLINGUISTICS
Second edition

In this series

P. H. MATTHEWS *Morphology* Second edition

B. COMRIE *Aspect*

R. M. KEMPSON *Semantic Theory*

T. BYNON *Historical Linguistics*

J. ALLWOOD, L.-G. ANDERSON and Ö. DAHL *Logic in Linguistics*

D. B. FRY *The Physics of Speech*

R. A. HUDSON *Sociolinguistics* Second edition

J. K. CHAMBERS and P. TRUDGILL *Dialectology*

A. J. ELLIOTT *Child Language*

P. H. MATTHEWS *Syntax*

A. RADFORD *Transformational Syntax*

L. BAUER *English Word-Formation*

S. C. LEVINSON *Pragmatics*

G. BROWN and G. YULE *Discourse Analysis*

R. HUDDLESTON *Introduction to the Grammar of English*

R. LASS *Phonology*

B. COMRIE *Tense*

W. KLEIN *Second Language Acquisition*

A. CRUTTENDEN *Intonation*

A. J. WOODS, P. FLETCHER and A. HUGHES *Statistics in Language Studies*

D. A. CRUSE *Lexical Semantics*

F. R. PALMER *Mood and Modality*

A. RADFORD *Transformational Grammar*

M. GARMAN *Psycholinguistics*

W. CROFT *Typology and Universals*

G. G. CORBETT *Gender*

H. J. GIEGERICH *English Phonology*

R. CANN *Formal Semantics*

P. J. HOPPER and E. C. TRAUGOTT *Grammaticalization*

J. LAVER *Principles of Phonetics*

F. R. PALMER *Grammatical Roles and Relations*

B. BLAKE *Case*

M. A. JONES *Foundations of French Syntax*

SOCIOLINGUISTICS

SECOND EDITION

R. A. HUDSON

PROFESSOR OF LINGUISTICS
UNIVERSITY COLLEGE LONDON

CAMBRIDGE
UNIVERSITY PRESS

Published by the Press Syndicate of the University of Cambridge
The Pitt Building, Trumpington Street, Cambridge CB2 1RP
40 West 20th Street, New York, NY 10011–4211, USA
10 Stamford Road, Oakleigh, Melbourne 3166, Australia

First published 1980
Second edition 1996

Printed in Great Britain at the University Press, Cambridge

A catalogue record for this book is available from the British Library

Library of Congress cataloguing in publication data

Hudson, Richard A.
Sociolinguistics / R. A. Hudson. – 2nd edn.
    p.   cm. – (Cambridge textbooks in linguistics)
Includes bibliographical references and index.
ISBN 0 521 56349 6 (hardback). – ISBN 0 521 56514 6 (paperback)
1. Sociolinguistics. 1. Title. 11. Series.
P40.HB 1996 95–44008 CIP
306.4'4 – dc20

First edition ISBN 0 521 22833 6 hardback
             ISBN 0 521 29668 4 paperback

ISBN 0 521 56349 6 hardback
ISBN 0 521 56514 6 paperback

KW

To LUCY, ALICE and GAYNOR

CONTENTS

Preface to the second edition   *page* xiii
Preface to the first edition   xv

1 Introduction   1
  1.1 Sociolinguistics   1
1.1.1 *A description*   1
1.1.2 *Sociolinguistics and linguistics*   2
1.1.3 *Sociolinguistics and the sociology of language*   4
  1.2 Sociolinguistic phenomena   5
1.2.1 *An imaginary world*   5
1.2.2 *A real but exotic world*   6
1.2.3 *A real and familiar world*   9
  1.3 Speakers and communities   10
1.3.1 *Conformity and individualism*   10
1.3.2 *The sociolinguistic development of the child*   14
  1.4 Summary and conclusions   17

2 Varieties of language   **20**
  2.1 Introduction   20
2.1.1 *Global and specific statements*   20
2.1.2 *Linguistic items*   21
2.1.3 *Varieties of language*   22
2.1.4 *'Speech communities'*   24
  2.2 Languages   30
2.2.1 *'Language' and 'dialect'*   30
2.2.2 *Standard languages*   32
2.2.3 *The delimitation of languages*   34
2.2.4 *The family tree model*   37
  2.3 Dialects   38
2.3.1 *Regional dialects and isoglosses*   38

2.3.2 *Diffusion and the wave theory*   39
2.3.3 *Social dialects*   41
2.3.4 *Types of linguistic item*   43
  2.4 Registers   45
2.4.1 *Registers and dialects*   45
2.4.2 *Diglossia*   49
  2.5 Mixture of varieties   51
2.5.1 *Code-switching*   51
2.5.2 *Code-mixing*   53
2.5.3 *Borrowing*   55
2.5.4 *Pidgins*   59
2.5.5 *Creoles*   63
  2.6 Conclusions   68

3 Language, culture and thought   **70**
  3.1 Introduction   70
3.1.1 *Culture*   71
3.1.2 *Thought*   72
3.1.3 *Language, culture and thought*   78
  3.2 Linguistic and cultural relativity   81
3.2.1 *Semantic relativity*   81
3.2.2 *Prototypes*   85
3.2.3 *Basic-level concepts*   88
3.2.4 *Conclusions*   90
  3.3 Language and thought   91
3.3.1 *Language and socialisation*   91
3.3.2 *The Sapir–Whorf hypothesis*   95
3.3.3 *Sexism in the language system*   102
  3.4 General conclusions   104

4 Speech as social interaction   **106**
  4.1 The social nature of speech   106
4.1.1 *Introduction*   106
4.1.2 *The classification of speech*   109
4.1.3 *Speech as skilled work*   112
4.1.4 *The norms governing speech*   116
4.1.5 *Conclusion*   119
  4.2 Speech as a signal of social identity   120
4.2.1 *Non-relational social categories*   120
4.2.2 *Power and solidarity*   122

Contents

4.2.3	*Linguistic signals of power and solidarity*	127
4.3	The structure of speech	132
4.3.1	*Entries and exits*	132
4.3.2	*Other kinds of structure in speech*	134
4.4	Verbal and non-verbal behaviour	136
4.4.1	*Relation-markers*	136
4.4.2	*Structure-markers*	138
4.4.3	*Content-markers*	139
4.5	Male/female differences in speech	140
5	**The quantitative study of speech**	**144**
5.1	Introduction	144
5.1.1	*The scope of quantitative studies of speech*	144
5.1.2	*Why study speech quantitatively?*	148
5.2	Methodology	150
5.2.1	*Problems of methodology*	150
5.2.2	*An example: New York*	155
5.2.3	*An example: Norwich*	159
5.2.4	*An example: Belfast*	163
5.2.5	*An example: Cardiff*	164
5.2.6	*An example: Detroit*	166
5.3	Linguistic variables	169
5.3.1	*Types of variable*	169
5.3.2	*Calculating scores for texts*	175
5.3.3	*Calculating scores for individuals and groups*	177
5.4	Influences on linguistic variables	181
5.4.1	*Linguistic context*	181
5.4.2	*The speaker's group membership*	184
5.4.3	*The speaker's degree of group membership*	190
5.4.4	*The speaker's sex*	193
5.4.5	*The situation and 'style'*	199
5.5	Summary	201
6	**Linguistic and social inequality**	**203**
6.1	Linguistic inequality	203
6.1.1	*Introduction*	203
6.1.2	*Three types of linguistic inequality*	205
6.2	Subjective inequality	206
6.2.1	*Language-based prejudice*	206
6.2.2	*Evaluation of language*	209

6.2.3 *Stereotypes and how to study them*   211
6.2.4 *Prejudice of teachers*   216
6.2.5 *Prejudice of pupils*   217
   6.3 Linguistic incompetence: strictly linguistic inequality   220
   6.4 Communicative incompetence: inequality in
        communication   224

   7 **Theoretical summary**   **228**
   7.1 Introduction   228
   7.2 The social functions of language   230
7.2.1 *Face*   230
7.2.2 *Solidarity and accommodation*   232
7.2.3 *Networks and multiple models*   234
7.2.4 *Social types and acts of identity*   237
7.2.5 *Power*   240
7.2.6 *Analogue relationships and variability*   241
   7.3 The structure of language   243
7.3.1 *Background*   243
7.3.2 *The history of the isolation of language*   244
7.3.3 *Evidence against the isolation of language*   245
7.3.4 *Two further sources of variability*   248
7.3.5 *Implications for theories of language structure*   252

        Bibliography   258
        Index   271

PREFACE TO THE SECOND EDITION

This edition is very different from the first – as it ought to be, after sixteen years! Over a third of the text is completely new; I have added a whole new chapter (7: Theoretical summary) to replace the very short 'Conclusions' in the first edition, and nine new sections to compensate for fourteen which I have removed.

Some of the changes were needed because of changes in my own ideas; the new theoretical summary is an attempt to explain these ideas. But most of them reflect developments in the field since 1979. Some ideas appear to have died: variable rules, panlectal grammars and restricted codes. Some new ideas have been born (or at least grown very fast): face, politeness, accommodation and prototypes. Some research areas have expanded enormously: sex differences of all kinds, and the relationship between language and thought; and some have turned into well-established separate disciplines which no longer need a place in this book: discourse analysis and pidgin and creole studies. The parts of sociolinguistics that were already bearing fruit in 1979 are still producing interesting and important findings.

Sociolinguistics is much more accessible now, thanks in part to a monumental research aid, the *Encyclopedia of Language and Linguistics*, which is very strong on sociolinguistics, plus other important sources such as the smaller *International Encyclopedia of Linguistics* and Labov's *Principles of Linguistic Change: Internal Factors* – not to mention a host of excellent textbooks which have appeared since my own (especially Fasold 1984, 1990, Holmes 1992, Wardhaugh 1986). Another major research aid which did not exist at all in 1979 was the internet, which has allowed me to conduct two tiny research projects without leaving my desk – one on sex differences (used in 5.4.4), and the other on naming (4.2.3).

Apart from these major additions and deletions I have changed numerous details. One very general change is the removal of sexist language, a source of great embarrassment to me now. In 1979 even sociolinguists wrote sentences like the following (from page 5 of the first edition): 'The difference between sociolinguistics and the sociology of language is very much one of emphasis, according to whether the investigator is more interested in language or society, and also according to whether he [!] has more skill in analysing linguistic or social structures.' How times have changed. I now believe firmly that every such sentence reinforces the assumption that the prototypical person is a man (see the new section 3.3.3!), so I have tried to ensure that my text is now completely bias-free. Maybe in another fifteen years we shall have a satisfactory replacement for the supposedly sex-neutral *he*, but meanwhile I have generally reworded to avoid the need for one.

Like the first edition, this is a rather personal book. It presents sociolinguistics through the eyes of a descriptive and theoretical linguist, making the most of the points at which sociolinguistics throws light on questions that interest me to do with the structure of language and the nature of linguistic competence. The result, for those interested in theoretical model-building, is a unified theory of some parts of social structure and of language structure. Those new to the subject may not be ready to go this far; and some experts may find my ideas unacceptable. No matter – the integration is all done in the last chapter, and (I think) the other chapters are reasonably free of way-out theoretical assumptions.

The following deserve special thanks: Penelope Eckert, Nikolas Coupland, all the students in my sociolinguistics class who have provided data and encouragement and the colleagues on the internet who have engaged in discussions of sexism, naming and other things.

PREFACE TO THE FIRST EDITION

I have written this book in the hope that it will do a number of different things, from informing and stimulating the newcomer to providing a theoretical framework within which the findings of sociolinguistics may be related to the theory of language structure (so-called 'theoretical linguistics'). If there is a bias in my selection of topics to cover, it is in favour of those topics which will be of most interest to students of language or linguistics, but I hope that others coming from sociology, social psychology and anthropology may be interested to see how the relations of language to society look to one whose training and research has been almost exclusively in structural linguistics. As a theoretical linguist myself, I have felt free to criticise the tradition within which I work, and the writing of this book has made it clear to me that there is much to criticise in this tradition. At the same time, I have tried to pick out the many positive contributions that a sociolinguistic viewpoint can make to the study of language.

My thinking on sociolinguistics is based on a course which I have been giving in London since 1970, on work with a number of stimulating graduate students, and on discussions with other sociolinguists (most of them British). It will be clear from the text and the references who has influenced me most, but I should like to mention in particular Bob Le Page, who first suggested the writing of this book and who spent a lot of time working through two quite different versions of it with me, discussing many of the theoretical issues and shaping my thinking on them. Other colleagues gave me helpful comments on various chapters – Thea Bynon, David Carmeli, Anne Holloway, John Holm, Joan Russell, Greg Smith, Adrian Stenton, Geoffrey Thornton and Peter Trudgill; and I had especially helpful and detailed comments from Geoff Sampson, Howard Giles and Jim and Lesley Milroy. I hope they approve of what I have done with their comments.

1
Introduction

1.1 Sociolinguistics

1.1.1 A description

We can define sociolinguistics as *the study of language in relation to society*, and this is how we shall be taking the term in this book. Sociolinguistics has become a recognised part of most courses at university level on 'linguistics' or 'language', and is indeed one of the main growth points in the study of language, from the point of view of both teaching and research. There are now major English-language journals devoted to research publications (*Language in Society, Language Variation and Change* and *International Journal of the Sociology of Language*) and a number of introductory textbooks, apart from the present one. Most of the growth in sociolinguistics has taken place since the late 1960s. This is not meant to imply that the study of language in relation to society is an invention of the 1960s – on the contrary, there is a long tradition in the study of dialects and in the general study of the relations between word-meaning and culture, both of which count as sociolinguistics by our definition. What is new is the *widespread* interest in sociolinguistics and the realisation that it can throw much light both on the nature of language and on the nature of society.

Like other subjects, sociolinguistics is partly empirical and partly theoretical – partly a matter of going out and amassing bodies of fact and partly of sitting back and thinking. The 'armchair' approach to sociolinguistics can be fairly productive, whether it is based on facts collected in a systematic way as part of research or simply on one's own experience. In particular, it allows the beginnings of an analytical framework to be worked out, containing terms such as LANGUAGE (a body of knowledge or rules), SPEECH (actual utterances), SPEAKER, ADDRESSEE, TOPIC and so on. And of course personal experience is a rich source of information on language in relation to society. However, it will soon become clear that the armchair approach is dangerous for two reasons if it is applied to personal experience alone. First, we may be seriously wrong in the way in which we interpret our own experience, since

1

most of us are not consciously aware of the vast range of variations in speech which we hear, and react to, in our everyday lives. And secondly, personal experience is a very limited base from which to generalise about language in society, since it does not take account of all the other societies where things are arranged very differently.

However, the reason why interest in sociolinguistics has grown so rapidly over the last decades is not because of the achievements in armchair theorising but because of the empirical discoveries made in the course of systematic research projects. Some of this research has taken place in 'exotic' communities, and this has produced facts which many readers of this book will find stimulating because they are so unexpectedly different from the kind of society which they already know. For instance, British people are generally surprised (and interested) to hear that there are societies where one's parents *must not* have the same mother-tongue (see below, 1.2.2). Other research projects, however, have been in the kind of complex, urban industrial society to which most readers will be accustomed, and this research too has provided some surprises, such as the discovery that differences between social classes are as clearly reflected in speech in America as they are in Britain, although the United States has an image of being much less class-conscious (the evidence for this claim will be discussed in chapter 5, especially 5.2.2).

It is important to recognise that much of the interest in sociolinguistics has come from people (such as educationalists) who have a *practical* concern for language, rather than a desire simply to understand better how this small area of the universe works. In particular, it became possible in the United States in the 1960s and 1970s to fund relatively large-scale research projects connected with the speech of underprivileged groups, on the grounds that the findings would make possible a more satisfactory educational policy. Chapter 6 is largely devoted to the issues raised in and by this research, but the research reported in chapter 5 would probably not have been possible in a different social climate, and the same may also be true of that reported in chapter 4, though perhaps to a lesser extent.

1.1.2   Sociolinguistics and linguistics
Throughout this book I shall refer to sociolinguists and linguists as separate people, but of course there are many sociolinguists who would also call themselves linguists, as well as the large number whose background is in sociology, anthropology or social psychology. The question of who is a sociolinguist and who is not, is neither interesting nor important; but it is important to ask whether there is a difference between sociolinguistics and linguistics and, if so, what it is. A widely held view is that there is such a difference, and that

linguistics differs from sociolinguistics in taking account only of the *structure* of language, to the exclusion of the social contexts in which it is learned and used. The task of linguistics, according to this view, is to work out 'the rules of language X', after which sociolinguists may enter the scene and study any points at which these rules make contact with society – such as where alternative ways of expressing the same thing are chosen by different social groups. This view is typical of the whole 'structural' school of linguistics which has dominated twentieth-century linguistics, including transformational-generative linguistics (the variety developed since 1957 by Noam Chomsky).

However, not all students of language would accept this view. Some would argue that since speech is (obviously) social behaviour, to study it without reference to society would be like studying courtship behaviour without relating the behaviour of one partner to that of the other. There are two particularly good reasons for accepting this view. The first is that we cannot take the notion 'language X' for granted, since this in itself is a social notion in so far as it is defined in terms of a group of people who speak X. As we shall see in chapter 2, the problem is that this group will in all probability be defined, in a complete circle, as 'the group who speak X', especially when we focus on detailed differences between dialects and try to define 'dialect X' instead of 'language X'. This argument has been developed especially by William Labov (1972a: viii). The second reason is that speech has a social function, both as a means of communication and also as a way of identifying social groups, and to study speech without reference to the society which uses it is to exclude the possibility of finding social explanations for the structures that are used. This view is typical of J. R. Firth (for example, 1950, 1964), who founded the 'London School' of linguistics, and whose followers include Michael Halliday (1985) but it is still not widely accepted by linguists.

This book will argue that the findings of sociolinguistics are highly relevant to the theory of language structure – for instance, in relation to the nature of meaning (3.2) and of grammar (7.3). The view I prefer is therefore the second one, according to which linguistics ignores society at its peril. I point this out to warn the reader against possible bias, but it is also clear that there is a big difference between recognising that one *should* take account of the social dimension of language and knowing *how* to do so.

I shall refer throughout to 'sociolinguists' and 'linguists' as though they were separate individuals, but these terms can simply be used to reflect the relative amount of attention given to the social side of language, without taking the distinction too seriously. There is no denying that remarkable progress has been made in the study of language structure within the structural tradition, by people who would call themselves 'linguists' and not 'sociolinguists'.

Moreover, it is clear that some areas of language, such as those covered in this book, relate more directly to social factors than others do. Those who concentrate on other areas, taking a more or less 'asocial' approach, we can call 'linguists', as opposed to 'sociolinguists'. However, although I am not arguing that the topics covered in this book are the only ones which should be studied, I do believe that all who study language, from whatever point of view, should be much more aware of the social context of their subject matter than is often the case, and the topics covered here seem most relevant in this context.

1.1.3 Sociolinguistics and the sociology of language

I defined sociolinguistics as 'the study of language in relation to society', implying (intentionally) that sociolinguistics is part of the study of language. Thus, the value of sociolinguistics is the light which it throws on the nature of language in general, or on the characteristics of some particular language. As we might expect, students of society have found that facts about language can illuminate their understanding – after all, it is hard to think of any characteristic of a society which is as distinctive as its language, or as important for its functioning. 'The study of society in relation to language' (the converse of our definition of sociolinguistics) defines what is generally called THE SOCIOLOGY OF LANGUAGE.

The difference between sociolinguistics and the sociology of language is very much one of emphasis, according to whether the investigator is more interested in language or society, and also according to whether they have more skill in analysing linguistic or social structures. There is a very large area of overlap between the two and its seems pointless to try to divide the disciplines more clearly than at present. Much of what follows in this book could equally well have been written in a textbook on the sociology of language. On the other hand, there are some issues which such a textbook ought to include which this one will not, notably most of what is called 'macro' sociology of language, dealing with the relations between society and languages as wholes. This is an important area of research from the point of view of sociology (and politics), since it raises issues such as the effects of multilingualism on economic development and the possible language policies a government may adopt. However, such 'macro' studies generally throw less light on the nature of language than the more 'micro' ones described in this book, because the notion of 'language X' is usually left unanalysed. (There is a good discussion of the relations between sociolinguistics and the sociology of language in the introduction to Trudgill 1978.) For more information on the sociology of language, see Gibbons 1992 (a brief overview) and Fasold 1984 (the main textbook).

4

1.2   Sociolinguistic phenomena

1.2.1   An imaginary world

What, then, is there to say about language in relation to society? It may be helpful to start by trying to imagine a society (and a language) about which there is very *little* to say. The little world described below is completely imaginary, and sociolinguists would agree that it is highly unlikely that any such world either does or even could exist, given what we know about both language and society.

In our imaginary world there is a society which is clearly defined by some natural boundary, impassable in either direction. The purpose of postulating this boundary is to guarantee, on the one hand, that no members of other communities join this one, bringing their own languages with them, and, on the other, that members of this community never leave it and take their language to another, thereby complicating the perfect coincidence between language and community.

Everybody in this society has exactly the same language – they know the same constructions and the same words, with the same pronunciation and the same range of meanings for every single word in the language. (Any deviation from such an exact identity raises the possibility of statements such as 'Person A knows pronunciation M, but Person B knows pronunciation N, for the same word', which would be a statement about language in relation to society.) An obvious problem is that very young members of the society, just learning to talk, must necessarily be different from everybody else. We might get round this problem by saying that child language is the domain of a branch of psychology rather than sociology, and that psychology can provide general principles of language acquisition which will allow us to predict every respect in which the language of children in this society deviates from the language of the adults. If psychology were able to provide the necessary principles, then there would be a good deal to say about language in relation to individual development, but nothing about language in relation to society. Needless to say, no psychologist would dream of claiming that this was possible, even in principle.

A consequence of the complete absence of any differences between members of this community is that language change is thereby ruled out, since such change normally involves a difference between the oldest and youngest generations, so that when the former all die only the forms used by the latter survive. Since change seems to affect every language so far studied, this makes the language of our imaginary community unique. The only way to allow for change in a totally homogeneous community is to assume that every change affects every member of the community absolutely and simultaneously: one day, nobody has the new form, the next day, everybody has it. (It is very hard

5

to see any mechanism which could explain such change, short of community-wide telepathy!)

Another characteristic of the community we are considering is that *circumstances* have no influence on what people say, either with respect to its content or its form. There are no 'formal' and 'informal' situations, requiring different kinds of vocabulary (such as *receive* versus *get*) or different pronunciations for words (like *not* versus *-n't*) (see 2.4, 5.4.5). Nor are there any 'discussions' and 'arguments', or 'requests' and 'demands', each requiring not only particular forms but also particular meanings. Nor are there any differences between the beginnings, middles and ends of conversations, such as would require greetings and farewells. None of these differences due to circumstances exist because if they did they would require statements about society – in particular, about social interaction, the topic of chapter 4. Indeed, if we discount any influence of the social context, it is doubtful if speech is possible at all, since spoken messages are generally geared specifically to the needs of the audience.

Finally, we must assume that there is no connection between the culture of the postulated community and the meanings which its language (especially its vocabulary) allows it to express. The language must therefore contain no words such as *cricket* or *priest*, whose meanings could be stated only with reference to a partial description of the culture, as will be argued in 3.2. To assume otherwise would be to allow rich and interesting statements about language in relation to society, since culture is one of the most important characteristics of society. Exactly what kinds of concepts the members of this community *would* be able to express is not clear – possibly they would only be able to assert logical truths such as 'If p and q, then p', since any other kinds of word are likely to involve some reference to the community's culture.

All in all, our blue-print for a community is an unpromising one. All the restrictions imposed on it were necessary in order to guarantee that there should be nothing to say about its language in relation to society, beyond the simple statement 'Such-and-such community speak language X'. However, it will be noticed that this statement is precisely the kind which is generally made by linguists (or laypeople) about a language, and exhausts what they feel obliged to say about the language in relation to society. The purpose of this section has been to show that the only kind of community (or language) for which such a statement could be remotely adequate is a fictitious one.

1.2.2 *A real but exotic world*

We now turn to a real world, in which there is a great deal to be said about language in relation to society. It is the very exotic world of the north-west Amazon, described by A. P. Sorensen (1971) and J. Jackson (1974) (though we shall see in 1.2.3 that things are not so very different in the kind of society to which most of us are accustomed).

Geographically, the area in question is half in Brazil and half in Colombia, coinciding more or less with the area in which a language called Tukano can be relied on as a LINGUA FRANCA (i.e. a trade language widely spoken as a non-native language). It is a large area, but sparsely inhabited; around 10,000 people in an area the size of England. Most of the people are indigenous Indians, divided into over twenty tribes, which are in turn grouped into five 'phratries' (groups of related tribes). There are two crucial facts to be remembered about this community. First, each tribe speaks a different language – sufficiently different to be mutually incomprehensible and, in some cases, genetically unrelated (i.e. not descended from a common 'parent' language). Indeed, the *only* criterion by which tribes can be distinguished from each other is by their language. The second fact is that the five phratries (and thus all twenty-odd tribes) are exogamous (i.e. a man must not marry a woman from the same phratry or tribe). Putting these two facts together, it is easy to see the main linguistic consequence: a man's wife *must* speak a different language from him.

We now add a third fact: marriage is patrilocal (the husband and wife live where the husband was brought up), and there is a rule that the wife should not only live where the husband was brought up, but should also use his language in speaking to their children (a custom that might be called 'patrilingual marriage'). The linguistic consequence of this rule is that a child's mother does not teach her own language to the child, but rather a language which she speaks only as a foreigner – as though everyone in Britain learned their English from a foreign au-pair girl. One can thus hardly call the children's first language their 'mother-tongue' except by a stretch of the imagination. The reports of this community do not mention any widespread disruption in language learning or general 'deterioration' of the languages concerned, so we can assume that a language can be transmitted efficiently and accurately even under these apparently adverse circumstances, through the influence of the father, the rest of the father's relatives and the older children. It is perhaps worth pointing out that the wife goes to live in a 'long-house' in which the husband's brothers and parents also live, so there is no shortage of contacts with native speakers of the father's language.

What is there to say about language in relation to such a society? First, there is the question of relating languages as wholes to speakers, assuming for simplicity that it is possible to talk usefully about 'languages as wholes' (contrary to what we shall argue in 2.2). For any given language X, it will first be necessary to define who are its native speakers, but since this means referring to some tribe, and tribes are primarily defined with reference to language, there is clearly a problem. The solution is either to list all the long-houses belonging to the tribe concerned, or to specify the geographical area (or areas) where the tribe lives. (Most tribes do in fact have their own territory, which does not overlap with that of other tribes.) However, it will have to be borne in mind that about a quarter of the native speakers of language X will be made up of the   married women who are dispersed among the other tribes, and similarly about a quarter of the people living in the area designated as 'language X territory' will be *non-native* speakers of X, being wives from other tribes. Indeed, any given long-house is likely to contain native speakers of a variety of languages, on the assumption that brothers need not be attracted to girls of the same 'other' tribe. In addition to the native speakers of language X, there will be   people who speak it as non-natives, with every degree of fluency from almost native-speaker to minimal. Thus anyone wishing to write a grammar for   language X will need to say precisely for whom the grammar is claimed to be true – just for the native speakers left at home in the tribal area, or for all native speakers including those dispersed among the other tribes, or for all speakers, native or non-native, in the tribal area.

Secondly, there is the question of discourse: how is speech used in social inter-action? There are questions which arise out of the number of languages avail-able: for instance, how do people get by when they travel around within the area, as they very often do? Are they expected to use the language of the long-house which they are visiting? Apparently not – the choice of language is based solely on the convenience of the people concerned (except for the rule requiring wives to use their husbands' language when speaking to their chil-dren). If visitors do not know the long-house language, but someone there knows their language, they will use the visitors' language when speaking to them. What about language itself as a subject of conversation? Here too practi-cal needs are put first, namely the need to know as many languages as possible in order to be able to travel and (for young people) to find a partner. It is quite normal to talk about a language, learning its vocabulary and phrases, and this continues into old age; yet people generally do not know how many languages they can speak, and do not think of language learning as a way of gaining pres-tige. Perhaps this is what we might expect in a society where everyone can be expected to speak *at least* (i) their father's language, (ii) their mother's language (which she will certainly have taught her children with a view to their seeking partners among her tribe) and (iii) the lingua franca, Tukano (which may also be the father's or mother's language). However, in addition to the aspects of dis-course which are directly related to multilingualism, there are many other things to be said about the relations between speech and the social circumstances in this complex Amazonian society. For instance, there is a rule that if you are listening to someone whom you respect, at least for the first few minutes, you should repeat after them, word-for-word, everything they say.

Thirdly, there is the question of the relation of language to culture, on which we have little information in the reports on the north-west Amazon referred to above, but on which we can make some safe guesses. For instance, it would be surprising if any of the languages concerned lacked a word for 'long-house' or 'tribe', and we might reasonably expect a word for 'phratry' (though such higher-level concepts often lack names, as we shall see in 3.3.1). Similarly, we may predict that each language will have words to express most concepts relevant to the culture, and that most words in each language will express cultural concepts, definable only in terms of the culture concerned.

In the world of the north-west Amazon there is probably nothing that linguists could satisfactorily say about any language without at the same time making some fairly complicated statement about it in relation to society. In particular, they could not say *which* language they were describing by referring to some predefined community who use it (in the way in which one might feel entitled to talk about, say, 'British English' or 'Birmingham English'). The main source of this complexity is the rule of 'linguistic exogamy', which might not be expected to be very widespread in the world. However, the other source is the amount of individual bilingualism (or, more accurately, multilingualism), which makes it hard to decide who is a speaker of a given language and who is not. This characteristic, widespread multilingualism, is anything but exceptional in the world as a whole, as an armchair sociolinguist can easily deduce from the fact that there are some six thousand languages in the world, but only about 160 nation states. At least some states must therefore contain a very large number of languages, and probably most contain a fair number, with an average around forty. In view of the need for communication with neighbouring communities and government agencies, it is fair to assume that many members of most communities are multilingual. It is worthwhile bearing this conclusion in mind in reading the next section, since it shows that the monolingual communities familiar to many of us may in fact be highly exceptional and even 'exotic' from a global perspective.

1.2.3 A real and familiar world

Readers are now invited to consider the world in which they themselves grew up. It is unlikely that any reader has had a background quite as linguistically exciting as the one described above, but most of us will certainly find that there is more to be said about our own sociolinguistic worlds than might be expected and much of it is surprisingly interesting.

9

In order to focus their thinking, readers may find it helpful to imagine themselves, reasonably fluent in Tukano, sitting in a long-house in the north-west Amazon, telling the residents about their language, in the way that travelling Indians in the area are presumably asked to do if they reach a long-house unfamiliar with their language. The kind of information they would be expected to provide would cover both very general and very specific matters. Who else speaks the language? Where do the speakers live? Do they speak any other languages? What do they say when they first meet a stranger? What is the word meaning 'phratry'? What are the meals eaten at different times of day called? Are there any special ways of talking to young children? How do you count? Is there any way of showing that you're quoting what somebody else has told you? How do you show that the thing you're referring to is already known to the person you are talking to? Are there different ways of pronouncing any of the words according to where you come from? In answering every one of these questions, something will not only have been said about the language but also about one aspect or another of the society that uses it; and such questions could be multiplied by the inquisitive long-house residents until a complete description of the strangers' language has been provided.

The point of this exercise is to make readers aware of how much there is to say about their own language in relation to society. My hope is that, as they read this book, readers will keep their own background in mind and try to imagine what results would have been obtained if research projects comparable with those which will be described below were to be carried out in their language community.

1.3 Speakers and communities

1.3.1 Conformity and individualism

If sociolinguistics is about language in relation to society, we might expect a book on sociolinguistics to be mainly about large-scale social units such as tribes, nations and social classes. These will indeed be mentioned, and there will be a discussion of the relevance of some of them to language, especially in 5.4. However, society consists of individuals, and both sociologists and sociolinguists would agree that it is essential to keep individuals firmly in the centre of interest, and to avoid losing sight of them while talking about large-scale abstractions and movements. The individual speaker is important in sociolinguistics in much the same way that the individual cell is important in biology: if we don't understand how the individual works, to that extent we shan't be able to understand how collections of individuals behave either.

Moreover, there is an even more important reason for focussing on the individual in sociolinguistics, which does not apply to the cell in biology (or not to the same extent): we can be sure that *no two speakers have the same language, because no two speakers have the same experience of language.* The differences between speakers may vary from the very slight and trivial (in the case of twins brought up together, for instance) to total difference within whatever limits are set by universal characteristics of language. Unlike the individual cell, the individual speaker is presumably moulded much more by experience (as a listener) than by genetic make-up, and experience consists in fact of speech produced by other individual speakers, each of whom is unique. What we shall try to do in this book is to look at society from the inside, so to speak, taking the viewpoint of an individual member talking and listening to other individuals.

The uniqueness of each person's sociolinguistic past is not the only source of differences between speakers, however. We can imagine a person constructing a more or less unconscious mental map of the community in which they live, in which the people around them are arranged in a 'multi-dimensional space', i.e. showing similarities and differences relative to one another on a large number of different dimensions or parameters. Some of these dimensions involve linguistic differences – such as how some particular word is pronounced – and the map consequently covers linguistic parameters as well as variables of other types. The particular map which each individual draws will reflect their own personal experience, so people with different sociolinguistic backgrounds will be led to construct correspondingly different maps relevant to language and society.

However, the individual is not simply a 'social automaton' controlled by this map, nor is the map itself just a direct and unselective record of past experience (like a tape-recording or video). Rather individuals *filter* their experience of new situations through their existing map and two people could both hear the same person talking, but be affected in different ways. For instance a Briton and an American could watch the same American film, but learn quite different facts from it about language – what for the American viewer counts as a new fact about how poor whites in the Deep South talk might count for the Briton simply as a new fact about how Americans talk. From this point of view, we may expect differences in existing maps to lead to differences in later ones, even where the experience on which the changes are based is objectively the same in both cases.

To complete this picture of the sources of differences between individuals, we can return to the multi-dimensional space to which we referred above. There is ample evidence, which we shall review in chapter 5, that society is structured, from a sociolinguistic point of view, in terms of a multi-dimensional space. One need only think of the rather obvious ways in which people can be classified more or less independently according to the dimensions of age, region of origin, social class (or profession) and sex, to see an example of a four-dimensional space, each dimension of which is relevant to language. Once we have constructed a model of how this multi-dimensional space looks from our point of view, we then have to *choose* where to locate *ourselves* in it. Language is only one part of the picture, of course, but a particularly important part because it gives us a very clearly structured set of symbols which we can use in locating ourselves in the world. The people around us belong to a variety of social types (for example, old males are very different from young females), and we have to decide where we ourselves belong among these types. If different types speak differently we can use our own speech to signal this choice. In other words, at each utterance our speech can be seen as an ACT OF IDENTITY in a multi-dimensional space (Le Page and Tabouret-Keller 1985).

Against this background of the last few paragraphs, in which we have emphasised the scope for individual variation among speakers, we may be impressed by the amount of *agreement* that is often found among speakers, and which we shall also illustrate in chapter 5. It is important to point out that the degree of similarity generally found between speakers goes well beyond what is needed for efficient communication. For instance, contrary to what was predicted by Ferdinand de Saussure, father of the structural tradition in linguistics, it is not sufficient to keep two adjacent vowel phonemes distinct from each other: our particular pronunciations of them must be *precisely* the same as those of the people we take as models. Similarly, our syntactic restrictions on the use of particular words will be more or less exact copies of the restrictions applied by other people (for example, all English speakers agree in restricting *probable* to use with a *that*-clause, in contrast with its synonym *likely* which can be used either with a *that*-clause or with an infinitive: *It's likely/probable that we'll be late*, or *We're likely to be late*, but not **We're probable to be late*).

Perhaps the show-piece for the triumph of conformity over efficient communication is the area of irregular morphology, where the existence of irregular verbs or nouns in a language like English has *no* pay-off from the point of view of communication (it makes life easier for neither the speaker nor the hearer, nor even for the language learner). The only explanation for the continued existence of such irregularities must be the need for each of us to be seen to be conforming to the same rules, in detail, as those we take as models. As is well known, children tend to use regular forms (such as *goed* for *went*), but later *abandon* these forms simply in order to conform with older people.

The two 'forces' which we have now considered, one leading to individual differences and the other leading to similarities between individuals, may be referred to for convenience as INDIVIDUALISM and CONFORMITY. The amount of variation actually found within any given community will depend on the relative strengths of these two forces, so that conformity will predominate in some communities and individualism in others. The terms FOCUSSING and DIFFUSION have been suggested for these two kinds of situations (Le Page and Tabouret-Keller 1985). Focussing is found where there is a high degree of contact among speakers and agreement on linguistic norms, and is typical of very closely knit small communities (such as the working-class networks in Belfast discussed in 5.4.3), or of societies where there is a highly standardised written language such as English or French. Diffusion, on the other hand, is found where neither of these conditions holds, an extreme example being Romany, the gipsy language. Of course, there is no question of a clear distinction between focussing and diffusion; rather they are the names for the two ends of a scale on which any society, or part of it, may be located.

Interestingly, it has never been suggested that individuals can be more or less conformist so far as language is concerned, though it is of course conceivable that such differences exist. In order to show that they do, it would be necessary to find differences in, for instance, the extent to which individuals maintain irregularity in their morphology. It would not be enough to show that some individuals reject the model of their parents (as they clearly do), since this is probably because they are conforming to a *different* model (that of their peers) rather than to no model at all. There may also be individual differences in willingness to create new vocabulary or to use language metaphorically, in which case the 'creative' individual would be going beyond the accepted norms, and perhaps breaking them under special circumstances (for example, in poetry). However, such creativity seems to take place against the background of a normal, conformist language system.

Conformity extends to some unexpected areas of our linguistic behaviour, of which perhaps the most surprising is swearing. Native speakers of English all know expressions like *shit* and *bloody*, and for each one we know exactly how it is used (for example, *shit* is either a noun or an exclamation, whereas *bloody* can only be used as an adjective; and *shit* is 'stronger' than *bloody*). We learn these words in just the same way as we learn the rest of our language, by hearing them used by other people, and like many other parts of language their function is to express an emotion (compare *Oh dear!* and *Hurray!*, which are not swear words). What makes swearing different is that the emotions expressed are both strong and negative, emotions which are socially dangerous; and what makes it interesting is that our society provides us with a list of words which are suitable for expressing such emotions precisely because they come with the label 'Danger – Do not use!' – dangerous words for expressing dangerous emotions. The words concerned are typically linked through their meaning to socially dangerous areas of life – religion, substances that come out of our bodies and sex;

13

and the extent to which our society sees these words as dangerous can be seen in the fact that swear words are ranked with sex and violence as the three dangerous elements in terms of which TV shows, films and videos are classified. (A readable and thoughtful discussion of these issues can be found in chapter 3 of Anderson and Trudgill 1990, and Apte 1994 is a survey of the research literature.)

As regards conformity, the main relevance of swearing is that we meekly use the resources provided by our language even when we are expressing strong (and antisocial) feelings; and we always follow the grammatical rules (for example, I doubt if any English speaker would ever use *Bloody!* as an exclamation). On the other hand, our individualism is relevant as well because we choose to ignore the 'do not use!' rule – a nice example of the principle that rules exist in order to be broken!

1.3.2 *The sociolinguistic development of the child*

Although we may assume that each speaker has a unique experience of language, and on this basis develops a unique grammar, a number of generalisations can be made about the stages through which people may be expected to pass in their sociolinguistic development. However, it should be emphasised from the outset that the following generalisations must all be treated as tentative hypotheses rather than established research findings, since they are based on a very small body of research supported by anecdotal evidence.

The first generalisation concerns the linguistic models which the child follows. For many children, the pattern is as follows: first parents, then peers, then adults. Within the 'peers as models' phase we can distinguish between childhood and adolescence, giving four life-phases: babyhood, childhood, adolescence and adulthood. The sociolinguistic evidence for these distinctions is summarised in Chambers (1995: 151ff.). The following is a very rough summary which obviously ignores a lot of important subtleties and details.

- Babyhood. The models are parents and other carers, who use 'baby-talk' (words like *gee-gee*, 'horse', and constructions like *Baby go night-night now*).

- Childhood. The models are other children of the same age or somewhat older, and if these children speak differently from the parents, the children's model generally is the one which is actually adopted. At this stage children are extremely conservative in their language; their main concern seems to be the same as the older children (with some attempts to imitate teenagers as well). This leads to what is called 'AGE-GRADING' (Hockett 1950), a pattern of use in which linguistic items are used by people of a particular age, who then stop using it when they grow older. The language used by primary-school children is full of archaic forms which were in use by children of the same age centuries ago – ancient counting-rhymes, skipping songs, truce-terms (for calling a truce in a 'battle'), names for playground games, taunts, challenges and so on. (Opie and Opie 1959 is a classsic survey of this language in England.) Another example of age-grading is found in the speech of black American children, who use archaic forms which were part of the creole out of which the English of black Americans is widely believed to have developed (Dillard 1976). Perhaps because of this obsessive conformism with the local models, children can learn a new dialect or language perfectly (i.e. just as though it had been their first language).

Two other facts about this stage are important. Firstly, children tend very strongly to prefer members of their own sex, so it is very easy for girls and boys to develop differently. As we shall see in 4.5, men and women tend to perpetuate these differences in the way they use language. And secondly, children are also learning to recognise the social significance of different linguistic norms, as we shall see below.

- Adolescence. The models now are other adolescents, but the foundations of language have already been laid – for most people (perhaps all) it is too late to learn a new language or dialect perfectly (Chambers 1995: 160). This is the stage at which children prepare to be the next generation of adults. Unlike children, adolescents aim to be different from all previous adolescents, which gives rise to the constantly changing picture of teenage slang (Chambers 1995: 171). It is essential to the self-respect of a fourteen-year old to be different from the ex-teenage twenty-year olds (not to mention ex-ex-teenage fifty-year olds!); but of course it is also essential to be in step with other 'relevant' adolescents, identified in terms of alternative life-style models. Maybe teenage gangs and social types are a preparation for the complexities of adult life, but whatever their reason they have a profound effect on the speech of adolescents (as we shall see in a case-study in 5.2.6).

- Adulthood. Our models are other adults, with current adolescents as a potential source of inspiration (or offence). Work, parenthood and other social activities bring us into contact with other adults who offer competing models which we may either avoid or copy, for reasons that we shall explore in later chapters. There is still scope for change, and in particular for learning to use more or less standard speech for work purposes under the pressures of the 'linguistic market-place' (Bourdieu and Boltanski 1975, explained well in Chambers 1995: 177ff.). However, by now we are all more or less stable linguistically, with a personal language which defines our place in the social world in terms of region, age, sex, social class and other characteristics.

After this overview of the main stages we can return to the earlier years to ask how children adapt to the very varied linguistic world into which they are born. First, at what age do children become aware of the social significance of different speech forms? They appear to be aware of different speech forms, and the fact that there are social differences between them, from an early age. Children brought up in a bilingual environment have been reported as being aware that two separate language systems were being used even at eighteen months (see Romaine 1989, chapter 5, for a convenient summary). Some anecdotes suggest that this may happen even earlier, though others put the age later. For instance, Robbins Burling reports (1959) that his son learned Garo (a tribal language of north-eastern India) from his nanny at the same time as he learned English from his parents, and that he was about two years three months before he realised that different people spoke different languages; only then would he work out who was likely to understand his Garo before speaking. Before this – by eighteen months – he had noticed that many things had more than one word to express them, such as English *milk* and Garo *dut*, but he had not yet made the considerable abstraction to the existence of two separate systems. As for dialect differences, there is little evidence relevant to young children, but it seems a fair assumption that they are at least capable of being aware of such differences by the time they start to model themselves on their peers, and will be aware of dialect differences to the extent that the speech of their parents and of their peers is different.

Assuming that a child has learned that two different languages or varieties are different systems, each used by a different range of people, how long does it take to become aware of the positive and negative prejudices that grown-ups have towards some of these varieties? And how long does it take children to adopt these prejudices themselves? Again the evidence is sketchy, and to some extent contradictory, but we shall see (6.2.5) that there is some evidence at least which suggests strongly that there are communities in which many children as early as age three have not only already become aware of such prejudices, but have adopted them themselves. On the other hand, this is clearly not the same thing as claiming that four-year-olds have fully developed adult prejudices, and we may safely assume on the basis of other evidence that their prejudices go on developing throughout childhood and adolescence. Indeed, there seems to be no reason for thinking that the process ever stops completely.

What about the child's own speech? How does this develop in relation to the social environment? It is clear that children from an extremely early age adapt their speech to its social context (Andersen 1990). As soon as they start to speak they speak differently to different people (Giles and Powesland 1975: 139), which is hardly surprising if we think of their speech as just one aspect of social behaviour, and remember that they behave differently towards different people from very soon after birth. Moreover, from a very early age – in the first year, before they have learned any of the adult forms – they use different noises for different purposes, such as asking for something or saying the equivalent of 'I say, just look at that!' (Halliday 1975). Similarly, a child of twenty-three months was reported as deliberately separating her syllables off to make them clearer when she was being misunderstood (Weeks 1971).

By age three the children of bilingual parents will probably be reasonably efficient at keeping the two languages separate from each other in their own speech, and any three-year-old may have started practising a range of roles such as baby, doctor or cowboy (Weeks 1971). The role of 'baby' is a particularly interesting one, as children get *better* at playing it, rather than worse, as one might expect from a naive view of baby-talk as a left-over from their own babyhood (Berko Gleason 1973, Sachs and Devin 1976). A four-year-old is already remarkably versatile. As Jean Berko Gleason puts it (1973), 'Four-year olds may whine at their mothers, engage in intricate verbal play with their peers, and reserve their narrative, discursive tales for their grown-up friends.' There is no reason to think that there is any end-point in the process of acquiring new styles of speaking, or of becoming more sophisticated in the use of the styles we already have.

1.4   Summary and conclusions

In the second section of this introductory chapter we considered three very different societies and showed that it is much harder than one might think to separate language from its social background. We are all used to thinking of languages like English, French and Japanese as relatively independent of the societies that speak them; so, for instance, we could in principle learn about French vocabulary and grammar without learning anything at all about

French people. But as soon as we start to consider language as an object of research, social questions are hard to ignore.

It would be wrong to imply that such questions are always centre-stage. For some kinds of work on language they can safely be kept in the background, and in fact this has probably been true of most work on language over the last two thousand years (since linguistics started in Ancient Greece and India). This is done simply by loading all the social information into the language-label. Instead of saying 'The people who live in England typically say *cat* for "cat"' and 'The people who live in England typically say *dog* for "dog"', we say 'The people who live in England typically speak English' and 'The English for "cat" is *cat*' and 'The English for "dog" is *dog*'. It is easy to see how enormously useful these language-labels are for any work on language; but at the same time it is important to bear in mind that they are socially problematic. Where exactly are the boundaries of English? For example, what about Afro-Caribbean pidgins and creoles? (The following sentence is part of Nigerian Pidgin (Todd 1994): 'A bin kam, kariam go', meaning 'I came and carried it away'; is it English? We shall discuss this example further in 2.5.5.) And what about all the variation within English? Sometimes these questions hardly matter, and it's important not to get sidetracked by them from the matter in hand. This kind of work is what we can call 'non-social linguistics'.

In sociolinguistics, in contrast, the social questions are in full focus, though they share the stage with the same kinds of question that linguistics studies. Sociolinguists flourish where linguists flounder, wherever there is variability within a community, or fuzzy boundaries between communities (or between languages), or words that are tied to particular social situations or to particular cultural beliefs. Over the few decades of its existence sociolinguistics has developed ways of analysing and thinking about the links between such things, and there are even the beginnings of some theoretical frameworks. In short, sociolinguistics and non-social linguistics complement one another – sociolinguistics takes over where non-social linguistics gives up, and vice versa. However, the findings of sociolinguistics, as described in this book, challenge a number of widely held views. Chapter 2 proposes reasons for questioning the assumption that languages are discrete, identifiable entities, consisting of dialects which can further be subdivided until the individual is reached, as the locus of the 'smallest dialect'. Chapter 3 shows that 'knowledge of language' may not in fact be clearly distinct, or distinct at all (even unclearly), from 'knowledge of culture'. Chapter 4 indicates that speech is not clearly different in kind from other aspects of social behaviour, but that some aspects of language structure can be described properly only by reference to speech as social behaviour. Chapter 5, in some ways the core of the book, is about variability in the forms we use when speaking. It shows that there is no such thing as a homogeneous grammar, whether for an individual or for a community, but that speakers make extraordinarily subtle use of the available variability in order to locate themselves in society. Chapter 6 deals with the complex notion of 'linguistic equality', which linguists have tended to oversimplify. The last chapter offers a theoretical perspective which accommodates the various insights described in earlier chapters, but shows that some of these insights cast doubt on some of the most popular approaches to language.

2
Varieties of language

2.1 Introduction

2.1.1 *Global and specific statements*

Our purpose in this chapter is to see how far it is possible to describe the relations of language to society in terms of 'global' linguistic categories such as 'language X' or 'dialect Y' and global social categories like 'community Z'. To the extent that it is possible, the relations concerned can be handled in terms of these global categories, and need make no reference to the individual linguistic items, such as items of vocabulary, contained in 'language X' or to the individual members of 'community Z'. On the other hand, we shall see that it is not always possible to do so without loss of accuracy and that at least some linguistic items are socially unique – that is, there are no other items that are used by precisely the same range of speakers or under precisely the same range of circumstances. Similarly, as we saw in the last chapter, we may assume that every individual in a community has a unique language when we probe the details. To the extent that different linguistic items have different relations to society (in terms of people and circumstances), it is obviously necessary to describe these relations separately for each item. Thus on the one hand there are statements about global categories, like whole languages, and on the other hand there are statements about individual linguistic items; and in each case the statement refers to speakers either as members of some community or as individuals.

The questions that arise are complex and surprisingly hard to answer, but they are important to anyone interested in the nature of language in general or in the relations of language to society in particular. How should global linguistic categories like 'language X' be defined? How should particular instances of them be delimited? Indeed, do such categories correspond to any kind of objective reality in terms of which these questions make sense? Can distinct types of global category (for example, 'language' versus 'dialect') be distinguished? How are global categories related to one another? What do they consist of (i.e. what are they categories *of*)? How should communities be defined and delimited for these purposes? Do communities defined on a linguistic basis have any kind of objective reality? And so on. It is still far too early to give definite answers to most of these questions, but it is possible to cast serious doubt on some widely accepted answers.

Briefly, we shall be able to show that things are much more complex than many of us linguists think, though it may well be that readers with less professional commitment to linguistics will find that their current common-sense view of language fits the facts quite well. On the other hand, many lay people are prepared to ask the 'professionals' questions such as 'Where is real Cockney spoken?' and 'Is Jamaican creole a kind of English or not?', assuming that these questions are really meaningful, whereas we shall see that they are not the kind of question that can be investigated scientifically. Thus there may be some surprises in this chapter, both for the professional and for the lay reader, at least as far as the conclusions are concerned, though many of the facts on which these conclusions are based are unsurprising.

2.1.2 Linguistic items

The discussion will be easier if we have some technical terms to use, as we need to distance ourselves somewhat from the concepts represented by the words *language* and *dialect*, which are a reasonable reflection of our lay culture, called 'common-sense knowledge' (see 3.1.1), but not helpful in sociolinguistics. First, we need a term for the individual 'bits of language' to which some sociolinguistic statements need to refer, where more global statements are not possible. We have already used the term LINGUISTIC ITEM (2.1.1) and shall continue to use it as a technical term.

What is a linguistic item? The answer to this question concerns the theory of language structure, and people will give different answers according to which theory they think gives the best view of language structure. Everyone would accept that there are items of vocabulary (called 'lexical items' or 'lexemes'), and that there are also sound-patterns within them and larger syntactic patterns in which they are used. For convenience we can call them 'lexical items', 'sounds' and 'constructions', and we shall see that sociolinguists have studied all three. As far as sociolinguistics is concerned, there is no important difference among them, as much the same kinds of social variation and social links are possible in each case; but non-social linguists generally treat them very differently in their theoretical models of how language 'works'. A typical view is that lexical items are listed (in a lexicon), but that sounds and constructions are defined ('generated') by general rules or principles. For example, the lexical items *cat*, *dog* and *horse* are simply listed, along with their meanings and their various other characteristics (word-class, pronunciation, etc. – just as in any dictionary); but there is no list which contains the pattern 'word-final /r/' (as in *car* and *daughter* in accents of English where /r/ is pronounced) or the construction 'bare relative clause' (as in *the book I bought*, in contrast with a 'wh-relative clause' *the book which I bought*). Although we can recognise these patterns when they occur, and talk about them, they don't really exist in a grammar in the way that the lexical items do.

This contrast between lexical and other kinds of items immediately raises a theoretical problem: if they are treated so differently in the grammar, why should they be similar sociolinguistically? And how do the social facts combine with the linguistic ones? It is reasonably easy to include social facts about lexical items along with the linguistic facts; after all, this is what any good dictionary does with social information about dialect or style differences. But how can we extend the same treatment to sounds and constructions if these aren't recognised individually in a grammar? This is one of many challenges that sociolinguistics poses for the theories that have been developed in non-social linguistics.

Later in this chapter we shall see evidence that different linguistic items in 'the same language' can have quite different social distributions (in terms of speakers and circumstances), and we may assume that it is possible for the social distribution of a linguistic item to be *unique*. In fact it is much harder to demonstrate this than to show differences between selected items, since we should need to compare the item suspected of being unique with every other item in the same language, just to make sure that no other has the same distribution. For example, it is easy to show that the distribution of the words used in England for *she* (*she, her, hoo, shoo*) is quite different from that for the words for *am* (*am, is, be, bin*) (see the maps in Wakelin 1978: 21, 23). What is not easy, is to show that none of these forms has the same distribution (i.e. is used by exactly the same speakers under the same circumstances) as any other word. There is, however, no known mechanism which could prevent items from having unique distributions, so it seems fair to assume that at least some of them do.

2.1.3   *Varieties of language*

If one thinks of 'language' as a phenomenon including all the languages of the world, the term VARIETY OF LANGUAGE (or just VARIETY for short) can be used to refer to different manifestations of it, in just the same way as one might take 'music' as a general phenomenon and then distinguish different 'varieties of music'. What makes one variety of language different from another is the linguistic items that it includes, so we may define a variety of language as *a set of linguistic items with similar social distribution*. This definition allows us to call any of the following 'varieties of language': English,

French, London English, the English of football commentaries, the languages used by the members of a particular long-house in the north-west Amazon, the language or languages used by a particular person.

It will be seen from this list that the very general notion 'variety' includes examples of what would normally be called languages, dialects and registers (a term meaning roughly 'style', which we shall discuss in section 2.4). The advantage of having a general term to cover all these concepts is that it allows us to ask what basis there is for the distinctions among them – for instance, why do we call some varieties different languages and others different dialects of the same language? Sections 2.2, 2.3 and 2.4 will be occupied with precisely such questions, and will lead to the conclusion that there is *no* consistent basis for making the distinctions concerned. This leaves us only with the general term 'variety' for referring to things which in non-technical terms we call 'languages', 'dialects' or 'styles'.

This conclusion may seem rather radical, but the definition of 'variety' given above, and the examples given in the list, suggest even greater departures from the linguistic tradition. It will be noticed that it is consistent with the definition to treat all the languages of some multilingual speaker, or community, as a single variety, since all the linguistic items concerned have a similar social distribution – they are used by the same speaker or community. That is, a variety may be much larger than a lay 'language', including a number of different languages. Conversely, according to the definition a variety may contain just a handful of items, or even in the extreme case a single item, if it is defined in terms of the range of speakers or circumstances with which it is associated. For instance, one might define a variety consisting of those items used solely by some particular family or village. Thus a variety can be much smaller than a 'language', or even than a 'dialect'. The flexibility of the term 'variety' allows us to ask what basis there is for postulating the kinds of 'package' of linguistic items to which we conventionally give labels like 'language', 'dialect' or 'register'. Is it because the items form themselves into natural bundles, bound together by a tight set of interlocking structural relations of some kind, as has always been suggested by the 'structuralist' tradition of the twentieth century? The answer given in the following sections is again negative: the bundles into which linguistic items can be grouped are quite loosely tied, and it is easy for items to move between them, to the extent that bundles may in fact be muddled up. The extreme cases of this will be discussed in section 2.5.

In conclusion, discussions of language in relation to society will consist of statements which refer, on the 'language' side, to either individual linguistic items or varieties, which are sets of such items. There are no restrictions on the

23

relations among varieties – they may overlap and one variety may include another. The defining characteristic of each variety is the relevant relation to society – in other words, by whom, and when, the items concerned are used. It is an empirical question to what extent the traditional notions of 'language', 'dialect' and 'register' are matched by varieties defined in this way. As we shall see in the following sections, the match is only approximate at best, and in some societies (and individuals) it may be extremely hard to identify varieties corresponding even roughly to traditional notions.

2.1.4 'Speech communities'

It may be helpful at this point to discuss the kind of community to which varieties or items may be related. The term SPEECH COMMUNITY is widely used by sociolinguists to refer to a community based on language, but LINGUISTIC COMMUNITY is also used with the same meaning. If speech communities can be delimited, then they can be studied, and it may be possible to find interesting differences between communities which correlate with differences in their language. The study of speech communities has therefore interested linguists for some time, at least since Leonard Bloomfield wrote a chapter on speech communities in his book *Language* (1933: ch. 3). However, there has been considerable confusion and disagreement over exactly what a speech community is, as the following survey shows.

(1) The simplest definition of 'speech community' is that of John Lyons (1970: 326):

> Speech community: all the people who use a given language (or dialect).

According to this definition, speech communities may overlap (where there are bilingual individuals) and need not have any social or cultural unity. Clearly it is possible to delimit speech communities in this sense only to the extent that it is possible to delimit languages and dialects without referring to the community that speaks them.

(2) A more complex definition is given by Charles Hockett (1958: 8):

> Each language defines a speech community: the whole set of people who communicate with each other, either directly or indirectly, via the common language.

Here the criterion of communication within the community is added, so that if two communities both spoke the same language but had no contact with each other at all, they would count as different speech communities.

(3) The next definition shifts the emphasis entirely from shared language to communication. A simple form of it was given by Leonard Bloomfield (1933: 42):

> A speech community is a group of people who interact by means of speech.

This leaves open the possibility that some interact by means of one language, and others by means of another. This possibility is explicitly recognised in the definition given by John Gumperz (1962):

> We will define [linguistic community] as a social group which may be either monolingual or multilingual, held together by frequency of social interaction patterns and set off from the surrounding areas by weaknesses in the lines of communication.

(4) A later definition by Gumperz, however, introduces the requirement that there should be some specifically linguistic differences between the members of the speech community and those outside it (1968):

> the speech community: any human aggregate characterised by regular and frequent interaction by means of a shared body of verbal signs and set off from similar aggregates by significant differences in language use.

Unlike definition (2), this does not require that there should be just one language per speech community. The effect of putting emphasis on communication and interaction, as in these last two definitions, is that different speech communities will tend not to overlap much, in contrast with the earlier definitions where overlap automatically results from bilingualism.

(5) A different definition puts the emphasis on shared attitudes and knowledge, rather than on shared linguistic behaviour. It is given by William Labov (1972a: 120):

> The speech community is not defined by any marked agreement in the use of language elements, so much as by participation in a set of shared norms; these norms may be observed in overt types of evaluative behaviour [see 6.2 below], and by the uniformity of abstract patterns of variation which are invariant in respect to particular levels of usage [see 5.4.1].

Rather similar definitions, referring to shared norms and abstract patterns of variation rather than to shared speech behaviour, have been given by Dell Hymes (1972) and Michael Halliday (1972). It will be seen that this kind of definition puts emphasis on the speech community as a group of people who *feel* themselves to be a community in some sense, rather than a group which only the linguist and outsider could know about, as in some of the earlier definitions.

(6) Lastly, there is an approach which avoids the term 'speech community' altogether, but refers to groups in society which have distinctive speech characteristics as well as other social characteristics. It should be noted that the groups are those which the individual speaker perceives to exist, and not necessarily those which a sociologist might discover by objective methods; and the groups need not exhaust the whole population, but may represent the *clear* cases of certain social types (i.e. the 'prototypes', in the sense of 3.2.2). This approach has been advocated by Robert Le Page (Le Page and Tabouret-Keller 1985):

> Each individual creates the systems for his verbal behaviour so that they shall resemble those of the group or groups with which from time to time he may wish to be identified, to the extent that
> a. he can identify the groups,
> b. he has both opportunity and ability to observe and analyse their behavioural systems,
> c. his motivation is sufficiently strong to impel him to choose, and to adapt his behaviour accordingly,
> d. he is still able to adapt his behaviour.

This is the view mentioned in 1.3.1, according to which individuals 'locate themselves in a multi-dimensional space', the dimensions being defined by the groups they can identify in their society. Unlike the 'speech communities' defined in (3), (4) and (5), these groups very definitely overlap. For instance a child may identify groups on the basis of sex, age, geography and race, and each grouping may contribute something to the particular combination of linguistic items which they select as their own language.

Our last quotation, by Dwight Bolinger, identifies these 'personal' groups as speech communities, and stresses the unlimited amount of complexity that is possible (Bolinger 1975: 333):

> There is no limit to the ways in which human beings league themselves together for self-identification, security, gain, amusement, worship, or any of the other purposes that are held in common; consequently there is no limit to the number and variety of speech communities that are to be found in society.

According to this view, any population (whether of a city, a village or whole state) may be expected to contain a very large number of speech communities indeed, with overlapping memberships and overlapping language systems. Indeed, Le Page's proviso a (to the extent that 'he can identify the groups') raises the possibility that different members of the population may be aware of different groups. If we take the position that speech communities should have some kind of psychological reality for their members (as in definition (5) above), then it follows that we must identify different speech communities in the same population according to the person whose viewpoint we are taking.

We have thus moved from a very simple definition of 'speech community' to a very complex one. How do we evaluate these different definitions? One answer, of course, is that they are all 'correct', since each of them allows us to define a set of people who have something in common linguistically – a language or dialect, interaction by means of speech, a given range of varieties and rules for using them, a given range of attitudes to varieties and items. The sets of people defined on the basis of different factors may of course differ radically – one criterion allows overlapping sets, another forbids them, and so on – but there is no need to try to reconcile the different definitions with one another, as they are simply trying to reflect different phenomena. On the other hand, the fact remains that they all purport to be definitions of the same thing – the 'speech community' – and the tone of some of the definitions given above (notably that of Labov in (5)) implies that it is a matter of finding the 'true' definition ('the speech community is not defined by . . . so much as by . . . '). Moreover, the word 'community' implies more than the existence of some common property; after all, nobody would talk of the 'community' of all the people whose names begin with the letter *h*, or who have overdrawn bank accounts. To qualify as a 'community', a set of people presumably needs to be distinguished from the rest of the world by more than one property, and some of these properties have to be important from the point of view of the members' social lives. The question, then, is which of the definitions of 'speech community' lead to genuine communities in this sense.

It might be thought that they *all* do. Even taking the simplest of the definitions, according to which a speech community is simply the set of people who use a given language or dialect, it is hard to imagine such a community having nothing *but* the common language or dialect to set them off from other people – nothing in their culture, nothing to do with their history, and so on. As soon as the factor of interaction comes in, of course, it goes without saying that there will be other shared characteristics in addition to the interaction. This answer has the attraction of resolving the apparent conflict between the definitions of 'speech community', but leads inevitably to the conclusion that different speech communities intersect in complex ways with one another – for example, a community defined in terms of interaction may contain parts of several communities defined in terms of shared language varieties. It will be seen that this is in fact precisely the notion of 'speech community' as defined in

(6), so we may take (6) as the most comprehensive view which subsumes all the others, and therefore makes them unnecessary.

This conclusion may seem very satisfactory, since it reconciles conflicting definitions with one another and replaces them all by a single definition. However, it raises a serious problem, since the notion 'speech community' thus defined is very much less easy to use for making generalisations about language and speech than the kinds of community defined by the earlier definitions. What would help the sociolinguist most would be a way of identifying some kind of natural speech community with reference to which it would be possible to make all relevant generalisations, and much of sociolinguistics has in fact been carried out on the assumption that this is possible. For example, the context of Labov's definition of 'speech community' given above is a discussion of his work in New York City, which he claims can be treated as a single speech community with reference to which a large number of generalisations can be made. Indeed, he goes so far as to propose that this community shares a single 'community grammar'. Our preferred definition of 'speech community' predicts that there can be no single set of people, such as all those living in New York City, which will provide a reference point for a large number of generalisations about linguistic items: on the contrary, different generalisations will be true of differently delimited communities. It will be seen that this conclusion is amply supported by the facts and arguments of the following sections.

More seriously still, it is doubtful whether the notion 'speech community' is helpful at all. The term may in fact mislead us by implying the existence of 'real' communities 'out there', which we could discover if only we knew how. There are good reasons for rejecting this assumption:

(1) Mismatch between subjective and objective reality.
According to definition (6), communities exist only to the extent that we are aware of them, so their reality is only subjective, not objective – and may be only very loosely based on objective reality. We all have hazy notions of the way people speak in distant places of which we have little direct experience – notions such as 'Northerner' (or 'Southerner'), 'American' (or 'British'), 'Irish', 'Australian' and so on. No self-respecting dialectologist would recognise a dialect area called 'Northern' (or 'Southern') English, but some lay people certainly think in such terms, so the least we can say is that if objective communities exist, they are different from the communities that we recognise subjectively.

(2) Evidence against community grammars.
The assumption behind all the definitions except (6) is that members of the community are linguistically 'the same' in some sense, either in their use of language

or in what they know and think about language. Peter Trudgill considers this assumption (Trudgill 1983b), and rejects it on the grounds that people do not even know the linguistic details of other people who live in the same city, let alone people who live hundreds of miles away. He illustrates this conclusion from his work in Norwich, which we shall discuss later (see 5.2.3). No doubt we could illustrate the same point even for members of the same family, especially if differences between generations are taken into account.

(3) Evidence for networks.
We shall see a great deal of evidence for the importance of social networks in people's linguistic behaviour (5.4.3). A typical social network has a small cluster of people near the centre and a collection of others 'hanging on' more or less closely, and perhaps hanging on to other neighbouring networks at the same time. A community, in the sense intended by all our definitions, has a boundary (even if a hazy one), but social networks have no boundaries, not even hazy ones.

(4) Small size of the most important communities.
The last problem with the general notion of 'speech community' is that if we are looking for social groups that are clearly relevant to a person's language, by far the most important ones are also very small – their family, their friends, their neighbours, their colleagues at school or work, any clubs or local organisations they belong to. These are the most important sources of linguistic influence, especially on children, even in these days of mass communications, but they are far smaller than the 'speech communities' that linguists have tended to invoke.

The conclusion would therefore seem to be that our sociolinguistic world is not organised in terms of objective 'speech communities', even though we may think subjectively in terms of communities or social types such as 'Londoner' and 'American'. This means that the search for a 'true' definition of the speech community, or for the 'true' boundaries around some assumed speech community, is just a wild goose chase.

This discussion of speech communities has raised the fundamental question: 'Where is language?' Is it 'in' the community or 'in' the individual? The position adopted throughout this book is that language must be 'in the individual' for various reasons – because each individual is unique, because individuals use language so as to locate themselves in a multi-dimensional social space, and for a number of other reasons which will emerge later. This view is widely held by linguists, and the following quotation is fairly typical:

> . . . language, while existing to serve a social function (communication) is nevertheless seated in the minds of individuals. (Guy 1980)

The reader should know, however, that this position is controversial. Unfortunately it appears to be opposed to the view of William Labov, who (as we shall see) is the most influential of all sociolinguists. Labov takes a very clear position on this issue, as witness these remarks in a discussion of the English spoken in the American city of Philadelphia:

> . . . the English language is a property of the English speech community, which is in turn composed of many nested subcommunities. There is no doubt that Philadelphia speakers of English are members of the larger community of American English speakers, and the even larger community of all speakers of English. It might also be said that Philadelphia is in turn composed of many smaller subcommunities. But the data presented here show that the linguistic world is not indefinitely complicated. (1989: 2)

> I began this paper with a question about the possible objects of linguistic description. As far as I can see, the individual speaker is not such an object. This essay, like other studies of sociolinguistic variation, shows that individual behavior can be understood only as a reflection of the grammar of the speech community. Language is not a property of the individual, but of the community. Any description of a language must take the speech community as its object if it is to do justice to the elegance and regularity of linguistic structure. (1989: 52)

The context of these remarks is a long (and impressive) discussion of variations in a single complicated feature of the English spoken in Philadelphia, in which he shows that a representative sample of speakers hardly varies at all even on the finest details. His data are beyond dispute, but they only seem to show that individuals in Philadelphia are very similar as far as this one feature is concerned. It does not follow that Philadelphians agree on all features, nor that every human being belongs clearly to a single community, nor that every community (however defined) will show the same amount of internal agreement. Moreover, the existence of agreement among speakers does not show that 'language is not a property of the individual', any more than similarities of height or income in some population show that height and income are not really properties of the individual.

2.2   Languages

2.2.1   'Language' and 'dialect'

We shall spend the rest of this chapter looking at the most widely recognised types of language variety: 'language', 'dialect' and 'register'. We shall see that all three types are extremely problematic, both from the point of view of finding a general definition for each one which will distinguish it from the others, and also from the point of view of finding criteria for delimiting varieties.

We first need to consider the concept 'language'. What does it mean to say that some variety is a language? This is first of all a question about popular usage: what do ordinary people mean when they say that some variety is a language? Having answered the question in this form, we may or may not wish to take 'language' as a technical term, and say how we propose to use it in sociolinguistics. We shall want to do so if we find that popular usage reflects some kind of reality to which we should like to refer in sociolinguistics, but if we come to the conclusion that popular usage reflects no such reality, then there will be no point in defining 'language' more explicitly in order to use it as a technical term.

One thing that is not in question is the importance of studying popular usage of the term 'language' simply as part of English vocabulary, along with 'well-spoken', 'chat' and other vocabulary which reflects the parts of our culture which are related to language and speech. It is part of our culture to make a distinction between 'languages' and 'dialects' – in fact, we make *two* separate, distinctions using these terms, and we may draw conclusions from this fact about our culturally inherited view of language (in the same way that we can use vocabulary as evidence for other aspects of culture – see 3.2.1).

We may contrast our culture in this respect with others where no such distinction is made. For example, according to Einar Haugen (1966), this was the case in England until the term *dialect* was borrowed in the Renaissance, as a learned word from Greek. In fact, we may see our distinction between 'language' and 'dialect' as due to the influence of Greek culture, since the distinction was developed in Greek because of the existence of a number of clearly distinct written varieties in use in Classical Greece, each associated with a different area and used for a different kind of literature. Thus the meanings of the Greek terms which were translated as 'language' and 'dialect' were in fact quite different from the meanings these words have in English now. Their equivalents in French are perhaps more similar, since the French word *dialecte* refers only to regional varieties which are written and have a literature, in contrast with regional varieties which are not written, which are called *patois*. The point of this discussion is to show that there is nothing absolute about the distinction which English happens to make between 'languages' and 'dialects' (and for readers familiar with some language other than English, this discussion will hardly have been necessary).

What then is the difference, for English speakers, between a language and a dialect? There are two separate ways of distinguishing them, and this ambiguity is a source of great confusion. (Haugen (1966) argues that the reason for the ambiguity, and the resulting confusion, is precisely the fact that 'dialect' was borrowed from Greek, where the same ambiguity existed.) On the one hand, there is a difference of *size*, because a language is larger than a dialect. That is, a variety called a language contains more items than one called a dialect. This is the sense in which we may refer to English as a language, containing the sum total of all the terms in all its dialects, with 'Standard English' as one dialect among many others (Yorkshire English, Indian English, etc.). Hence the greater 'size' of the language English.

The other contrast between 'language' and 'dialect' is a question of *prestige*, a language having prestige which a dialect lacks. If we apply the terms in this sense, Standard English (for example, the kind of English used in this book) is not a dialect at all, but a language, whereas the varieties which are not used in formal writing are dialects. Whether some variety is called a language or a dialect depends on how much prestige one thinks it has, and for most people this is a clear-cut matter, which depends on whether it is used in formal writing. Accordingly, people in Britain habitually refer to languages which are unwritten (or which they think are unwritten) as dialects, or 'mere dialects', irrespective of whether there is a (proper) language to which they are related. (It would be nonsense to use 'dialect' in this way intending its 'size' sense, of course.) The fact that we put so much weight on whether or not it is written in distinguishing between 'language' and 'dialect' is one of the interesting things that the terms show us about British culture, and we shall return to the importance of writing in 2.2.2.

2.2.2 Standard languages

It is probably fair to say that the only kind of variety which would count as a 'proper language' (in the second sense of 'language') is a *standard language*. Standard languages are interesting in as much as they have a rather special relation to society – one which is quite abnormal when seen against the context of the tens (or hundreds?) of thousands of years during which language has been used. Whereas one thinks of normal language development as taking place in a rather haphazard way, largely below the threshold of consciousness of the speakers, standard languages are the result of a direct and deliberate intervention by society. This intervention, called 'standardisation', produces a standard language where before there were just 'dialects' (in the second sense, i.e. non-standard varieties).

The notion 'standard language' is somewhat imprecise, but a typical standard language will have passed through the following processes (Haugen 1966; for a somewhat different list, see Garvin and Mathiot 1956 and Garvin 1959).

(1) *Selection* – somehow or other a particular variety must have been selected as the one to be developed into a standard language. It may be an existing variety, such as the one used in an important political or commercial centre, but it could be an amalgam of various varieties. The choice is a matter of great social and political importance, as the chosen variety necessarily gains prestige and so the people who already speak it share in this prestige. However, in some cases the chosen variety has been one with no native speakers at all – for instance, Classical Hebrew in Israel and the two modern standards for Norwegian (Haugen 1994).

(2) *Codification* – some agency such as an academy must have written dictionaries and grammar books to 'fix' the variety, so that everyone agrees on what is correct. Once codification has taken place, it becomes necessary for any ambitious citizen to learn the correct forms and not to use in writing any 'incorrect' forms that may exist in their native variety.

(3) *Elaboration of function* – it must be possible to use the selected variety in all the functions associated with central government and with writing: for example, in parliament and law courts, in bureaucratic, educational and scientific documents of all kinds and, of course, in various forms of literature. This may require extra linguistic items to be added to the variety, especially technical words, but it is also necessary to develop new conventions for *using* existing forms – how to formulate examination questions, how to write formal letters and so on.

(4) *Acceptance* – the variety has to be accepted by the relevant population as *the* variety of the community – usually, in fact, as the national language. Once this has happened, the standard language serves as a strong unifying force for the state, as a symbol of its independence of other states (assuming that its standard is unique and not shared with others), and as a marker of its difference from other states. It is precisely this symbolic function that makes states go to some lengths to develop one.

This analysis of the factors typically involved in standardisation has been quite widely accepted by sociolinguists (for more details and examples, see Fasold 1984, Milroy and Milroy 1985, Haugen 1994). However, there is ample scope for debate and disagreement about the *desirability* of certain aspects of standardisation. For instance, it is not essential either that standardisation should involve matters of *pronunciation* as well as of writing (Macaulay 1973), or that the standard language should be presented as the only 'correct' variety (a point argued by many linguists and sociolinguists).

The present section on standard languages is the only part of this book that deals in any detail with the large-scale issues of the sociology of language (see 1.1.3), but it has been included for three reasons. Firstly, it is relevant to the discussion of the second meaning of 'language' introduced in 2.2.1 (where 'language' = 'standard language'). Secondly, it is interesting to see that language can be deliberately manipulated by society. Thirdly, and perhaps most importantly, it brings out the *unusual* character of standard languages, which are perhaps the *least* interesting kind of language for anyone interested in the nature of human language (as most linguists are). For instance, one might almost describe standard languages as pathological in their lack of diversity. To see language in its 'natural' state, one must find a variety which is neither a standard language, nor a dialect subordinate to a standard (since these too show pathological features, notably the difficulty of making judgments in terms of the non-standard dialect without being influenced by the standard one). The irony, of course, is that academic linguistics is likely to arise only in a society with a standard language, such as Britain, the United States or France, and the *first* language to which linguists pay attention is their own – a standard one.

2.2.3   *The delimitation of languages*

We now return to the question posed at the beginning of 2.2: what does it mean to say of some variety that it is a language? We can now clarify the question by distinguishing between the two meanings of 'language' based, respectively, on prestige and size. We have already given an answer on the basis of prestige: a language is a standard language. In principle this distinction is an absolute one: either a variety is a standard language, or it is not. (It is clear, however, that some languages are more standard than others; for instance, Standard French has been more rigidly codified than Standard English.) When we turn to the other distinction, based on size, the situation is very different, since everything becomes relative – for example, in comparison with one variety a chosen variety may be large, yet compared with another it may be small. The variety containing all the items used in (English-speaking) Britain looks large compared with, say, Standard English or Cockney, but only small compared with the variety which consists of all the items used in any of the 'English-speaking' countries. This being so, the claim that a particular variety is a language, in the 'size' sense, amounts to very little. Is there, then, any way in which the distinction between 'language' and 'dialect' based on size can be made less relative? (To anticipate, our answer is that there is not.)

The obvious candidate for an extra criterion is that of *mutual intelligibility*. If the speakers of two varieties can understand each other, then the varieties concerned are instances of the same language; otherwise they are not. This is a widely used criterion, but it cannot be taken seriously because there are such serious problems in its application (Simpson 1994a).

(1) Even *popular usage* does not correspond consistently to this criterion, since varieties which we (as lay people) call different languages may be mutually intelligible (for example, the Scandinavian languages, excluding Finnish and Lapp) and varieties which we call instances of the same language may not (for example, the so-called 'dialects' of Chinese). Popular usage tends to reflect the other definition of language, based on prestige, so that if two varieties are both standard languages, or are subordinate to different standards, they must be different languages, and conversely they must be the same language if they are both subordinate to the same standard. This explains the difference between our ideas on the varieties of Scandinavia and of China: each Scandinavian country has a separate standard language (indeed, as we have just seen, Norway has *two*), whereas the whole of China only has one.

(2) Mutual intelligibility is a matter of *degree*, ranging from total intelligibility down to total unintelligibility. How high up this scale do two varieties need to be in order to count as members of the same language? This is clearly a question which is best avoided, rather than answered, since any answer must be arbitrary.

(3) Varieties may be arranged in a DIALECT CONTINUUM, a chain of adjacent varieties in which each pair of adjacent varieties are mutually intelligible, but pairs taken from opposite ends of the chain are not. One such continuum is said to stretch from Amsterdam through Germany to Vienna, and another from Calais to the south of Italy. The criterion of mutual intelligibility is, however, based on a relationship between languages that is logically different from that of sameness of language, which it is supposed to illuminate. If A is the same language as B, and B is the same language as C, then A and C must also be the same language, and so on. 'Sameness of language' is therefore a transitive relation, but 'mutual intelligibility' is an intransitive one: if A and B are mutually intelligible, and B and C are mutually intelligible, C and A are not necessarily mutually intelligible. The problem is that an intransitive relation cannot be used to elucidate a transitive relation.

(4) Mutual intelligibility is not really a relation between varieties, but between people, since it is they, and not the varieties, that understand one another. This being so, the degree of mutual intelligibility depends not just on the amount of overlap between the items in the two varieties, but on qualities of the people

concerned. One highly relevant quality is *motivation*: how much does person A want to understand person B? This will depend on numerous factors such as how much A likes B, how far they wish to emphasise the cultural differences or similarities between them and so on. Motivation is important because understanding another person always requires effort on the part of the hearer – as witness the possibility of 'switching off' when one's motivation is low. The greater the difference between the varieties concerned, the more effort is needed, so if A cannot understand B, this simply tells us that the task was too great for A's motivation, and we do not know what would have happened if their motivation had been higher. Another relevant quality of the hearer is *experience*: how much experience have they had of the variety to which they are listening? Obviously, the greater the previous experience, the greater the likelihood of understanding it.

Both of these qualities raise another problem regarding the use of mutual intelligibility as a criterion, namely that it *need not be reciprocal*, since A and B need not have the same degree of motivation for understanding each other, nor need they have the same amount of previous experience of each other's varieties. Typically, it is easier for non-standard speakers to understand standard speakers than the other way round, partly because the former will have had more experience of the standard variety (notably through the media) than vice versa, and partly because they may be motivated to minimise the cultural differences between themselves and the standard speakers (though this is by no means necessarily so), while standard speakers may want to emphasise these differences.

In conclusion, mutual intelligibility does not work as a criterion for delimiting languages in the 'size' sense. There is no other criterion which is worth considering as an alternative, so we must conclude (with Matthews 1979: 47) that *there is no real distinction to be drawn between 'language' and 'dialect'* (except with reference to prestige, where it would be better to use the term 'standard (language)', rather than just 'language'). In other words, the search for language boundaries is a waste of time. Where the boundary between two languages is clear to sociolinguists, it is clear to everybody else as well – for example, there is no doubt that the languages spoken on opposite sides of the English Channel are different, but you don't need to be a sociolinguist to be sure of that. And where a boundary is unclear to ordinary people, it is equally unclear to sociolinguists. We can't assume that the phenomenon 'language' always reaches us neatly packaged into 'language-sized' bundles. All we can assume is that there are varieties of language, and that a given variety may be relatively similar to some other varieties and relatively different from others.

2.2.4   The family tree model

A convenient way of representing the relationships among varieties is in terms of the *family tree model*, which was developed in the nineteenth century as an aid in the historical study of languages (for an excellent discussion, see Bynon 1977: 63). This model allows one to show how closely a number of varieties are related to one another – that is, how far each has diverged from the others as a result of historical changes. For instance, one might take English, German, Welsh, French and Hindu as the varieties to be related. By building a tree structure on top of these varieties, as in Figure 2.1, one can show that English is related most closely to German, less closely to Welsh and French and still less closely to Hindi. (For a fuller picture of the relations among these and many other 'Indo-European' languages, see Crystal 1987: 296–301.)

Chinese has been added to show that it is not related *at all* to the other languages. If one includes two varieties in the same tree there is an assumption that they are both 'descended', through historical changes, from a common 'ancestor' variety, which could be named on the diagram. Thus we could add the name 'Proto-Indo-European' to the node at the top of the tree, showing that all the varieties named at the bottom (except Chinese) are descended from this one variety. Similarly, we could label the node dominating English and German 'Proto-Germanic', to give a name to the variety from which they are both descended.

The main value of the family tree model for historical linguistics is that it clarifies the historical relations among the varieties concerned, and in particular that it gives a clear idea of the relative chronology of the historical changes by which the varieties concerned have diverged. From the present point of view, however, the advantage is that a family tree shows a *hierarchical* relation among varieties which makes no distinction between 'languages' and 'dialects'. Indeed, it is common in historical linguistics to refer to the varieties which are descended from Latin as 'dialects' of Latin (or 'the Romance dialects'), although they include such obvious 'languages' (in the prestige sense) as Standard French. If we had wished to add Yorkshire English and Cockney to

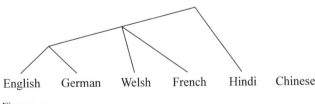

English   German   Welsh   French   Hindi   Chinese

Figure 2.1

our list of varieties, we would simply have added them below English, without giving them a different status from the others.

Apart from the attraction which we have just noted, however, the family tree model has little to recommend it to the sociolinguist, since it represents a gross simplification of the relations between varieties. In particular, it makes no allowances for one variety *influencing* another, which can lead in extreme cases to *convergence* – a single variety being descended from two separate varieties. We shall see in 2.5 that this does in fact happen, and in 2.3.2 we shall introduce a better model, the 'wave theory'.

2.3 Dialects

2.3.1 *Regional dialects and isoglosses*

Having rejected the distinction between 'language' and 'dialect' (except with reference to prestige), we can now turn to an even more fundamental question: how clear are the boundaries between varieties? The hierarchical model of the family tree implies that the boundaries between varieties are clear at all levels of the tree. Is this so? In particular, is it possible to continue such a tree downwards, revealing smaller and smaller varieties, until one comes to the level of the individual speaker (the 'idiolect')? The answer must be no.

If we consider the most straightforward variety differences based on geography, it should be possible, if the family tree model is right, to identify what are called REGIONAL DIALECTS within any larger variety such as English. Fortunately, there is a vast amount of evidence bearing on this question, produced by the discipline called DIALECTOLOGY, particularly by its branch called DIALECT GEOGRAPHY (see, for example, Bloomfield 1993: ch. 19, Chambers and Trudgill 1980, Hocket 1958: ch. 56; see also 5.4.2 below). Since the nineteenth century, dialectologists in Europe and the United States (and, on a smaller scale, in Britain) have been studying the geographical distribution of linguistic items, such as pairs of synonymous words (for example, *pail* versus *bucket*), or different pronunciations of the same word, such as *farm* with or without the /r/. Their results are plotted on a map, showing which items were found in which villages (since dialect geography tends to concentrate on rural areas to avoid the complexities of towns). The dialect geographer may then draw a line between the area where one item was found and areas where others were found, showing a boundary for each area called an ISOGLOSS (from Greek *iso-* 'same' and *gloss-* 'tongue').

The family tree model allows a very important prediction to be made regarding isoglosses, namely that they should not intersect. Distinctions can add further subdivisions within a variety, but they cannot subdivide two varieties at the same time for the simple reason that a tree diagram can show subclassification, but not cross-classification. You cannot use a tree, for example, to divide English both on a north–south axis and also on an east–west axis. (Try it!) According to the family tree model, then, isoglosses should never intersect, because if they did they would be dividing the same population in two contradictory ways (just as if we first split it according to sex and then according to age, which is impossible to show in a single tree). Unfortunately this prediction is wrong; in fact, it could hardly be further from reality, because cross-classification is the normal, most common relationship among isoglosses. To take just one example, there are two isoglosses in southern England which intersect, as shown in Map 2.1 on p. 40 (based on Trudgill 1974/1983: 171 and Wakelin 1978: 9). One isogloss separates the area (to the north) where *come* is pronounced with the same vowel as *stood*, from the area where it has the open vowel [ʌ], as in Received Pronunciation (RP), the prestige accent of England. The other isogloss separates the area (to the north-east) where *r* of *farm* is not pronounced, from the area where it is. The only way to reconcile this kind of pattern with the family tree model would be to give priority to one isogloss over the other, but such a choice would be arbitrary and would in any case leave the subordinate isoglosses unconnected, each representing a subdivision of a different variety, whereas in fact each clearly represents a single phenomenon. Examples like this could be multiplied almost indefinitely (for another particularly clear example, see the map in Bolinger 1975: 349; and for a scholarly review, see Sankoff 1973a).

From such findings many dialectologists have drawn the conclusion that each item has its own distribution through the population of speakers, and that there is no reason to expect different items to have identical distributions (Bynon 1977: 190). This seems to be the only reasonable conclusion to draw from the data. But this leads to the further conclusion that isoglosses need not delimit varieties, except in the trivial sense where varieties each consist of just one item; and if we cannot rely on isoglosses to delimit varieties, what can we use?

There seems to be no alternative, and we find ourselves in a similar position to the earlier one in our discussion of languages: there is no way of delimiting varieties, and we must therefore conclude that varieties do not exist. All that exists are people and items, and people may be more or less similar to one another in the items they have in their language. Though unexciting, this conclusion is at least true, and raises incidental questions such as what determines the amount and kind of similarity between people.

2.3.2 Diffusion and the wave theory

An alternative to the family tree model was developed as early as the nineteenth century to account for the kind of phenomenon we have just been considering. It is called the WAVE THEORY, and is based on the assumption that changes in language spread outwards from centres of influence to the surrounding areas in much the same way that a wave spreads from the place where a stone is dropped into a pool. This view of language change is accepted by all scholars, both in historical linguistics (Allan 1994, Simpson 1994b) and in sociolinguistics (Trudgill 1975/1983, 1986).

The wave theory explains why isoglosses intersect by postulating different geographical foci for the spread of different items. The isogloss between two items like *farm* with and without the /r/ shows where the influence of one item stops and the other takes over; on the assumption that one of the items represents an innovation, this means that the isogloss marks the furthest points which the influence of the new item has reached at the time when the dialectologist collected the data. There is no reason why innovations leading to any two different isoglosses should have started in the same place – or for that matter in the same period – so there is no particular reason why their isoglosses should not intersect. To return to the analogy, if two or more stones are dropped into a pool, there is no reason why they should fall in the same place, and there could be many different centres of influence from which ripples spread and intersect. Moreover, these centres may change with time, as different influences wax and wane. Each centre represents the source of a different innovative item from which 'waves' spread out in different directions.

The analogy fails in that waves of linguistic influence 'freeze' and stop expanding, because the influence at their point of origin is no longer strong enough to sustain them. In other words, in terms of the theory of acts of identity (see 1.3.1), the influence of an item stops when individuals choose for some reason not to identify themselves with the group which uses it. This means that – unlike the waves in a pool – the location of an isogloss may be the same

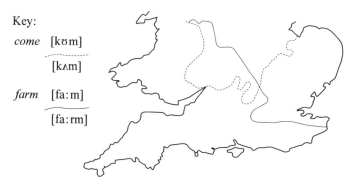

Key:

come [kʊm]

[kʌm]

farm [faːm]

[faːrm]

Map 2.1

one year as it was a century before since the strength of influence of the group with which it is associated may still not be strong enough to make it move any further. Moreover, an item need not be an innovation in order to influence people, since its effects depend on the social standing of the group associated with it, rather than on its newness. It is quite possible for a relatively archaic form to oust a newer one after the latter has spread. For example, in some areas of the United States the pronunciation of words like *farm* with an /r/ is currently replacing the pronunciation without /r/, although the latter is in fact the innovation (as the spelling suggests) – we shall discuss New York City as an example of such an area in 5.2.2.

Because of these reservations it seems best to abandon the analogy of the stones dropping in a pool. A more helpful analogy would perhaps be one involving different species of plants sown in a field, each spreading outwards by dispersing its seeds over a particular area. In the analogy, each item would be represented by a different species, with its own rate of seed dispersal, and an isogloss would be represented by the limit of spread of a given species. Different species would be able to coexist on the same spot (a relaxation of the normal laws of botany), but it might be necessary to designate certain species as being in competition with one another, corresponding to items which provide alternative ways of saying the same thing (like the two pronunciations of *farm*). The advantages of this analogy are that there is no need for the distribution of species in a field to be in constant change with respect to every item, and that every item may be represented in the analogy, and not just those which are innovative.

In terms of this new analogy, a linguistic innovation is a new species which has arisen (either by mutation or by being brought in from outside), and which may or may not prosper. If it does, it may spread and replace some or all of its competitors, but if it does not it may either die out or remain confined to a very small area of the field (i.e. to a very small speech community). Whether or not a species thrives depends on how strongly its representatives grow (i.e. on the power and influence of its speech community): the bigger the plants, the more seeds they produce, and the better the chances of the species conquering new territory.

2.3.3 *Social dialects*

Dialect differences are not, of course, only geographical, as has been implied in the discussion so far. There are two main sources of extra complexity. Firstly, there is geographical *mobility* – people move from one place to another, taking their dialects with them even if they modify them in the course of time to fit their new surroundings. Thus simply plotting speakers on a map may produce a more or less untidy pattern according to how mobile the population is (a problem which is generally avoided in dialectology by selecting as informants people who were born and bred in the place where they are now living).

The second source of complexity is the fact that geography is only one of the relevant factors, others being social class, sex and age (see 5.4.2). Dialectologists, therefore, speak of SOCIAL DIALECTS, or SOCIOLECTS, to refer to non-regional differences. Because of these other factors, a speaker may be more similar in language to people from the same social group in a different area than to people from a different social group in the same area. Indeed, one of the characteristics of the hierarchical social structure of a country like Britain is that social class takes precedence over geography as a determinant of speech, so that there is far more geographical variation among people in the lower social classes than there is amongst those at the 'top' of the social heap. This has gone so far that people who have passed through the public school system (or would like to sound as though they had) typically have *no* regional traits at all in their language. This is a peculiarity of Britain however, and is not found in other countries such as the United States or Germany, where 'top people' show their region of origin at least through their pronunciation, though possibly in few other features of their language.

Pronunciation seems in general to be more sensitive to regional and social differences than grammar and vocabulary, so we make a distinction between accent and dialect, with ACCENT referring to nothing but pronunciation and DIALECT referring to every other aspect of language. This allows us to distinguish between the standard dialect and non-standard dialects, while making separate statements about pronunciation in terms of accents (Wells 1982). Thus in Britain we may say that many people use a regional accent but standard dialect, and a select few use an RP accent with the same standard dialect. Great confusion results if the standard dialect, which is a matter of vocabulary, syntax and morphology, is referred to as 'RP'.

All I have done in this section is to introduce the terms 'social dialect' and 'accent', pointing out that there are linguistic differences between speakers which are due not only to geography but also to other social factors. The problems with delimiting regional dialects can also be paralleled for social dialects, as we shall see in chapter 5. It would be hard to draw isoglosses for social dialects, since one would need to plot them on a many-dimensional map, but there is no reason to doubt that, could such a map be drawn, we should again find that each isogloss follows a unique path. Consequently we must reject the notions represented by both 'social dialect' and 'accent', for the same reason as we rejected the notion of a regional dialect, except as a very rough and ready way of referring to phenomena.

2.3.4 Types of linguistic item

One of the most interesting questions which this whole discussion of varieties raises is whether all linguistic items are subject to variation in the same way. In referring to the notion 'accent' we have already suggested that there may be a general difference between items of pronunciation and other items (morphology, syntax, vocabulary), in that pronunciation is less liable to standardisation. Given the special connection between standardisation and writing, it would not be surprising if this were so.

Pronunciation seems to have a different social function from other types of item. For example, despite the manifest influence of the United States on Britain, its influence on British English is restricted almost entirely to vocabulary and appears to have had no effect at all on the pronunciation of even the most susceptible groups, such as teenagers. As Trudgill (1983c) has shown, even radio disc-jockeys and pop singers only put on American accents when singing or disc-jockeying!

It may be, then, that pronunciation and other items play different roles in the individual's acts of identity to which we referred above. For instance, it could be that we use pronunciation in order to identify our origins (or to *imply* that we originated from some group, whether we really did or not). In contrast, we might use morphology, syntax and vocabulary in order to identify our current status in society, such as the amount of education we have had. At present this is conjecture, but there is enough evidence for differences between pronunciation and other areas of language to make it worth looking for general explanations. As already suggested, the difference may be simply an artefact of the standardisation process, so it is important to look for evidence from societies not affected by standardisation. If such differences are found even there, then we may assume that we have discovered a fundamental, and rather mysterious, fact about language.

Pursuing this 'social' comparison of the major divisions of language, is there any evidence for the view that syntax is more resistant to variation than either morphology or vocabulary? It is certainly the case that examples of syntactic differences within a variety are much less frequently quoted in the literature than differences in either pronunciation or morphology, which are in any case hard to keep separate (for example, is the difference between *-ing* and *-in'* in words like *coming* a difference in pronunciation or in morphology?). Moreover, differences in vocabulary are also much more frequently discussed in the literature of dialectology than are differences in syntax. It seems, then, that there is a difference between syntax and the rest of language which needs to be explained. (For more discussion of these types of variable item, see 5.3.1.)

It is important to be wary about this apparent difference, however. For one thing, the lack of references in the literature to syntactic differences could be due to the difficulty of studying such differences, since where they exist the evidence for them is relatively rare in ordinary speech and is hard to elicit directly compared, in particular, with vocabulary items. Secondly, the apparent stability of syntax could be an illusion, because there are relatively few syntactic items (i.e. constructions) compared with vocabulary items, so that even if the same *proportion* of syntactic items varied the result would be a smaller number. Thirdly, even if there is a difference between syntax and the rest of language, this could again be an artefact of the process of standardisation. However, notwithstanding all these qualifications, there does seem to be a greater tendency to uniformity in syntax than in other areas of language, which is hard to explain. Could there be a tendency for people to actively *suppress* alternatives in syntax, while positively seeking them in vocabulary?

Evidence for such a view comes from two sources. Syntactic items are rather commonly diffused across 'language' boundaries into adjacent areas. (Features which are shared in this way, and cannot be explained as the result of a common heritage from a parent language, are called AREAL FEATURES (Simpson 1994b).) For example, three adjacent languages in the Balkans (Bulgarian, Romanian and Albanian) all have the rather unusual property of a suffixed definite article; thus in Albanian *mik* is 'friend' and *mik-u* 'the friend'. This shared feature can only be explained by diffusion in the relatively recent past (at least since Latin, from which Romanian is derived). Features presumably spread across language boundaries as the result of bilingualism, and the prevalence of syntactic features among areal features may be due to the tendency among bilingual individuals to mix languages in mid-sentence (2.5.1). The more similar the sentence-structures are in the two languages, the easier this is; so language-mixing may encourage the suppression of syntactic differences. The areal diffusion of syntactic features is otherwise rather hard to understand, since syntax generally seems to be relatively impervious to historical change.

Another piece of evidence for the view that we actively suppress alternatives in syntax is reported by John Gumperz and Robert Wilson (1971) from Kupwar, a small village in India, whose 3,000 inhabitants between them speak three languages: Marathi and Urdu, which are both Indo-European, and Kannada, which is not. (A small number also speak a non-Indo-European, language, Telugu.) As usual in India, the village is divided into clearly distinct groups (castes), each of which can be identified by its language. However, the different groups obviously need to communicate with each other, and bilingualism (or trilingualism) is common, especially among the men. These languages have coexisted in this way for centuries, but in spite of this contact they are still totally distinct in *vocabulary*. Gumperz and Wilson suggest that the reason for this is that the linguistic differences serve as a useful symbol of the caste differences, which are very strictly maintained; thus vocabulary has the role of distinguishing social groups, without which the demands of efficiency in communication would presumably have gradually eroded the differences in vocabulary over the centuries. As far as *syntax* is concerned, however, the three main languages have become much more similar in Kupwar than they are elsewhere. For example, in standard Kannada, sentences like *The postman is my best friend* do not contain a word for 'is', whereas in Urdu and Marathi they do; but in the Kannada of Kupwar there is a word for *is*, on the model of Urdu and Marathi. This example seems to support our hypothesis that differences in syntax tend to be suppressed, whereas those in vocabulary and pronunciation tend to be favoured and used as markers of social differences. There do not appear to be any examples of communities in which this relationship is reversed, with less variation in vocabulary and pronunciation than in syntax.

A very tentative hypothesis thus emerges regarding the different types of linguistic items and their relations to society, according to which *syntax* is the marker of cohesion in society, with individuals trying to eliminate alternatives in syntax from their individual language. In contrast, *vocabulary* is a marker of divisions in society, and individuals may actively cultivate alternatives in order to make more subtle social distinctions. *Pronunciation* reflects the permanent social group with which the speaker identifies. This results in a tendency for individuals to suppress alternatives, but in contrast to the tendency with syntax, different groups suppress different alternatives in order to distinguish themselves from each other, and individuals keep some alternatives 'alive' in order to be able to identify their origins even more precisely, by using them in a particular and distinctive proportion relative to other alternatives. Unbelievable though this may at first seem, it is certainly one way in which pronunciation variables are used, as we shall see in chapter 5.

The main reason for putting the above suggestions forward here is to show that it is possible to formulate interesting and researchable hypotheses against the background of the view of language which we are developing, in spite of our rejection of the concepts 'language X', 'dialect X' or even 'variety X'.

2.4 Registers

2.4.1 *Registers and dialects*

The term REGISTER is widely used in sociolinguistics to refer to 'varieties according to use', in contrast with dialects, defined as 'varieties according to user' (Cheshire 1992, Downes 1994, Biber 1988). The distinction is needed because the same person may use very different linguistic items to express more or less the same meaning on different occasions, and the concept of 'dialect' cannot reasonably be extended to include such variation. For instance, in writing one letter a person might start: 'I am writing to inform you that . . . ', but in another the same person might write: 'I just wanted to let you know that . . . '. Such examples could be multiplied endlessly, and suggest that the amount of variation due to register differences (if it could somehow be quantified) may be quite comparable with that due to differences in dialect.

We can interpret register differences in terms of the model of acts of identity in much the same way as for dialect differences. Each time we speak or write we not only locate ourselves in relation to the rest of society, but we also relate our act of communication itself to a complex classificatory scheme of communicative behaviour. This scheme takes the form of a multi-dimensional matrix, just like the map of our society which we each build in our mind (see 1.3.1). At the risk of slight oversimplification, we may say that your dialect shows who (or what) you *are*, whilst your register shows what you are *doing* (though these concepts are much less distinct than the slogan implies, as we shall see on page 47).

The 'dimensions' on which an act of communication may be located are no less complex than those relevant to the social location of the speaker. Michael Halliday (1978: 33) distinguishes three general types of dimension: 'field', 'mode' and 'tenor'. FIELD is concerned with the *purpose* and *subject-matter* of the communication; MODE refers to the *means* by which communication takes place – notably, by speech or writing; and TENOR depends on the *relations* between participants. Once again, a slogan may help: field refers to 'why' and 'about what' a communication takes place; mode is about 'how'; and tenor is about 'to whom' (i.e. how the speaker views the person addressed). In terms of this model, the two examples of letter-openings cited above would differ in tenor, one being impersonal (addressed to someone with whom the writer only has formal relations) and the other personal, but their field and mode are the same.

According to this model, register differences are at least three-dimensional. Another widely used model has been proposed by Dell Hymes (1972), in which no less than thirteen separate variables determine the linguistic items selected by a speaker, apart from the variable of 'dialect'. It is very doubtful if even this number reflects all the complexities of register differences. Nevertheless, each of these models provides a framework within which any relevant dimensions of similarity and difference may be located. For example, the relations between speaker and 'addressee' involve more than one such dimension (as we shall see in 4.2.2), including the dimension of 'power', on which the addressee is subordinate, equal or superior to the speaker, and the dimension called 'solidarity', which distinguishes relatively intimate relations from more distant ones. In English speakers locate themselves on these two dimensions in relation to addressees largely by choosing among the alternative ways of naming the addressee – *Mr Smith, sir, John, mate* and so on.

We have so far presented the concept of 'register' in the way in which it is normally used, as the name of one kind of variety that is parallel to 'dialect'. However, we have already shown that dialects do not exist as discrete varieties, so we must ask whether registers do. The answer is, predictably, that they do not seem to have any more reality than dialects. For example, it is easy to see that the selection of items within a given sentence reflects different factors, depending on which items are involved. One item may, for instance, reflect the formality of the occasion, while another reflects the expertise of the speaker and addressee. This is the case in a sentence like *We obtained some sodium chloride*, where *obtained* is a formal word (in contrast with *got*) and *sodium chloride* is a technical expression (in contrast with *salt*). The dimension of formality is totally independent of the dimension of technicality, so four combinations of formality with technicality can be illustrated by the following perfectly normal sentences:

formal, technical	*We obtained some sodium chloride.*
formal, non-technical	*We obtained some salt.*
informal, technical	*We got some sodium chloride.*
informal, non-technical	*We got some salt.*

Simple examples like these suggest that different linguistic items are sensitive to different aspects of the act of communication, in the same way that different items react to different properties of the speaker (5.4.2). We can only speak of registers as varieties in the rather weak sense of sets of linguistic items which all have the same social distribution, i.e. all occur under the same circumstances. This is a far cry from the notion of variety in which speakers stick to one variety throughout a stretch of speech, speaking 'one dialect' (perhaps the only one they can speak) and 'one register'. However, it is also probably fair to say that those who use the term 'register' have never really intended it to be taken in this sense, as witness the fact that all the models presented lay great stress on the need for multi-dimensional analysis of registers.

Another point of similarity between dialects and registers is that they overlap considerably – one person's dialect is another person's register. For example, the items which one person uses under all circumstances, however informal, may be used by someone else only on the most formal occasions. This is the relation between 'native' speakers of standard and non-standard dialects.

Forms which are part of the standard speaker's 'dialect' are part of a special 'register' for the non-standard speaker – a serious social inequality (6.3).

In conclusion, we have now developed a model of language which is radically different from the one based on the notion 'variety'. In the latter, any given text may reasonably be expected to represent just one variety (though it is recognised that 'code-switching' may take place; see 2.5), and for any given variety it is possible to write a grammar – a description covering all types of linguistic item found in texts which represent that variety.

We may call this the VARIETY-BASED view of language in contrast with the ITEM-BASED view which we have developed so far in this book. Figure 2.2 illustrates the variety-based view. It shows just two linguistic items, related in some kind of linguistic structure (shown by the diagonal lines), but of course the reality involves tens of thousands of items for each speaker – possibly hundreds of thousands if they are multilingual. The little stick person is meant to stand for one of the many social categories that linguistic items may be related to – for example, one particular type of person. The horizontal line shows the relationship between this social category and the linguistic items; in most cases the relationship is that this kind of person is the typical speaker of this kind of language, but other relationships are also possible as we shall see in 4.2. The circle around the two linguistic items stands for a variety of language which in this case we have called 'language L'. The main point to notice in this diagram is that linguistic items are not linked directly to social categories, but only indirectly via language L; it is whole languages (or other varieties), and not individual linguistic items, that have social significance. This is actually equivalent to denying the need for sociolinguistics (as opposed to the sociology of language).

Now compare this with Figure 2.3, for the item-based view. Here the organisation of the linguistic items is the same, but the dotted circle shows that language L plays a much less important role – in fact, in the case illustrated it plays no role at all, because each item is linked directly to the social category

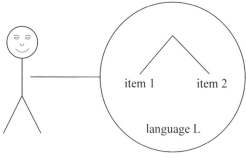

Figure 2.2

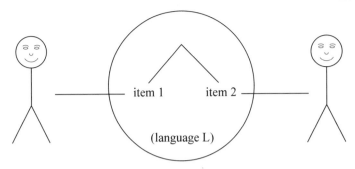

Figure 2.3

which is relevant to it. In this view the notion 'linguistic variety' is an optional extra, available when needed to capture generalisations that apply to very large collections of linguistic items, but by no means the only mechanism, or even the most important mechanism, for linking linguistic items to their social context.

2.4.2   *Diglossia*

Having emphasised the theoretical possibility of each individual linguistic item having its own unique social distribution among the various circumstances of use, it is now important to report that this possibility need not be exploited, and that in some societies there is a relatively simple arrangement called DIGLOSSIA in which at least one type of social restriction on items can be expressed in terms of large-scale 'varieties', rather than item by item. The term 'diglossia' was introduced into the English-language literature on sociolinguistics by Charles Ferguson (1959) in order to describe the situation found in places like Greece, the Arabic-speaking world in general, German-speaking Switzerland and the island of Haiti – a list which can easily be extended (A. Hudson 1994). In all these societies there are two distinct varieties, sufficiently distinct for lay people to call them separate languages, of which one is used only on formal and public occasions while the other is used by *everybody* under normal, everyday circumstances. The two varieties are normally called 'High' and 'Low', or 'standard' and 'vernacular'. Ferguson's definition of diglossia is as follows:

> Diglossia is a relatively stable language situation in which, in addition to the primary dialects of the language (which may include a standard or regional standards), there is a very divergent, highly codified (often grammatically more complex) superposed variety, the vehicle of a large and respected body of written literature, either of an earlier period or in another speech community, which is learned largely by formal education

49

and is used for most written and formal spoken purposes but is not used
by any sector of the community for ordinary conversation.

For example, in an Arabic-speaking diglossic community, the language used
at home is a local version of Arabic (there may be very great differences between
one 'dialect' of Arabic and another, to the point of mutual incomprehensibility),
with little variation between the most educated and the least educated speakers.
However, in a lecture at a university, or a sermon in a mosque, the only possibility is Standard Arabic, a variety different at all levels from the local vernacular,
and felt to be so different from the 'Low' variety that it is taught in schools in
the way that foreign languages are taught in English-speaking societies.
Likewise, when children learn to read and write, it is the standard language,
and not the local vernacular, which they are taught.

The most obvious difference between diglossic and English-speaking societies
is that no one in the former has the advantage of learning the High variety (as
used on formal occasions and in education) as their first language, since everyone speaks the Low variety at home. Consequently, the way to acquire a High
variety in such a society is not by being born into the right kind of family, but
by going to school. Of course, there are still differences between families in
their ability to afford education, so diglossia does not guarantee linguistic equality between poor and rich, but the differences emerge only in formal public situations requiring the High variety. We shall have more to say about the situation
in non-diglossic societies in 6.2 and 6.3.

It will be noticed that the definition of 'diglossia' given by Ferguson is quite
specific on several points. For example, he requires that the High and Low varieties should belong to the same language, for example, Standard (or Classical)
and Colloquial Arabic. However, some writers have extended the term to
cover situations which do not strictly count as diglossic according to this definition. Joshua Fishman, for example, refers to Paraguay as an example of a
diglossic community (1971: 75), although the High and Low varieties are
respectively Spanish and Guaraní, an Indian language totally unrelated to
Spanish. Since we have argued that there is no real distinction between varieties
of one language and of different languages, this relaxation seems quite
reasonable.

However, Fishman (following John Gumperz) also extends the term diglossia to include any society in which two or more varieties are used under distinct
circumstances (1971: 74). This may be a regrettable development, as it would
seem to make *every* society diglossic, including even English-speaking England
(i.e. excluding communities with other languages as their mother tongues),
where different so-called 'registers' and 'dialects' are used under different

circumstances (compare a sermon with a sports report, for example). The value of the concept of diglossia is that it can be used in sociolinguistic *typology* – that is, in the classification of communities according to the type of sociolinguistic pattern that prevails in them – and 'diglossia' provides a revealing contrast with the kind of pattern found in countries such as Britain and the United States, which we might call 'social-dialectia' to show that the 'varieties' concerned were social dialects, not registers.

Another important difference between Ferguson's classic diglossia and social-dialectia is that the varieties concerned are more sharply distinguished in the former. Whereas social dialects turn out to dissolve into a myriad of independently varying items, the items involved in diglossia all vary together so that their variations can be generalised satisfactorily in terms of large-scale varieties. However, even in diglossic communities it would be surprising if there were no intermediate cases, and the distinction between the types of community is probably less clear than this discussion implies.

2.5   Mixture of varieties

2.5.1   Code-switching

We have been concerned so far in this chapter with the status of 'varieties' in the language system – to what extent is our collection of linguistic items compartmentalised into separate varieties, each with its own social links, and to what extent are social links restricted to these large-scale varieties, rather than the individual linguistic items? The effect of the earlier discussion was to give varieties a relatively unimportant role in the language system, though we did not deny their existence altogether. We now turn to a different kind of question about varieties: even when we can recognise varieties as clearly distinct languages (for example, English versus Spanish), to what extent do their speakers keep them separate? This divides into two separate questions: do they keep them separate in speech? and do they keep them separate as language systems? The first two sections are concerned with the first question: are languages always kept separate in speech? Here too we find that the variety-based view is far too rigid to do justice to human linguistic behaviour.

We start with CODE-SWITCHING, which is the inevitable consequence of bilingualism (or, more generally, multilingualism). (For a brief but very helpful survey see McCormick 1994a. Romaine 1989 is a good book-length discussion of this and other consequences of bilingualism.) Anyone who speaks more than one language chooses between them according to circumstances. The first consideration, of course, is which language will be comprehensible to the person addressed; generally speaking, speakers choose a language which the other person can understand (though interesting exceptions arise for example in religious ceremonies). But what about members of a community where every-body speaks the same range of languages? In community multilingualism the different languages are always used in different circumstances, and the choice is always controlled by social rules. Typically one language is reserved exclusively for use at home and another is used in the wider community (for example, when shopping); for example, according to Denison (1971), everyone in the village of Sauris, in northern Italy, spoke German within the family, Saurian (a dialect of Italian) informally within the village, and standard Italian to outsiders and in more formal village settings (school, church, work). Because of this linguistic division of labour, each individual could expect to switch codes (i.e. languages) several times in the course of a day. (The term 'code-switching' is preferred to 'language-switching' in order to accommodate other kinds of variety: dialects and registers.)

More precisely, this kind of code-switching is called SITUATIONAL code-switching because the switches between languages always coincide with changes from one external situation (for example, talking to members of the family) to another (for example, talking to the neighbours). The choice of language is con-trolled by rules, which members of the community learn from their experience, so these rules are part of their total linguistic knowledge. Now a very obvious question arises: why should a whole community bother to learn three different languages, when just one language would do? If everyone in Sauris knows stan-dard Italian, why don't they stick to this all the time and let the local German and Italian dialects disappear? No doubt Saurians themselves have a clear answer: standard Italian would just feel wrong at home. The rules link the lan-guages to different communities (home, Sauris, Italy), so each language also symbolises that community. Speaking standard Italian at home would be like wearing a suit, and speaking German in the village would be like wearing beach-clothes in church. In short, each language has a social function which no other language could fulfil. These social functions are more or less arbitrary results of history, but they are no less real for that. The same seems to be typical of bilingual communities in general. The main reason for preserving the lan-guages is because of the social distinctions that they symbolise. (We saw another example of the same pattern in the discussion of the Indian village Kupwar, where three languages are used in order to maintain the caste system – see 2.3.4.)

Given this heavy symbolic load that languages bear, it is entirely to be expected that bilingual speakers will use their choice of language in order to define the situation, rather than letting the situation define the choice of lan-guages. In clear cases, we can tell what situation we are in just by looking around us; for example, if we are in a lecture-room full of people, or having breakfast with our family, classifying the situation is easy, and if language choice varies with the situation it is clearly the situation that decides the language, not the other way round. But in some cases the situation is less clear, either because it is ambiguous or because the speaker decides to ignore the observable external situation and focus instead on less observable characteristics of the people concerned. Such cases, where it is the choice of language that determines the situation, are called METAPHORICAL CODE-SWITCHING (Blom and Gumperz 1971).

An example which is quoted by Jan-Petter Blom and John Gumperz arose out of their research in a town in northern Norway, Hemnesberget, where there is a diglossic situation, with one of the two standard Norwegian languages (Bokmål) as the High variety and a local dialect, Ranamal, as the Low one.

> In the course of a morning spent at the community administration office, we noticed that clerks used both standard and dialect phrases, depending on whether they were talking about official affairs or not. Likewise, when residents step up to a clerk's desk, greeting and inquiries about family affairs tend to be exchanged in the dialect, while the business part of the transaction is carried on in the standard. (Blom and Gumperz 1971: 425)

Examples like this show that speakers are able to manipulate the norms governing the use of varieties in just the same way as they can manipulate those governing the meanings of words by using them metaphorically. This is something everyone knows from everyday experience, but it is worth explicit reference in a book on sociolinguistic theory because it helps to avoid the trap of seeing speakers as sociolinguistic robots able to talk only within the constraints laid down by the norms of their society.

2.5.2 Code-mixing

In code-switching the point at which the languages change corresponds to a point where the situation changes, either on its own or precisely because the language changes. There are other cases, however, where a fluent bilingual talking to another fluent bilingual changes language without any change at all in the situation. This kind of alternation is called CODE-MIXING (or CONVERSATIONAL CODE-SWITCHING, a rather unhelpful name). The purpose of code-mixing seems to be to symbolise a somewhat ambiguous situation for which neither language on its own would be quite right. To get the right effect the speakers balance the two languages against each other as a kind of linguistic cocktail – a few words of one language, then a few words of the other, then back to the first for a few more words and so on. The changes generally take place more or less randomly as far as subject-matter is concerned, but they seem to be limited by the sentence-structure, as we shall see.

The following is an extract from the speech of a Puerto-Rican speaker living in New York, quoted by William Labov (1971). The stretches in Spanish are translated in brackets.

> Por eso cada [therefore each . . .], you know it's nothing to be proud of, porque yo no estoy [because I'm not] proud of it, as a matter of fact I hate it, pero viene Vierne y Sabado yo estoy, tu me ve hacia mi, sola [but come (?) Friday and Saturday I am, you see me, you look at me, alone] with a, aqui solita, a veces que Frankie me deja [here alone, sometimes Frankie leaves me], you know a stick or something . . .

Examples like these are interesting since they show that the syntactic categories used in classifying linguistic items may be independent of their social descriptions. For instance, in the above extract the Spanish verb *estoy* 'am' needs to be followed by an adjective, but in this case it is an English adjective (*proud*). This supports the view that at least some syntactic (and other) categories used in analysing language are universal rather than tied to particular languages.

An even clearer example of conversational code-switching within a single sentence is quoted by Gillian Sankoff, from a speech by an entrepreneur in a village in New Guinea (Sankoff 1972: 45). Here the languages concerned are a language called Buang and Neo-Melanesian Pidgin, or Tok Pisin (to which we shall return in 2.5.3). In Buang, negation is marked by using *su* before the predicate (i.e. the verb and its objects), and *re* after it; but in one sentence (which is too long to quote here) the predicate was mostly in English, but was enclosed within the Buang *su . . . re* construction. Again we may conclude that items from languages even as different as Buang and Neo-Melanesian Pidgin are classified, by speakers as well as by linguists, in terms of a common set of syntactic categories (in this case something like the category 'predicate').

An important question about code-mixing is what syntactic constraints apply to it, and attempts to answer this question have constituted one of the main points of contact over the last few years between sociolinguistics and non-social linguistics. There is no doubt that there are syntactic constraints; people who belong to code-mixing communities can judge whether particular constructed code-mixed examples are permitted or not, and these judgments are on the whole born out by studies of texts. For example, both Spanish and English have a word which is used just before an infinitive (*to* in English, *a* in Spanish), and language-change is possible after either – *to* can be followed by a Spanish infinitive, and *a* by an English one. But what is apparently not possible is for a

Spanish verb which is normally followed by *a* to be followed by *to* instead (Blake 1987). This example is typical and could be multiplied from the growing literature.

The reason why code-mixing has interested non-social linguists is that these restrictions call for an explanation. Are they peculiarities of each language pair involved in mixing, or are there more general patterns that apply to all code-mixing – and if there are, what are they and why do they exist? The research is still in its infancy and the results are quite inconclusive, but it is hard to avoid the conclusion that constraints vary from community to community (see, for example, Clyne 1987, Choi 1991) in spite of the enthusiastic attempts to provide universal explanations (see, for example, di Sciullo et al.. 1986, Belazi et al.. 1994).

2.5.3   *Borrowing*

Another way in which different languages may become mixed up with each other is through the process of BORROWING (Heath 1994). At this point, however, we are shifting our view from speech to language-systems. Whereas code-switching and code-mixing involved mixing languages in speech, borrowing involves mixing the systems themselves, because an item is 'borrowed' from one language to become part of the other language. Everyday examples abound – words for foods, plants, institutions, music and so on, which most people can recognise as borrowings (or LOAN-WORDS), and for which they can even name the source language. For most English speakers the following would probably be included: *karaoke* (Japanese), *paella* (Spanish), *schnapps* (German), *eisteddfod* (Welsh), *sputnik* (Russian) and *fait accompli* (French).

Examples like these are relevant to sociolinguistics because of their 'double-allegiance': we treat them as ordinary English words, used in ordinary English sentences, but at the same time we know that they are modelled on words in other languages, which gives them a more or less foreign 'flavour'. We can make this rather vague description more precise by building on the discussion of code-switching and code-mixing, where we agreed that each language has a distinctive symbolic value for people who use it regularly because of its links to particular kinds of people or kinds of situation. The same can be true, to a more limited extent, of languages that we do not use regularly, and which we may hardly know at all – languages that we associate with holidays, particular kinds of culture and so on. One reason for using a word from such a language is to pretend, just for a moment, to be a native speaker with whatever social characteristics we associate with the stereotype. Another reason, of course, is that there is simply no other available word, in which case the link to the country may be irrelevant, or at least unintended. (In some countries all loan-words are frowned upon because of their foreign associations, so steps have to be taken to invent native words with the same meaning.)

It is important to distinguish examples like these from the enormous number of words which are borrowings only in the historical sense, and which ordinary people no longer associate with any other language. Such words account for more than half of the vocabulary of English, which has borrowed a great deal from Latin, Greek and French. Words like *money, car, church* and *letter* can all be traced to borrowings from these languages, but none of us are aware of this and use them just like any other English word, without any trace of foreign associations. However it is also important to recognise that borrowings can keep their foreign associations for a very long time, whether or not we recognise them as loans. It is very easy to show this in English, where so-called 'Latinate' vocabulary is quite distinct in spelling, in morphology and in register. For example, in 2.4.1 we contrasted *get* and *obtain* as informal and formal; what we did not mention is that *obtain* was once a borrowing from Latin, whereas *get* is not. (Actually, *get* was also borrowed, but it was borrowed from Old Norse.) At the time of the borrowing Latin was the language of scholarship, the law and so on – in fact, it was the High language in a diglossic situation, with English as the Low (and French in between as the language of the Court). This being so, *obtain* had the prestige of Latin when it was borrowed – and it still has, many centuries later, even though most people do not know its origin. The same is true of most Latinate vocabulary in modern English. In sum we certainly cannot call these words 'borrowings', in the strict sense of words that ordinary users know to be borrowed, but we can at least explain the 'High' status which sets them off from the historically non-Latinate vocabulary as a relic of the mediaeval diglossia in which Latin was High.

It may be helpful to diagram these distinctions. Figure 2.4 shows the knowledge-structure for someone who knows *fait accompli*, uses it as an ordinary English word(-pair) (for example, *It's a fait accompli*), but recognises it as a French loan (for example, by using a semi-French pronunciation). The arrow pointing from the French *fait accompli* to the English one shows that the person concerned knows the historical connection between the two.

Now contrast this with Figure 2.5, for the difference between *get* and *obtain*. Here we assume that the person concerned may or may not know that *obtain* has a link to Latin (hence the question mark), but the social category to which it is linked is the same as it would have been with that link. The link to a specific Latin word is no longer known.

One curious and importance consequence of borrowing is that (once again) the boundaries between languages come into question. We have assumed so

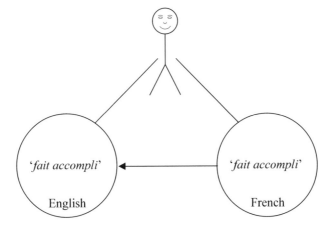

Figure 2.4

far that a loan word is definitely part of the borrowing language, but this is in fact a matter of degree. It is common for items to be *assimilated* in some degree to the items already in the borrowing variety, with foreign sounds being replaced by native sounds and so on. For instance, the word *restaurant* lost its uvular *r* when it was borrowed from French into English, so that it would occur with a uvular *r* in an English sentence only as an example of code-

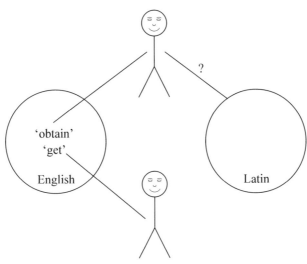

Figure 2.5

switching. On the other hand, assimilation need not be total, and in *restaurant* many English speakers still have a nasal vowel at the end, which would not have been there had the word not been borrowed from French. Words like this make it very hard to draw the neat line round 'English' which is required by any description of 'the English phoneme system', since the English system gets mixed up with systems from other languages. On the other hand, this partial assimilation of borrowed words is an extremely common phenomenon both in English and in other languages. (Consider, in British English, the velar fricative at the end of *loch* and the voiceless lateral fricatives in *Llangollen*, both of which are very unusual in English words.)

The completely unassimilated loan-word is at one end of a scale which has at the other end items bearing no formal resemblance to the foreign words on which they are based. Such items are called LOAN TRANSLATIONS (or 'calques'). For example, the English *superman* is a loan translation of the German *Übermensch*, and the expression *I've told him I don't know how many times* is a direct translation of the French *Je le lui ai dit je ne sais pas combien de fois* (Bloomfield 1933: 457). What these examples illustrate is that borrowing may involve the levels of syntax and semantics without involving pronunciation at all, which brings us back to the question of areal features, discussed in 2.3.4, where we saw that it is common for features of syntax to be borrowed from one language into neighbouring ones, via people who are bilingual in both. We now have three mechanisms which may help to explain how this happens. First, there is a tendency to eliminate alternatives in syntax (see 2.3.4). Then there is the existence of specific loan-translations like those just quoted, which may then act as models from which regular 'native' constructions can be developed. And third, there is code-mixing (2.5.2), which encourages the languages concerned to become more similar in their syntax so that items from each may be more easily substituted for one another within the same sentence; if both languages put the object on the same side of the verb, for example, code-mixing is easier than if one puts it before and the other after.

The question is, whether there are any aspects of language which *cannot* be borrowed from one language into another. The answer appears to be that there are not (Bynon 1977: 255). Even the inflectional morphology of a language may be borrowed, as witness a Tanzanian language called Mbugu which appears to have borrowed a Bantu inflectional system from one or more Bantu neighbours, although other aspects of its grammar are non-Bantu (Goodman 1971). Its non-Bantu features now include the personal pronouns and the numbers from one to six, which would normally be considered to be such 'basic' vocabulary as to be immune from borrowing (Bynon 1977: 253). In such cases there are of course problems for the family tree model, since it ought to be possible to fit the language into just one tree, whereas some features suggest that it ought to be in the Bantu tree, and others, like those mentioned above, indicate that it belongs in some other tree (possibly the tree for 'Cushitic' languages). How should one resolve the conflict? Can any general principles be applied in balancing the evidence of inflectional morphology against that of basic vocabulary? (It should be noted, incidentally, that the inflectional morphology is matched by Bantu-type rules of concord, which are presumably part of syntax.) One wonders whether there is *any* kind of external reality against which an answer to questions such as these might be measured.

Assuming that there are no parts of language which cannot be borrowed, it is still possible to ask questions which may distinguish one part from another. For example, are there any restrictions on the circumstances under which different parts of language may be borrowed? We might suspect, for instance, that some kinds of item will be borrowed only under conditions of widespread bilingualism, while others may occur where only a few members of a society are bilingual in the relevant languages. Aspects of the first type would count as least, and the second type as most, subject to borrowing, so we could set up a scale of accessibility to borrowing, on which inflectional morphology, and 'basic vocabulary' such as small numbers, would presumably be at the 'least accessible' end, and vocabulary for artefacts (like *aeroplane* or *hamburger*) at the other. A word for the number 'one', for instance, will be borrowed only when almost everyone speaks both the 'borrowing' and the 'source' languages, whereas a word for 'aeroplane' could easily be borrowed when nobody is fully proficient in the two languages, but one or two people are familiar enough with the source language to know the word for 'aeroplane'. However, the truth may turn out to be much more complex than is suggested by this hypothesis, which is in any case by no means simple as far as the organisation of linguistic items into separate levels, such as syntax, vocabulary and phonology, is concerned, since different vocabulary items are put at opposite ends of the scale. Thus borrowing is a phenomenon which may throw light on the internal organisation of language, and certainly on the relations of language to society, once the right research has been done.

2.5.4 *Pidgins*

There is yet another way, apart from code-switching and borrowing, in which varieties may get mixed up with each other, namely by the process of creating a new variety out of two (or more) existing ones. This process of 'variety-synthesis' may take a number of different forms, including for instance the creation of artificial auxiliary languages like Esperanto and Basic English (for which see Crystal 1987: 352–5). However, by far the most important manifestation is the process of pidginisation, whereby PIDGIN LANGUAGES, or PIDGINS, are created. These are varieties created for very practical and immediate purposes of communication between people who otherwise would have no common language whatsoever, and learned by one person from another within the communities concerned as the accepted way of communicating with members of the other community. (An excellent brief survey of the issues discussed here and in 2.5.5 is Aitchison 1994; for a scholarly survey in two volumes, see Holm 1988, 1989.)

Since the reason for wanting to communicate with members of the other communities is often trade, a pidgin may be what is called a TRADE LANGUAGE, but not all pidgins are restricted to being used as trade languages, nor are all trade languages pidgins. Instead, the ordinary language of some community in the area may be used by all the other communities as a trade language. It will be recalled from 1.2.2 that in the north-west Amazon area, Tukano is the language of one of the twenty-odd tribes but is also used as a trade language by all the others. Similarly, English and French are widely used as trade languages in many parts of Africa. In contrast with languages like this, a pidgin is a variety specially created for the purpose of communicating with some *other* group, and not used by *any* community for communication among themselves.

There are a large number of pidgin languages, spread through all the continents including Europe, where migrant workers in countries like Germany have developed pidgin varieties based on the local national language. Each pidgin is of course specially constructed to suit the needs of its users, which means that it has to have the terminology and constructions needed in whatever kinds of contact normally arise between the communities, but need not go beyond these demands to anticipate the odd occasion on which other kinds of situation arise. If the contacts concerned are restricted to the buying and selling of cattle, then only linguistic items to do with this are needed, so there will be no way of talking about the quality of vegetables, or the emotions, or any of the many other things about which one can talk in any normal language.

Another requirement of a pidgin is that it should be as simple to learn as possible, especially for those who benefit *least* from learning it, and the consequence of this is that the vocabulary is generally based on the vocabulary of the dominant group. For instance, a group of migrant workers from Turkey living in Germany will not benefit much from a pidgin whose vocabulary is based on Turkish, since few Germans would be willing to make the effort to learn it, consequently they take their vocabulary from German. Similarly, in a colonial situation where representatives of a foreign colonial power need to communicate with the local population in matters of trade or administration, and if it is in the interests of the local population to communicate, then the

pidgin which develops will be based on the vocabulary of the colonial power –
hence the very large number of pidgins spread round the globe based on
English, French, Portuguese and Dutch.

However, although the vocabulary of a pidgin may be based mainly on that
of one of the communities concerned, the 'dominant' variety, the pidgin is still
a compromise between this and the subordinate varieties, in that its syntax and
phonology may be similar to the latter, making the pidgin easier for the other
communities to learn than the dominant language in its ordinary form. As for
morphology, this is left out altogether, which again makes for ease of learning.
To the extent that differences of tense, number, case and so on are indicated at
all, they are marked by the addition of separate words. Indeed, one of the most
characteristic features of pidgins is the lack of morphology, and if some variety
is found to contain morphology, especially inflectional morphology, most specialists in this field would be reluctant to treat it as a pidgin (which does not of
course mean that every language without inflectional morphology must be a
pidgin).

The best way to illustrate these characteristics of pidgins is by discussing a
sentence from Tok Pisin, the English-based pidgin spoken in Papua New
Guinea (Todd 1994: 3178, 4622).

> Bai em i no lukim mi. 'He will not see me.'

The English origins of the vocabulary are not immediately obvious in the official
spelling, which reflects the words' current pronunciation rather than their
origins, so the following notes may be helpful.

Bai	From *by and by*, an adverb used instead of the auxiliary verb *will* to indicate future time.
em	From *him*, meaning 'he'.
i	From *he*, but obligatorily added to a verb whose subject is third person (like the English suffix -*s*).
no	From *no* or *not*, used instead of the verb *doesn't*.
luk-	From *look*, but means 'see'.
-im	From *him*, but added obligatorily whenever the verb has an object, in addition to this object.
mi	From *me*.

The example shows how different the syntax is from English, but how rigidly
rule-governed it is, in particular by the rules which require the redundant *i*
before the verb and -*im* added to it – a far cry from the idea of a makeshift
attempt at speaking English. Another point which emerges clearly is the

question of classification: is this a variety of English? Such cases highlight the general problem of deciding where the boundaries of languages lie.

Let us return to the more general question of the relation between pidgins and the societies which create them. As we have seen, pidgins are sometimes developed as trade languages, which we may take in a fairly broad sense as varieties used only for trade and administration. This is how Neo-Melanesian Pidgin or Tok Pisin (i.e., 'pidgin talk' – see 2.5.1) developed during the present century for communication between the English-speaking administrators of Papua New Guinea and the local population, who themselves speak a large number of mutually incomprehensible languages (one of which is Buang, which was involved in code-mixing with Tok Pisin in the example quoted in 2.5.2).

However, not all pidgins have arisen as trade languages, as Tok Pisin did. Another situation in which pidgins are needed is when people from different language backgrounds are thrown together and have to communicate with each other, and with a dominant group, in order to survive. This is the situation in which most Africans taken as slaves to the New World found themselves, since the slavers would break up tribal groups to minimise the risk of rebellion. Thus the only way in which the slaves could communicate either with each other or with their masters was through a pidgin which they generally learned from the slavers, based on the latter's language. Since most slaves had little opportunity to learn the ordinary language of their masters, this pidgin remained the only means of communication for most slaves for the rest of their lives. This had two consequences. One was that pidgins became very closely associated with slaves, and acquired a poor reputation as a result (and the slaves also got the reputation of being stupid since they could not speak a 'proper' language!). The other consequence was that pidgins were used in an increasingly wide range of situations, and so gradually acquired the status of creole languages (see 2.5.5).

It may be helpful to bring together some characteristics of pidgins which distinguish them from other types of variety and variety-mixture.
(1) A pidgin based on language X is not just an example of 'bad X', as one might describe the unsuccessful attempt of an individual foreigner to learn X. A pidgin is itself a language, with a community of speakers who pass it on from one generation to the next, and consequently with its own history. Indeed, it has even been suggested that many pidgins have a common origin in the Portuguese-based pidgin which developed in the Far East and West Africa during the sixteenth century, under the influence of Portuguese sailors, and that this Portuguese-based pidgin might in turn have had its roots in the 'Lingua Franca' developed in the Mediterranean as early as the Crusades. This suggestion represents one of a number of attempts to explain the existence of a fairly

large number of similar features which have been found in pidgins from many different parts of the world (Todd 1994).

(2) A pidgin is not simply the result of heavy borrowing from one variety into another, since there is no pre-existing variety into which items may be borrowed. An 'X-based pidgin' is not a variety of X which has borrowed a lot of syntactic constructions and phonological features from other varieties, since there may well be no model in these other varieties for any of the changes, such as the loss of inflections to which we referred above. Nor is it a variety of some other language which has borrowed a lot of vocabulary from X, since the syntax, phonology and morphology need not be the same as those of any of the other varieties involved. In any case, it is not clear which community would be the borrowers, since the pidgin is developed jointly by both sides of the communication gap, each trying to help bridge the gap. Of course, there is an interesting problem in relation to borrowing, since we *can* talk of borrowing into a pre-established pidgin, just as we can in connection with any other kind of variety, whereas we cannot invoke borrowing as a process in the establishment of the pidgin in the first place. The problem is that this implies too clear a distinction between the periods before and after the establishment of the pidgin.

(3) A pidgin, unlike ordinary languages, has no native speakers, which is a consequence of the fact that it is used only for communication between members of *different* communities. On the other hand, this distinction is not clear-cut since there are situations, such as those of slavery, where a community can come into existence with a pidgin as its only common variety, although all the members of the community learned it as a second language. The lack of a clearly defined group of native speakers has the effect of putting most pidgins near the 'diffuse' end of the scale contrasting 'focussing' and 'diffusion' (1.3.1), in contrast with highly focussed standard languages such as French, and this is another reason why pidgins are of such considerable interest to sociolinguists.

2.5.5 *Creoles*

A pidgin which has acquired native speakers is called a CREOLE LANGUAGE, or CREOLE, and the process whereby a pidgin turns into a creole is called 'creolisation'. It is easy to see how pidgins acquire native speakers, namely by being spoken by couples who have children and rear them together. This happened on a large scale among the African slaves taken to the New World, and is happening on a somewhat smaller scale in urban communities in places like Papua New Guinea.

From a social point of view, creoles are of more interest than pidgins. Most creole languages are spoken by the descendants of African slaves and are of great interest, both to their speakers and to others, as one of the main sources of information on their origins, and as a symbol of their identity. A similar interest is shown by people who speak varieties whose origins are in a creole, but which have since been 'decreolised', i.e. moved towards the dominant variety at the expense of most distinctive characteristics of the creole. It is possible that the English of black people in the United States is such a variety, and because of this creoles and decreolised languages are of particular interest to many American linguists (see 1.3.2, 5.4.2 and, a good survey, Fasold 1990). Another reason for the interest in creoles is that there are minority groups, such as West Indian immigrants in Britain, whose members speak some form of creole. If their creole is one based on the majority language of the country into which they have immigrated – for example, an English-based creole in the case of immigrants to Britain – then serious educational problems may arise if neither teachers nor taught can be sure if this creole is a different language from the majority one or a dialect of it. If the former, it may be appropriate to use second-language teaching methods to teach the majority language, but this is by no means an appropriate method if it is a dialect. Consequently research is needed in order to establish the extent of the difference between the creole and the majority language. Similar problems arise in countries where the majority language is itself a creole, if the language expected by the education system is the standard version of the language on which the creole is based, as in many Caribbean countries. The problem is not helped, of course, by the fact that the difference between 'same' and 'different' is rather meaningless when applied to language varieties, as we argued in 2.2, so it may be that a more realistic model of language might help to solve some of these problems.

From the point of view of what they tell us about language, however, creoles are of less immediate interest, since they are just ordinary languages like any others, except in their origins. There are just two qualifications to be made to this claim, both of which are matters of language change: creoles, unlike ordinary language, arise through a process called (naturally enough) creolisation, and they are likely to gradually lose their identity by decreolisation (Aitchison 1994: 3184–6). It is only in between these two stages that they are ordinary languages.

Taking DECREOLISATION first, this is what happens when a creole is spoken in a country where other people speak the creole's lexical source-language (for example, English). Since the latter has so much more prestige than the creole, creole speakers tend to shift towards it, producing a range of intermediate varieties. Sociolinguists call the creole the BASILECT and the prestige language the ACROLECT, with the intermediate varieties lumped together as MESOLECTS. This range of varieties spanning the gap between basilect and acrolect is called a 'POST-CREOLE CONTINUUM'.

This term reflects an interesting factual claim about the relationships among the mesolects. Like the acrolect and basilect, each mesolect is a vast collection of items which could (in principle at least) constitute the entire language of a group of speakers. The basilect is likely to be as different from the acrolect as Tok Pisin is from English, so it is easy to see that thousands of items must vary and that, linguistically speaking, most of them are quite independent of one another: the way in which future time is expressed has nothing to do with the form of the pronoun *I* or *me*, and so on through the grammar and vocabulary. Each mesolect represents one combination of basilect and acrolect items, so it is easy to imagine a rather chaotic scene in which different mesolects combine items in completely different ways. The claim that lies behind the term 'continuum', however, is that the relations are actually much more orderly, and there is at least a strong tendency for mesolects to line up along a single scale from most basilectal to most acrolectal.

For example, here is a series of alternative ways of saying 'I came and carried it away' that are allowed by the post-creole continuum of Nigeria (Todd 1994: 3181):

(1)   A bin kam, kariam go.
(2)   A kom, kariam go.
(3)   A kom, kariam awe.
(4)   A kem and kari it awe.

If these examples are typical, then there are at least four degrees of 'height' from the lowest basilect (1) to the highest mesolect (4). Each of the linguistic items concerned can be given an index to show the range of heights that it covers:

bin kam	(1)	kariam	(1–3)	go	(1–2)
kom	(2–3)	kari it	(4)	awe	(3–4)
kem	(4)				

Each mesolect represents a consistent selection on this scale, in which all the items are allowed to have the same relative height. If this is so, then no mesolect allows *bin kam* (1) and also *awe* (3–4), nor is there one which combines either *bin kam* or *kom* as well as *kari it*.

Post-creole continuums have been reported from several countries, perhaps the best documented being the one in Guyana (Bickerton 1975). They are clearly of great interest socially, if we can take them as evidence for a general tendency for such communities to create single-scale social ranking systems, although a more chaotic pattern is so easy to imagine. However, what makes post-creole continuums particularly interesting for a sociolinguist is the clear evidence they give for the independent social classification of single linguistic items. The scale of 'height' in the last paragraph applies to individual items, with each item assigned a particular range on the scale. Notions like 'dialect' are of no help at all in this kind of situation, and what is actually needed is a way of giving detailed social information about individual items. This conclusion should come as no surprise after the discussion above about the centrality of individual linguistic items.

We turn now to the other peculiarity of creoles, the process of CREOLISATION. As we noted at the beginning of this section, a creole is a pidgin that has native speakers. As it stands, this is simply a fact about how we use the words *pidgin* and *creole*, and it is a matter of fact whether having native speakers entails any other differences between creoles and their pidgin sources. Tok Pisin has just recently gone through this process of 'acquiring native speakers' (a nice reversal of the usual process whereby native speakers acquire a language!). Imagine a couple in New Guinea who speak Tok Pisin to each other for lack of any other common language, but who each have some other language as their native language. They have a baby, who starts to speak Tok Pisin. (As we saw in the north-west Amazon, it is possible for a child's first language to be a language which is not the mother's native language.) The essential difference between the baby and the parents is that the baby is learning Tok Pisin as its first language, whereas when they learned it they already knew another language. The question is whether this difference necessarily affects the outcome of the learning process. In other words, will the Tok Pisin which the child eventually speaks as an adult be different in essential ways from the Tok Pisin spoken by its parents?

The answer to this question is the subject of an intense debate not only among creole specialists but also among non-social linguists. On the one hand, are the linguists who, following Noam Chomsky (1986), believe that every child is genetically prepared ('programmed') to learn a human language like English or Japanese; in other words, that our ability to learn language is innate. When children are born into a family where the only language they hear is a mere pidgin, their genes push them to up-grade it to a full language by enriching it with relative clauses and other complexities not needed in a mere pidgin. The main proponent of this view is Derek Bickerton (1981, 1988), who calls the genetic predisposition to learn a full language the 'bioprogram'. On the other side of the debate are the majority of sociolinguists and creolists, who are less impressed by Chomsky's arguments for an innate language faculty. They question Bickerton's factual claims about differences between creoles and pidgins, and also his claims about similarities between creolisation and the processes of ordinary first-language acquisition (Aitchison 1994: 3185). In any case the kinds of feature which Bickerton assumes to be innate seem very different from those which Chomsky has argued for, so the two views conflict rather than support one another. (For a helpful review of this debate, see Romaine 1988.)

A somewhat different view is that pidgins can become richer to the extent of being similar to ordinary languages without the intervention of infant language-learners. On this view, the only difference between a creole and an enriched pidgin is that the former has native speakers and the latter does not. We have seen that some pidgins are already sufficiently developed to be used as standard languages, as in the case of Tok Pisin. One particularly interesting piece of research has been done on Tok Pisin in this connection, by Gillian Sankoff and Penelope Brown (1976), who studied the recent history of relative clauses in Tok Pisin and showed how a consistent marker of relative clauses was gradually developed out of the word *ia* (based ultimately on the English *here*), which is now put both before and after many relative clauses.

> Na pik *ia* ol ikilim bipo *ia* bai ikamap olsem draipela ston.
> (Now pig here past kill people here future become huge stone)
> 'And this pig which they had killed before would turn into a huge stone.'
> (Sankoff and Brown 1976: 632)

This construction may illustrate the influence of the syntax of the local languages on that of the pidgin, since Buang, for instance, has a word which is used both as a demonstrative and as a marker of relative clauses in the same way as *ia*. What is particularly interesting about this research is that speakers of a pidgin continue to develop it, using whatever resources are available, in a process that does not depend on creolisation. Indeed, Sankoff and Brown have evidence that it had started at least ten years before there were any significant numbers of native speakers of Tok Pisin. Again, there is no research evidence of changes that have happened during creolisation which cannot be matched by changes to a pidgin without native speakers.

The conclusion to which this discussion seems to lead is that there is no clear difference between pidgins and creoles, apart from the fact that creoles have native speakers and pidgins do not. No other differences between pidgins and creoles seem necessarily to follow from this one. Since we have also claimed that creoles are just ordinary languages (with some reservations about creole continua) and that pidgins are rather peculiar, it follows that the distinction between the 'normal' and the 'peculiar' (as represented by early stages of pidginisation) is unclear, and is in fact a continuum rather than a qualitative difference. Moreover, it is clear that there is no moment in time at which a particular pidgin suddenly comes into existence, but rather a process of variety-creation called pidginisation, by which a pidgin is gradually built up out of nothing. We might well ask whether this process is essentially different from what happens in everyday interaction between people who think they speak the same language, but who are in fact constantly accommodating their speech and language to each other's needs. (Compare the suggestion by Robert Le Page (1977b) that 'every speech act is . . . the reflex of an "instant pidgin" related to the linguistic competence of more than one person'.) For instance a parallel may be drawn between the New Guinea natives learning an approximation to English vocabulary from each other and the local English speakers, on the one hand, and students of linguistics learning an approximation to the vocabulary of their teachers from each other and from their teachers, on the other. In both cases it is clear who has to do the bulk of the learning, though the dominant group may sometimes use the forms which they know the subordinate group use, in order to make things easier for them. In both cases what develops is a variety of language which is passed on from one person to another, developed out of countless encounters between teachers and students and between students themselves. The reader of this book may be amused at the idea of being a speaker of 'pidgin linguistics', but the suggestion is intended to be taken quite seriously.

2.6   Conclusions

This chapter has ranged over several types of language variety, including 'languages', 'dialects' (both regional and social), 'registers', 'standard languages', 'High' and 'Low' varieties in diglossia, 'pidgins' and 'creoles'. We have come to essentially negative conclusions about varieties. Firstly, there are considerable problems in delimiting one variety from another of the same type (for example, one language from another, or one dialect from another). Secondly, there are serious problems in delimiting one *type* of variety from another – languages from dialects, or dialects from registers, or 'ordinary languages' from creoles, or creoles from pidgins. (We could have shown similar uncertainties on the border between 'standard' and 'non-standard' varieties.) Thirdly, we have suggested that the only satisfactory way to solve these problems is to avoid the notion 'variety' altogether as an analytical or theoretical concept, and to focus instead on the individual linguistic item. For each item some kind of 'social description' is needed, saying roughly who uses it and when: in some cases an item's social description will be unique, whereas in others it may be possible to generalise across a more or less large number of items. The nearest this approach comes to the concept of 'variety' is in these sets of items with similar social descriptions, but their characteristics are rather different from those of varieties like languages and dialects. On the other hand, it is still possible to use terms like 'variety' and 'language' in an informal way, as they have been used in the last few sections, without intending them to be taken seriously as theoretical constructs.

We also came to rather similar conclusions regarding the concept 'speech community', which seems to exist only to the extent that people have identified it and can locate themselves in relation to it. Since different individuals will identify different communities in this way, we have to give up any attempt to find objective and absolute criteria for defining speech communities. This leaves us, on the one hand, with individuals speakers and their range of linguistic items and, on the other, with communities defined primarily without reference to language.

Having reduced the subject-matter of sociolinguistics to the study of individual linguistic items of particular speakers, we may ask what kinds of generalisation it is possible to make. We have seen that there are many general questions to which it would be interesting to have answers, such as whether different kinds of linguistic items are related to different aspects of society. I have suggested some answers to this question, and to others raised in this chapter, but at this stage they can be little more than speculative. However, it should now be clear that such questions are worth asking, and that future research will provide answers supported by empirical evidence.

3
Language, culture and thought

3.1 Introduction
3.1.1 Culture
In the last chapter we saw that the phenomenon of language does not have natural divisions between 'varieties' of language, which we could call 'languages', 'dialects' or 'registers', though there may be natural internal divisions within it on the basis of 'levels' of language, such as vocabulary, syntax, morphology and phonology. We now turn to the external relations of language, to ask whether there are natural boundaries between the phenomena covered by the term 'language' and other kinds of phenomena, notably those called 'culture' and 'thought'. Once again we shall arrive at a somewhat complex answer, but it is one which emphasises the similarities between language and other phenomena rather than the differences, and which also stresses the close connections between the phenomena rather than their independence. For instance, I shall argue that many of the properties of language looked at in the last chapter are also properties of culture in general, and that meaning is best studied in relation to culture and thought. To the extent that these conclusions are correct, they present a challenge to the view which has dominated twentieth-century linguistics, that language is both unique and autonomous. The autonomous view of language has recently been challenged strongly from a different direction, by linguists whose main interest is in meaning and who collectively refer to themselves as 'Cognitive linguists'. Cognitive linguistics now has its own journal with the same name. The 'classics' are Lakoff 1987 and Langacker 1990, and a useful survey is Taylor 1989.

To avoid confusion we must start with some matters of terminology. First, the word CULTURE is taken in the sense in which it is used by cultural anthropologists, according to whom culture is something that everybody has, in contrast with the 'culture' which is found only in 'cultured' circles – in opera houses, universities and the like. The term is used differently by different anthropologists, but always refers to some characteristics shared by a community, especially those which might distinguish it from other communities. Some

70

anthropologists are interested in what is called 'material culture' – the artefacts of the community, such as its pottery, its vehicles or its clothing. However, we shall follow Ward Goodenough in taking culture as socially acquired *knowledge*:

> As I see it, a society's culture consists of whatever it is one has to know
> or believe in order to operate in a manner acceptable to its
> members . . . Culture, being what people have to learn as distinct from
> their biological heritage, must consist of the end-product of learning:
> knowledge, in a most general . . . sense of the term. (Goodenough 1957)

As Goodenough points out, we must take 'knowledge' here in a broad sense, to include both 'know-how' and 'know-that' – for instance, to cover both the ability to tie knots and the knowledge that one pound coin buys as much as ten ten-penny coins. One attraction of taking this view, widely accepted among anthropologists, is that it will allow us to compare culture with language, which we are also taking to be a kind of knowledge.

If culture is knowledge, it can exist only inside people's heads so there is a problem in studying it: how can one know what the cultural knowledge of Mr X is? Worse still, how can one know what the culture of community X is? Does one need to examine the cultural knowledge of every member of the community? And what if there are differences between people? Problems like these are completely familiar to the student of linguistics, of course, and the solutions are much the same whether one is interested in culture or in language. Firstly, we can observe people's natural behaviour (i.e. outside artificial experimental situations) and draw our own conclusions about the knowledge that must underlie it. Secondly, we can arrange interviews and ask people more or less direct questions about their knowledge, taking their answers with a pinch of salt if need be. Thirdly, we can use ourselves as informants. And fourthly, we can conduct psychological experiments of one kind or another, such as measuring the length of time it takes people to perform certain tasks in order to develop a measure of the relative complexity of the knowledge involved. (For more discussion of methodology, see 5.2.) All these methods can be used, and have been used in both cultural anthropology and linguistics.

Having discovered the relevant facts about a number of individuals, there is a problem of generalisation in both disciplines – to what extent may we assume that the people studied are representative of the community as a whole? And to what extent may we assume that if two people share one item of knowledge, they will also share some other item? In discussing linguistic items in chapter 2 we came to the conclusion that generalisations are very hard to make, across both people and linguistic items, and the same would certainly be true of items of cultural knowledge (Sankoff 1971). In short, problems of methodology that exist in the study of language are also found in the study of culture.

Before leaving the question of culture, we should note that the knowledge included in a culture need not be factually or objectively correct in order to count. For instance, some people think that strenuous exercise shortens life and others think the opposite, but so long as we can show that each view is learned socially (i.e. from other people), they both count as items of culture. Lay people's knowledge is often referred to as COMMON-SENSE KNOWLEDGE, and is the kind which is of most interest to anthropologists, just as linguists are more interested in day-to-day usage than in prescriptive grammars or dictionaries. On the other hand, the specialist knowledge of scientist or scholar is also a part of culture, and one of the most interesting questions in the study of culture is about the relations between common sense and specialist knowledge, since it is clear that influence goes in both directions. For example, one of the problems in writing this book is that there is a good deal of common-sense knowledge about language in any culture, some of which is right and some badly wrong, but it is hard to predict the particular beliefs of each reader. And a similar problem in sociolinguistics itself is that sociolinguists know in principle that some of their beliefs about language may be wrong and unhelpful, while others may be near enough to the truth to be built into a theory; but we do not know in advance which are which.

3.1.2 *Thought*

The term 'thought' covers a number of different types of mental activity, and lies in the province of cognitive psychology. To help our discussion, I shall distinguish first between MEMORY and INFERENCE, and then between CONCEPTS and PROPOSITIONS, as the objects of memory or inference. The terms should be self-explanatory, if propositions are thought of as roughly equivalent to statements and concepts as general categories in terms of which propositions are formulated and experience is processed. For instance, the English words *oil, water, float* and *on* may be taken as the names of concepts (two substances, one state and one relation), and the sentence *Oil floats on water* can be seen as the 'name' of the proposition 'oil floats on water', i.e. that one of the substances maintains the state of floating in the 'on' relation to the other substance. This proposition may be either remembered (already stored in memory) or inferred (worked out), i.e. it may either be something we already know, or something we discover (and probably add to our memory, so that next time it will be there as knowledge). Similarly, a concept may either exist in our memory, as a category used in thinking, or may be created as a new category which could then be stored away in memory. When we come to the relations of language to thought we shall find it important to distinguish these various kinds of 'thought'.

What then is the relation between thought and culture? Given the definition of culture as 'socially acquired knowledge', it is easy to see that culture is one part of memory, namely the part which is 'acquired socially', in contrast with that which does not involve other people. This distinction is anything but clear, so we must not put too much weight on it, but it might distinguish between propositions which are known to be true from one's own experience and those which have been learned from other people. An example of the first kind would be 'I had sausages for lunch today', which is excluded from the notion 'culture'; whereas a proposition like 'Columbus discovered America' clearly belongs to culture, as something one has learned from other people. Similarly, some concepts are cultural and others are not. We create the former because we see that others around us make use of them in their thinking, as may be illustrated by the concepts which students of linguistics or sociolinguistics build up because they find that their teachers are using them. (In most cases there is a word for such concepts, so the main clue the student has to the existence of a concept such as 'diglossia' is the existence of the word.) A non-cultural concept, on the other hand, is one which we build without reference to other people, as a convenient way of interpreting our experience – 'me', or 'the way my wife talks', or 'the smell of paint'.

To the extent that a distinction can be made between cultural and non-cultural knowledge, it concerns the source of such knowledge. If it means an approximation to the concepts or propositions in other people's minds, it is cultural, but otherwise not. One of the most interesting things about cultural knowledge is the extent to which people can interpret each other's behaviour and arrive at more or less the same concepts or propositions. For instance, millions of people every year attend concerts of various kinds in Britain, but with very few exceptions they appear to share the same concepts for categorising concerts (pop, classical, jazz and so on), and the same propositions about what constitutes appropriate behaviour during each type (for instance, during a classical concert audience participation is very closely restricted as to what may be done and when). If people did not share such detailed knowledge, their behaviour in concerts could not be as predictable as it in fact is, especially since the conventions are somewhat arbitrary.

On the other hand, it does not follow that non-cultural knowledge must differ from person to person, since different people can arrive at similar conclusions on the basis of similar experiences of the universe or similar genetic predispositions. For instance, if we find that all human beings have a concept 'vertical dimension', there is no need to assume that they have all learned it from other people in order to establish a chain of connections between them; it is much more likely that it is because they all live in a world dominated by gravity and full of human beings who walk upright; or even that it is inborn and needs no learning. (See Clark and Clark 1977: ch. 14, especially page 534, for an excellent discussion of similarities in non-cultural concepts.)

Thus we find that there are three kinds of knowledge:

(1) *cultural knowledge*, which is learned from other people;

(2) *shared non-cultural knowledge*, which is shared by people within the same community or the world over, but is not learned from each other;

(3) *non-shared non-cultural knowledge*, which is unique to the individual.

It is not difficult to find a place for language in this schema. Most of language is cultural knowledge, since it has to be learned from others, but some is shared non-cultural knowledge. We shall return to this point below, in 3.1.3.

The reader may be sceptical about the possibility of actually studying thought, as opposed to speculating about it, so it may be helpful to refer very briefly to the vast amount of such research that has been carried out, and the conclusions to which it has led. We might pick out for special mention one particular development in the study of concepts to which we shall be referring in a later discussion of meaning (3.2.3).

The 'classical' theory of concepts is that each one consists of a set of features ('criterial features') which are necessary and sufficient for something to count as an instance of that concept. For example, the concept 'bird' would consist of a set of features referring to wings, eggs and so on. These features are all 'necessary', so every bird must have the whole range, and they are 'sufficient' for counting as a bird. There are a number of problems with this theory, not least the fact that it is very hard, or even impossible, to decide what is covered by the words *and so on*. Is flying necessary? If so, what about ostriches and penguins? Are just wings and eggs sufficient? If so, where do butterflies fit in? What about the number of legs? Can we contemplate a mythical four-legged bird? And so the problems multiply, without throwing much light on what we really mean by 'bird'. The problems suggest that it may be wrong to look for this kind of definition in the first place. On the other hand, it does seem clear that we define concepts in terms of separate features (such as having wings, flying and laying eggs), each of which is recognised separately, rather than by some kind of global process which doesn't involve this kind of detailed analysis. What is needed is a theory of concepts which combines the feature-based analysis of concepts with a more flexible approach to membership which makes it less important to decide which features are necessary and sufficient.

The most promising approach is based on the work of the psychologist Eleanor Rosch, who showed that at least some concepts are organised around clear cases, or PROTOTYPES. In this theory, a concept has a feature-based definition, but the definition applies to the prototype, an abstract description of the most typical examples, with other examples fitting in as best they can. The prototype for 'bird' has all the features we associate with typical birds – laying eggs, flying, having two wings and two legs, building a nest and having about the size of a blackbird. Compared with this model, blackbirds and sparrows are very 'good' birds but ostriches are very 'bad', because they are exceptional in very many respects. Ostriches are classified as birds because they do have some bird-features, and they are nearer to the prototype 'bird' than they are to the prototype of any other comparable concept (animal, fish, insect, etc.), but they are exceptional.

These examples show how the idea of prototypes applies to the relationship between general concepts ('bird') and their subconcepts ('blackbird', 'ostrich'); but the same is true of concepts and their individual members. For example, individual blackbirds are occasionally albino, but they are still blackbirds, though exceptional. Every day we come across objects that are hard to classify because they are equally poor examples of a number of different categories – is it rain or drizzle? sand or shingle? a tree or a shrub? a booklet or a leaflet? a child or a teenager? a linguist or a sociologist? The same principle applies as between concepts and their subconcepts: if we have to classify, we choose the concept that provides the best and most relevant fit. Interestingly, one of the clearest (and earliest) demonstrations of this uncertainty was provided by William Labov, whose work on dialect differences has dominated sociolinguistics (as we shall see in chapter 5). Labov showed that the concepts 'cup', 'mug', 'bowl' and 'vase' were based on prototypes each of which was defined by a number of features including its shape (ratio of height to width) and its function. His evidence was the ways in which people classified various invented examples which varied these features systematically (Labov 1973, 1978).

The discussion so far has been more or less uncontroversial. All I have done is to point out that some 'instances' of a concept are better, i.e. more typical, than others are, and that this applies whether the 'instances' are other general concepts (such as 'blackbird') or individual examples. These observations are called 'prototype effects'. We now have to ask what theoretical conclusions can be drawn about the definitions of concepts themselves. In brief, there is no agreed answer, and a good deal of disagreement. One answer is that the various features mentioned in a definition must be somehow ranked or graded for importance, to reflect the ranking or grading of the instances (see Jackendoff 1983: 115ff. for a good discussion of this and other theories). Another is that concepts have a complex 'radial' structure in which subconcepts are grouped round a central core (Lakoff 1987). My own preference is for a much simpler theory in which everything that we know about a concept has the same status, without any attempt to distinguish its 'criterial' features from the rest, but where exceptions are allowed freely (Hudson 1990, 1995).

There is a good deal of evidence in favour of the prototype theory of concepts as opposed to the 'criterial feature' theory. Some of the evidence comes from experimentation; for instance, it takes people less time to verify a sentence like *X is a bird* if the word *X* is the name of a typical bird than if it is a word like *ostrich* or *penguin*, names of very atypical birds (Rosch 1976). Evidence has also come from experiments in which people were asked to rate members of more general categories according to how typical they were of the category concerned. This exercise was significant because there was a large measure of agreement among people as to the relative ranking of the items. For instance, it was generally agreed that robins and swallows were the most typical birds from a list of eight, and chickens and penguins the least typical; among items of furniture, chairs and dressers were most typical, and radios and ashtrays the least; apples and plums were most typical instances of fruit, and coconuts and olives the least; trousers and coats were most typical items of clothing, and purses and bracelets least typical (Clark and Clark 1977: 464). If the concepts 'bird', 'furniture', 'fruit' and 'clothing' were each defined by a set of criterial features, there would be no way to explain why some things satisfied the features more than others. Instead one would expect a clear distinction between members and non-members of the categories concerned.

One of the attractions of the prototype theory for an anthropologist or sociolinguist is that it is not too hard to understand how people can *learn* such concepts from each other. Imagine a baby, without language, learning the concept 'place for sleeping in' – a clear example of a cultural concept, since it depends on what other people expect the baby to do, and not just on what it wants to do itself. The 'prototype' place for sleeping is of course the baby's own cot, and as long as the baby can identify this as the place, *par excellence*, for sleeping in, its main concept-formation task is over. Other places can then be subsumed under the concept as the need arises – other cots, or grown-up beds, or beds made up on the floor, or back seats of cars and so on. In some cases the concept will be extended only temporarily, but if the same situation arises again the baby may store the new kind of sleeping place in its memory and might even replace the original prototype with the new one. The point of this example is to show that a prototype-based concept can be learned on the basis of a very small number of instances – perhaps a single one – and without any kind of formal definition, whereas a feature-based definition would be very much harder to learn since a much larger number of cases, plus a number of non-cases, would be needed before the learner could work out which features were necessary and which were not.

Another attraction of the prototype theory is that it allows for the kind of creative flexibility in the application of concepts which we find in real life – in other words, it predicts that the boundaries of concepts will be fuzzy, as they in fact are. For example, let us assume that we have two concepts 'fruit' and 'vegetable', built partly on the basis of other people's speech but also on the basis of our own non-linguistic experience – for instance, fruits are typically eaten as dessert or between meals, typically grow on trees or bushes and are typically sweet or sour, while vegetables are typically eaten with the meat course, typically grow on or under the ground and are typically savoury. An apple has all the characteristics of a prototypical fruit, and a cabbage all those of a prototypical vegetable, but there are anomalous cases such as tomatoes and rhubarb which might count as either, according to which criterion seems most relevant to the occasion concerned. The task of the person applying the concept 'fruit', for example, is not simply to look for the defining characteristics of fruit in the tomato or rhubarb, but to show initiative and sensitivity to the needs of the occasion in deciding between the criteria available. Compared with the feature-based model, the prototype model puts more burden on the user, but gives virtually unlimited freedom to apply concepts creatively.

A third attraction which the prototype theory offers sociolinguists is the possibility of using the theory in explaining how people categorise the social variables to which they relate language – variables such as the kind of person who is speaking and the circumstances in which they are doing so. As we saw in the last chapter, people learn that certain linguistic items are associated with certain types of people or circumstances, but we did not discuss how people categorise speakers and circumstances. If concepts are based on defining features, any speaker or set of circumstances should be equally easy to classify. On the other hand, if they are based on prototypes, all we need do when learning a new linguistic item is to work out what kind of speaker *typically* uses it, or what are the typical circumstances under which it is used, leaving the unclear, borderline cases to look after themselves as the need arises.

This is indeed the basis for a well-established system of analysis developed by Joshua Fishman, in terms of what are called DOMAINS – concepts such as 'home', 'school', 'work', 'religion' and so on (see Fishman 1971, Fasold 1984: 183). The assumption underlying this system is that the choice of language in a bilingual community varies from domain to domain, and that domains are *congruent* combinations of a particular kind of speaker and addressee, in a particular kind of place, talking about a particular kind of topic. If a teacher is talking about history to a pupil, and they are in school, the contributory factors are congruent and define a domain – that of 'school' – and there will be no difficulty in deciding which language to use. If, however, we make one of the factors incongruent – by moving the scenario into the pupil's home, for instance – the interaction is no longer covered unambiguously by any one domain, so the speaker has to use intelligence and imagination in deciding which language to use.

It should have become very clear from this discussion of the prototype theory of concepts that sociolinguists stand to learn a lot from cognitive psychology and psycholinguistics. Any attempt to erect boundaries between 'the psychological' and 'the sociological' approaches to language is likely to be to the detriment of both.

3.1.3   *Language, culture and thought*

The main purpose of the two previous sections was to clarify the terminology relating to culture and thought, and the relations between them. We have said little about language as such, so we can now try to fit language into the picture described so far. Let us see first of all what that picture looks like.

As we have seen, culture may be defined as the kind of knowledge which we learn from other people, either by direct instruction or by watching their behaviour. Since we learn our culture from those around us, we may assume that we share it with them, so this kind of knowledge is likely to play a major role when we communicate with them, and in particular when we use language. The same will be true for any knowledge that we share with other people, regardless of whether we learned it from them or not; for example, even if we are born knowing about things such as verticality and the basic lay-out of people's faces, such shared knowledge is equally important for language (as witness the meanings of words like *up* and *face*).

This knowledge can be broken down into small units which we have called 'concepts' and 'propositions'. Most words express concepts – the concept of 'bird', or 'walking', or 'language', for instance – so it is easy to see how important concepts are to language. Similarly, sentences generally express propositions, for example, the proposition that Columbus discovered America, or that oil floats on water. Our shared knowledge consists of concepts as well as propositions; 'diglossia' and 'bird' are concepts but they are just as much part of our cultural knowledge as the belief that diglossia is found in Switzerland and that birds fly. Indeed, as this example shows, concepts and propositions are inextricably linked, because propositions provide the links between concepts that give them content. The only thing that distinguishes the concept 'bird' from all other concepts is that it is mentioned in propositions like 'birds fly', which links it to the concept of flying. In short, our knowledge consists of a vast network of concepts interrelated by propositions (Hudson 1990, 1995; Aitchison 1987: 194ff.; Weischedel 1994).

The idea of knowledge as a network is fairly uncontroversial, though it is often studied in a more fragmentary way. There are three points of controversy that need to be considered, however. We have already considered the question of the nature of concepts, when we discussed the choice between 'classical' and 'prototype-based' concepts. The outcome of that discussion was a negative verdict on the idea that concepts have a definition, a set of necessary and sufficient propositions which are distinct from all the other propositions that mention them. Any proposition may be 'overridden' in exceptional cases, so although typical birds do fly, some exceptional birds do not. A second question involves the distinction between concepts and 'percepts', which are the outcome of direct perception, such as a smell, a taste, a sound or a particular sight. These do not seem to depend on propositions for their content in the way that concepts like 'bird' or 'diglossia' do, but they can be involved in propositions – for example, the proposition that the smell of paint is less pleasant than the smell of roses. For present purposes we can ignore the distinction between concepts and percepts, and we shall also ignore the third distinction, between 'knowing that' and 'knowing how', sometimes called declarative and procedural knowledge. Knowing how to ride a bicycle, or how to speak English, is probably a different kind of knowledge from knowing that a bicycle has two wheels or that *cat* is an English word; but the issue is complicated and not directly relevant here.

We can now turn to language. There are three points at which language makes contact with knowledge, and more specifically with the kind of knowledge that we call 'culture'. As a distinguished anthropologist said, 'a society's language is an aspect of its culture . . . The relation of language to culture is that of part to whole' (Goodenough 1957).

(1) Language consists of *concepts* and *propositions*. In whichever way we understand the notion 'linguistic items' (see 2.1.2), we can see them as the categories which we use to analyse our experience, i.e. as concepts. For instance, each lexical item represents a combination of phonological, syntactic and semantic properties in just the same way that the concept 'fruit' represents a combination of properties to do with when the object is eaten, where it grows and whether it is sweet or savoury; similarly, a syntactic construction is defined by a complex combination of properties in much the same way as the concept 'table' is defined by a particular arrangement of vertical and horizontal pieces. Moreover, it is

increasingly clear that many (if not all) linguistic items are defined in terms of prototypes, just like non-linguistic concepts, which is why it is often impossible to draw a hard and fast distinction between 'good' and 'bad' sentences. For instance, the typical subject of a verb like *cook* is the person who does the cooking (*Mary cooked the meat*), but it can also be the instrument (*The oven cooked the meat*) or even the thing cooked (*The meat cooked well*). The prototype subject of *cook* combines a number of different properties, including being 'agent' and 'having primary responsibility', but it is possible to generalise from this combination to cases where the subject merely has primary responsibility for the cooking, such as *The oven cooked the meat*. If even this feature is absent, the sentence becomes much less acceptable, as in *?The saucepan cooked the meat*. (For detailed discussion of examples like this, and arguments for a prototypical approach to linguistic items, see Lakoff 1977.)

(2) *Meanings are concepts and propositions.* There is considerable controversy over the definition of 'meaning', but there is widespread agreement that the meaning of a linguistic item is its *sense*, that is, what is permanent about its relation to the world, rather than its *referents*, the objects or events to which it refers on particular occasions. More controversially, however, we can go on to identify the sense of an item with the concept to which it is related in the speaker's memory – in other words, with the concept that the item expresses. For instance, the sense of the word *cat* is the concept 'cat', which may well have existed in the person's memory before they ever learned the word to express it (for this view see Clark and Clark 1977: 439, 449, Barrett 1994). More complex items such as sentences express propositions rather than concepts, but again these are part of knowledge – in fact, they are the main vehicle for transferring knowledge from one person's mind to another's.

(3) *Understanding and using speech involves the whole of knowledge.* Points (1) and (2) recognise that a hearer or speaker needs to know the relevant linguistic concepts (words, constructions and so on), and also the concepts and propositions that serve as their meanings. But we also use a great deal of knowledge which has nothing in itself to do with language. This is the province of pragmatics (for example, Levinson 1983, Sperber and Wilson 1986), the study of how we use language. If I hear someone else say 'He kissed her', I have to use a great deal of non-linguistic knowledge in order to work out who the people concerned are, when the reported event happened, how reliable the report is, what conclusions can be drawn, and so on. Similar questions have to be considered by the speaker; if I want to tell someone that I think John loves Mary, how do I do it most effectively? The mental processes that take place in our minds are

called 'inference': the hearer infers what the speaker intends, and the speaker infers the best way to express the message. Inference is like a mental calculation – if A, B and C are true, what follows? – and everything we know is grist for its mill.

(4) *Linguistically relevant social categories are concepts.* As was pointed out at the end of 3.1.2, we may assume that we categorise speakers and circumstances in terms of concepts based, as usual, on prototypes. In the previous chapter we argued that speakers locate themselves in a multi-dimensional space in relation to the rest of their society, and locate each act of speaking in a multi-dimensional space relative to the rest of their social lives. We can now suggest that each 'dimension' is defined by a particular concept of a typical type of person or typical situation. This view allows us to predict many phenomena which are in fact found in sociolinguistics, such as the 'domains' discussed in the previous section, the 'metaphorical code-switching' discussed in 2.5.1 and the different degrees to which people's speech identifies them with particular groups (chapter 5, especially 5.4.3, and 7.2.6).

3.2   Linguistic and cultural relativity

3.2.1   *Semantic relativity*

Having clarified some of the connections between language, culture and thought, attention can now be paid to the two issues which have dominated the study of language in relation to culture and thought. Firstly, to what extent do cultures (including languages) differ from one another? Are they all in some sense cut to the same mould, reflecting a common underlying 'humanity', or do they differ arbitrarily and unrestrictedly from one another, reflecting the fact that different people live in very different intellectual and physical worlds? This is the question of RELATIVITY, and in this section we shall concentrate on how far meanings may differ from variety to variety and whether there are any connections between differences in meaning and differences in culture. The second issue is DETERMINISM (to which we turn in 3.3), which is concerned with the influence of language on thought.

One aspect of relativity is very easily demonstrated since we can point to items in some languages which certainly express meanings not expressed in others. This can be seen in the difficulties of translating between languages that are associated with different cultures, and consequently have names for different ranges of customs (*birthday-party*), objects (*hovercraft, sausage*), institutions (*university*) and so on. A moment's thought will show how large a proportion of everyday vocabulary is tied to culture-specific concepts – concepts which simply do not exist in other cultures. This is especially true if concepts get their content from all the propositions that mention them, as I suggested above, because then the details will become much more important. For example, the English words *brown, monkey, chair, jug* and *carpet* are all more or less untranslatable into French, in the sense that no single French word expresses precisely the same concept as the corresponding English word; different words must be chosen on different occasions even though it is apparently the same concept that is expressed in each case by the English word (Lyons 1981: 67).

The conclusion to which examples like these point is that different languages do not simply provide different ways of expressing the same ideas, but they are also different in the more fundamental (and interesting) sense that the ideas that can be expressed differ from language to language. We can call this kind of variability SEMANTIC RELATIVITY. English has a word for 'carpet', but French doesn't, and so on (including an equal number of examples of concepts for which English has no word, of course). All we have shown so far is that there are some examples of these mismatches between meanings that are expressible in different languages, so the important question is how far-reaching semantic relativity is. The simplest view is that there are no limits at all on the variation, apart from whatever limits there are on human concept-formation. (Obviously a concept that is inconceivable, if there are such things, cannot even be conceived, let alone expressed in language.) Is this view correct? We shall consider some limits that have been proposed.

One possibility is that all the concepts that serve as word-meanings in different languages are simply different ways of combining a limited range of rather basic 'components'. For example, the English verb *eat* is translated into German in two different ways, according to whether the eater is a human (*essen*) or an animal (*fressen*). Clearly both of these German verbs has a more specific meaning than *eat*, but the concepts 'human' and 'animal' exist in English as well (among other things as the meanings of the words *human* and *animal*) so the difference between the two languages lies simply in how the concepts 'human', 'animal' and 'eat' are combined into word-meanings. If all differences can be explained in this way, relativity will actually be very limited indeed. This possibility leads to a search for universal components of meaning in terms of which all meanings can be expressed. It lay behind the 'componential analysis' which used to be described in introductions to semantics (for example, Kempson 1977), according to which concepts like 'man' could be decomposed into the components 'male', 'human' and 'adult'. It has also stimulated some interesting attempts to develop a universal semantic vocabulary for defining all words in all languages (Wierzbicka 1980). However, as soon as this kind of analysis is applied to concepts like 'carpet' it becomes apparent that at least the immediate 'components' of culture-specific concepts must themselves be further culture-specific concepts. The goal of a small universal vocabulary still looks very remote.

Another possible limit to semantic relativity is that it only applies to vocabulary. Maybe the meanings that are expressed by inflectional morphology or by syntactic constructions vary less? Once again this is a matter of fact, to be decided by careful analysis of particular cases, and not something we can decide simply by thinking hard. Some of the most interesting work has been done on languages which strike us as extremely exotic (one of which we shall consider shortly), but even work on English dialects has produced evidence of surprising variation. For example, in Irish English there is no single form which corresponds in meaning to the mainland combination *have* + past participle (for example, *I have eaten*). Sometimes the equivalent is *be after* (for example, *I am after seeing him* = 'I have just seen him'), at other times it is the present tense (for example, *I know his family all me life* = 'I've known his family all my life') and at others again by *have* + object + past participle (for example, *I've it pronounced wrong* = 'I've pronounced it wrongly') (Harris 1993). None of these patterns has a meaning which is as broad as that of mainland *have* + past participle. Admittedly we might react by saying that even the latter has not just one meaning but a range of distinct meanings, each corresponding to the meaning of one of the Irish English constructions; but this still leaves subtle differences between the two. For example, Irish English only uses the *have* + object + past participle construction when the verb refers to an event that takes some time (for example, *John has his dinner eaten*) but not to a momentary one (for example, *John has the ball kicked*) (Milroy and Milroy 1985: 88): its sense is therefore something like 'extended event which is now past'. No such restriction applies to any of the mainland English constructions, so this construction must have a sense which cannot be expressed precisely by any mainland English construction. The conclusion, then, is that even different varieties of 'the same language' (English) may allow different concepts to be expressed by grammatical constructions.

Not surprisingly, such differences are much more dramatic when we consider languages from more exotic cultures. A particularly interesting example is discussed in Casad and Langacker 1985. This article is a detailed discussion of two affixes that are widely used in a Uto-Aztecan language called Cora spoken in Mexico. They are *u-* and *a-*, which can very approximately be translated as 'inside' and 'outside', but this translation is so approximate as to be almost useless as we shall see. We can start with two different one-word sentences which can both be used when describing a dog, to say that its tail is chopped short.

(1)   u-h-kí-tya-pu'u.

(2)   a-h-kí-tya-pu'u.

The crucial difference between these two sentences is the position of the speaker in relation to the dog. Sentence (1) is used by a speaker who is standing behind the dog, and sentence (2) by one who is standing to one side of the dog. This immediately establishes our main point, which is that a prefix in one language (Cora) expresses a meaning which cannot be expressed by prefixes in another language (English) – indeed, it is hard to think how this particular meaning difference could be expressed at all in English. (Maybe 'I see by looking at that dog from the back/side that its tail is chopped short'?)

If we consider other examples of *u*- and *a*- and look for a common meaning, it turns out to be a matter of visual geometry. The Cora use *u*- with things that are in the direct line of vision, when looking towards the highest point, while *a*- is used for things that are outside that line of vision. An essential fact about the Cora is that they live in a mountainous area, and this system is used primarily when looking at mountains to distinguish things that are on a direct line to the peak from things that are off to one side. As far as the dog is concerned, the 'peak' is the dog's rump, so *u*- is correct when the tail is between the speaker and the rump, but not otherwise. The system has enormous ramifications; for example, because *u*- means 'in line of vision' it is also used to mean 'inside' (as our original translation suggested). Therefore *u*- is used if something is inside an enclosure. Now another background fact about the Cora people is that they live in the open air, so anything in an enclosure is invisible (in contrast with our urban view, where we see most things from indoors), and *u*- is also used when the thing described is invisible. Consequently, if a Cora wants to refer to a place which is out of sight on the other side of the river, they say *u-tavan* (where *tavan* means 'across the river'), but to refer to someone who is standing on the beach and therefore visible, they say *a-tavan*. If we were forced to apply *inside* and *outside* to these two cases, we would probably use *inside* for the person on the beach ('inside' the river) and *outside* to the other case, but this would of course be precisely the reverse of the Cora usage, if we persist in translating *u*- as 'inside' and *a*- as 'outside'.

The general conclusion seems clear. Even if we concentrate on grammatical constructions, affixes and the like, we still find dramatic differences from language to language in the kinds of meaning that can be expressed. It is hard to avoid the conclusion that semantic relativity is limited only by the limits of cultural variation, and it is at any rate certain that there is much more semantic variation between languages than most of us are aware of. Having made this point, however, it is important to restore the balance by showing how easy it is to exaggerate the differences between languages. If we analyse meanings correctly, we may discover unsuspected similarities. We now consider two analytical aids, 'prototypes' and 'basic level concepts'.

3.2.2 Prototypes

If meanings are examined in relation to prototypes (explained in 3.1.2), it can be shown that there are fewer differences if we focus on the prototypes around which the meanings of words are organised than if we try to cover the extensions of the prototypes as well. To illustrate this we shall consider the analysis of kinship terminology. The main development to which we shall refer is due to the anthropologist Floyd Lounsbury, who arrived at the notion of meanings centred on prototypes independently of the psychological work of Eleanor Rosch referred to in 3.1.2 (see especially Lounsbury 1969, Burling 1970: 49, Schusky 1994). Let us start by looking at the kinds of data which confront a linguist or anthropologist studying kinship terminology.

In various societies, including the Seminole Indians of Oklahoma and Florida and the inhabitants of the Trobriand Islands (to the east of Papua New Guinea), the same term (X) may be used to refer to the following relations:

(1) father
(2) father's brother (English *uncle*)
(3) father's sister's son (English *cousin*)
(4) father's mother's sister's son (English?)
(5) father's sister's daughter's son (English?)
(6) father's father's brother's son (English?)
(7) father's father's sister's son's son (English?)

The English terms in parentheses, where there are any, are not at all accurate translations, as they have wider senses than the meanings given. For instance, *uncle* refers either to one's father's brother or to one's mother's brother, whereas X cannot be used to refer to one's mother's brother. Moreover, for most of us there is simply no term in English to refer to senses (4)–(7), though no doubt those who are sufficiently expert in these matters (a small minority in Britain) could construct some compound like *second cousin twice removed*. It is hardly worth emphasising that there is no term in English which has the same meaning as X in these languages.

Not only is the meaning of X baffling for any ordinary English speaker, but it would also puzzle an analyst in search of common features defining the people that can be referred to as one's X. One common feature is that the person concerned must be male, but beyond that it is hard to see any set of defining characteristics of the set covered by X. (It should be noted that X does not mean 'male blood relative on one's father's side' since it does *not* include 'father's father', for example.) However, if one takes the 'prototype' approach instead of looking for defining features, things look very different. According to Lounsbury, all of these meanings may be predicted by assuming that the basic meaning (the prototype) is simply 'father', and that the other meanings are derived from this by applying any of the following three equivalence rules:

A. A man's sister is equivalent to his mother.
B. Siblings (i.e. brothers or sisters) of the same sex are equivalent to each other.
C. Half-siblings are equivalent to full-siblings.

These three rules are needed to predict the meanings of other kinship terms in the same languages, and only these rules are needed.

To start with an easy example, 'father's brother' (2) is derived from 'father' by rule B, since the father and his brother are siblings of the same sex and are therefore equivalent. For 'father's sister's son' (3), we first apply rule B, converting 'father' into 'father's brother', then rule C, replacing 'brother' by 'mother's son' (a way of referring to a half-brother), giving 'father's mother's son', and finally rule A, replacing 'father's mother' by 'father's sister', giving the desired relationship 'father's sister's son'. Table 3.1 shows how meaning (7), 'father's father's sister's son's son', can be derived from 'father'.

One striking thing about this analysis is that the basic meaning of term X is now exactly the same as that of English *father*, and the differences between them are due to the existence of rules of derivation which exist in other languages but not in English. (It should be noted that the English word *father* too has secondary, derived, meanings, such as 'priest' and 'adoptive father'.) This discovery opens the possibility that if we compare the prototype meanings of kinship terminology from different languages (assuming that we can identify such meanings for them all), we shall find that there are relatively few variations

Table 3.1. *Derivation of kinship terms in certain languages*

Rule	Meaning
prototype	father
B sibling = sibling	father's brother
C half-sibling = full	father's father's son
B sibling = sibling	father's father's brother's son
C half-sibling = full	father's father's mother's son's son
A sister = mother	father's father's sister's son's son

on a few very general patterns, though we may expect differences in the rules of derivation. The differences in those rules cannot be dismissed as unimportant, of course, because they can have dramatic and far-reaching consequences, but at least we seem to have restricted the kinds of differences between kinship terminologies in different languages, and no longer see them as evidence for extreme relativity.

It would be wrong, however, to leave the impression that the prototype approach makes all kinship systems look the same except for their derivation rules, since this is certainly not the case. Even prototype meanings may be closely related to the social organisation of the society concerned. For instance, there is an Australian tribe called the Njamal whose marriage customs refer to a unit which anthropologists call 'moiety', since it divides the tribe into two halves (cf. French *moitié* 'half'). (The following account is based on Burling 1970: 21.) In Njamal society, your moiety is always the same as your father's, but different from your mother's since the rules require husbands and wives to belong to different moieties. The importance of moiety differences is reflected not only in the derivation rules (which are formulated so as not to mix relatives from different moieties under the same term) but *also* in the prototype meanings. For instance, there are four words referring basically to members of your parents' generation: one each, as one would expect, for 'father' and 'mother', but also one for 'mother's brother' and one for 'father's sister'. Why should these two relations be picked out for special treatment, to the exclusion, say, of 'father's brother'? The answer is presumably that they provide a basic sex contrast independent of the moiety contrast (for instance, your father and your father's sister are of your own moiety but of opposite sexes, and your mother and her brother are of the other moiety but of different sexes). In contrast, your father's brother is both of the same moiety and of the same sex as your father, and would therefore not be a usefully distinct prototype.

Even if we take the prototype approach to kinship terminology, there is still ample scope for reflecting differences in social organisation, either in the prototypes themselves or in the rules for deriving other meanings from them. (For example, the concept 'father' itself can be defined in terms of a number of different factors such as biological paternity and status as guardian, and such factors may be given different emphases in different societies.) Moreover, it seems likely that a concept like 'moiety' will need to be referred to in defining prototypes in languages like Njamal, but not in languages which are associated with other kinds of social system, so we cannot even be sure that the 'semantic components' referred to in prototypes are 'universal' in any very significant sense.

One final point about the notion 'prototype' itself. We have considered three different ways in which a word's prototypical meaning may be extended.

Firstly, a speaker or hearer may exploit the creative flexibility that we discussed earlier (3.1.2), by making an original extension to the meaning; in some cases the originality merits the name 'metaphorical' (for example, when applying an established prototype to a totally exotic object which fits it only poorly). Secondly, there may be accepted and clear rules for extending meanings, as in the case of Lounsbury's analysis of kinship terminology, and we may perhaps assume that at least some of the extended meanings are worked out afresh each time, rather than being stored in the speaker's memory. And thirdly, there are words whose meanings centre on some prototype but whose extended meanings are presumably stored in memory as well. For instance, we must assume that the sense of *father* which allows it to be applied to a Catholic priest is stored in memory, although it is derived, at least historically, from the primary biological meaning of *father*. There are many interesting and important questions to be asked about the relations among these three types of extension, which we cannot pursue here, but any reader who is at all familiar with the study of *word-formation* will see that the ways in which prototype meanings are extended can be matched in word formation. Take, for example, the ways in which 'ordinal' numbers are formed. For instance, a speaker who says *twenty-seventh* is presumably creating a new form by applying a rule (case 2), one who says *first* or *second* must be extracting a form from memory (case 3), and one who wants to refer to an example numbered *3a* and refers to it as the *3a-th example* is acting creatively (case 1).

3.2.3 Basic-level concepts

We have seen that focussing on components and prototypes has the effect of reducing the extent to which languages express different meanings. We now come to another theory developed by the psychologist Eleanor Rosch (who, it will be recalled, developed the notion of prototype in psychology), which suggests that there may be less difference than might be expected in the *organisation* of word-meanings (see e.g. Clark and Clark 1977, Rosch 1976; the theory was anticipated in some respects by Brown 1958a, 1958b). It starts from the natural assumption that the way in which a language structures the world, through the meanings which it distinguishes, depends partly on the way in which the world itself is structured and partly on the communicative needs of its speakers. The notion of the 'prototype' arises from the fact that in the world itself features do not combine randomly, but tend to occur in complex bundles. For instance, a thing which has feathers is likely also to have two legs, to fly, to lay eggs and to have a beak. All we are doing when we create a concept of a prototype is to recognise this fact about the world, while allowing for the fact that there are exceptional cases. It can be argued that this is a more efficient approach than working out watertight categories with their respective sufficient and necessary defining features.

Another consequence which Rosch draws from her basic assumption is that there should be what she calls BASIC-LEVEL CONCEPTS, in contrast with other concepts which are either more general or more specific. Assuming that there is at least some hierarchical structure in our concepts, with more general ones like 'furniture' subsuming less general ones like 'chair', it should be possible to work out which level in the hierarchy gives the most information (i.e. involves the greatest number of facts per concept). For instance, it is much more informative to say 'I bought a chair' than 'I bought a piece of furniture', because *chair* implies several physical features (a horizontal surface, legs, a vertical back), whereas there are no such features shared by all pieces of furniture, and similarly *chair* carries information about function, in terms of a 'motor programme', telling one what to do with it, in contrast with *furniture*, which only carries the vaguest of functional information. On the other hand, *kitchen chair* conveys only one extra fact compared with *chair*, a fact which in any case would normally be of little relevance to the situation. Accordingly, *chair* is a 'basic level' concept, in the sense that it is the category that comes to mind most naturally when we have to refer to an object which could equally truly be described as a piece of furniture, a chair or a kitchen chair. There is obvious support for this conclusion in the fact that *chair* is just one word, in contrast with both *kitchen chair* and *piece of furniture*, but the main evidence comes from the ways in which speakers use these terms, as studied by Rosch.

The relevance of basic-level concepts to the question of relativity is two-fold. First, if it is true that concepts tend to be organised hierarchically around basic ones, we should expect to see similarities between languages in the hierarchical organisation of their vocabulary. This prediction has been confirmed by studies of 'folk biology' carried out by the anthropologist Brent Berlin and colleagues (summarised in Clark and Clark 1977: 528), who found that in a wide variety of languages the names for plants and animals are organised into five or six levels of which the third from the top is the 'basic' one. For instance, English has a hierarchy represented by terms like *plant, tree, pine, Ponderosa pine* and *northern Ponderosa pine*, and in this hierarchy the third level, represented by *pine*, is the lowest at which a single word is used, suggesting that it is basic. Rather amazingly, Berlin and his colleagues found that all the languages they studied had about the same number of level-three terms in the 'biology' hierarchy – about 500. Taken together, these findings represent a high degree of similarity between languages in their semantic structure, even though the particular concepts concerned might be quite different according to the kinds of plants and animals found where the particular language was spoken.

The second connection between basic-level concepts and relativity is that they offer an additional area with respect to which people may *differ* in their language, thus making the relativity of language look rather greater. People differ in the particular concepts which they treat as basic. For instance, research done by Rosch showed that people who live in towns treat 'tree' rather than, say, 'pine' as basic (Rosch 1976) – presumably because they are less familiar with the specific properties of pine trees than the country-dwellers with whom Berlin and his colleagues mainly worked. Conversely, we might expect that 'Ponderosa pine' might be the basic level for a forester, and that this would be reflected by an abbreviation of the name to a single word, *Ponderosa* (Clark and Clark 1977: 553). (An alternative name for 'pine' is *pine tree*, and it would be interesting to know whether those who treat 'tree' as the basic level concept are more likely than country-dwellers to use this longer form for 'pine'.)

3.2.4 *Conclusions*

The main conclusion of this section is that the meanings that languages can express vary about as much as the associated cultures do. For example, kinship terms reflect the kinship systems of their users, and vary to the extent that these do; if every language has a word which (basically) means 'father', this is because every culture recognises a special place in a person's life for their father. Conceptual distinctions that are very important in everyday life, such as the Cora inside/outside distinction, may be expressed in very central parts of the grammar. And so on, through the various examples we have considered. Not surprisingly, perhaps, the results become more interesting as the analyses become more sophisticated; so if we use tools such as prototype and basic-level analysis to push behind the surface details we find unsuspected similarities as well as differences.

Having said all this, however, it is important to restore the balance by stressing the separateness of the language's semantic system from the rest of the culture. Alongside these examples where we can see deep cultural explanations for the language's semantic structure, we must remember others which seem to have nothing to do with anything else in the culture. Take the German verbs for 'eat', *essen* and *fressen*, which we discussed earlier. German forces a speaker to pay attention to whether the eater is a person or an animal, whereas English doesn't; but there seems to be nothing else in the two cultures which reflects this difference. The same can be true even of far-reaching semantic differences. For example, according to Hawkins (1986: 29), the case of *eat* is typical of a lot of verbs in English and German. The same is true of *dig*, *know*, *put* and *put on*, for example, all of which have to be translated by a range of different German verbs with more specific meanings. Maybe this difference reflects a profound difference between German- and English-speaking cultures, but there is no evidence for one. What these examples show is that semantic differences between languages can be profound without necessarily being related to anything else in the culture.

The converse is also true. General cultural differences can be profound without necessarily being reflected in the language's semantic structure. Modern pluralist societies are rich in cultural differences between subgroups, all of whom speak basically the same language, with the same semantic structures. Some of the cultural differences do emerge in the subgroups' language, but language is rather conservative and the central parts change only slowly. A particularly dramatic example of the mismatch between culture and language is the need for a sex-neutral alternative to *he* and *she*, for use in sentences like 'If the visitor does not know the long-house language, but someone their knows *his*, they will use the visitor's when speaking to *him*' (from p. 9 of the first edition of this book). A new subculture has developed since I wrote this, but the language has not changed to suit our needs. Some languages (for example, Japanese) have a sex-neutral third-person pronoun, but English did not have one in 1979, and still doesn't. Similarly, some of us believe that humans are animals, and that chimpanzees (for example) are much more similar to us than they are to inanimate objects; but regardless of our beliefs, if we speak English we all have to make a fundamental choice between *who* and *what*, and between *someone* and *something*, which classifies chimps with stones rather than with us (Hudson 1995).

Our conclusion, then, is that the semantic system of a language is linked to the culture of its speakers – but only loosely. But the main point is that semantic systems vary enormously, and to roughly the same extent as cultures, so semantic relativity seems to be correct. As a research strategy, it is better to start from the assumption that semantic systems can vary without restriction, and then to look for restrictions, than to assume from the start that languages are simply different ways of expressing the same range of meanings, and then to look for variation.

3.3   Language and thought
3.3.1   *Language and socialisation*

We now turn to the question of *linguistic determinism*. To what extent, and in what ways, does language determine thought? This question is normally answered with reference to the SAPIR-WHORF HYPOTHESIS, according to which language determines thought to a very great extent and in many ways, and we shall discuss this hypothesis in the next section. This hypothesis is very controversial, so we shall prepare for it by considering related ideas that are more widely accepted.

One point of contact between language and thought is its use by an older generation to transmit its culture to a younger one. In other words, speech is an instrument of SOCIALISATION – the process by which children are turned into fully competent members of their society (Cazden 1994). However a good deal of culture is transmitted verbally, and it is often said the development of the faculty of language by the human species made it possible for 'biological evolution', working on genes, to be replaced as the dominant factor in our development by 'cultural evolution', working on our minds. There is no need to labour the point that speech is a crucial component in the process of socialisation.

It is obvious that language allows our socialisers to teach us facts (for example, 'Beethoven was a composer'; 'Germs make us ill'), and to name our concepts. The question is whether language can be said to build these concepts in the first place, or whether it reflects concepts which would have been there in any case. The answer seems to be 'A bit of each'.

We can be sure that some concepts are independent of language. Some we learned as babies before we started to speak towards the end of the first year of life, and others were formed later, but must have developed without recourse to language since we still have no words for them in our adult vocabulary. For instance, we have a concept for the kinds of things we buy at a newsagent (or a tobacconist, or a 'do-it-yourself' shop), but no name for any of these concepts, in contrast with concepts for things bought in other kinds of shop, for example, *groceries*. Whether or not there is a name for these concepts seems to have little to do with our ability to learn them. Similarly, we can see the similarities among nails, screws, rivets, nuts and bolts – they have similar functions, they are all made of metal and we might expect people to store them together – but there is no name for this concept. Examples like this are easy to multiply, and warn us against the danger of assuming that concepts only exist when there is specific linguistic evidence for them. Interestingly, it seems that such 'lexical gaps' tend to occur at the levels above the 'basic' one (see 3.2.3). (Gaps below this level are harder to identify, since they can easily be filled by a compound form like *Ponderosa pine*.)

On the other hand, we can be equally sure that there are other concepts which we should not have if it were not for language. The most obvious cases are those which relate to language as a phenomenon – the concepts 'language', 'meaning', 'word' and so on. However, there are other concepts which we learn *after* we have learned their names, and for which the name is our main evidence. For instance, Clark and Clark (1977: 486) quote an incident where a mother said to her five-year-old child, 'We have to keep the screen door closed, honey, so the flies won't come in. Flies bring germs into the house with them.' When the child was asked afterwards what germs were, the answer was 'Something the flies play with'! This example illustrates nicely the way in which a new word may act as evidence that an unknown concept exists, leaving the learner with the problem of somehow working out what that concept is, making use of any evidence that may be available. Many students of linguistics must find themselves doing just this on occasions, when they come across terms like *complementiser* or even *empirical*.

Moreover, we learn many concepts by being told about them, especially during our formal education, so we do in fact learn them through language, whether or not we could have learned them without it. If it were not for language we should probably not have concepts to which we could attach words like *peninsula*, *feudal*, *metabolism*, *classical* or *factor*. One of the main functions of education is to teach concepts, and technical terminology is the teacher's most important teaching aid in this task. The examples discussed so far have all depended simply on the existence in the language's vocabulary of some lexical item which guides the learner to a new concept, its meaning. However, it is rather obvious that the extent of the effect will depend on how often the item is used. If a word is used often, a child has more opportunities for learning its meaning accurately, and gets more practice in making the relevant distinctions in talking about the world. Take, for example, the difference between *east* and *west*. In familiar western languages these terms exist, but we don't use them very often and, indeed, most of the time we don't think at all easily in such terms. In contrast, we use *left* and *right* rather often and children learn to make this distinction long before they learn the East/West distinction. If we have two cups and a tea-pot on a table and need to pick out one of the cups, we might well call it the cup on the right of the pot, but we would surely never call it the one to the east of the pot (even if this were true)!

We might expect the same to be true everywhere, but according to Pedersen 1995 it is not. In some communities it is quite normal to apply the compass-points system (North, South, East, West) to 'table-top' layouts, and there are even some languages (in Australia) which have no general terms for 'left' and 'right'. Pedersen describes a 'compass-points' society of Tamil speakers in southern India, but de Léon (1994) reports another one, speaking Tzotzil (a Mayan language) in Mexico. Rather remarkably, de Léon found that children as young as five could apply the compass-points system efficiently, at an age when European children cannot use 'left' and 'right' correctly. For example, when de Léon asked a child to talk about a collection of toy animals and objects, a typical child would talk about 'the ball to the East of the pig'! This is very surprising, as one would expect the points of the compass to be much harder to learn and to apply than the left/right distinction.

We do not know whether the use of language causes the speakers to think either in terms of compass-points or in terms of left/right, but we do know that the two things are closely related to each other, thanks to Pedersen's careful work in India. His Tamil community is especially interesting because different speakers use different *linguistic* strategies for their table-top description. Some people consistently used a left/right approach, and others consistently used compass-points; very few people mixed the two. This allowed him to divide his subjects into two 'orientation' groups who in other respects were similar – same general culture, same language (apart from this preference), same immediate environment (apart from a contrast between villagers and city-dwellers which is an unfortunate irrelevance in the research).

The main focus of Pedersen's research was on how his subjects thought about the objects – how they remembered them and how they solved problems connected with them. The experiments were designed to force subjects to choose between the two orientations, and the crucial piece of apparatus was a second table containing similar objects. The subject had to turn through 180° when moving from the first table to the second, which reversed the relationship between East/West and left/right: for example, if East was to the right on table 1, it would be to the left on table 2.

In one of the experiments the subject was asked to look at a single card on table 1 and to pick out one of four cards on table 2 which was 'the same' as the one on table 1. The cards all had the same pattern – two different shapes next to each other – but those on table 2 each pointed in a different direction, so the subject had to pick the one which had the same orientation as the one on table 1. There were two correct answers, according to whether orientation was defined in terms of compass points or in terms of left/right, and the relevant result was that the choice between these two correlated strongly with language use. People who used the East/West system in their normal speech (when describing objects on the table) also used it in selecting a card from table 2, and those who preferred the left/right contrast in speech also preferred it in selection. This test showed that the two groups of subjects tend to think in different ways about the objects, as well as using different words to describe them.

The other tests confirmed this tendency in more sophisticated ways, but Pedersen is careful to stress that his evidence does not prove that the language-use in itself causes the differences in thinking. Another explanation, which cannot be ruled out, is that there is some influence which causes them both (such as the difference between rural and urban life, or even formal education, which seems to encourage the left/right distinction). However it seems reasonable to assume that the habitual language use, repeated perhaps dozens of times a day, reinforces the effects of these other influences; and of course we cannot rule out the possibility that it is the language differences themselves which are the primary cause of the thinking differences.

In conclusion, language seems to be more important in learning some concepts than others, and one general principle may be that language becomes more important as the concepts concerned get further from one's immediate sensory experience – in other words, more abstract (as in the germs example). Another principle may be that the influence of language is more important where there are alternative ways of interpreting experience (as in the choice between East/West and left/right). If we combine this conclusion with semantic relativity, we have evidence that language does influence thought: the concepts that people learn through language may be different according to the language through which they learn them. We have already considered a clear example of this in discussing the distinction between languages and dialects in 2.2.1, where I suggested that the reason why we assume that dialects and languages are distinct may be because modern English has different names for them; if we had been brought up speaking English before the Greek word *dialect* was introduced we might well not have made this assumption, and there would have been no need to question the reality of the distinction. It is very easy indeed to multiply examples like this, especially if we concentrate on abstract nouns like *mind*, *spirit*, *nature*, *fun* and *sport*.

3.3.2 The Sapir–Whorf Hypothesis

Finally we come to the celebrated 'Sapir–Whorf Hypothesis', so named after the American linguist Edward Sapir (1884–1939) and his student Benjamin Lee Whorf (1897–1941). Both Sapir and Whorf worked extensively on American Indian languages and made important contributions to our knowledge of those languages and also to linguistic theory (among other things). The work most clearly relevant to the hypothesis was done in the 1930s, towards the end of their respective careers, so their ideas represent the results of two distinguished lifetimes devoted to the serious study of language and culture and cannot be dismissed lightly. Both Sapir and Whorf are well worth reading in the original; their articles are available in Mandelbaum 1949 and Carroll 1956. A thorough survey of the literature is now available in Lucy 1992a.

Here is one of the most famous quotations in which Whorf (1940) laid out his view on the relationship between language and thought:

> . . . the background linguistic system (in other words the grammar) of
> each language is not merely a reproducing instrument for voicing ideas
> but rather is itself the shaper of ideas, the program and guide for the
> individual's mental activity, for his analysis of impressions, for his
> synthesis of his mental stock in trade. Formulation of ideas is not an
> independent process, strictly rational in the old sense, but is part of a
> particular grammar, and differs, from slightly to greatly, between
> different grammars. We dissect nature along lines laid down by our
> native language. The categories and types that we isolate from the world
> of phenomena we do not find there because they stare every observer in
> the face; on the contrary, the world is presented in a kaleidoscopic flux of
> impressions which has to be organised by our minds – and this means
> largely by the linguistic systems in our minds. We cut nature up and
> organize it into concepts, and ascribe significances as we do, largely
> because we are parties to an agreement to organize it in this way – an
> agreement that holds throughout our speech community and is codified
> in the patterns of our language. The agreement is, of course an implicit
> and unstated one, BUT ITS TERMS ARE ABSOLUTELY OBLIGATORY; we
> cannot talk at all except by subscribing to the organisation and
> classification of data which the agreement decrees . . . We are thus
> introduced to a new principle of relativity, which holds that all observers
> are not led by the same physical evidence to the same picture of the
> universe, unless their linguistic backgrounds are similar, or can in some
> way be calibrated.

The most important point to notice here is that Whorf is talking about how our thinking is affected by the *grammar* of our language. Grammar involves conceptual distinctions that are very general and that we use very frequently (for example, the distinction between singular and plural nouns, an example which we shall discuss below). Whorf's claim is that we do not only apply these distinction when putting thoughts into words, but that they affect the way in which we understand our experiences at all times, whether or not we are using language. If Whorf is right, the effects of our grammatical system will be much more pervasive and important than those of individual lexical items. The effect of vocabulary is uncontroversial and rather obvious, but the Sapir–Whorf hypothesis is much more far-reaching, and controversial.

What exactly is the hypothesis, and why is it still alive but controversial over fifty years later? These questions are related: the hypothesis is extraordinarily hard to test, and one of the reasons for this is that neither Sapir nor Whorf ever formulated it sufficiently precisely. This passage is one of the clearer statements, but is typical in its frustrating blend of overstatement and caution.

On the one hand, it claims that our grammar is the only thing that influences our thinking – 'the background linguistic system . . . of each language is . . .

itself *the* shaper of ideas . . . We dissect nature along lines laid down by our native language . . . all observers are not led by the same physical evidence to the same picture of the universe, *unless* their linguistic backgrounds are similar . . . ' In other words, the *only* kind of experience that influences our thought processes is linguistic experience. It is this view that is implied by the phrase *linguistic determinism*, containing the word *determinism* which is often contrasted with 'free will' in discussions of human behaviour. If linguistic determinism is right, then our language provides the only framework of ideas within which we can think. But it must be wrong if, as our earlier discussion suggested, we form some concepts without any help at all from language. Moreover the very fact that we can talk about these things seems to suggest that we can escape from the prison of our language if only to look at the prison from outside. It would therefore be fair to describe the view of linguistic determinism as 'largely discredited' (Hill 1988: 16).

On the other hand, Whorf also qualifies the claim by adding *largely*: 'the world is presented in a kaleidoscopic flux of impressions which has to be organised in our minds – and this means *largely* by the linguistic systems in our minds. We cut nature up and organize it into concepts, and ascribe significance as we do, *largely* because we are parties to an agreement to organize it this way . . . ' This is a very different claim, because it allows other kinds of experience also to play some part, albeit a minor one. However, even in this weaker version the hypothesis is still controversial because of the important influence that it ascribes to grammar, rather than to vocabulary. The extent to which linguists accept this view depends largely on the extent to which they accept that the grammars of different languages can express different meanings. The hypothesis is completely empty if one believes that different languages are just different codes for expressing the same range of meanings; on this assumption there are simply no differences between languages that could influence thought, and there is nothing to discuss. However, our earlier discussion of Irish English and Cora (3.2.1) suggested that the meanings that can be expressed by grammatical patterns can vary enormously, so there is indeed an interesting and important question. Do these differences have any effect beyond the use of language itself? We can call this the question of linguistic 'influence' – a much weaker idea than 'determinism', but still an important one.

This is not the kind of question that a training in linguistics allows one to investigate, but cognitive psychology has methods for exploring thought patterns, so this research involves a mixture of linguistics (for the analysis of the linguistic patterns) and psychology, with a serious contribution from anthropology on the cultural background of the people studied. A great deal of work has in fact been done, but all I shall do here is to summarise two of the most interesting projects, an old one which is rather easy to summarise and a recent one which is more complicated.

We start, then, with a research project carried out in the 1950s (Carroll and Casagrande 1958; see Lucy 1992a: 198ff. for a useful summary and critique). It involved a comparison of English with Navajo (an Athabascan language spoken by about 200,000 people in Arizona, New Mexico and Utah; the name is sometimes spelled *Navaho*). The relevant grammatical fact about Navajo is that verbs of 'handling' show the shape of the thing to which they are applied; for example, 'Please hand it to me' is translated differently according to whether the object concerned is a long flexible object such as a piece of string (*šaṅléh*), a long rigid object such as a stick (*šaṅtííh*), a flat flexible material such as paper or cloth (*šanilcóós*) and so on. In other words, in Navajo the speaker and hearer are forced by the grammar of Navajo to pay attention to the shapes of the objects they refer to in a way that has no parallel in English. The question, then, is whether this has any effect on observable behaviour beyond the choice of verbs of handling.

One standard psychological test is called a 'triads sorting task', in which the 'subjects' (the people who take part in the experiment) are shown two objects and asked to group a third object with one of them on the basis of similarity. The objects in each triad are chosen so that the third is similar to each of the first two in a different respect – for example, it might be similar to one of them in size and to the other in colour. The subject's choice shows which of these two 'dimensions' of classification is more important in this particular triad, and after a large number of triads it may be possible to draw general conclusions about the relative importance of different dimensions. In research on how children's concepts develop, American and European psychologists had discovered that shape developed later than size and colour; but Navajo children as young as three used the handling verbs correctly so at least this area of their thinking paid attention to shape. Caroll and Casagrande's prediction was that this would generalise beyond language to the sorting task. This prediction turned out to be right when they compared the sorting behaviour of a group of children whose dominant language was Navajo with an English-dominant group (who were otherwise similar) living in the same Navajo community. The Navajo speakers paid more attention to shape than the English speakers. Since the dominant language was the only thing that distinguished these two groups, these results suggested strongly that the language did influence the children's non-verbal behaviour, so the stress on shape in Navajo grammar had spread well beyond the use of language to affect other parts of the children's conceptual systems. Grammar did indeed influence thought.

However this was not the end of the research, because the next step was to compare these two groups with other non-Navajo children in order to separate the effects of grammar from those of culture. How did the two Navajo groups compare with children from other cultures? They applied the same test to English-speaking children in middle-class Boston, expecting to find that they too would pay less attention to shape than the Navajo speakers had done; but in this case the results proved otherwise: the middle-class children performed in just the same way as the Navajo-speakers. On the other hand, when they applied the test to English-speaking children in working-class Harlem, they got the same results as they had found for the English-speaking Navajo children. The most obvious interpretation of these results is that the effects of a middle-class upbringing are similar to those of learning to speak Navajo. The relevant part of middle-class childhood is presumably the range of toys whose purpose is specifically to draw attention to shapes (building blocks, jigsaw puzzles and so on), and these toys are as large a part of a middle-class child's experience as the verbs of handling are in a Navajo-speaking child's. In contrast, the English-speaking children in Harlem and in the Navajo community were raised in families which were too poor for such things, so nothing focussed their attention on shapes.

The general conclusion to which this research points, then, is that grammar does influence our thinking in ways that go beyond the use of language, but that it is only one of the things that does – contrary to the extreme view of 'linguistic determinism'. We now turn to the more recent research project which supports the same view. This is a very careful study by John Lucy (Lucy 1992b) which was carried out over a decade of work with a community in Mexico whose language is Yucatec Maya. (Nearly everyone in the village studied spoke Maya and very little Spanish, the official state language.)

Once again the purpose was to compare the cognitive effects of speaking this language with those of speaking English, and specifically the work focussed on a very general grammatical difference between the two languages, their treatment of number differences in nouns. English requires every noun to be either singular or plural (*man* or *men*, *dog* or *dogs*, *hammer* or *hammers*, *table* or *tables*, *cake* or *cakes* and so on). In contrast, the marking of plurality is optional in Maya, so *pèek'*, for example, means either 'dog' or 'dogs'. It is possible to distinguish a group from a single individual by means of an optional element *-ó'ob'*, so *pèek'-ó'ob'* means 'dogs', not 'dog', but this marking is optional. The first difference, then, between English and Maya is that English forces us to pay attention to the distinction between 'one' and 'more than one' in a way that Mayan does not.

A second important difference is that Mayan speakers actually use the plural marker *-ó'ob'* much more often with animate nouns (words for people and animals) than with discrete inanimates (for example, words for hammers, tables, trees and so on); and in both languages the 'number' of a substance like mud, milk and bread (a 'non-discrete inanimate') is hardly ever marked for number, even though the substances can in fact be distributed in separate 'portions'; for example, if there were several lumps of mud on the floor we should still describe the floor as having simply 'mud' on it. Lucy takes these quantitative differences as part of the grammatical system of Mayan although strictly speaking the grammar may simply say that the plural marker is *optional* in all cases; this is a weak point in the argument, but his assumption is reasonable. At least we can say that it reflects the observable linguistic behaviour of Mayan speakers.

The experiment in this case involved twelve Mayan men, whose performance was later compared with twelve English-speaking students at Chicago University. Each subject did a range of tasks all connected with pictures which had been specially constructed to contain animals, instruments (examples of discrete inanimates) and substances (non-discrete inanimates). The pictures differed according to which of these occurred singly or in groups, and the tasks were designed to show how far the subjects paid attention to the 'single/group' distinction in each case. In the first task, for example, the subject simply described the contents of the current picture while looking at it; in the second he recalled its contents from memory; in the third he compared one picture with a range of slightly different pictures; and so on. Readers might like to test themselves on the pictures in Figure 3.1.

In a nutshell the results confirmed that both the grammatical differences between Mayan and English had an effect on how they treated the pictures. The fact that number-differences are always optional in Mayan, in contrast with English, is reflected in the greater overall attention that the English speakers paid to the single/group contrast. But more interesting than this was the effect of the second difference, which is that Mayan makes a fundamental distinction between animate and inanimate, showing plurality for animates (humans or animals) much more than for inanimates, whether discrete (implements) or non-discrete (lumps of dough and other substances). This difference too was reflected in the strong tendency for Mayans to pay far more attention to the number of animals than to the number of implements in the pictures. In contrast, the English-speaking subjects gave much more equal treatment to the animals and to the implements. For example, in describing the picture that was in front of them the English speakers mentioned how many animals there were about the same number of times as they mentioned the

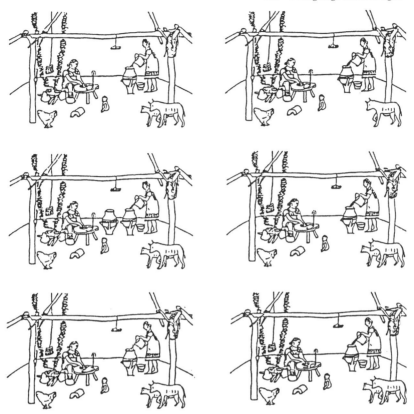

Figure 3.1. Taken from Lucy 1992b: 170

number of implements, but ignored the number of substances; whereas the Mayan speakers only mentioned the number of implements about as often as they mentioned the number of substances.

In conclusion, it seems that there is good evidence that some semantic contrasts which are expressed by grammar are also applied outside the strictly linguistic realm of language use. Whether or not a person applies these contrasts in general life seems to depend on how their language expresses the contrasts concerned (obligatorily, often, rarely or not at all), so it seems reasonable to assume that language is the cause and the 'thought-patterns' are the effect. In short, language does affect thought in ways that go beyond the rather obvious effects of specific lexical items. On the other hand, language is not the only kind of experience which does affect thought, so we have moved a long way from the idea of 'linguistic determinism'.

3.3.3   *Sexism in the language system*

The conclusion that we have just reached has important social consequences. We all like to think that the way we think about the world is objectively correct, even if there are large areas of ignorance. But what if our thinking is influenced, in ways that we are completely unaware of, by our language? This could be all for the better if the influence of language is healthy; for example, if our language offers only one way of referring to all humans (using words like *who, someone, person* and so on), then to that extent it may encourage us to treat all humans equally. But what if our language reflects outmoded ways of thinking which we now reject morally? Can the language system act as a serious brake on progress?

This question has been raised by the recent changes in our view of women and their place in society. The women's movement aims at a major shift in culture from the Bad Old Days when women were powerless and generally subordinate to men to a new era where we all have equal rights and status. The problem is that the languages which we have inherited were all developed in the Bad Old Days, so the question is whether they force us all to think along the old lines without realising it. Do languages discriminate against women? More precisely, do the ways in which languages allow us to refer to males and females discriminate against females? (In principle we could ask a similar question about discrimination against males, but nobody has even tried to argue that case so we don't need to consider it!) The list of relevant publications grows ever longer; Graddol and Swann 1989 and McCormick 1994b are helpful surveys.

Some examples are quite clear, such as the English distinction between *Mrs* and *Miss* which is not paralleled by a pair of male titles showing whether or not the bearer is married. This implies (unfairly) that it is more important for a woman than for a man to show whether they are married, but it is fairly easily remedied by the introduction of a new word, *Ms*, whose success is unexpected considering how odd a word it is in both spelling and pronunciation. What is more worrying, in the light of the Sapir–Whorf hypothesis, is the existence of more general trends that run right through a language rather than being confined to individual lexical items; these are more likely to have an effect on speakers' thinking partly because they are pervasive, and partly because they are subtle and therefore below consciousness. In English, and many other languages, there are two such tendencies that have been studied recently.

One tendency involves words that are clearly restricted in reference to one sex or the other, with female words tending to have less favourable meanings. A classic pair is *master* and *mistress*, where the male meaning is 'good' and the female is 'bad'; specifically, a mistress but not a master is a partner for extramarital sex. This sexual use of the female word is typical (Graddol and Swann

1989: 110): apparently North American English has no fewer than 220 words for a sexually promiscuous woman, but only twenty for sexually promiscuous men, and London school children had a rich vocabulary of insult terms for girls, all related to sexual behaviour, but very few specifically for boys. These trends may be changing; for example, in 1987 North American female students had a rich vocabulary of sexual insults for men, including some which had historically been reserved for women (*bitch, whore* and *slut*), but they have a long way to go!

The other unfair tendency involves the notion of prototype. As we saw in 3.1.2, the concepts that we use as word-meanings tend to centre on clear cases, so their definition is a description of the most typical examples; for example, a bird is typically very much like a sparrow or robin, which leaves ostriches and penguins as untypical birds. How does this apply to a word like *doctor*, which appears to be sex-neutral? A little thought shows that the prototype doctor must be male – when the doctor's sex is not directly relevant we are much more likely to specify it for a female than for a male. The same seems to be true of most names for professions, with a few obvious exceptions like *nurse*. It is true that this bias against females is in the concepts that the words express, and not in the words themselves; but this conceptual inequality reinforces itself by its effect on our speech. Every time we refer to a female as a woman doctor we reinforce the bias, as we do every time we refer to a male simply as a doctor.

Any discussion of language bias against women must discuss the words *man* and *he*, which both illustrate the problem of the last paragraph. On the one hand, each of these words could reasonably be claimed to have two distinct meanings, one of which is genuinely neutral for sex; so *man* means either 'person' or 'male adult', and *he* either 'the person just mentioned' or 'the male just mentioned'. On the other hand, the way in which people actually use the supposedly sex-neutral meanings shows that they take the male as the prototype even for the sex-neutral concept. The literature is full of telling examples like the following:

> As for man, he is no different from the rest. His back aches, he ruptures easily, his women have difficulties in childbirth . . . (Graddol and Swann 1989: 104)

The generic use of *man* meaning 'mankind' is rather special, and does not show that *man* can mean simply 'person'; for example, we can never apply it to an individual female (as witness the badness of examples like *Mary Brown was the first man to have a baby in that ward*, where *person* would have been fine). The use of *he* is more pervasive and therefore potentially more dangerous. Here is a very typical example in a discussion of conversational turn-taking (taken, once again, from the first edition of this book):

> Conversely, the other person looks down when he is about to start speaking, in anticipation of his change of role . . .

It is extraordinary how insensitive even sociolinguists were to such things until recently. Here is a telling example produced by Labov himself, which he would certainly have avoided nowadays:

> We must somehow become witness to the everyday speech which the informant will use as soon as the door is closed behind us: the style in which he argues with his wife, scolds his children, or passes the time of day with his friends. (Labov 1966: 99, quoted in Graddol and Swann 1989: 109)

This example illustrates the dilemma of those of us who want to eliminate linguistic bias against females. The mention of the wife shows that the bias is a deep conceptual one, as Labov must have been thinking of the typical informant as male, but the pronoun *he* surely encourages this bias. Simply avoiding sex-neutral *he* will not in itself dispose of the bias, but it is a step in the right direction. An even better step would be the invention of a genuinely neutral pronoun distinct from both *he* and *she*, comparable with *Ms* for *Miss* and *Mrs*, and the most promising candidate is *they*. This has been used for centuries after non-specific pronouns like *anyone* and *everyone* (for example, Shakespeare's 'God send every one their heart's desire!', (*Much Ado About Nothing*), quoted in Graddol and Swann 1989: 105), but it still feels very awkward in other contexts. This may be a case where linguists should agree to change language in their own practice rather than simply describing it, in the hope that their practice will spread. However it is important to be realistic about what can be achieved. A genuinely sex-neutral pronoun will not in itself guarantee that women will be treated equally with men. Evidence for this comes from languages such as Farsi (modern Persian) which already have such pronouns but are spoken in societies where men and women are treated very unequally (Ardehali 1994).

3.4   General conclusions

This chapter has been mainly about the semantics of human languages and how the semantic patterns relate to other kinds of knowledge that we have. The most general conclusion is probably that semantics is inseparable from the rest of knowledge, a conclusion which is shared by cognitive linguists but denied by many other linguists (and some psychologists); so it is interesting if only because it is controversial. However, we have spelled out some more specific consequences as well, which it may be helpful to bring together at this point:

- The meanings of words and sentences, like most of cultural knowledge, are concepts and propositions. An important part of our total knowledge is a network of concepts linked by propositions, and the meanings that we can express in language form a portion of that network. There is no boundary between meanings and general knowledge.

- Concepts are prototypes, i.e. clear typical cases; so the propositions that mention a particular concept are typically true but they allow exceptions. This is true not only of linguistic meanings but also in general cognition, so it also applies to other concepts that sociolinguists try to study, namely those that people develop for classifying people and situations.

- The meanings that can be expressed directly by language vary from language to language, and according to the hypothesis of semantic relativity, they can vary as much as cultures can vary. This is true not only of word-meanings but also of meanings that are expressed by grammatical patterns (for example, the 'inside' and 'outside' prefixes of Cora). Some apparent variation may turn out to disappear in a more sophisticated analysis (for example, an analysis using prototypes and derivational rules), but there is no evidence that language is any more uniform than cultures in general are.

- Some cultural concepts, including some of our most important abstract concepts, are learned through language, so language is an important 'instrument of socialisation'. The same is true of more general 'thought patterns', which may be influenced by the grammatical patterns of the language concerned. These concepts and thought patterns seem to affect our behaviour not only when talking, but also in other activities. On the other hand, language is only one influence on our thinking, so we have rejected 'linguistic determinism'.

All of these conclusions involve the relations between language and culture, and since culture is an important aspect of society, they all fall within our definition of sociolinguistics as the study of language in relation to society.

4
Speech as social interaction

4.1 The social nature of speech

4.1.1 Introduction

In this chapter we shall focus on what we have been referring to as 'speech' – that is, shorter or longer strings of linguistic items uttered on particular occasions for particular purposes. We shall ignore various kinds of spoken texts, in order to concentrate on what is called FACE-TO-FACE INTERACTION – in other words, what happens when we talk to someone else who is facing us. Although we shall exclude all kinds of important but impersonal communication such as the mass media, this still leaves a wide range of activities: conversations, quarrels, jokes, committee meetings, interviews, seductions, introductions, lessons, teasing, chit-chat and a host of others.

One of the main questions we must again ask concerns the balance between the social and the individual. For *language*, our knowledge of linguistic items and their meanings, the balance is in favour of the social, since we learn our language by listening to others, although each individual's language is unique because of our different individual experiences. What about the balance in the case of speech? Ferdinand de Saussure claimed that speech was totally individual, in that it depended only on the 'will of the speaker' (1916/1959: 19), and conversely that language was entirely social, being identical from one member of a speech community to another. He was clearly wrong about language, but was he any nearer to the truth about speech? We shall see that he was not.

We have seen that speech is crucial in a number of social activities, including socialisation (see 3.3.1), and it is hardly necessary to stress the general importance of speech in social life. Speech allows us to communicate with each other at a much more sophisticated level than would otherwise be possible, and since communication is a social activity it could be said that speech is also social. Although this is true, it is not directly relevant to de Saussure's claim about speech being individual, since he was referring to the knowledge involved in speech, rather than the uses to which that activity is put, holding that speech involved no social constraints, in contrast with language, which was entirely so

constrained. For de Saussure so long as a speaker knew the relevant language –
which meant knowing which sound-sequences were allowed to be used for
which meanings – they would be able to speak it properly simply by applying
it as they chose. What we need to show, therefore, is that we have to learn social
constraints on speech over and above those which are part of our language.

It is clear that there are many such constraints, which may differ from society
to society. For example, in Britain we are required to respond when someone
else greets us; when we refer to someone, we are required to take account of
what the addressee already knows about them; when we address a person, we
must choose our words carefully, to show the social relations between us; when
someone else is talking we are required to keep more or less silent (but not
totally so). However, the same is not necessarily true in all societies, as we shall
see, so the constraints are learned through socialisation. Our task in the present
chapter is to consider the types of constraint that we accept from the society in
which we live, and to relate them to what we do as individuals – either obeying
or flouting the social constraints, and, in situations where custom offers no
guidelines, using our own initiative. By the end of the chapter, it should be
clear that the balance between society and individual is in favour of the latter
as far as speech is concerned – so to that extent de Saussure was right – but
that there are far more social constraints on our speech than we may at first
realise.

Another thing which will become apparent is that the distinction between
'language' and 'social constraints on speech' is anything but clear, since many
of the constraints discussed below refer to specific linguistic items, or more or
less large classes of items, and could therefore be treated as part of language
along with what we know about meanings. This is not surprising, since many
items have meanings which refer specifically to aspects of the speech-events in
which they are used – notably all the items with DEICTIC meanings, referring
to the speaker (*I, we*), the addressee (*you*), the time of speaking (present/past
tense, *today*, etc.) and the place of speaking (*here*, etc.). Moreover, we have
seen (2.4) that many items are restricted in their use to certain social circumstances (for example, *get* versus *obtain*), and we took it for granted that such
information was part of our language. Consequently, it would be natural to
make the same assumption about the information that the French word *tu*
'you' is to be used only to intimates (and small children and animals). And
having made that decision, it is only a small step to including in 'language' similar information about whole classes of items, such as the class of first names in
English, which are also to be used only to intimates (in contrast with names
like *Mr Brown*). (For further discussion of the restrictions on French
pronouns and English proper nouns, see 4.2.2 below.)

It is easy to see how 'language' and 'social constraints on speech' merge, and it will also be clear from several points in the discussion below that social constraints on speech can apply not just to speech but to social behaviour in general. (This conclusion supports the view put forward in chapter 3 that there is no clear distinction between 'language' and other aspects of thought, especially in matters of meaning.) The accepted term for aspects of behaviour through which people influence and react to each other is SOCIAL INTERACTION, and speech is only one aspect of such behaviour, closely meshed with other aspects. One of the leading investigators in this field, Michael Argyle (a social psychologist), has described the field as follows (Argyle 1973: 9):

> One achievement of recent research has been to establish the basic
> elements of which social interaction consists; current research is
> concerned with finding out precisely how these elements function. It is
> now agreed that the list consists of various signals: verbal and non-
> verbal, tactile, visible and audible – various kinds of bodily contact,
> proximity, orientation, bodily posture, physical appearance, facial
> expression, movement of head and hands, direction of gaze, timing of
> speech, emotional tone of speech, speech errors, type of utterance and
> linguistic structure of utterance. Each of these elements can be further
> analysed and divided into categories or dimensions; each plays a
> distinctive role in social interaction, though they are closely
> interconnected.

In 4.4 below we shall look in more detail at some of the non-verbal aspects of social interaction and see how they relate to speech.

The study of speech as part of social interaction has involved many different disciplines, including social psychology, sociology, anthropology, ethology (the study of behaviour in animals), philosophy, artificial intelligence (the study of human intelligence via computer simulation), sociolinguistics and linguistics. Each discipline brings a different range of questions and methods to bear on the study, and all can learn a lot from the others. The main methods used in the study are introspection and participant observation (discussed in 5.2.6), with a certain amount of experimentation (by social psychologists and ethologists) and computer simulation (by artificial intelligence workers). One of the most important contributions has been made by anthropologists who engage in what is called THE ETHNOGRAPHY OF SPEAKING or THE ETHNOGRAPHY OF COMMUNICATION, a field dominated by the work of Dell Hymes (see, for example, Hymes 1972, 1974, Sherzer 1992, Schiffrin 1994: ch. 5). The importance of this work has been to provide data on societies other than the advanced western ones in which most linguists live, and to make it clear how much variety there is in the social constraints on speech. Most readers may expect some surprises in the next few pages, but relativity is not unlimited in this field any more than it was in the field of meaning (3.2), as we shall see below.

4.1.2   The classification of speech

Speech plays many different roles in social interaction. The anthropologist Bronislav Malinowski claimed that 'in its primitive uses, language functions as a link in concerted human activity, as a piece of human behaviour. It is a mode of action and not an instrument of reflection' (Malinowski 1923). An example of this would be the kind of speech used by people shifting furniture: *To you . . . now up a bit . .* and so on, where the speech acts as a control on people's physical activity, in contrast to its function in a lecture where it is intended to influence the thoughts rather than the actions of the listeners. Another use of speech is simply to establish or reinforce social relations – what Malinowski called PHATIC COMMUNION, the kind of chit-chat that people engage in simply in order to show that they recognise each other's presence. We might add many other uses of speech to this list – speech to obtain information (for example, (*Where's the tea-pot?*), for expressing emotions *What a lovely hat!*), for its own sake (*She sells sea-shells by the sea-shore*) and so on. We shall not try to develop a proper classification of speech functions at this level, but just restrict ourselves to noting that speech in social interaction does not have just one function such as communicating propositions which the hearer does not already know.

One particular approach to the functional classification of speech certainly ought to be mentioned, however, as it has been extremely influential. This is the approach based on SPEECH-ACTS, which has been developed in the main by philosophers and linguists following the British philosopher J. L. Austin (Austin 1962, Schriffin 1994: ch. 3). Austin argued that the study of meaning should not concentrate on bald statements such as *Snow is white*, taken out of context, since language is typically used, in speech, for many other functions – when we speak we make suggestions, promises, invitations, requests, prohibitions and so on. Indeed, in some cases we use speech to perform an action (as Malinowski had argued), in the extreme sense that the speech is itself the action which it reports – for instance, *I name this ship 'Saucy Sue'* has to be said if the naming is to be accomplished. Such bits of speech are called PERFORMATIVE UTTERANCES. It can be seen that an account of all these different functions of speech must be formulated in terms of a general theory of social activity, and this is what Austin and his followers tried to provide.

One of the achievements of work on speech acts has been to draw attention to the extensive vocabulary that ordinary English provides for talking about utterances – verbs like *say*, *promise* and *persuade*. The following examples are just a small selection of the available terms in English (Dixon 1991: 140ff):

general:	speaking, talking
manner:	saying, shouting, whispering
flow of information:	agreeing, announcing, asking, discussing, explaining, ordering, reminding, reporting, suggesting, telling
source:	acting, reading, reciting, mimicking
speaker evaluation:	apologising, boasting, complaining, criticising, grumbling, joking, thanking
hearer evaluation:	flattering, promising, teasing, threatening, warning
effect on hearer:	cajoling, dissuading, persuading

What these examples show is, firstly, that the classification of speech-acts is of great interest and importance to English speakers, and secondly that there is no single basis for classification. We can classify on the basis of: manner of speaking (for example, whispering versus shouting), how information flows between speaker and hearer (for example, asking versus telling), where the words originate from (acting, reciting versus spontaneous speech), how the speaker evaluates the content (for example, apologising versus boasting), how the hearer evaluates it (for example, promising versus threatening), and the effect it has on the hearer, i.e. its 'perlocutionary force' (for example, persuading and dissuading). We can even combine two or three of these bases; for example, preaching and lecturing are defined both by their manner and by the flow of information. Even the length of units classified – our 'speech-acts' – varies vastly, from these complex categories like preaching and lecturing, which apply to long stretches of speech, to the manner-based categories (for example, whispering) which can apply just to single words. Some of these bases for classification appear to be much more important than others. For example, we have very few words specifically for describing the effects of speech-acts, as opposed to words like *depress*, *annoy* and so on which can be applied to the emotional effect of any kind of event, and not just to those of speech-acts.

If speech-act categories are cultural concepts we might expect them to vary from one society to another, and that is what we do find. For a simple example, take the speech-act verb *baptise* and its synonym *christen*, which express meanings which are bound very specifically to a Christian culture in which baptism plays a part. It is interesting to compare the concepts reflected in English with those of very different cultures such as that of the Tzeltal Indians (a branch of the Maya of Mexico), reported by Brian Stross (1974). Tzeltal also has a rich terminology for classifying speech-acts, but compared with English the classifications have quite different bases, which means that we have to translate each Tzeltal lexical item by a whole phrase in English. Here are some examples:

> 'talk in which things are offered for sale'

> 'talk in which the speaker has spread the blame for something, so that he alone is not blamed'

> 'inhaled talk, talk produced while breathing inwards'

> 'speech occurring at night or late evening'

> 'speech by someone who comes to another's house and spends time talking even though the other is quite ill'

These meanings may look very strange, but most of them are comparable to the meanings of familiar English words: *haggle*, 'argue about something, especially about the price of something being bought'; *waffle*, 'talk or write a lot without saying very much that is clear or important'; *mutter*, 'speak very quietly so that you cannot easily be heard, often because you are complaining about something or because you are speaking to yourself'. (These definitions are taken from the *Collins Cobuild English Language Dictionary*.) Most of the Tzeltal words have meanings that take account of the same kinds of characteristics as some English words, though the particular meanings are different. The last two Tzeltal examples stand out as completely different from the meaning of any single English lexical item.

What this discussion of speech-acts has shown is that they are very varied. This variation is socially very important – it is vital to know whether the speaker is joking or serious, telling us a fact or asking for information and so on – so it is not surprising to find a rich set of categories that can be described in words. It is not just sociolinguists who like to talk about talking, and it is interesting to compare the classificatory systems that different languages recognise. Some of the categories have been studied by philosophers as 'illocutionary forces' and 'perlocutionary forces', but the categories that fall under these terms are only a small selection of the total range and may not have any special claim to being fundamental; nor can we be sure that the categories which our language recognises are the only important ones for us as students of speech behaviour. All we can be sure of is that people's behaviour varies according to what kind of speech-act they consider themselves to be performing, and that some of this variation is systematic.

4.1.3   Speech as skilled work

We have just seen that speech is so important to us that we give it special treatment in our culture as an object to be classified and talked about; and we may assume that the same is true of every human culture. We can now go further by showing that our speech is controlled by rules that we learn as part of our culture, just like the grammar and vocabulary that make up our language.

The first point to establish is that speech is not an automatic reflex like sneezing or a spontaneous expression of emotion like laughing; it is skilled work. It is *work*, since it requires effort, and its degree of success depends on the effort that is made. It is *skilled* in that it requires the 'know-how' type of knowledge, which is applied more or less successfully according to how much practice one has had (and according to other factors such as intelligence). Putting these two characteristics together, we can predict that speech may be more successful at some times than at others, and some people may be better at it than others. There is no doubt that this is the case: we all know that sometimes we get 'tongue-tied' or 'drop a brick', and that some people are more likely than others to be stuck for 'the right thing to say'.

If speech is skilled work, the same is true of other aspects of social interaction in face-to-face communication (or 'focussed interaction'): 'it is fruitful to look upon the behaviour of people engaged in focussed interaction as an organised, skilled performance, analogous to skills such as car driving' (Argyle and Kendon 1967). Just as some people are better drivers than others (to the extent that some pass the driving test and others fail), so some people are better at social interaction than others. However, there are two major caveats. Firstly, success in speech varies considerably according to the type of speech-act required. Some people are good at intellectual debate and poor at phatic communion, and vice versa; and we shall see (6.4) that children who are highly skilled in verbal games may flounder in the classroom or in a formal interview. Secondly, it is not obvious how success should be measured, except against the intentions of the speaker. For instance, if a chatterbox is with a person who habitually stays silent while others do the talking, each may consider themselves more successful than the other, according to how they balance the need to fill 'awkward' gaps against the need to avoid triviality. The same two caveats apply equally, of course, to other aspects of social interaction.

This is not the place to try to specify the particular kinds of skill needed for successful speech, since they presumably include all the general skills needed for social interaction plus all the specifically linguistic skills concerned with the use of linguistic items. They vary from very specific skills, dealing with particular linguistic items (e.g. when to say *sir*) or with particular situations (for example, how to conduct a business transaction on an expensive transatlantic telephone call), to much more general skills, such as how to avoid ambiguity. We may perhaps think of these skills arranged hierarchically, with the most specific ones at the bottom and the most general at the top, and assume that in dealing with a particular situation the speaker will look for a specific skill in preference to a more general one, since the latter will always involve more cognitive effort and may be less successful. For instance, in asking for a ticket on a bus, it is easier and safer to use what you know about buying bus-tickets, or buying transport tickets in general, than to use a more general rule for requesting anything from anybody (for example, by saying *Excuse me, would you mind selling me a ticket to . . .*). We may guess that one of the reasons why some people perform particularly well in some situations is that they have learned very specific skills for use in those situations.

We started this chapter by asking whether de Saussure was right to see speech as purely individual. We can now answer this question by pointing, first, to the evidence given above that speech is socially classified in terms of types of speech-act, and second, to the fact that these speech-act types are learned as part of our socialisation. For example, we learn how to order a meal in a restaurant by watching other people doing it, in much the same way that we learn vocabulary and grammatical constructions. The clearest evidence for this learning is that rules and skills vary from society to society, as we shall see in the next subsection.

Speech, then, is an acquired skill; but it is also work. Talking takes energy, both physical and mental, and can leave us feeling tired. Sometimes we are too tired to engage in it. The same is true, of course, of all social interaction, which raises an important question: why are we willing to do it? and why are we willing to accept the restrictions placed on us by our society's social rules? It is easy to see why we bother to say things that help us to get things that we want, but why do we bother with phatic communion and why do we worry about how we dress up our requests in speech? The question of motivation is one of the basic questions of social psychology and sociology, so we cannot expect a simple answer, but a particularly influential (and attractive) theory is based on the term 'FACE', which is used in much the same way as in the expressions *to lose face* and *to save face*, meaning something like 'self-respect' or 'dignity'. The theory was developed by Erving Goffman, an American sociologist (1955, 1967, 1969), who called the work needed to maintain face 'face-work'.

The basic idea of the theory is this: we lead unavoidably social lives, since we depend on each other, but as far as possible we try to lead our lives without losing our own face. However, our face is a very fragile thing which other people can very easily damage, so we lead our social lives according to the Golden

Rule ('Do to others as you would like them to do to you!') by looking after other people's faces in the hope that they will look after ours. The principle is described as follows in a standard sociology text-book:

> Much of what we usually call 'politeness' or 'etiquette' in social gatherings consists of disregarding aspects of behaviour that might otherwise lead to a 'loss of face'. Episodes in an individual's past, or personal characteristics that might produce embarrassment if mentioned, are not commented on or referred to . . . Tact is a sort of protective device which each party involved employs in the expectation that, in return, their own weaknesses will not be deliberately exposed to general view. (Giddens 1989/1993: 93)

Face is something that other people give to us, which is why we have to be so careful to give it to them (unless we consciously choose to insult them, which is exceptional behaviour).

For sociolinguists the most relevant discussion of face is by Brown and Levinson (1978/1987), who distinguish two kinds of face. They call them 'positive' and 'negative', but these terms can be misleading because both kinds of face are valuable; instead, I shall call them 'solidarity-face' and 'power-face', to show the close link to the important concepts of 'power' and 'solidarity' that we shall introduce in 4.2.2. Both kinds could be described as 'respect', but this word has a different sense in each case. Solidarity-face is respect as in *I respect you for* . . . , i.e. the appreciation and approval that others show for the kind of person we are, for our behaviour, for our values and so on. If something threatens our solidarity-face we feel embarrassment or shame. Power-face is respect as in *I respect your right to* . . . , which is a 'negative' agreement not to interfere. This is the basis for most formal politeness, such as standing back to let someone else pass. When our power-face is threatened we feel offended. Each kind of face is the basis for a different kind of 'politeness' (a term which now has a rather more general sense than the ordinary one which contrasts it with rudeness). Solidarity-politeness shows respect for the person, whereas power-politeness respects their rights.

It is interesting to see how much of language is geared to looking after the two kinds of politeness, and we shall consider some of these ways in more detail below. For solidarity-politeness we have a wide range of ways of showing intimacy and affection – words used for addressing the other person (for example, *mate, love, darling*, not to mention greetings like *Hi!*) and others used to show solidarity-politeness towards the person referred to (for example, *William* or even *Bill* as opposed to *Mr Brown*). For showing power-politeness there are different 'address' words (for example, *sir, please*), and all the euphemisms that protect the other person from being offended (for example, *spend a penny, pass away*). (As we saw in 1.3.1, swear words are inherently offensive, so they have the opposite effect.) Allan and Burridge (1991) discuss euphemisms explicitly in terms of the theory of face.

The theory of face is part of a larger theory of social interaction, in which speech is only one component (Giddens 1989/93: ch. 4 is a good introduction). This theory starts by distinguishing 'unfocussed' and 'focussed' interaction, according to whether or not the people concerned consider themselves to be 'together' in more than a purely physical sense. Most interactions in modern cities are unfocussed, with strangers passing in the street or sitting next to each other on buses. The main consideration in these cases is to preserve each other's power-face. One obvious example is that we try to keep out of each other's way, but another is that we avoid eye-contact. Unfocussed interaction is a recent creation of modern social patterns for which our genes have presumably given us little preparation.

In contrast, focussed interaction has been the basis for social groups since the earliest times; in fact, it is the basis for all primate species (including humans) that live in groups, such as chimpanzees. It is focussed interaction that provides most of our face even in modern societies, so it also provides most of the serious threats to face. This is where solidarity-face becomes so important because we care about what our friends and family think of us; and power-face can be threatened in many ways (not least by parents imposing restrictions on children). One reason why we avoid eye-contact in unfocussed interaction is probably that it is so important as a way of negotiating our way through focussed interactions, and it is interesting to learn that some chimpanzees (bonobos) also use eye-contact socially (to initiate joint action). It is even more interesting to learn that a member of this species is the only primate to have learned spontaneously to use a communication-system invented by humans (Williams et al. 1994). However one of the many other ways in which primates keep group-life harmonious is by grooming each other, and it is easy to see parallels to this in our selective use of physical contact with other people to show affection (solidarity-face). Humans have a rich 'vocabulary' for non-verbal communication – smiles, frowns, winks, nods, gestures and body-movements (Key 1992) – most of which are shared not only by all human societies but also by some primates (Whiten 1994: 3331). It seems likely, therefore, that some of the skills needed for face-work are innate, as is our general need to maintain face.

Returning to our original question about motivation, it may now be possible to explain why we put so much effort into the skilled work involved in speaking. We need to save our own face by saving the face of everyone we talk to, so we need to manage our behaviour, both verbal and non-verbal, very carefully.

115

This does not mean that speech will be the same the world over, even if we ignore differences of vocabulary and grammar. Far from it, as we shall see in the next subsection. Each society recognises its own norms for saving face, so our face-work consists in recognising these norms and applying them effectively. The consequences of failure in face-work have been dramatically described by Goffman (1957):

> A person who chronically makes himself and others uneasy in
> conversation and perpetually kills encounters is a faulty interactant; he is
> likely to have such a baleful effect upon the social life around him that he
> may just as well be called a faulty person.

If we see speech, and social interaction in general, as skilled work, we may say that failure such as Goffman describes here is due to lack of either skill or motivation (or both). As we now see, both skill and motivation to work are due to the society in which a person lives, and (to the extent that they influence speech) we may conclude that de Saussure was wrong in thinking of speech simply as an individual activity, owing nothing to society.

4.1.4   The norms governing speech

Skill in speaking depends on a variety of factors, including a knowledge of the relevant rules governing speech. Such rules are of various types, dealing with different aspects of speech, but all we can do here is to mention a few examples. The rules chosen vary from one society to another, which makes it easier to see that there *are* rules, but this should not be taken to imply that all rules are similarly variable. (It is possible that there are widespread, if not universal rules, though the emphasis in the literature is on differences rather than similarities between cultures.) We shall call such roles NORMS because they define normal behaviour for the society concerned, without specific penalties against those who do not follow them.

First, there are norms governing the sheer quantity of speech that people produce, varying from very little to very much. Dell Hymes describes a society where very little speech is the norm (Hymes 1971b):

> Peter Gardener (1966) did some fieldwork . . . in southern India, among
> a tribal people called the Puliya, describing their socialization patterns.
> There is no agriculture and no industry, and the society is neither
> particularly cooperative nor particularly competitive; so children are led
> neither to be particularly interdependent nor to be aggressively
> competitive with each other, but simply to busy themselves with their
> own concerns in reasonable spatial proximity. He observed that, by the
> time a man was forty, he practically stopped speaking altogether. He had

no reason to speak. People there, in fact, just didn't talk much and seldom seemed to find anything much to talk about, and he saw this as a consequence of the particular kind of socialization pattern.

We may contrast this society with one in Roti, a small island in eastern Indonesia, described by James Fox (1974):

> For a Rotinese the pleasure of life is talk – not simply an idle chatter that passes time, but the more formal taking of sides in endless dispute, argument and repartee or the rivalling of one another in eloquent and balanced phrases on ceremonial occasions . . . Lack of talk is an indication of distress. Rotinese repeatedly explain that if their 'hearts' are confused or dejected, they keep silent. Contrarily, to be involved with someone requires active verbal encounter.

According to Besnier (1994) much the same is true of typical Jewish east-coast Americans. There may be problems when people from societies with different norms meet, as shown by the following anecdote quoted by Coulthard (1977: 49), where other instances of different norms relating to quantity of speech may also be found:

> An . . . enthnographer describes staying with in-laws in Denmark and being joined by an American friend who, despite warnings, insisted on talking with American intensity until 'at 9 o'clock my in-laws retired to bed; they just couldn't stand it any more'.

Another kind of norm controls the number of people who talk at once in a conversation. Most readers would probably accept the principle that only one person should speak (otherwise there must be more than one conversation taking place, as at a party), but apparently this norm is not universal. The practices in a village in Antigua, in the West Indies, are described by Karl Reisman (1974):

> Antiguan conventions appear, on the surface, almost anarchic. Fundamentally, there is no regular requirement for two or more voices not to be going at the same time. The start of a new voice is not in itself a signal for the voice speaking either to stop or to institute a process which will decide who is to have the floor. When someone enters a casual group, for example, no opening is necessarily made for him; nor is there any pause or other formal signal that he is being included. No one appears to pay any attention. When he feels ready he will simply begin speaking. He may be heard, he may not. That is, the other voices may eventually stop and listen, or some of them may; eyes may or may not turn to him. If he is not heard the first time he will try again, and yet again (often with the same remark). Eventually he will be heard or give up.

Similarly, most readers would accept that there must be a limit on the number of interruptions permissible in a conversation; not so in Antigua:

> In a brief conversation with me, about three minutes, a girl called to someone on the street, made a remark to a small boy, sang a little, told a child to go to school, sang some more, told a child to go buy bread, etc., all the while continuing the thread of her conversation about her sister.

Other norms refer to the information which participants in a conversation give each other. If our only concern is to communicate as efficiently as possible, then information should flow freely. This may be the pattern in some societies, as suggested by some theories of pragmatics (for example, Grice 1975, Sperber and Wilson 1986), but we cannot take it for granted. After all, information is an important commodity, and new information is particularly valuable as the substance of interesting conversations and a source of status for those who give it away. Those who have information that others don't know are in a powerful position, and may decide to ration the flow in a way that contradicts our more rational expectations. In familiar societies this is an individual matter (and we probably all know individuals who enjoy making others work hard for their information); but in some societies the process is institutionalised. For example,

> gossips on Nukulaelae Atoll frequently withhold important pieces of information, such as the identity of a person, from their gossip narratives, thus manipulating their audiences into asking for the missing information, sometimes over the space of several turns, as information is revealed in small doses, requiring further questioning (Besnier 1994; see also Besnier 1989).

Similarly, according to Elinor Keenan (1977), in at least one part of Madagascar the norm is waived under many circumstances. For instance, it would be quite normal to refer to one's own sister as 'a girl' (Keenan quotes a specific occasion when a boy said to her – in Malagasy – 'There is a girl who is coming', referring to his own sister). Or again,

> if A asks B 'Where is your mother?' and B responds 'She is either in the house or at the market', B's utterance is not usually taken to imply that B is unable to provide more specific information needed by the hearer. The implicature is not made, because the expectation that speakers will satisfy informational needs is not a basic norm.

There are a number of reasons why speakers are so uninformative in this community. One is that they are afraid that identifying an individual may bring the person to the attention of evil forces, or get them into trouble in other ways.

Another reason is the shortage of news in small isolated villages. Consequently, there is no reluctance to give information when it is easily available to anyone – for instance, if there is a pot of rice cooking over a fire, people will refer to it as 'the rice' since anyone can see that there is rice there. Clearly, different norms for speech in different societies can often be explained by reference to other aspects of their cultures and cannot, therefore, be satisfactorily studied in isolation.

Finally, there are very specific norms which may vary from society to society, such as the way one answers the telephone. To take another example, in Germany the hostess at a formal dinner party would probably say to her guests *Ich darf jetzt bitten, Platz zu nehmen* ('I may now ask (you) to take (your) places'), using a declarative construction, in contrast with the interrogative that might be used by an English hostess: *May I ask you to come and sit down now?* Other examples of quite specific constraints will be mentioned in the following sections.

The diversity in the norms for speech are matched in the area of non-verbal communication. For example, a raised eyebrow may mean various things according to the culture and social circumstances: greeting, invitation, warning, scepticism, disdain, doubt, interest, intrigue or disgust. Conversely, different actions can have the same meaning in different communities. It has even been claimed that people brought up in the southern states smile differently from other Americans! On the other hand, behind all this diversity there appear to be some features that are universal, such as the obvious indications of 'up' and 'down' (Key 1992). As noted earlier, we may share some of these features with our primate relatives, in which case the explanation for the similarities is presumably genetic; so non-verbal communication offers the same range of learned and innate patterns as we seem to find in language.

4.1.5   *Conclusion*

This discussion has shown that de Saussure was wrong in seeing speech as the product of the individual's will, unconstrained by society. This might be nearer the truth for certain aspects of speech in Antigua, but it is far from true in the societies familiar to most readers (and to de Saussure himself).

Society controls our speech in two ways. Firstly, by providing a set of *norms*, which we learn to follow (or occasionally to flout) more or less skilfully, but which vary from society to society, though some may be universal. For instance, even in Madagascar the norm of informativeness seems to apply *unless* it conflicts with other principles (of safeguarding individuals or keeping news to oneself), and this norm may in fact be recognised by all societies in spite of these apparent counter examples. Secondly, society provides the *motivation* for adhering to these norms, and for putting effort into speech (as in social interaction in general). The theory of face-work explains this motivation, and could explain why it is that speech can run as smoothly as it usually does, given the possibilities for misunderstanding and other difficulties that exist.

In addition to controlling it in these two ways, society takes a great interest in speech, and in particular provides a set of concepts for thinking and talking about it. This terminology makes socialisation easier, just as in other areas of life. For example, one speech-category is 'lesson', and one of the things that primary-school children have to learn, by explicit instruction, is not to interrupt in the middle of a lesson (in contrast with all other kinds of speech in which they are involved). More precisely, if they do want to interrupt they must do it in a way which gives the teacher control, by raising their hand and awaiting permission. Similarly, they learn that a discussion has a purpose and an outcome but a chat doesn't; so discussions should not be interrupted or diverted, but chats can be all the better for being both interrupted and diverted.

We have referred in very general terms to 'society', but it would be wrong to give the impression that societies are any more homogeneous with respect to the ways in which they control speech than they are with respect to the linguistic items which their members use. There is no reason to believe that this is so, and we may expect just as much variation in norms of speech as in linguistic items. Similarly, it is likely that people use speech like linguistic items in order to locate themselves in relation to the social groups that they can identify in the world around them. In one group they swear, shout and argue, and in another they hardly talk at all.

4.2   Speech as a signal of social identity

4.2.1   *Non-relational social categories*

Every language seems to have linguistic items that reflect social characteristics of the speaker, of the addressee or of the relation between them. Consequently speech which contains such items tells a hearer how the speaker sees these characteristics, and misuse constitutes a violation of the norms that govern speech. The norms reviewed below are the best known and the most widely studied of those that govern speech.

The simplest cases are linguistic items which reflect the social characteristics of just one person, either speaker or addressee. One of the oddest cases described in the ethnographic literature is that of the Abipon of Argentina, who according to Hymes (1972) add -*in* to the end of *every* word if either the speaker or addressee is a member of the warrior class. Similarly, the Yana language of California contained special forms for use in speech either by or to women

(Sapir 1929). However, in most cases the norm refers specifically only to the speaker or to the hearer.

As far as speakers are concerned, the commonest characteristic to be reflected by specific linguistic items is sex (Trudgill 1974/1983: 78ff., Graddol and Swann 1989: 42ff., McCormick 1994b, Bainbridge 1994). For instance, in the Koasati language spoken in Louisiana there are quite regular morphological differences between the verb forms used by males and females, with males typically adding -*s* to the end of the female forms (for example, males say *lakáws* where females say *lakáw*, both meaning 'he is lifting it'). A rather different kind of sex-marker is found in the Island Carib language of Central America, whose history is specially likely to show sex differences since the Island Caribs may be descended from Carib-speaking males and Arawak females whose males were slaughtered by the Caribs. (Arawak is unrelated to Carib.) In modern Island Carib, males and females differ in various aspects of their common language, including the genders given to abstract nouns, which are treated as grammatically masculine by female speakers and feminine by male ones (Taylor 1951: 103).

Japanese is an important language for studying the linguistic classification of the speaker. By the end of the feudal period, which lasted until 1867, some forms were exclusively for use by female speakers and others were only used by members of the ruling warrior class (Shibatani 1990: 124). Since then the rules have changed, but sex differences remain very clear (Shibatani 1990: 371ff.). It is perhaps not too surprising that the word which refers to the speaker ('I/me') varies according to the speaker's sex – there are in fact several words, varying in terms of formality, but *boku* is used only by males and *atasi* only by females. More surprisingly, the word for 'you' also varies with the sex of the speaker, though once again formality is relevant: only males use *kimi anta* or *omae*, and only females *anta*. These restrictions have a historical explanation, but nowadays they are simply arbitrary facts that Japanese children have to learn. A particularly interesting difference, from this point of view, is the rule which allows females to omit the word *da*, 'is/are' in certain (common) types of sentence. For example, *kirei da yo*, 'It's pretty', is the only form available for males, whereas females normally say *Kirei yo*, and are said to sound 'blunt and masculine' if they use the other. As we shall see shortly, the omission of the word for 'is/are' is characteristic of 'baby-talk', so it is interesting to speculate about whether this originated as an example of women being treated like children. All these distinctions (and others) are tied specifically to the speaker's sex, and must be signalled in some way in every Japanese speaker's internal grammar.

The most extraordinary of all the distinctions that have been reported is probably found among the Nootka Indians of Vancouver Island (Sapir 1915).

Nootka apparently provides special word-forms for use when speaking either to or about people with various kinds of deformity or abnormality, namely 'children, unusually fat or heavy people, unusually short adults, those suffering from some defect of the eye, hunchbacks, those that are lame, left-handed persons and circumcised males'. For example, in talking either to or about a person with a squint a suffix is added to verbs, and all sibilant sounds ([s] and [c]) are changed into voiceless laterals (like the Welsh sound written '*ll*').

4.2.2   Power and solidarity

Speech may also reflect the social relations between the speaker and addressee, most particularly the POWER and SOLIDARITY manifested in that relationship. (These terms and the related concepts were introduced into sociolinguistics by the social psychologist Roger Brown – see Brown and Ford 1961 and Brown and Gilman 1960, the 'classic' papers on linguistic markers of social relations.) 'Power' is self-explanatory, but 'solidarity' is harder to define. It concerns the social distance between people – how much experience they have shared, how many social characteristics they share (religion, sex, age, region of origin, race, occupation, interests, etc.), how far they are prepared to share intimacies, and other factors.

For the English speaker, the clearest linguistic markers of social relations are personal names, such as *John* and *Mr Brown*. Each person has a number of different names by which they may be addressed, including first and family names, and possibly a title (such as *Mr* or *Professor*). Let us consider just two possible combinations: the first name on its own (for example, *John*), and the title followed by the family name (for example, *Mr Brown*). How does one decide whether to address John Brown as *John* or as *Mr Brown*? The answer must refer to both power and solidarity, as Brown and Ford found in their study of American middle-class usage. Once again the notion of prototypes is useful, since we can define two prototypical situations in which *John* and *Mr Brown* respectively would be used, and then we can relate other situations to them. *John* is used if there is high solidarity between the speaker and John Brown, and John Brown has less power than the speaker – in other words, if John Brown is a *close subordinate*. A clear example is when John Brown is the speaker's son. On the other hand, *Mr Brown* is used if there is low solidarity and John Brown has more power than the speaker – if he is a *distant superior*, such as a company boss or a headmaster whom the speaker knows only from a distance. It seems unlikely that there would be any disagreement among English speakers as to the names appropriate to these two situations, which are shown in Figure 4.1. In this diagram the length of the line is meant to indicate

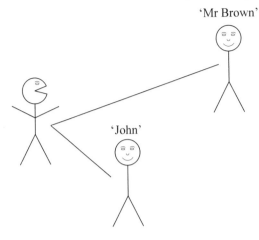

Figure 4.1

the social distance between the speaker and the person addressed, while the vertical direction of the line indicates power relationships.

There is less agreement, and less certainty, over the names to be used in intermediate situations. What do you call John Brown if he is a close superior (for example, the man for whom you have been working for thirty years), or a distant equal (for example, a stranger of your own age to whom you have just been introduced)? The answer will no doubt vary from person to person, but we are all guided by our experience of other people's behaviour so we can expect to find regularities not only in each person's behaviour but also across individuals. The fact remains, however, that we are all rather uncertain about the choice of names when dealing with cases other than the clear ones.

One of the advantages of signalling power and solidarity by our choice of names is that we can avoid such problems simply by not using *any* name to address the person concerned. However, other languages have other devices for signalling power and solidarity which in this respect are less accommodating (as we shall see in 4.2.3), such as the use in French of the pronouns *tu* and *vous*, both meaning 'you' and both singular, (although *vous* is also plural). The norms for choosing between *tu* and *vous* in the singular are precisely the same as those for choosing between first name only and title plus family name in English, *tu* being used prototypically to a close subordinate, and *vous* to a distant superior, with other situations resolved in relation to these. In contrast with the English system, however, it is much harder to avoid the problems of choice in French, since to do so it would be necessary to avoid making any reference at all to the person addressed.

123

The studies by Brown and Gilman show that there have been considerable changes through time in the norms for using the French pronouns, which derived from Latin pronouns where the distinction was one of number only (*tu* 'you, singular', *vos* 'you, plural'). It is unclear why the pronouns' meanings changed in this way. Brown and Gilman link it to the complexities of the history of the Roman Empire, but since their work was published this kind of change has been found in languages all over the world, as reported by Penelope Brown (a different Brown!) and Stephen Levinson (1978/1987: 198ff.). Their explanation is based on the theory of face which we considered in section 4.1.3. By using a plural pronoun for 'you', the speaker protects the other person's power-face in two ways. First, the plural pronoun picks out the other person less directly than the singular form does, because of its ambiguity. The intended referent could, in principle, be some group of people rather than the individual actually targeted. This kind of indirectness is a common strategy for giving the other person an 'out', an alternative interpretation which protects them against any threats to their face which may be in the message. The second effect of using a plural pronoun is to pretend that the person addressed is the representative of a larger group ('you and your group'), which obviously puts them in a position of greater power.

The choice of pronouns in French involves both power and solidarity, but it seems that the relative importance of these two relationships has changed over the centuries. For instance, it was normal until quite recently for French children to call their father *vous*, in recognition of his greater power, but in the very different circumstances of modern urban society it is usual for them to call him *tu* because of the high solidarity.

Linguistic signalling of power and solidarity is sufficiently well studied for at least four possible linguistic universals to be suggested. The first is that every language might be expected to have some way of signalling differences in either power or solidarity or both, which could be explained by reference to the extreme importance of both power and solidarity in face-to-face relations between individuals, and the need for each individual to make it clear how they see those relations.

Secondly, power and solidarity are very often expressed by the same range of forms – for example, by the same range of alternative pronouns – though this may not always be so. For example, the language Mijikenda (which is spoken in north-east Kenya) allows speakers the same two options for 'you' addressed to one person as French does, one of which is the plural 'you', the word which can also be used for addressing more than one person (McGivney 1993). But unlike other languages with this pronoun choice, the choice seems to be based on considerations of solidarity alone, without any role for power. The sole basis for the choice is the relative generation of the speaker and the addressee (which, as we shall see shortly, is definitely not a matter of power), and since it is a tightly-knit society most people know precisely how other people fit into the scheme of generations. The choice of pronouns reflects the 'generation gap' very strictly: if you belong to the same generation as my parents, I (as a Mijikenda speaker) must use the plural 'you' regardless of your age, power, status, familiarity and other things which might be relevant. (For instance, if you are my father's brother I have to use the plural form even if you are in fact younger than me, as can happen.)

This much of the system could be interpreted either in terms of solidarity (same versus different generation) or in terms of power (higher versus lower generation), but the next fact removes the second possibility: I also have to use the plural 'you' if you belong to the same generation as my children. In other words, the choice of pronouns is always reciprocal, so power (which is non-reciprocal by definition) must be irrelevant. To confirm this, we can ask what happens between grandparents and grandchildren, where the power differences are even more extreme. Since neither belongs to the same generation as the intervening generation, and since the plural pronoun would imply the opposite, they have to use the singular pronoun to each other; and by the same logic great-grandparents and great-grandchildren use the plural pronoun! The system is impressive for its consistency, but the most important point to notice about it is that the choice of pronouns is always reciprocal, and therefore completely uninfluenced by considerations of power.

Returning to our second universal, then, we cannot claim that any form which expresses power must also express solidarity, and vice versa. However, we may be able to make a somewhat weaker claim: that power and solidarity tend strongly to be expressed by the same forms. This is certainly true of very many languages, and it may be that we can explain why Mijikenda is different by referring to the 'purity' of its criteria for pronoun choice. In most societies pronoun choice is based on a rather diffuse notion of solidarity which is hard to separate from power; but if generation is the only criterion there is no reason why power should enter the picture at all.

Thirdly, it seems that wherever power and solidarity are reflected in the same range of forms, the form which expresses high solidarity also expresses greater power on the part of the speaker, and vice versa; i.e. the conflict-free prototypes are a close subordinate and a distant superior. This pairing is NEVER reversed, linking a close superior to a distant subordinate. This widely observed fact can be explained in two ways (both of which may be true). One is that this combination of intimacy and dominance is typical of the relationship between a parent and a child, which is clearly one of the most fundamental relationships in society

(Brown and Levinson 1978/1987: 46). What counts is the way parents address and talk about children, rather than vice versa, because parents talk long before the child does. A second explanation is that solidarity inevitably increases through time as two people get to know each other better, so the question is when it is sufficient to justify more intimate language. If power is unequal, it is likely to be the superior who decides this, so there may be a period where the superior uses intimate forms to the subordinate while the latter is still using the distant forms, but the reverse will never be true (Brown and Ford 1961).

Lastly, there is a generalisation about the use of names which follows from the third universal. In every society at least two kinds of name are available for use within a family in identifying people as unique individuals or in addressing them: given names (for example, *John*) and role-based names (for example, *Mum*). These are distributed unequally, with a strong tendency for given names to be applied to junior relatives and role-based names to senior relatives. What seems to be universally true is that this pattern is never reversed completely, but there are interesting variations on it even within English-speaking society. In some families parents encourage their children to call them by their given names (a very exotic practice, it seems!), while in others parents call their sons 'son'; one possible interpretation of these practices is that in the first case the parents accept the same powerlessness as their children, while in the second they allow their sons (but not their daughters!) to share in their own power.

Other societies show more systematic and dramatic variations on the basic theme. (The following data come from contributors to the internet list language-culture@cs.uchicago.edu, from Mitchell (1975: 159) on North Africa and from Melia Linggi on Iban.) In Chinese all junior relatives are normally named with a role-based name ('son', 'niece', etc.), a practice which is also common in Polish; in Japanese adults are rarely called by their given name, and names based on family roles are used extensively even outside the family. India shows a wide variety of practices: for example, some communities in Bombay call mothers exclusively by a name based on their motherhood (for example, 'X's mother', where X is her first child), and in Maharashtra husbands give their wives a new name on marriage – an interesting example which presumably shows how naming a person can be used to assert dominance over them. In some communities (for example, the Iban tribe of Malaysia) there are no family names as such, but there is an adult alternative to a given name which is used outside the family: 'father of X' (like the Bombay pattern), where X is the oldest child. Perhaps the most fascinating naming pattern of all is reported from North Africa, Puerto-Rican Spanish in New York and throughout the Indian subcontinent: small children are addressed as parents! Sometimes a son is called 'daddy' and a daughter 'mummy'; in other cultures the word for 'mummy' is applied to both sexes. At present we can only marvel at the rich variety of data, but this is no substitute for understanding why these apparently strange practices exist.

4.2.3 *Linguistic signals of power and solidarity*

In English the main markers of power and solidarity might fairly be described as peripheral to the system of English as a whole, in the sense that proper names used as vocatives (i.e. to address someone) could be handled in a separate section of the grammar with little or no consequence for any other parts of it. (In fact, we shall see below that things are not quite as simple as that even in English.) English-speaking readers might think, therefore, that the same is true of all languages, but this is by no means the case. It is common for the power-solidarity contrast to be quite crucial, and for the grammar of such a language to refer to it at many points. What follows is a brief survey of some of the better known types of linguistic signal of power–solidarity (as we shall call the contrast for convenience, without wishing to imply that both power and solidarity are involved necessarily and equally in all cases). A fuller discussion may be found in Brown and Levinson (1978/1987).

One of the easiest ways of showing that power–solidarity relationships are central to the grammar is by pointing out that even in English they are not restricted to vocatives. If I am talking about John Brown, I have exactly the same choice between *John* and *Mr Brown* as I do when I am addressing him directly; if he is my friend I address him with 'Hello, John' and talk about him with 'I saw John yesterday', but if he is a distant superior I say 'Hello, Mr Brown' and 'I saw Mr Brown yesterday'. In some cases it is important to contrast these two cases so we can call the first 'vocative' and the second 'referring'; and for present purposes the important point is that referring names are part of the ordinary sentence structure, covered by the ordinary grammar. Even if vocatives are too peripheral for inclusion, ordinary referring names are not, so a grammar of English must allow both *John* and *Mr Brown* and should explain the difference between them.

Having distinguished vocative and referring names, however, we must also recognise their similarities. Figure 4.2 shows a speaker, S, talking to someone else (A, for 'addressee') about some person R (for 'referent', what a word refers to); the curved line is a notation that I have used elsewhere (Hudson 1995a) to show the referent relationship. A and R are each related to S in terms of both solidarity, shown by the straight lines, and power, shown by the angled lines (meaning 'up, down or level'). The diagram implies that A and R are different people, but this need not be so – I can talk to you about yourself – and we shall mention this special case below.

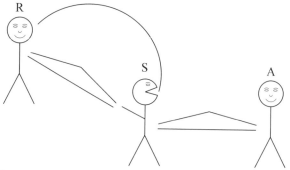

Figure 4.2

In the following discussion we shall use 'X' to stand for either A or R except where these need to be distinguished. The question, then, is how languages reveal the power–solidarity relations between S and X. Briefly, the answers that have been found are:

(1)   via the expression for X,
(2)   via the expression for S,
(3)   via the verb,
(4)   via general vocabulary level.

(1)   The expression for X

The linguistic expressions that S can apply to X include not only names but also personal pronouns (*you*, *he*) and ordinary common nouns (*mother*, *woman*). The choice is always controlled by general principles rather than left to the speaker's whim, and one of the controlling questions is the nature of the power–solidarity relationships between S and X.

In English S can use various vocatives to John Brown, including *you* (*Hey, you!*) or a common noun such as *waiter* as well as the names *John* or *Mr Brown*, or the role-based name *dad* which we mentioned above. It is clear to any English speaker that these imply very different relationships between S and X. In non-vocative uses, on the other hand, English allows less choice and power–solidarity relationships are generally irrelevant except for the choice of names mentioned above. A description like *the teacher's hat* gives no indication of S's relationship to its referent, X.

In some languages even noun-phrases like this can be marked linguistically for power–solidarity; for example, Japanese has an 'honorific' prefix *o-* which can be attached to a noun to show respect for its referent – for example, the Japanese for rice wine, which is called *sake* in the west, is *o-sake*! The prefix allows one to show respect for a person via their possessions; for example, the normal word for 'hat', *boosi*, would normally be expanded to *o-boosi* if the hat belonged to a superior (Shibatani 1990: 374). Moreover, languages can have very different rules for the use of names, as we saw in the previous section, so we should not take the English system for granted. Where English speakers would use a given name such as *John*, some languages (for example, Chinese and Japanese) prefer a role-based name such as 'mother' or 'older brother'. The choice always gives information about power–solidarity, but the details vary from society to society according to how power and solidarity are balanced against each other. Calling X by a given name can show solidarity, affection and so on; but it can also show dominance; and conversely the use of a role-based name can show respect but it can also deny X's individuality, which is a denial of both solidarity and power.

A particularly important case is where a pronoun meaning 'you' is used to refer to X – i.e. where X is not only R but also A. In modern English *you* is neutral for power-solidarity, but this is a recent development resulting from the loss of *thou* (which survives in some English dialects). In earlier English *thou* was used to close subordinates and *you* to distant superiors, just like *tu* and *vous* in French (4.2.2).

(2)   The expression for S

Another way to define the relationship between S and X is by the choice of expression for S – in other words, by alternatives for *I* or *me*. This is much less widespread, but does occur. A particularly elaborate example is Persian, which offers a vast range of alternatives (Jahangiri 1980: 174, 210; Jahangiri and Hudson 1982: 56). The basic form is *man* or *mâ* (which also means 'we', and may imply more humility than *man*), but there are about ten others which are based on common nouns with meanings like 'slave', 'despised' and 'one who prays for you'. Japanese too has a range of alternative words for 'I'.

(3)   The verb

So far we have considered the nouns and pronouns which can be used to address X or to refer to X. These are where we might expect speakers to express information about their relationships to X. However, there is another possibility which is particularly interesting for a grammarian, and which is even better evidence for the inseparability of sociolinguistics and grammar. In some languages, this information is located in the main verb of the sentence concerned. This is relevant to any theory of language structure because the verb is also the collecting point for so much other information in the sentence (for example, tense, negation, questions and commands are typically shown in the verb, and some are restricted to the main verb), and in all modern theories of grammar the main verb is the structural 'root' (or 'head') of the whole sentence, with the subject, object, adjuncts and so on (including subordinate clauses) all dependent on it. A simple, and familiar, example is the form of the imperative verb in Italian, which shows not only that the sentence is imperative (a command, invitation or whatever), but also whether the person addressed is an intimate or not: *Parlami!*, 'Speak to me!', is used to an intimate, whereas when talking to a superior one would say *Mi Parli!*

Admittedly Italian also has a pronoun contrast (like the French *tu*/*vous* contrast) between *tu* and *lei*, both meaning 'you', so one might interpret the verb difference as a consequence of two distinct 'understood' subject pronouns which arises only when A and R are the same. This interpretation is not possible in Japanese, however, where the endings attached to verbs show the solidarity relationship of S to A regardless of what is being talked about. For example, the 'plain' way to say 'Taro came' is *Taroo ga ki-ta*, but the 'distant' form is *Taroo ga ki-masi-ta*, with the suffix *-masi* added to the verb. In Japanese, therefore, S shows social distance (or lack of it) in every single sentence, regardless of topic. Interestingly for a grammarian, however, it is only once per complete sentence, since distant forms are only used as main verbs, i.e. as the root verb of the whole sentence. Subordinate verbs (in relative clauses, temporal clauses, reported clauses and so on) are always left in their neutral form. Once again, then, we find an important similarity between 'social information' and other kinds of information shown by verbs. (Shibatani 1990 is a clear introduction and the source of all these examples and those in the next paragraph; the interpretation in terms of power and solidarity is based on Wetzel 1994.)

In addition to the distant forms which show lack of solidarity with A, Japanese also allows the speaker to show power relations to R through the choice of one of two verb-forms. According to Shibatani these 'power' forms show respect to someone referred to in the sentence, but differ according to whether this person is referred to by the subject or by the object. In either case an extra auxiliary verb is used which allows the ordinary verb to be combined with the so-called 'honorific' prefix *o-* mentioned above. The following examples illustrate the processes involved. (The particles *ga* and *o* are used after the subject and object respectively, and have nothing to do with the 'honorification'.)

Sensei ga	*warat-ta.*		(no honorific)
Teacher	laughed.		
Sensei ga	*o-warai ni*	*nat-ta.*	(subject honorific)
Teacher	honoured-laugh	did	
Taroo ga	*sensei o*	*tasuke-ta.*	(no honorific)
Taroo	teacher	helped.	
Taroo ga	*sensei o*	*o-tasuke*	*si-ta.* (object honorific)
Taroo	teacher	honoured-help	did

This system can combine with the polite form discussed in the previous paragraph, for example, *Sensei ga o-warai ni nari-masi-ta*, 'The teacher laughed' (polite and subject honorific).

Japanese is not the only language in which social information is shown by the main verb. Another is Basque, where main verbs (but not subordinate verbs) show the speaker's social relationships to the person addressed (Trask 1995). If A is either a close kin or childhood friend of the speaker – a very restrictive condition on intimacy compared with most languages! – a special morpheme is added to the main verb. The form of this morpheme also shows A's sex. For example, the neutral way of saying 'She is English' is *ingelesa da*, but the verb *da* would become *duk* when speaking to a male intimate, and *dun* to a female. The same intimacy contrast is also made in the pronoun 'you' (intimate: *hi*, neutral: *zu*).

(4) General vocabulary level

A good example of this is found in Javanese (Geertz 1960), which offers a range of alternative forms, listed in the lexicon, for each of a large number of meanings. For instance, Geertz gives the alternative forms for the Javanese sentence meaning 'Are you going to eat rice and cassava now?' (which apparently may be translated word-for-word from English), and shows that there are two or three different words in Javanese for each word in the English except *to* and *cassava*. Geertz identifies just six 'style levels', each marked by a definable range of vocabulary items so that any given sentence can belong to just one of the levels. The function of style levels is to signal the power–solidarity relations between S and A, and specifically to build a 'wall of behavioural formality' to protect the addressee's power-face, which Geertz calls their 'inner life'. The higher the style level, the more walls there are to protect the addressee against the encroachment that any communication inevitably makes on privacy. English uses register distinctions of vocabulary in somewhat similar ways (2.4.1).

These various linguistic signals of power–solidarity relationships can be seen as ways in which speakers can show others how they locate themselves in their social world. Speakers in every language can use language to locate themselves in relation to the people they are talking to and also in relation to people they are talking about. In some languages central parts of the grammatical system are dedicated to this important social function, so it is important to bear these languages in mind as a corrective to the idea that the sole purpose of language is to convey messages efficiently.

4.3 The structure of speech

4.3.1 Entries and exits

Whenever regularly recurring patterns are identified in some kind of behaviour, we say that behaviour is structured by those patterns. There is no difficulty in establishing that speech is structured, since grammars and dictionaries are full of recurrent patterns of words, constructions and so on. These relatively short patterns, contained within the sentence, are obviously only a part of the total structure of speech since all sorts of longer patterns can be identified, such as the one consisting of a question followed by its answer, and even longer ones such as some piece of interaction between two people, with a clearly recognisable greeting at the beginning and a farewell at the end. What is controversial is the extent to which a hierarchical structure can be identified above the sentence, and we shall return to this question in the next section, after first looking at greetings and farewells, which offer the clearest examples of structure in speech.

The reasonable assumption that every language has a range of forms for use as greetings and farewells, is based on the social importance of 'entries' (into pieces of interaction) and 'exits'. (The terms 'entry' and 'exit', borrowed from the stage, reflect the fact that discussions of speech norms often compare them with the 'lines' that an actor recites on stage.) Erving Goffman, the originator of 'face-work' (see 4.1.4), suggests that a greeting is needed to show that the relation which existed at the end of the last encounter is still unchanged, in spite of the separation, and that a farewell is needed in order to 'sum up the effect of the encounter upon the relationship and show what the participants may expect of one another when they next meet' (Goffman 1955). Everything we have seen so far shows that relations between the participants in some piece of interaction are of the greatest interest to the participants themselves, and it is easy to see why it is important for each piece of interaction to begin and end with an indication of these relations. Goffman's own theory of face predicts that it will be even more important than the quotation above suggests. Wrapping up an encounter neatly by an appropriate farewell is not just an investment for future meetings with the same person. We also do it to people we are never likely to meet again – strangers who ask us the way, shop assistants who serve us and so on. Even in these cases there is a little ritual which we go through to leave both parties with their faces intact.

Although greetings and farewells (presumably) exist in all languages, they also vary enormously from language to language (and between dialects), so close translation-equivalents are often hard to find. For example, the French farewells *au revoir* and *adieu* can both be translated by *good-bye*, but they differ according to whether or not the people concerned expect to meet again.

However there are recurrent themes (Ferguson 1976). One, which is hardly surprising in view of the previous discussion, is that greetings and farewells often show power and solidarity relations (for example, *Hi!* versus *Good morning*). Another is that they frequently reflect the time of day or a public festival (*Good morning, Good afternoon, Happy Easter, Happy New Year*); this presumably adds to solidarity-face by emphasising the similar experiences currently being shared. Some of these formulae are made up out of ordinary words used in fairly ordinary ways (for example, *Happy Easter*) but others are opaque without etymological help (for example, *Good-bye*, from *God be with you*; *'Bye!* is even more opaque, of course). None of them really expresses a claim about how the world is, nor even a claim about how the speaker feels, so truth and sincerity do not really count (in contrast with a sentence like *I'm pleased to see you* or *I hope you have a good journey*). Nevertheless the rituals are critically important and have to be performed in the finest detail if we are to avoid embarrassment, offense or ridicule.

Furthermore, the sheer length of a greeting is generally proportional to the length of time since the last meeting (i.e. a greeting to a friend last seen ten years ago will be longer than one to a friend seen yesterday) and to the importance of the relationship (i.e. a friend will receive a longer greeting than a mere acquaintance). Goffman's explanation for the role of greetings might lead us to expect that there will only be the briefest of greeting, or none at all, where no previous relation has existed, and this seems to be the case: witness the lack of greetings when people approach strangers to ask for information. Similarly we might predict (correctly) that longer greetings will be used when people are less certain of their relations, and therefore need more reassurance.

Goffman's predictions may be based on a rather American style of social behaviour, since there is at least one society to which they appear not to apply, namely the Apache Indians, studied by K. H. Basso (1970). Instead of using speech, in the form of greetings, to assure each other that relations are just as they were before the separation, they wait until they are sure that relations really *are* the same before they speak to each other at all, at least in situations where there is reason to think that relations may have changed, as when children return after a year in boarding-school. Many British or American parents might chatter hard with their children as soon as they come off the bus, but Apache parents apparently wait and say nothing for up to fifteen minutes, while they assess the effect of the year's schooling on their children's behaviour. Thus the Apache do not use greetings in the way that Goffman predicts, but do confirm his more general claim that it is important for people to know how they stand in relation to others before they start to talk.

4.3.2 *Other kinds of structure in speech*

There has been a great deal of research in the last few decades on other aspects of what is called DISCOURSE STRUCTURE – the structure of speech above the sentence level (Schiffrin 1994). It is clear that there is no lack of different kinds of structure linking sentences together in coherent wholes, but there is no agreed single theoretical framework for the analysis of these coherent patterns. The most obvious fact about discourse structure is that many different kinds of structure run through discourse, and any attempt to reduce them to a single type is bound to fail.

One kind of structure is based on the fact that people take *turns* at speaking in most kinds of interaction, so that speech is divided up into separate stretches spoken by different speakers. In studying this aspect of discourse one can ask questions such as whether 'turns' are taken strictly in sequence or overlap one another, how speakers show that they are about to finish speaking, how listeners show that they would like to start, who decides who should speak next, who does most of the talking, who speaks to whom and so on. The work on this aspect of discourse has mostly been done either by social psychologists interested in group dynamics (for a representative selection of papers, see Argyle 1973) , or by sociologists of the 'Conversation Analysis' school (Schiffrin 1994: ch. 7). Research has shown that turn-taking is a very highly skilled activity indeed. As we shall see, it involves many kinds of behaviour as well as speech (for example, eye-movements), all of which are coordinated with split-second timing and reacted to with great accuracy by other participants. One particular type of turn-taking structure is characterised by ADJACENCY PAIRS – a type of utterance by one speaker which requires a particular type of utterance by another. The most obvious adjacency pair is a sequence of question followed by answer, but there are many others, such as greeting + greeting, complaint + apology, summons + answer, invitation + acceptance and so on.

A second type of structure in discourse is based on *topic*, which clearly bears little relation to the type based on turn-taking, since speakers frequently change topics in the middle of their turn. It is tempting to think that topic-based structure is hierarchical, in the sense that a given text should be analysable into successively smaller units on the basis of topic. This temptation is reinforced by the writing practices to which highly literate people (such as any reader of this book) are accustomed. For instance, this book has a very clear hierarchical structure based on topic, with chapters as the largest units, sections as the next largest, then subsections (for example, the present one, which is 4.3.2), then paragraphs and finally sentences, all neatly delimited by one kind of typographic convention or another. In imposing this structure on the book, I have tried to make it reflect the topics discussed, so that the present sentence is an illustration of one kind of structure, dealt with in the present paragraph, which is part of the subsection on types of discourse structure other than entries and exits, which is one part of the section dealing with discourse structure, and that in turn is part of the chapter dealing with speech as social interaction.

Some researchers have claimed to be able to find a similar hierarchical structure in other kinds of discourse, both spoken and written. For instance, John Sinclair and Malcolm Coulthard (1975) analysed tape-recordings of a number of lessons from secondary schools, and identified a hierarchical discourse structure with 'lesson' as the largest unit, then 'transaction', then 'exchange', then 'move' and finally 'act', corresponding very roughly with the syntactic unit 'clause' (see Coulthard 1977 for a survey of other proposals for hierarchical analyses of discourse). However convincing we may find these proposals, it seems clear that there is no such hierarchical structure in certain kinds of interaction, but rather the topic 'drifts' gradually from one subject to another – perhaps starting off with a film about sheep-farming in Wales, leading to a sheep-dog trial somebody saw on holiday, and from there into further details of the holiday and a comparison with a holiday spent in Spain and so on. Moreover it seems unlikely that participants in such a conversation have any clear plan at the start about the shape it will take, as would seem to be implied by the notion of a hierarchical structure.

On the other hand, speakers do tend to stick to the same topic and may feel obliged to give a special signal if they are changing it (for example, *Oh, by the way, on a completely different matter, . . .*). The reason for sticking to a given topic, or only drifting gradually away from it, is partly that this increases the chances of other participants being interested in what is said, and partly because it increases their chances of understanding the discourse, because for any given topic we all have a large amount of information about how the world works which we can exploit both as speakers and hearers. Speakers who keep to the same topic can take most of this information for granted. For example, if we all know we are talking about the holiday someone had last year, a speaker can say simply *The food was disappointing* and we all know which food they mean. If the topic for each sentence were different from that of the previous one, none of this information could be taken for granted. In short, sticking to one topic makes speech much easier both for speaker and for addressee.

The conclusion to which we seem to be led on the topic-based structure of discourse is that some kinds of discourse may have a hierarchical structure, especially if entirely under the control of one person who has the opportunity to plan the entire discourse before starting (for example, a book or a lecture), but that most discourse probably has a much looser kind of structure. This is characterised by the change of topic through time, and consists only of the *current* topic at any given moment. An analyst can therefore trace the ways in which the topic has varied in the discourse from time to time, either by gradual drift or by abrupt change. In the words of Harvey Sacks, one of the founders of Conversation Analysis:

> a general feature for topical organization is movement from topic to topic, not by a topic-close followed by a topic-beginning, but by a stepwise move, which involves linking up whatever is being introduced to what has just been talked about, such that, as far as anybody knows, a new topic has not been started, though we're far from wherever we began. (Quoted from Sacks' lecture notes in Schiffrin 1994: 261)

A third type of discourse structure is based on what we know about the structure of the world – what we might call *encyclopedic* structure, which gives form to what we have been referring to as 'the current topic'. If the current topic is a holiday, we know there are various 'subtopics' which are generally considered relevant, such as accommodation, weather, activities and travel, each of which can be further subdivided – for example, 'activities' might include sight-seeing, swimming, other sports, night-life and shopping. Alternatively, other subtopics might cut across these, spoiling the neat hierarchical organisation implied so far – for instance, 'food' might cut across 'accommodation' and 'activities', since you can eat either in your hotel or in a restaurant. To take a different kind of example, if we were describing a flat we could make use of one of two kinds of encyclopedic knowledge. We could either take the architect's viewpoint, and describe it statically: *There are four rooms, forming a square, . . .* , or we could take the point of view of someone visiting the flat and being shown around it: *First you come into a hall, then you go down a corridor on your left, . . .* Interestingly, according to the research of Linde and Labov (1975), most people take the visitor's viewpoint.

Other types of structure can be identified in discourse in addition to those based on turn-taking, topic and encyclopedic knowledge. It should be clear from the discussion that there is no chance of reducing all these structures to a single type, and that the structures of discourse are complex mixtures of norms specific to speech and general knowledge of the world. It is hard to see how the study of discourse structure can be anything but interdisciplinary.

4.4   Verbal and non-verbal behaviour
4.4.1   Relation-markers

This section considers the relations between verbal and non-verbal behaviour in social interaction. The phonetician David Abercrombie claimed that 'we speak with our vocal organs, but we converse with our entire bodies' (Abercrombie 1968), and we shall see in what sense this is true. Non-verbal behaviour is involved in the two aspects of speech considered in this chapter – marking relations between speaker and addressee (4.2) and the structure of discourse (4.3); and it is also involved in the communication of 'content', that is, propositions and referents.

One very obvious aspect of non-verbal behaviour which helps to reflect power–solidarity is the physical distance between the people concerned, the subject-matter of PROXEMICS (Pocheptsov 1994). It would be a safe hypothesis that physical distance is proportional to social distance in all cultures, so that people who feel close in spirit will put themselves relatively near to each other when interacting. At one end of the scale are courting couples, and at the other end impersonal and formal occasions where speakers may be long distances from their addressees, as in theatres, or unable to see them at all, as on radio and television. What varies from culture to culture is the distance which is thought appropriate for a particular degree of solidarity. For instance, Arabs generally set the distance lower than Americans. This claim is supported by research (Watson and Graves 1966) in which comparisons were made between Arab and American students in an American university. The students were asked to converse in pairs in a room where they could be observed without their knowledge, and records were kept of their movements – how close to each other they sat, how they oriented themselves towards each other, how much they touched each other, how much they looked at each other, and how loudly they talked. Sixteen Arabs and sixteen Americans were studied in this way, with Arabs talking to Arabs and Americans to Americans. When the results were compared it was found that 'Arabs confronted each other more directly than Americans when conversing . . . , they sat closer to each other . . . , they were more likely to touch each other . . . , they looked each other more squarely in the eye . . . , and they conversed more loudly than Americans.'

As we noticed in 4.1.4, such cultural differences can lead to serious misunderstandings, and it is easy to see how physical distance relates to solidarity- and power-face. We get (and give) solidarity-face by physical contact (touching, stroking, grooming), and intimacies of the close family and between lovers are the ultimate in showing acceptance, so the closer we are the more we can bolster each other's solidarity-face. On the other hand, being physically close to another person is also an intrusion on their personal territory and a threat to their power-face. What is needed is a very delicate balancing act: too near and we are intrusive, too far and we are cold. We don't make these decisions unaided, but learn them from those around us; this is very helpful when we are dealing with our own group, but a source of problems when dealing with strangers.

Another kind of non-verbal behaviour that is very important for power-solidarity (and other socially important emotions) is what we do with our face – in the literal sense this time! We give out social signals with our mouths (smiling, showing disgust), our eyes (eye-contact) and our eye-brows (frowning, showing surprise). These signals are particularly interesting and important because some of them seem to be universal (as Darwin claimed over a hundred years ago). For example, Ekman studied an isolated community in New Guinea which had hitherto had virtually no contact with the outside world, and found that they used much the same facial expressions as Europeans to express six basic emotions (happiness, sadness, anger, disgust, fear and surprise); and Eibl-Eibesfeld found much the same in six infants who had been born both blind and deaf, who could not have learned these reactions from others (Ekman and Friesen 1971 and Eibl-Eibesfeld 1973, both in Giddens 1989/1993: 92).

Even more interestingly, human smiles can probably be traced back to the ancestors we share with chimpanzees, which also smile in friendly greetings. More generally the same may be true of other parts of non-verbal behaviour:

> Visual signals are also used [by chimpanzees] in combination with other modalities, such as vocalization and touch. For example, after fights, chimpanzees may attempt reconciliations which start with the gesture of an outstretched hand and are commonly completed with a kiss and grooming, reminiscent of the human tendency to 'kiss and make up': in a different context, support is expressed to a nervous individual during conflicts through an embrace rather than a kiss, again suggesting basic patterns shared with humans. (Whiten 1994: 3331)

In short, whatever our genes may (or may not) do for our spoken language, they clearly have a lot of influence on the non-verbal communicative framework within which speech takes place.

4.4.2 *Structure-markers*

Non-verbal behaviour also helps to mark the structure of the inter-action. One of the main kinds of structure considered above (4.3.1) was the pattern of behaviour associated with 'entries' and 'exits', where non-verbal behaviour is just as clearly patterned as verbal behaviour. Some aspects of the former are relatively conventionalised, such as hand-shaking, which in some cultures is replaced by nose-rubbing or supplemented by kissing or embracing, according to the relation between the participants. In Britain hand-shaking seems to be used to show that a relation is being given a fresh start, rather than as a sign of intimacy. Thus it is used to patch up quarrels between friends, or when one is introduced to a stranger, or to anyone not seen for a long time. In other cultures the rules for shaking hands are clearly different, so once again we find scope for relativity in the norms governing behaviour. An interesting example is the difference between British and Wolof (Senegal) practice when greeting a *group* of people. In Britain non-verbal behaviour is generally restricted to an occasional nod to some individuals in the group and the verbal greeting is directed to the group as a whole, whereas the Wolof use the appropriate non-verbal and verbal greeting behaviour separately towards each individual in the group (Irvine 1974).

Apart from entries and exits, non-verbal cues are important for structuring discourse as far as turn-taking is concerned. As we saw (4.3.2), one of the questions to be asked about turn-taking is how speakers signal that they are ready to stop and let the other person start. Eye-movements are one such cue. Research has shown that we normally look at the other person's eyes for much longer periods when we are listening than when speaking, so when we are about to stop speaking (and start listening) we look up at the other person's eyes, in anticipation of our next role as listener. Conversely, the other person looks down when about to start speaking, in anticipation of the change of role (Argyle and Dean 1965, Kendon 1967). Eye-movement is not the only signal of an approaching change of speaker. In some institutions (notably schools, conferences and parliaments), there are other, formalised, signals, such as a would-be speaker raising their hand. Less formalised signals include moving forward in one's chair or clearing one's throat. Equally, there are ways of countering such moves if the speaker does not want to yield the floor – such as deliberately looking away so that the would-be speaker cannot catch one's eye.

4.4.3   *Content-markers*

Finally we come to the use of non-verbal behaviour for marking content. Again there is one very obvious instance of this in most cultures – the use of head movements to indicate 'yes' or 'no'. There are cultural differences in the particular head-movements used for each meaning – for 'yes', some cultures (for example, Western Europe and the United States) use a top-to-bottom movement, others (for example, Eastern Mediterranean) use a bottom-to-top movement and still others (for example, the Indian subcontinent) use a diagonal movement. However, the use of a head-movement to mean 'yes' or 'no' seems sufficiently widespread to risk the hypothesis that it is universal, though it is hard to see why it should be.

Many other gestures also help to mark content (McNeill 1992). People may count on their fingers, and in some societies this is a recognised way of displaying numbers. Indeed, in East Africa there are differences between tribes in the rules for doing this, depending, for instance, on whether 'one' is indicated by the thumb or the little finger (Omondi 1976). There are also differences between the same tribes in the gestures used to show the height of a child, according to whether or not a hand is put, palm downwards, at the height of the top of the child's head. (Some tribes believe this could stunt the child's growth.) Every culture presumably has its own repertoire of gestures for commenting on people and objects, such as the various gestures in British culture for suggesting that someone else is crazy, or for saying that food is just right. Finally, one should not forget the gesture of pointing (done with different fingers in different societies), which is often associated with the use of demonstratives like *this* or *that* and *here* or *there*. It must be rather rare for *this* to be contrasted with *that* (for example, *This is bigger than that*) without some kind of gesture as an accompaniment, even if it is only a nod of the head in the direction of the thing in question. Somewhat surprisingly, pointing is something that chimpanzees do *not* do naturally, though they can be taught to do it and they naturally point with their eyes – i.e. by looking at the thing they want to draw attention to.

It would not be inappropriate to compare you when speaking with the conductor of a large orchestra consisting of the various speech-organs and other visible organs of your body over which you have control. A successful performance requires the conductor to keep all these various organs moving in exact coordination with one another, whatever the speed of the performance and whatever the number of separate organs involved at one moment. To make your job even more taxing, you have to coordinate your performance with that of other conductors who are each conducting their own orchestras (that is, with other participants). It is no wonder that people sometimes find it easier to slip into fixed routines, nearer to music played from a score than to extemporised music like jazz. Nor is it surprising that the study of speech is still so rudimentary.

4.5 Male/female differences in speech

In the last chapter (3.3.3) we saw that males and females may be treated very differently in the cultural systems that languages help to perpetuate. Furthermore, we saw earlier in this chapter (4.2.1) how some languages provide distinct forms for use by male and female speakers. Our current agenda is a different kind of contrast between males and females. Do they use speech differently? More specifically, do they have different priorities and purposes in conversation? Once again there has been a flurry of research activity over the last decade or so which suggests that, at least in some societies, they do. More precisely, there seem to be rather general 'interaction styles' which tend to be associated with one sex or the other, though individuals may of course be exceptions. If this is true, then it matters to everyone; and the general book-reading public has taken a keen interest in the whole question of male/female differences in speech, and of miscommunications more generally, thanks in part to two best-sellers by the American sociolinguist Deborah Tannen (1986, 1990). These books, like a good deal of the research they discuss, focus on middle-class America so it is important to bear in mind that they may not be directly relevant to other societies.

The general consensus seems to be that men are more concerned with power and women with solidarity. For men,

> conversations are negotiations in which people try to achieve and maintain the upper hand if they can, and protect themselves from others' attempts to put them down and push them around. Life, then, is a contest, a struggle to preserve independence and avoid failure.

In contrast, for women

> conversations are negotiations for closeness in which people try to seek and give confirmation and support, and to reach consensus. They try to protect themselves from others' attempts to push them away. Life, then, is a community, a struggle to preserve intimacy and avoid isolation. Though there are hierarchies in this world too, they are hierarchies more of friendship than of power and accomplishment. (Tannen 1990: 24–25)

This generalised difference explains a number of differences in behaviour, though at present we have little more than our own experience (and a host of reported examples) as evidence for these differences.

One such difference involves the preferred relations between speaker and addressee. Men are said to prefer a one-to-many pattern, where a single speaker has the rest of the group as audience, while women tend to break a larger group into a number of smaller conversation groups (McCormick 1994b: 1357). (It is interesting to remember the pattern reported from Antigua in 4.1.4, which is yet another possibility – the group stays united but everyone talks at the same time. This example reminds us to treat generalisations based on middle-class America with caution as the basis for universal conclusions.) The same sex difference seems to apply to small boys and girls when talking in single-sex groups (Tannen 1990: 43), which reminds us that children have plenty of opportunities for developing these different patterns when playing in single-sex groups (1.3.2), regardless of whether the differences are dictated by our genes.

One consequence of this difference which presumably has major implications for men's and women's career prospects is that the male style prepares them better for public speaking – asking questions after lectures, talking in committees, presenting verbal reports and so on – while the female style is more 'private', suitable for establishing rapport (hence Tannen's terms 'report-speaking' and 'rapport-speaking' (1990: 70)). Tannen says that the first question after her public lectures always comes from a male, as do most of the questions, even though she generally talks about male/female conversation differences to audiences which are mainly female!

Another difference in behaviour is that females tend to put more effort than men into keeping a conversation going by giving supportive feedback (for example, *yeah*, *mhm*) and asking questions (McCormick 1994b: 1357). For example, one of the earliest studies (which has only just been published as Hirschman 1994) compared two men and two women talking to each other in all possible pairings, and found that the women used *mhm* (two syllables, first low in pitch then high) thirty-three times as often as the men! This feedback can involve interruptions, which are just as frequent in single-sex groups among women as among men, but the reasons for interrupting seem to be fundamentally different for the two sexes, because when males and females are together males interrupt women far more often than the other way round (Zimmerman and West 1975, quoted in McCormick 1994: 1357). One interpretation of these findings is that males use interruptions in order to assert their dominance, and in the absence of a better alternative we have to accept this.

Males and females seem to be different even in the things they talk about. This is not just a matter of general topics such as football versus families, but of the people discussed. An easy way of measuring these differences is to count the pronouns used. In the early study mentioned above (Hirschman 1994), the women used *we* and *you* far more than the men, who tended to prefer *I*. In other words, the women tended to include the person addressed among the people discussed, whereas the men tended to focus on themselves. The research in this area is still frustratingly sparse, so we cannot yet be sure to what extent findings like these are typical; but if they are, they raise important social and moral questions (especially for us males!)

These general conclusions are very easy to integrate into the framework of ideas that we are gradually building. Everyone has to pay attention to face, both solidarity-face and power-face, but males and females strike different balances between the two. Females give priority to solidarity and concentrate on building and maintaining the social bonds that hold communities together; for males, priority goes to power, the struggle for independence. These differences put females at a disadvantage in the world of work (at least as it has been developed by males), and males at a disadvantage in the family and other important places where relationships are at a premium; and they are a potential source of misunderstanding wherever males and females have to communicate. These conclusions may be vastly too simple, or even wrong, but the issues that they try to summarise are obviously of enormous importance and interest.

5
The quantitative study of speech

5.1 Introduction

5.1.1 The scope of quantitative studies of speech

For some sociolinguists the work we shall be describing in this chapter *is* sociolinguistics (see, for example, Trudgill 1978: 11), though the value of the work covered in the preceding chapters is generally acknowledged. The development of quantitative studies of speech has coincided with that of sociolingustics and, for many linguists whose main interest is the structure of language, this part of sociolinguistics apparently makes the most relevant contribution, providing new data which need to be reconciled with current linguistic theories.

Quantitative studies of speech seem particularly relevant to theoretical linguistics because they involve precisely those aspects of language – sounds, word-forms and constructions – which theoretical linguists consider central. In chapter 2 we discussed the notion 'speech variety', covering the notions 'language', 'dialect' and 'register', but many theoretical linguists think that these concepts are not problematic, and therefore not particularly important. In chapter 3 we explored the relations of language to culture and thought, an area that theoretical linguists have traditionally left to anthropologists and psychologists. Chapter 4 was about discourse, and showed (among other things) that speakers match their speech to fit the needs of the occasion. The aspects of speech referred to were mainly on the fringe of what many linguists would call language structure – vocatives, greetings, alternative pronoun-forms and so on, not to mention non-verbal behaviour. Not surprisingly, perhaps, many linguists believe that discourse-markers are the concern only of specialists in discourse.

The work that we shall review in the present chapter is much more central to the theory of language structure as traditionally conceived. It is based largely on familiar languages, especially English, even though the varieties studied tend to be non-standard; and it is concerned with variations in the form of words and constructions, topics which are at the heart of structural linguistics.

144

For instance, there are some speakers who never give words like *house* and *hit* an [h], in contrast with other speakers who always do, so presumably these two groups of speakers have different language systems, one with an element [h], and the other without it. But for many speakers, the [h] comes and goes in such words – sometimes *house* has [h], at other times it does not. What are we to make of their language system? And what do we make of the fact that [h] sometimes appears in words like *apple*, where the people who regularly pronounce [h] in *house* and *hit* never have it? Similarly, there have been studies of the rules for making sentences negative. For some people, indefinite noun phrases after a negative *not* contain *any* (*I didn't eat any apples*), for others they contain *no* (*I didn't eat no apples*), and many speakers sometimes apply one rule and sometimes the other. What is the relation between these people's grammars? Exactly what kinds of differences are there between them – for instance, do they differ in morphology, in syntax or in semantics? And how should we allow for the people who alternate between the two systems? Questions such as these clearly lie at the heart of theoretical linguistics.

The work we shall be reviewing here is often called 'Labovian sociolinguistics' or 'the Labovian paradigm' (where *paradigm* means something like 'approach') in contrast with 'Chomskian linguistics' and 'the Chomskian paradigm', as the two American linguists William Labov and Noam Chomsky are the main advocates of the two contrasted positions. Let's start with the points of agreement between Labov and Chomsky. They are both linguists, so their main interest is in the   nature of language; Labov himself prefers to describe his work not as sociolinguistics but just as plain linguistics (Labov 1972a: 183–4). Moreover, they both see language as a complex system (with a grammar and a lexicon whose structures can be investigated); indeed, at one time Labov accepted many of Chomsky's theories about language structure and used them in his own work (Labov 1972a, 1972b). For both of them, linguistics is a search for theoretical explanations rather than for mere facts, and both expect theories to be sufficiently general to apply to all languages.

These areas of agreement are very important, and it is quite possible to see their work as complementary rather than conflicting. This view is encouraged by the fact that Labov's main focus of interest is in how languages change, i.e. historical linguistics, which is quite marginal to Chomsky's interest in the nature of language systems – and especially those parts which never change because they are universal. Labov's most recent book is called *Principles of Linguistic Change* (1994), whereas Chomsky has never written at length about change. On the other hand, this interest in historical linguistics does not keep Labov entirely out of the same territory as Chomsky, because one of his main claims is that we cannot understand how languages change unless we have an accurate view of what language systems are like; so most of his work has actually been devoted to the study of living languages, and especially to the study of ordinary colloquial English. This kind of work is what we mean by 'Labovian socio-linguistics'.

The most obvious difference between them is over questions of method: what kind of data should we use as evidence, and what kinds of patterns should we pay attention to? They agree that for most purposes we can trust native speakers' judgments (Labov 1975: 31); for example, if you want to know the past tense of *wash*, you can probably trust any native speaker of English (including yourself, if you are one). But what about the cases where you can't trust native speakers (for example, because different speakers give different answers, or because you suspect they are biased)? Chomsky has not really addressed the question, but Labov has (especially in Labov 1972a: ch. 8), and his most general answer is that we should use as many different methods as possible, preferring results which are supported by them all. He has himself used a lot of different methods, but the family of methods described below are the core of the 'Labovian paradigm'. In a nutshell, the data are examples of ordinary speech produced (as far as possible) under ordinary conditions, and the patterns studied include quantitative patterns – i.e. how often various linguistic forms are used. This chapter will expand the nutshell somewhat, but Milroy 1987 is a reliable and much more thorough review.

We can start with some general comments on how this work is carried out. In some respects the work is just a continuation of a long line of careful studies of dialectologists (surveyed in Sankoff 1973) and phoneticians. As in this earlier work, investigators focus on a predetermined list of LINGUISTIC VARIABLES – elements which are known in advance to have different realisations, such as words which have more than one pronunciation (*house* with or without [h], *either* starting with [i:] or with [ai] and so on). For each variable, there is a list of its VARIANTS – the alternative forms known to be used – and the investigator goes through a collection of data noting which variants were used for each variable in the list.

The aim of this branch of sociolinguistics, like that of the 'dialect geography' branch of dialectology, is explicitly *comparative* – to compare texts or people with one another. Each predetermined variable provides a separate dimension on which texts may be compared. For instance, we might have a hundred tape-recordings of different people talking in similar circumstances, and a list of ten linguistic variables for which we know different people use different variants. When we have gone through the tapes identifying the variants for each variable, we can group the speakers on the basis of their use of variants – distinguishing for instance between people who use [h] in words like *house* and those who do not, between those who use *any* and those who use *no* after a negative, and so on. (Section 5.3 will show that the distinctions are not in fact so straightforward, but this complication can be ignored for the time being.) These groupings are similar in function to the dialect geographer's isoglosses (2.3.1) and (like iso-glosses) typically *do not coincide with one another*. That is, it is unlikely that a hundred speakers will fall into precisely, or even approximately, the same groupings on the basis of any two of the different variables, just as it is unlikely that two different isoglosses will follow the same route.

It should be clear that this way of studying linguistic variables in texts is pre-cisely what is demanded by the view of language which has emerged from the previous chapters of this book, which have shown that individual speakers choose among the available variants of all the available variables in order to locate themselves in a highly complex multi-dimensional social space. We have seen many examples of different linguistic variables which reflect different social contrasts. For instance, in the sentence *John'll be extremely narked*, each word except *be* relates to a different dimension in this social space: *John* (rather than, say, *Mr Brown*) locates the speaker relative to John, *'ll* (rather than *will*) locates the occasion on the casual–formal dimension, *extremely* locates the speaker (I assume) on the educated–uneducated dimension, and *narked* (a regionalism meaning 'angry') locates the speaker regionally. In some cases it may be fairly safe to use speakers' introspective judgments as evidence for distinguishing these different variables, but ultimately it should be possible to test any hypoth-esis formed in this way against what is found in texts. This is the purpose of studying texts – to test hypotheses about relations among linguistic and social variables. The fact that as investigators we start with a predetermined list of lin-guistic variables and their variants shows that we expect the variants in this list actually to occur in texts of the sort collected, and we also generally start with a range of hypotheses about the social variables to which the linguistic variables are related, such as region, social class or sex. All the work reported here is based on such hypotheses, and could hardly have been carried out without them.

On the other hand, the study of texts is very time-consuming, and for purely practical reasons the studies carried out so far have concentrated on linguistic variables which occur relatively frequently and which are relatively easy to iden-tify. The frequency requirement tends to rule out the study of individual words, except for those like pronouns which occur very frequently; and instead of studying, say, how the word *house* is pronounced one asks how words spelt with *h* are pronounced, i.e. each of the linguistic variables tends to include a whole class of words (though we shall note a number of studies which have treated individual words with interesting results). The frequency requirement also rules out many syntactic constructions, since those which are known to vary may only occur a few times each day (or week!) in the speech of a given person. The other criterion, that variables should be easy to identify, favours cases where it is clear that two forms are just different ways of saying the same thing such as alternative pronunciations of the same word. The two criteria may conflict – for example, individual words are good variables in that they are easy to identify, but poor from the point of view of frequency – and most instances of this type of work represent a compromise which has weaknesses of one kind or another. However, there is no doubt (as I hope to show in this chapter) that the method has given rise to interesting and important results.

It is necessary, at this point, to mention the notation that is commonly used in the literature. Linguistic variables are given within parentheses: (h) would therefore represent the variable presence or absence of [h] in words like *house*, and (*no/any*) might be used as the name of the variable involved in *I didn't eat any/ no apples*. We shall extend this convention by writing the name of a particular variant after the name of the variable concerned, separated by a colon. Thus, cases of the (h) variable where [h] is pronounced would be written (h):[h], in contrast with cases where it was absent, written (h):ø ('ø' is the symbol normally used in linguistics to represent 'zero' – i.e. the absence of some element).

5.1.2 Why study speech quantitatively?

If each text contained instances of only one variant for each variable, then it could be located in the relevant multi-dimensional linguistic space without using quantitative methods. For instance, if we were investigating (h) and (*no/any*) in a number of texts, we might (conceivably) find that some of the texts contained instances of (h):[h], but no instances of (h):ø, and that the other texts contained (h):ø, but no instances of (h):[h]; and similarly for the two variants of (*no/any*). In this case, each variable would define just two clearly distinct groups of texts, and the only complexity would be in the interaction between the two variables – on the basis of what we know about most English-speaking communities, we might expect (h):[h] to tend to occur in the same texts as (*no/any*):*any* and (h):ø to occur with (*no/any*):*no*, i.e. we might expect to find sentences like *We didn't see no 'ouses* and *We didn't see any houses*, but we might be less sure about *We didn't see no houses* and *We didn't see any 'ouses*. The study of a large number of texts would give us some indication of the extent to which these two linguistic variables are sensitive to the same social variables. If we found that (h):[h] was always found in the same texts as (*no/ any*):*any*, and that (h):ø and (*no/any*):*no* always occurred in the same texts, then we should be justified in concluding that both the linguistic variables were in fact sensitive to precisely the same social variable. Having come to this conclusion, we might then look at the social background to the texts, so far as we knew it, and try to decide what this social variable was. Let us imagine that we found that all the texts with (h):[h] and (*no/any*):*any* were produced by people who were paid by their employers once a month (whom we might call 'middle class', for short) and all the others by weekly wage earners ('working class'). It would then be reasonable to conclude that the relevant social variable was social class, a conclusion that could be reached without any use of quantitative mathematical techniques.

Of course, the sociolinguistic world is not like this at all. Different variants of the same variable do occur together in the same text, and texts can be arranged on a continuous scale according to how *often* each variant occurs. For instance, in a study of the use of negatives by various groups of adolescents in the United States, Labov found that (*no/any*):*no* and (*no/any*):*any* occurred together in many of the texts he collected, with (*no/any*):*no* accounting for between about 80 and 100 per cent of the cases, according to the text (Labov 1972b: 181). Similarly, Peter Trudgill studied (h) in Norwich (England), and found that (h):[h] made up between 40 and 100 per cent of the occurrences of (h), according to the text concerned (Trudgill 1974: 131). The *relations* between different linguistic variables are also a matter of degree, some being more closely related than others; and the same is true of relations between linguistic and social variables. It is rare indeed to find any linguistic variable whose variations *exactly* match those of any other linguistic or social variable, though it is common to find variables which match each other sufficiently closely to convince one that there is some kind of causal connection between them. Furthermore, social variables themselves are typically continuous rather than discrete – people are more or less wealthy, or manly, or educated, rather than falling into clearly discrete (and internally homogeneous) social groups.

All these facts call for a quantitative treatment of the data, using appropriate statistical techniques. Labov is undoubtedly the leader in this field, but he was not in fact the first person to study linguistic variables in a community. The 'classic' study was done at the start of the century by Louis Gauchat in a Swiss village, where he found clear differences between individual speakers (Gauchat 1905); he listed the variants used by each speaker, but he could not collect continuous texts so there are no text-based frequencies, only figures on how many people used which variants.

The same is true of another study in a very different part of the world, Tokyo (Kindaichi 1942, reported in Shibatani 1990: 171). This broke new ground in a number of ways, but perhaps the most interesting is that it was done in a city (in contrast with traditional rural dialectology) and was designed so as to study the effect on language of sex and social class, two of the most important social distinctions which later work has recognised. Kindaichi focussed on just one linguistic variable – the pronunciation of the phoneme /g/ in the middle of a word (for example, /kago/, 'card'). The traditional pronunciation is [ŋ] (a velar nasal, like the /n/ in *finger*) but having noticed that young people in Tokyo were replacing this by [g] he set out to study the pronunciation of seventy high-school students by getting them to read a list of words while he noted their pronunciation. Even this very unsophisticated method produced results which confirmed his observations, and showed that the change was being led by middle-class girls.

Somewhat later the same technique was used (independently of Labov) in two American studies. The first of these was in a 'semi-rural' community in New England, and focussed on how children pronounced the *ing* suffix in words like *talking*, with [n] or [ŋ] (Fischer 1958); it turned out that the latter pronunciation was used more by girls than by boys, more by 'model' boys than by 'typical' boys, and more in formal situations than in informal ones. The second study was in North Carolina, focussing on the presence or absence of [r] in words like *car* and *card* (Levine and Crockett 1966); the results showed that most people sometimes pronounced the [r] and sometimes didn't, but more interestingly, they showed that the effect of social class was clear, but complicated. High social status was linked both to the use of [r] and to its non-use, suggesting the coexistence in this community of two competing standards.

This then is the intellectual background to Labov's earliest work, starting with the research that he did for his Masters dissertation in the island of Martha's Vineyard off the New England coast (1963). Perhaps the most obvious difference between Labov's work and the earlier studies is that he used a tape-recorder to record continuous speech; this may seem a trivial matter of technology, but he himself has often said how important this change was, because for the first time it became possible to make a permanent recording of ordinary speech. This in turn made it possible to ask how consistent speakers are in their speech, rather than assuming that their one pronunciation of a word in a word-list is the only one they ever use. The use of tape-recorders is central to the Labovian research paradigm, which the next section describes in more detail.

5.2   Methodology

5.2.1   Problems of methodology

Methodology is both important and problematic at all stages in a sociolinguistic text study. The stages in such a study are:

(1)   selecting speakers, circumstances and linguistic variables;
(2)   collecting the texts;

150

(3) identifying the linguistic variables and their variants in the texts;
(4) processing the figures;
(5) interpreting the results.

The stages inevitably follow in the order stated, but there is usually some cyclicity involving one or two small-scale pilot studies before the main study. Moreover, all the texts need not be collected before processing starts, nor need all the variables be identified before the figures for some of them are processed. The order in which operations are carried out is less important than the methods applied at each stage.

(1) The *selection* of speakers, circumstances and linguistic variables involves some extremely important decisions, which are to a certain extent dictated by the expected results. For instance, we might start with the hypothesis that men and women in a particular community differ in their use of a particular set of linguistic variables, and that older and younger members of the same community differ with respect to some other set. In order to test these hypotheses, we clearly need to have speakers who represent all four possible combinations of age and sex, but we also need to make sure that other factors do not interfere with the results. For instance, if all the men selected were manual workers and all the women were 'white-collar' professionals, linguistic differences between them might result either from their occupation or from their sex, and no firm conclusion could be reached. Similarly, it is important that all the speech should be collected under the same circumstances, so far as this is possible.

There is a major problem of definition at this stage, both for the social variables and for the linguistic variables themselves. How do we define 'manual worker'? How do we distinguish 'old' from 'young'? How do we define circumstances precisely enough to keep them constant? How do we define the (h) variable? (If we define it with reference to orthography, then we should (wrongly) expect (h):[h] in words like *hour*; if we define it with reference to 'standard' speech, this presupposes that we can define 'standard' speech and can decide, for instance, whether *horizon* and *hotel* contain [h] in standard speech and so on.) For that matter, how do we define [h] and ø, the variants of (h)? (That is, how much of a puff of breath does there have to be before we recognise an [h]?) Worse still, there are major problems in defining the community to be studied, since 'speech communities' are not self-defining, as we saw in 2.1.4. There are no easy answers to any of these questions, but somehow the would-be researcher has to provide solutions which are at least reasonably satisfactory, to avoid the real danger that the results will be valueless because of ambiguities in defining the variables.

One of the problems of any research is that the value of the results depends to a great extent on the accuracy of the initial predictions. Suppose some linguistic variable is in fact sensitive to the speaker's age, but the researcher thinks the relevant factor is social class, not age. On this assumption the speakers might just as well all be from the same age-group – or, worse still, their age simply doesn't matter and need not be controlled. A collection of speakers based on social class will certainly not throw much light on the sociolinguistics of the variable concerned, and the research risks being a waste of time. A sensitive researcher may be able to avoid such a gross mistake, but it is much harder to avoid biasing the results in more subtle ways. To take an easy example, if the speaker's age is relevant, how should speakers be grouped by age? Should the main cut-off points be around twenty, forty and sixty, or thirty, fifty and seventy (or some completely different pattern)? There is no general solution of these problems, which are in any case shared by any kind of data-based research; but what everyone agrees is that false hypothesis is better than no hypothesis at all. A good researcher starts with an open mind (maybe the pet hypothesis will turn out to be wrong), but not with an empty one!

(2) After a decision has been reached as to what speakers will be appropriate under what circumstances, the *collection* of texts necessitates finding appropriate speakers who are willing to participate. Typically, this means finding people willing to be interviewed and recorded for about an hour in their homes, but many alternatives are described in the literature. This may mean gaining the confidence of a group of people and then obtaining their permission to tape-record them talking under otherwise ordinary circumstances (or the particularly ingenious alternative described on page 156). One practical problem is how to obtain tape-recordings which are sufficiently clear to be used later for identifying phonetic variants, without allowing the recorder to dominate the scene so much that it converts the conversation into the equivalent of a radio interview, thereby losing any chance of tapping the speaker's most natural kind of speech. There are no simple solutions, but with ingenuity (one of Labov's most noticeable characteristics) a satisfactory compromise can usually be found.

(3) The *identification* of variants of the selected variables is the stage where one might expect the least difficulty, since we already know what the variants to be distinguished are, and all we need do is listen for them. However, there is a considerable degree of subjectivity in recognising phonetic variants (as opposed to 'higher-level' variants like (*no/any*)), and different researchers can produce different analyses of the same text, even when they are all highly trained phoneticians (Knowles 1978).

One may also need to record information about the linguistic environment in which each instance of a variable is used, since this often influences the choice of one variant rather than another (see 5.4.1), but this is only possible if there is already a clear hypothesis as to which aspects of that environment are relevant. There may also be problems in identifying the linguistic environments – for instance, we may want to distinguish between cases where (h) occurs after a word-boundary (for example, *house*) and where it occurs within a word (for example, *behind*), but then have difficulty in deciding whether or not there is a word-boundary before the (h) in *greenhouse* and *summer-house*. Yet another problem at this stage is that it can be hard to decide which words or constructions should count as instances of some variable – we alluded to this problem briefly in connection with (h) (should *hour* be treated as an instance?), but it arises with virtually every variable and leads to problems in interpreting the results as we shall see in 5.5.1.

(4) The *processing* of the figures involves counting the number of identified occurrences of each variant in each text, and comparing the figures for different texts. The obvious first step is to reduce all the figures to percentages, since this makes comparison much easier. For instance, it is much easier to compare '80 per cent (h):[h]' and '65 per cent (h):[h]' with one another than to compare '73 out of 91 (h):[h]' and '97 out of 150 (h):[h]'.

The next step is to discover which differences between texts are statistically significant – i.e. roughly speaking which need to be taken seriously. Some differences are so small that they can easily be explained by chance, and no other explanation is needed. For example, if I toss a coin ten times and it lands four times one way up and six times the other, we need not assume that the coin is biassed; even a perfectly balanced coin, without any bias whatever, will not necessarily share its landings exactly evenly between the two sides. Statistical tests tell us when a difference really does need to be explained, and generally give a result which is a number between 0 and 1. This is the probability that the difference concerned could arise by chance, with 0 as absolute impossibility and 1 as absolute certainty; for example, $p = 0.05$ means that the difference has a probability of 0.05, meaning that it is likely to occur by chance five times in every hundred experiments or samples. The greater the difference, the lower its probability and (of course), vice versa. Social scientists tend to take 0.05 as a threshold; a difference with a probability above this figure needs no further explanation.

For example, suppose we have counted all the occurrences of (h) in two texts, A and B, and the results are those in Table 5.1.

Table 5.1

	Raw figure Text A	Text B	Percentages Text A	Text B
(h): [h]	17	20	22	18
(h): ø	60	90	78	82
Total	77	110	100	100

How seriously should we take the rather small percentage differences between the two texts? A standard statistical test (called the chi-squared test) gives a clear answer: not at all seriously. It tells us that the probability of this difference occurring by chance is very high: $p = 0.5$, meaning that any two texts produced by the same person under the same circumstances have a fifty-fifty chance of being as different as this. But suppose these figures were actually based on only a small part of each text, and when we went on counting we produced the figures in Table 5.2, which are all precisely ten times the figures in Table 5.1. The percentages are all exactly the same as in Table 5.1, but this time we have to take even these small differences much more seriously because the chi-square test tells us that $p < 0.05$ (i.e. the probability is less than 0.05). This is because the raw figures are so much bigger; a 4 per cent difference in about a thousand cases is much more significant than the same difference in a hundred or so cases.

This is not the place to learn more about the statistics needed for sociolinguistics, but fortunately there are other books which can be recommended. One is Milroy 1987 (especially pages 134–42), and another is Butler 1985. A novice can read most of the literature without understanding much more than I have just explained; you can trust the author to have sorted the significant from the insignificant, and all you need to understand is what p means. However, the more you understand statistics the better you are prepared not only to evaluate research reports but also to undertake quantitative research of your own.

Table 5.2

	Raw figures Text A	Text B	Percentages Text A	Text B
(h): [h]	170	200	22	18
(h): ø	600	900	78	82
Total	770	110	100	100

(5) The *interpretation* of the results is in some ways the hardest stage of all, and it is certainly the stage where fact and certainty gives way to speculation and uncertainty. But it is of course also the most important stage, because figures are of absolutely no value until interpreted. However, interpretation is itself a process with many stages. It starts with mere description of the patterns that seem to emerge from the analysis, and aims ultimately for an explanation of them in terms of much higher and larger-scale generalisations. At the level of mere description we might be quite confident that speakers A and B are significantly different in their use of (h), but the same on some other variable such as (some/any). This is a worthwhile finding, but not very valuable unless we can generalise beyond these speakers and these variables. Why are A and B different? Is it because they are socially different in some way (for example, in terms of social class)? To answer this we need to see if this social difference generally goes with this particular linguistic difference. And why should (h) be sensitive to this difference when (some/any) is not? And why should this particular social difference be at all relevant to language anyway? And for that matter, why should /h/ be variable when, say, /m/ is not? And so on and on. There is probably no limit to the questions we can ask, and it is no surprise to learn that as yet we have very few firm answers to even the lower-level questions. We shall consider some of the most general questions in chapter 7, so we need say no more about them in this chapter.

5.2.2   *An example: New York*

To give an idea of the range of methodology, we shall consider five separate pieces of work based on different methods. They do not represent all the types of work that have been done; for instance, they are all studies of urban communities, whereas some work has been done (especially on creole languages) in rural communities, where the problems and methods are somewhat different. The first example is included mainly to illustrate the personal ingenuity of William Labov (1972a: ch. 2).

Labov's first empirical work, carried out in 1961 on a small island off the New England coast (called Martha's Vineyard), demonstrated the existence of systematic differences between speakers in their use of certain linguistic variables (1972a: chs. 1 and 7), after which he worked in a very different kind of community in New York. The latter work mainly consisted of individual interviews with selected speakers, of the kind described in 5.2.3, but it was preceded by a preliminary study in which the data were collected in just a few hours and which is a classic example of the method of *rapid anonymous observation*.

Labov wanted to test some hypotheses which he had already formulated about the use of a single linguistic variable, (r), in New York. This variable had been studied in North Carolina (5.1.2), and represents the presence or absence – (r):[r] versus (r):ø – of a consonantal /r/ sound in words like *farm* and *fair*, where the next sound is not a vowel in the same word (as in *very* or *red*). He was aware that New Yorkers sometimes use one variant and sometimes the other, which was of particular interest because the choice seemed to represent a change currently taking place, as New Yorkers moved from the previous norm of consistent (r):ø (as in British RP) towards a new and relatively consistent (r):[r] (as in many other United States accents). (The study of linguistic changes currently taking place has been one of Labov's recurrent interests ever since his Martha's Vineyard work; see Bynon 1977: ch. 5 and Labov 1994.) Labov predicted that the proportion of (r):ø would be highest in the speech of older people (since (r):[r] is an innovation in New York), and of lower-status people (since the new standard, (r):[r], is the result of influence from the high-status community outside New York). He further predicted that (r):ø would be most frequent when speakers were paying least attention to their speech, since they would then be worrying less about how their hearers were assessing their social status; and finally that the linguistic context of (r) would influence the variant used, (r):ø being favoured more by a following consonant than by a following word-boundary as could be predicted on general phonetic grounds from the widespread tendency to simplify consonant clusters.

The method used to collect data was very simple, but exactly suited the hypotheses to be tested. Labov walked round three New York department stores asking shop-assistants where some goods were that he in fact knew to be on the fourth floor. Predictably, each assistant would answer 'Fourth floor' 'or 'On the fourth floor'. He would then lean forward and pretend not to have heard the first answer, thus making the assistant say it again. By selecting the words *fourth* and *floor* he was able to test the hypothesis about the influence of linguistic context, because the (r) is followed by a consonant in *fourth* but not in *floor*. By asking for the answer to be repeated, he could test the hypothesis that the amount of attention to speech was relevant, since the assistant would clearly be more careful about the second utterance. The hypothesis about the influence of age could easily be tested by making a rough guess at the age of each assistant. Finally, Labov could test the hypothesis about social status by comparing the stores with each other, since they served different clienteles and could be ranked from high status (Saks, Fifth Avenue), through middle status (Macy's) to low status (S. Klein). This ranking could be made on the basis of a number of easy criteria, such as the prices of their goods and the newspapers in which they advertised. Within each store further distinctions could be made among the assistants according to their jobs – between floorwalkers, salesstaff and stockboys – and even between different floors within each store, since higher-status goods are generally stocked on higher floors.

The method of recording was to note the relevant details about each assistant secretly after the encounter, so that none of them realised that they were taking part in linguistic research. A weakness of the method is that it requires an investigator who is not only a good phonetician but also an actor. Its great strength, however, is its speed and effectiveness: in just six and a half hours Labov collected 'texts' from 264 subjects and identified the variants (stages B and C)!

When the figures were processed they confirmed most of Labov's hypotheses. Figure 5.1, for instance, shows the percent of (r) realised as (r):[r] for each word, taking 'first' and 'second' utterances separately in each of the stores. As predicted, the use of (r):[r] decreased from high-status to low-status store, as witness the general decrease in height of the columns from left to right. Similarly, the hypothesis about the influence of attention to speech is confirmed by the tendency for the column labelled '11' to be longer than that labelled '1' for each store, except that there was virtually no change between first and

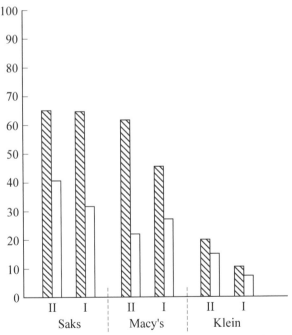

Figure 5.1 New York (r). Percentage of (r): [r] in first (I) and second (II) utterances of *fourth* (white) and *floor* (hatched) by assistants in three department stores (based on Labov 1972a: 52)

second utterance of *floor* in Saks, and a decrease of (r):[r] between first and second utterance of *fourth* in Macy's. Before seeking an explanation for such deviations, however, it is important to find out whether or not they are statistically significant. No statistical tests have in fact been applied to these figures, so we cannot know whether it is more likely that the deviations are due simply to random fluctuation or that there actually is some reason for them. There is clear support for the hypothesis that *fourth* and *floor* are different, since the white columns are consistently shorter than the hatched ones, i.e. the percentage of (r):[r] in *floor* is consistently higher than in *fourth*, as Labov predicted.

The hypothesis which was not confirmed in a direct and simply way was the one about age. It will be recalled that the original hypothesis was simply that older people would use the earlier variant, (r):ø, more than the younger people, who would favour the innovating form, (r):[r]. The relevant figures (see Figure 5.2) show that the hypothesis is confirmed for the high-status store, Saks and data for Klein are at least not too hard to reconcile with the hypothesis, since the slight rise between the middle-aged and the elderly may be insignificant. (Incidentally, it should be pointed out that the percentages shown in Figure 5.2 are not quite comparable with those in Figure 5.1, since they show the proportion of *assistants* in each group who used (r):[r] in both occurrences of both words, whereas Figure 5.1 shows the percentage of *utterances* of each word which contained (r):[r]; however, this difference is irrelevant for present purposes.) The problem is that the figures for Macy's show a clear trend but the trend is in the wrong direction, showing that at that store older people used (r):[r] considerably more than younger ones. This finding goes counter to Labov's hypothesis, and led him to revise the hypothesis in an interesting way by restricting it to people in the highest- and lowest-status groups. According to the revised hypothesis, these groups would be least likely to change their accents after adolescence, in contrast with the intermediate ones whose social aspirations might lead them to change accents in middle age in order to be more similar to the latest prestige accent. This is a clear example of the 'interpretation' stage of research, where the researcher goes beyond the processed figures and relates them to a general theory. The revised hypothesis was later tested and confirmed in Labov's main study of New York (Labov 1972a: ch. 5).

The study itself was replicated much later (in 1986) by Joy Fowler, using exactly the same methods as Labov (but replacing the low-status store by another one, because Klein had gone out of business). Her results were almost identical to Labov's (Labov 1994: 86ff.), except that the overall level of use of (r):[r] was about 10 per cent higher, showing that the new standard had increased its influence in the intervening twenty years. Labov comments that

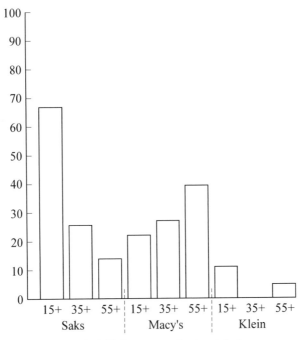

Figure 5.2 New York (r). Percentage of assistants in three age-groups and three stores using (r):[r] consistently (based on Labov 1972a: 59)

the speed of change has actually been somewhat slower than he had predicted after his work in the 1960s, but in other respects the later work supports his earlier work to a very impressive degree.

5.2.3 An example: Norwich

Another investigation, carried out in England by Peter Trudgill, provides an example of the 'classical Labovian method', using *structured interviews* (Trudgill 1974). The town selected was Norwich, of which Trudgill is a native – a fact which is highly relevant, since he not only had a good deal of 'inside' knowledge about the social structure of Norwich and its accent, but could use a Norwich accent himself when conducting the interviews, thereby encouraging speakers to speak more naturally than they might have done had he used RP. It is important to emphasise this kind of fact, since the influence of the interviewer's own speech on the interviewee is a potential problem when using formal interviews for collecting data.

The selection of speakers was carefully planned, taking account of what was already known about the social structure of Norwich. Four areas were first selected as representing different types of housing and a range of social status, then individuals were randomly selected from the electoral registers of these four areas and contacted at their homes to ask them to agree to be interviewed. Most were willing (only fifteen out of ninety-five people approached refused), but some had to be rejected for various reasons, such as that they had only moved into Norwich within the previous ten years. People who refused or were rejected were replaced at random by others, until a total of fifty adults who were willing and eligible had been identified. To these Trudgill added ten school children to broaden the age range, making sixty interviews in all. This may seem a small number on which to base general conclusions about the overall patterns of the 160,000 inhabitants of Norwich, but such a sample is statistically adequate to give a broad picture of patterns of variation, provided one does not want to take account of too many different social factors or to make too fine a set of discriminations. It is unrealistic to aim at very large samples because it takes so long to process the data collected (in contrast, say, with the data collected by market researchers). Lesley Milroy (1987: 21–2) points out that the most successful studies based on structured interviews have used fewer than a hundred speakers, and increasing the number of speakers tends to be counterproductive – the analytical work increases without much improvement in the results.

The circumstances under which speakers were to perform also needed to be selected. The preselection of speakers itself served to choose the circumstances, since a formal interview was the only feasible way to obtain the extensive data that was wanted. However, Trudgill followed Labov in structuring the interview so that it included a number of different types of circumstances. Most of the interview followed the usual pattern of an interview with a stranger, and could be expected to elicit a relatively formal style of speech. At one point the interviewee was asked to read a passage of continuous prose and a list of words, on the assumption that reading would produce a more formal style still, in which even more attention would be paid to speech. At other points, however, the interviewees' speech moved towards a less formal style – such as when interrupted by another family member, or asked to talk about a time when they had had a good laugh. Trudgill, following Labov, claims that there are a number of 'channel cues', such as a change in tempo or pitch-range, which can be used to identify this less formal type of speech, so that each interview could be divided (unequally) into four 'styles': 'casual' (identified by the channel cues), 'formal' (the bulk of the interview), 'reading-passage' and 'word-list'. These categories may be taken to represent part of the repertoire of accents available to the speaker for use under different circumstances.

The linguistic variables were selected in advance from what was already known about variation in Norwich. A total of sixteen variables was selected for study (three consonants and thirteen vowels), each of which showed a different pattern of variation. We shall look here at just one variable, (ng), the two pronunciations of the *ing* suffix which seem to apply throughout the English-speaking world. (It will be recalled that one of the first quantitative studies was a study of this variable in New England – see 5.1.2.)

There are two variants, (ng):[n] and (ng):[ŋ], of which (ng):[ŋ] is the one generally considered to represent standard English and RP, so we might predict in advance that (ng):[ŋ] will be used more often by high-status speakers than by low-status speakers, and more often under circumstances which draw attention to speech.

Trudgill's findings (Figure 5.3) clearly confirm these two hypotheses. Each of the five histograms (i.e. groups of columns) represents the average scores for one group of speakers defined in terms of a variety of factors: occupation, income, education, housing, locality and father's occupation (Trudgill 1974: 36). Taken together, these factors are used to define a hierarchy of socio-economic classes. We shall have more to say later (5.4.2) about this kind of categorisation of speakers, but for the present they may be accepted as representing a hierarchy based on status. The findings confirm the hypothesis that (ng):[ŋ] is used more often by high-status people. Indeed, we can go further and make the hypothesis rather more precise: the use of (ng):[ŋ] in *casual* speech is below 20 per cent for members of the three 'working-class' groups of speakers, and above 60 per cent for members of the two 'middle-class' groups.

The hypothesis about the effect of the amount of attention paid to speech is also confirmed by the general rise in the proportion of (ng):[ŋ] from the 'casual' to 'word-list' styles. However, for middle-class speakers the main difference is between casual and formal styles, whilst for working-class speakers it is between formal and reading-passage styles. This raises interesting problems of interpretation, since it suggests that (at least with respect to this particular variable) middle-class speakers are sensitive to differences in the formality of what might be called unscripted conversation (using this term to cover both casual and formal styles), whereas working-class speakers are not, but are very sensitive indeed to differences between unscripted conversation and reading. If this hypothesis is true, could it be generalised to cover all variables, and not just (ng)? Some of the other variables show a somewhat similar pattern so the hypothesis looks reasonably promising, but it can be refined. There is no way in which the middle-class speakers could have increased their use of (ng):[ŋ] in reading compared with unscripted conversation, as they already used it nearly all the time, so it is possible that they are in

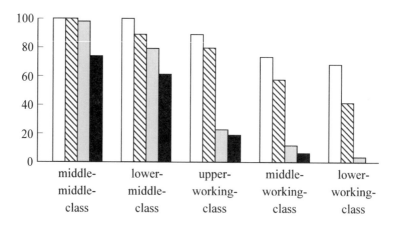

Figure 5.3 Norwich (ng). Proportion of (ng):[ŋ] in speech of five socio-economic classes in four styles: word-list (white), reading-passage (hatched), formal (dotted), casual (solid) (based on Trudgill 1947: 92)

principle just as sensitive as working-class speakers to differences between unscripted conversation and reading, and that their use of standard variants will be higher in the latter than in the former on variables where there is room for an increase. Just such a pattern is found in one of the other variables, the pronunciation of /t/ (which varies between standard [t] or [tʰ] and the non-standard glottal stop [ʔ] or [tʔ]): middle-class speakers increased their use of standard (t)[t] when reading just as sharply as working-class speakers did (Trudgill 1974: 96). On the other hand, even for middle-class speakers, there was very little change for the (t) variable between casual and formal styles, which seems to refute the first part of the hypothesis. Moreover, some other variables seem to show very little change at all between styles within any group of speakers, although different groups of speakers differ clearly in their use of those variables.

So far as Norwich is concerned, one must conclude (with Trudgill) that the influence of style differs according to (1) the linguistic variable in question, (2) the socio-economic class of the speaker, and (3) the particular style-differences in question, with differences within unscripted conversation not necessarily in step with those between unscripted conversation and reading. The problem remains how to fit such findings into a general explanatory theory, but there is little doubt that we should not even have been aware that a problem existed without such quantitative studies of carefully collected data.

5.2.4   An example: Belfast

The third investigation that we shall describe here is that by James and Lesley Milroy in Belfast, Northern Ireland, reported in Milroy (1980). The methods used are quite different from those of the classical Labovian approach, as exemplified by Trudgill's Norwich study, but rather similar to those used in the late 1960s by Labov himself in studies of the speech of black American adolescents (see especially Labov 1972b: ch. 7).

The main difference between the Milroys' work and that of Trudgill reported above is that Lesley Milroy, who did most of the field-work, was accepted as a friend by the groups whose speech she studied, which made it unnecessary to use the formal interview technique. This had the great attraction of allowing her to study genuinely casual speech, as used between friends, because the researcher's presence did not increase the formality of the situation. However 'casual' a stranger may try to be, an interview remains an interview, and there is no guarantee that what Labov and Trudgill referred to as 'casual' speech is at all close to the most relaxed speech of the speakers concerned. Another advantage of the method is that it opens new and exciting possibilities for the theoretical interpretation of sociolinguistic data. By becoming a friend, the investigator becomes part of a *network* of relations among the people being investigated, and can use the structure of this network as social data to which speech may be related. We shall return to this point below (5.4.3).

Before starting their research, the Milroys decided not to try to cover a complete spectrum of the socio-economic classes, but to exclude this dimension and concentrate on the speech of working-class people in Belfast. Three specific working-class areas were selected, all typical 'decayed core working-class areas with a high incidence of unemployment and other kinds of social malaise'. Behind these similarities, however, there were important differences between the areas. Two were unambiguously Protestant and one Catholic, and in one of the Protestant areas (Ballymacarrett) the traditional local industry, the ship-yard, was still employing local men, whereas the traditional employer of men in the other Protestant area (the Hammer) and the Catholic area (the Clonard) was the linen industry, which has declined, leaving men either unemployed or travelling outside the area to work. We shall see later that this difference in employment patterns is highly relevant to speech differences.

Within each area Lesley Milroy gradually built up a relationship with a particular group of people by being passed on from one to another as a 'friend of a friend' – a well-recognised status in this community, which confers a status almost equivalent to that of a member of the family. Of course, building and maintaining a large number of friendships makes heavy demands on a researcher's time and energy (not to mention courage and tact in a strife-ridden city like Belfast), and such research is not for the armchair sociologist. As a result of these efforts Lesley Milroy became accepted as a friend who could 'drop in' at certain houses at any time, to sit in the kitchen listening or taking part in the conversation for as long as she wanted and even to use her tape-recorder after explaining that she was interested in Belfast speech. Under such circumstances it seems unlikely that her presence, or even that of the tape-recorder, affected the way in which people spoke.

The Milroys processed these recordings in much the same way as Trudgill, identifying variants of a predetermined list of variables and comparing their frequencies across texts. The main interest of their findings is the light which they throw on the effect of the social network structure on speech, which will be discussed later in relation to the various social correlates of variations in speech (see 5.4.3).

5.2.5   An example: Cardiff

Our fourth example is a research project which was carried out in Cardiff, the capital of Wales, by Nikolas Coupland (1980, 1984, 1988). It will illustrate an important general principle which emerges from all these examples: the data-collection method should fit the question being investigated. No good research starts without a clear question, or set of questions, and different questions require different kinds of data, produced by different methods. In this case, the question with which Coupland started was: do we speak differently to different people? This possibility had been suggested by social psychologists in terms of a theory called 'Accommodation Theory' (Giles 1994), according to which we tend to 'accommodate' our speech to the speech of the people we are talking to, in the hope that they will like us more for doing so. Coupland's aim was to test this prediction by finding a situation in which one person spoke to a wide variety of people, of different types and speaking in different ways. If the theory was right, that person's own speech ought to vary accordingly. What Coupland needed, then, was just one person whose speech could be observed over time as they spoke to a variety of other people.

The speaker who Coupland chose was an assistant in a travel agency in the middle of Cardiff – a woman called Sue. She knew that he was interested in talk at work, and agreed to have a microphone located in front of her position at the counter, in the belief that Coupland was primarily interested in the speech of her customers. The customers did not know about the microphone, of course, which raised the ethical question of confidentiality, so Coupland (who was sitting in a corner of the shop) approached each customer as they left, to tell them that they had been recorded. None objected, and none accepted his offer of erasing their part of the tape. Coupland also used this encounter to ask the customers some basic sociological questions about their occupation and education which he later used to classify them. The recording was spread over a number of days, and Sue was given four days to get used to the tape-recorder. The recordings after these first four days produced fifty-one encounters. As one would expect under the circumstances, the individual encounters were short – between two and ten minutes – so there was hardly enough material to calculate figures for individuals. However, by lumping together people of similar social background Coupland managed to produce usable amounts of data on a range of frequent phonological variables. All the interactions took place in English, as Welsh is rarely used in Cardiff.

Sue was an ideal speaker for Coupland's purposes. She interacted with a wide range of people, covering a broad social spectrum, and the interactions involved a lot of speaking because the main commodity offered by a travel agent (unlike most other shops) is information. Furthermore she herself was from Cardiff and varied linguistically in the same way as her customers; and she was tied to a single position in the shop, so a single microphone would record both her speech and that of the customer – an important consideration if the two were to be compared. Another point in her favour was that her job was to relate to the customers in order to attract their business; in other words, she wanted the customers to like her, so if Accommodation Theory was right she would accommodate her speech to them. And lastly she was at her post for the whole day, so a large number of interactions could be recorded in a short time – a great benefit from Coupland's point of view. The example shows how ingenuity at the planning stage can produce data for a major research project in a matter of days rather than months.

The results confirmed Accommodation Theory, though not as simply as one might expect. There were two variables which were as predicted, where Sue's usage 'tracked' that of her customers quite closely: the more standard the customer's usage, the more standard Sue's usage. One of these variables was the (ng) variable that Trudgill studied in Norwich, but the other was a local Cardiff variable, (VtV), the pronunciation of /t/ between vowels (either as in RP or as a 'tap', sounding rather like a [d]). However the remaining variables showed less clear covariation between Sue's speech and that of her customers, which suggests that she may have (unconsciously) selected just these two variables for use in accommodation. If we think of accommodation as a way of reducing social distance, i.e. as a strategy for protecting solidarity-face, there is no reason to expect accommodation on every single variable; a few variables might well be singled out for accommodation, for use alongside the various other solidarity-supporting strategies that we have considered such as greetings and address-forms. This prediction is confirmed by a separate study by

Trudgill himself, who studied his own pronunciation (as interviewer) in his Norwich interviews (1983a: ch. 1). On the variable (t) his pronunciation tracked the interviewee's almost exactly, but on (a:) it was completely constant in spite of enormous differences from one interviewee to another.

As Coupland points out (1984: 65, 1988: 138ff.), his research leaves open an important question: was Sue accommodating linguistically or socially? Did accommodation consist in (1) making her speech more similar to her clients' speech – linguistic accommodation – or in (2) matching her social status (as indicated by her speech) to their social status – social accommodation? The two theories are distinguished in Figure 5.4 which shows two speakers accommodating to each other (shown by the extended 'equals' signs). Each produces speech (the string of x's) which implies a certain type of person (shown by the non-speaking figures), and presumably their aim in accommodating is to reduce the differences between these social types, as shown by the equals sign labelled 'social accommodation'. The theoretical question is whether this necessarily means that they make their speech more similar as well, involving the link labelled 'linguistic accommodation'. The two theories make very different predictions in cases where the speakers have different ways of locating themselves socially. What would Sue have done, for instance, if one of her customers had come from a different part of Britain (for example, from Birmingham)? Would she have started using Birmingham features in her own speech (linguistic accommodation) or would she have shifted towards their social class while staying within the Cardiff system (social accommodation)? At present we can only guess, but it is easy to imagine a research project which could answer the question.

5.2.6 An example: Detroit

Our last example takes us back to the United States, where Penelope Eckert did research in the early 1980s at a secondary school in the suburbs of Detroit which she calls 'Belten High' (1988, 1989, 1991, 1994). This example earns its place because of the interesting way in which it asks what social structures are relevant to language in this community, rather than assuming that we know the answer in advance. As in the earlier examples, it is impressive because of the researcher's clear view of the questions to be researched.

The population of Belten High is almost entirely white (unlike many Detroit schools), but Eckert found it to be deeply divided. Apart from the expected male–female division, there is a split (which applies to both sexes) between two polarised groups who are known (throughout the school) as the 'Jocks' and the 'Burnouts'. The Jocks are the 'good' pupils, who identify with the school; they

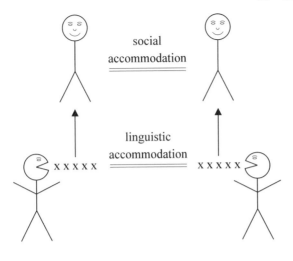

Figure 5.4

are the ones who do sport (hence their name), who support the out-of-hours activities at school, and who generally accept the school's values and culture. Most of their friends are within the same class of Belten High. The Burnouts are the exact opposite; instead of doing sport, they take drugs; instead of staying for school societies they leave the premises as soon as possible; and instead of accepting the school's culture, they reject it. Their life revolves around the world outside school, which is where they find many of their friends. These differences are made visible in many ways. The two groups dress differently, behave differently (for example, even the way they stand when waiting is different), and frequent different parts of the school. According to Eckert, the same polarisation is found in all American secondary schools, though the polarised groups have different names in other schools.

Eckert's research involved the 'ethnographic' methods which we described briefly in 4.1.1, and which were developed by anthropologists for studying unfamiliar societies. The researcher spends a lot of time in the society, as a 'participant observer', but the aim is not simply to study the things that can easily be observed. Rather, it is to understand the underlying system of ideas, values and so on, in much the same way that a linguist probes the underlying system of rules that lies behind the observable patterns of speech. In other words, the ethnographer tries to discover what makes members of the society 'tick'. This is what Eckert did – she spent two years in the school as an ethnographer (not as a teacher), watching the pupils, chatting to them and even interviewing them about their life in and out of school. She focussed on one year-group of

600 during their last two years at school and interviewed 118 of them. The following extract gives the flavour of the interviews:

> Yeah, burnouts get hassled, quite a bit. More than jocks. Sam got kicked out for getting in too much trouble. I mean, he used to get caught every day smoking in junior high. So he sort of got kicked out and Mike, I just, I don't know what happened to him. I think he just dropped out for the heck of it. Because they're pretty much bad burnouts from Detroit. So they don't really care. (Eckert 1991: 21)

These interviews provided ethnographic data as well as linguistic data, and allowed her to classify all her speakers according to the Jock–Burnout split as well as according to more conventional social-class distinctions based on their parents' occupation and so on. She found that only a third of the pupils were willing to identify themselves unambiguously either as Jocks or as Burnouts, but all the others recognised the groupings and could say how they related to them. Most pupils called themselves simply 'In-betweens', with some degree of allegiance to one or the other of the polarised types. As one might expect, the Jocks tended to come from middle-class families and the Burnouts from working-class families; but the link was sufficiently weak to allow Eckert to ask which classification was the more important in matters of language. Were sociolinguistic variables more closely related to the speaker's social class background, or to the Jock–Burnout contrast? According to Eckert , the best match is with the Jock–Burnout contrast. More precisely, this was true of the variables that she studied, though she could not of course study all possible variables to check whether any showed the opposite tendency.

The importance of this piece of research lies in the clear way in which it shows the dangers of taking social parameters for granted. Most previous studies had related linguistic variation to sex, age and social class, but Eckert showed how important it is to find out how the local community is organised socially rather than to impose these crude 'external' categories. In this case the local community is Belten High, and the most important social distinction is clearly the one between Jocks and Burnouts – a distinction which is only relevant to secondary schools, and maybe only to those in the United States. On the other hand, this distinction is also different from the local network structures that Milroy explored in her three communities in Belfast. The latter were based on social relationships among individuals, but the Jock–Burnout division is more a matter of ideology and life-style; two people with identical views and life-styles could belong to completely different social networks, but not to different groups on the Jock–Burnout contrast; and two Jocks need not know each other or interact at all. No doubt there were social networks in Belten High that were relevant to language but, without denying this possibility, Eckert has demonstrated that broad social 'types' (for example, 'Jock') are linguistically relevant as well. In 7.2 we shall see the importance of distinguishing clearly between groupings based on social types and those based on networks.

5.3   Linguistic variables
5.3.1   *Types of variable*

A variable is a collection of alternatives which have something in common. Most of the examples we have considered so far have been collections of alternative sounds which can be substituted for one another without changing the meaning of the word – for example, (ng) brings together the velar and alveolar nasals as alternative endings for the suffix -*ing*. Variables of this kind call out for a sociolinguistic explanation precisely because no other kind of explanation is relevant. In contrast, the difference between the same two sounds at the end of *sing* and *sin* is irrelevant to sociolinguistics because it can already be explained perfectly satisfactorily in terms of lexical items: these two forms belong to two different lexical items, each with its own meaning, syntax and so on. Once we understand these lexical differences it is obvious why we use *sing* on one occasion, and *sin* on another: because we choose our words to suit the meanings that we want to express. Similarly, sociolinguistics is irrelevant to the choice between *sing* and *sings* if this choice is already covered by the ordinary rules of grammar (*I sing* or *they sing*, but *she sings* or *John sings*), even though *sing* and *sings* both seem to have the same meaning. Linguists can handle these things satisfactorily without mentioning social context and social variables. For convenience, then, we can call linguistic variables that require a sociolinguistic explanation 'sociolinguistic variables'.

It may seem that this notion of sociolinguistic variables includes everything that sociolinguists might want to study, and in particular anything that we might want to count in texts; but this is not so. As we shall see in the next subsection, one of the essential characteristics of a typical sociolinguistic variable is that all of its variants can be recognised, and counted. For (r), there are two variants, [r] and ø (nothing). We can hear (r):[r] when it is used, and in principle we know when (r):ø occurs because we know which words could have contained (r):[r] (though we shall see below that even this is an oversimplification). When we hear *fourth floor* pronounced without any [r], we know there have been two occurrences of (r):ø, but we (obviously) don't recognise (r):ø every time we fail to hear [r]. But what about a socially sensitive word like *sir* (as in *Here you are, sir*)? Can we recognise a sociolinguistic variable (sir) whose variants are *sir* and nothing? If so, we must be able to decide on which occasions (sir):ø has occurred; but this decision would be virtually impossible to make since we do not know in which sentence-types or situations *sir* can be used. Unfortunately the same is true of all greetings, farewells, politeness forms, address-forms (for example, *John* in *Here you are, John*) and so on – in short, the parts of language that are the exclusive territory of sociolinguists. Until we understand these forms well enough to be able to predict exactly where they might have been used (but weren't) we cannot study them in terms of sociolinguistic variables. If we want to count them, the best we can do is to count their use in relation to some crude measure such as the total number of words or clauses.

What kinds of sociolinguistic variables are there? We can distinguish different types according to the level of language (phonetics, phonology, morphology, lexicon, syntax) at which the variants are *different*. Using this as the basis for classification, we may recognise the following theoretical possibilities:

- *Phonetic variables*, where the same phonological pattern has different phonetic realisations. These are uncontroversial, and examples abound in the literature. For example, the English phoneme /t/ has a range of alternative pronunciations (glottal stop, an r-like flap, a d-like tap, alveolar stop, alveolar aspirate with an s-like ending and so on), all of which count as pronunciations of the same phoneme.

- *Phonological variables*, where the same lexical item has alternative phonological structures. These too are uncontroversial and examples range from those which affect single lexical items (for example, *controversy* with stress on the first or second syllable) to large-scale differences which involve whole classes of lexical item such as those like *house* and *happy* with or without /h/.

- *Morphological variables*, where the same word has alternative morphological structures (defined in terms of roots and affixes). These certainly exist as well, as witness well-known examples like the presence or absence of the suffix -*s* on present-tense verbs in places like Norwich (where the local form is *she sing*, but people who use this also sometimes use the standard form *she sings*; see Trudgill 1990: 94). In some cases it is hard to decide whether a variable is morphological or phonological – for example, standard *did* is matched in most other dialects of English by *done*, but are these alternatives different in morphology as well as in phonology? Fortunately this uncertainty does not matter in our present state of ignorance but it may turn out to be important in the future.

• *Lexical variables*, where the same meaning can be expressed by two different lexical items – in other words, where two lexical items are at least partial synonyms. For example, compound pronouns like *nobody* and *somebody* seem to have exactly the same meaning as the corresponding forms with *-one* (*no one, someone*, etc.), but (as we shall see in 5.4.5) we prefer the *-body* forms in speech and the *-one* forms in writing (Edwards 1994). Similarly, traditional dialectology has always assumed that pairs like *sidewalk* and *pavement* are genuine synonyms. Lexical variables are particularly important in distinguishing registers, as illustrated in 2.4.1 by my example where *salt* and *get* were presented as alternatives to *sodium chloride* and *obtain*.

However, there are two reasons why this is a much more difficult area to research in terms of sociolinguistic variables. Lexical variables are tied to specific meanings which are unlikely to be expressed over and over again in a typical one-hour interview, so that much larger quantities of text are needed as a basis for quantitative generalisations. And secondly, word meanings are related in complex and subtle ways which can make it hard to decide whether the meanings of two words are the 'same' or 'different'. For instance, the meaning of *get* is much broader than that of *obtain* (for example, you can get a letter or a cold, but you can only obtain something that you intend to obtain); so the sentence *We got some salt* has a less specific meaning than *We obtained some salt*. This being so, there are two alternative explanations for the choice between them: the sociolinguistic explanation refers to style-levels (*got* is less formal than *obtained*) but the semantic explanation refers to generality of meaning (*got* is less specific than *obtained*). If we found the sentence *We obtained some salt* in a text, either or both of these explanations could be right. A similar example that has been discussed in print is the choice between *one* and *you* in sentences like *One/you never know(s) what might happen*, and similar contrasts in other languages; the debate is summarised conveniently in Fasold 1990: 254. But the point is that lexical variables are much less straightforward than variables at lower levels.

• *Syntactic variables*, where the same meaning is expressed by different syntactic structures. As in the case of lexical variables there are clear and agreed examples, but there is also a great deal of uncertainty (Milroy 1987: 150ff., Hudson forthcoming). One of

Labov's most influential (and impressive) articles, was 'Negative attraction and negative concord' (1972b), about pairs like *Nobody saw it* and *Didn't nobody see it*, which are clearly different in their syntax but express the same meaning. Another clear example of a syntactic variable is the range of patterns found at the start of English relative clauses, which may be introduced by *that*, by a wh-pronoun such as *who* or *which*, or by nothing at all (compare *the book that I bought, the book which I bought, the book I bought*). These are clearly alternative syntactic ways of expressing the same meaning, and occur frequently enough in texts to produce usable figures (Romaine 1980, 1982, Ball 1993).

Syntax is in fact rich in synonymous constructions, but the problem for the sociolinguist is that other disciplines may be able to offer better explanations for how we choose among them; or worse still, that a complete explanation may involve some (as yet unknown) combination of sociolinguistics with other disciplines. The most relevant other disciplines are psycholinguistics and discourse analysis. Suppose we have a text containing the sentence *The criminal was apprehended by a policeman who happened to be passing at the time*, whose content could also have been expressed by *A policeman who happened to be passing at the time apprehended the criminal*. This active/passive choice has to be explained, but how? A sociolinguist might try to relate the use of the passive to style level (passives being relatively formal), a psycholinguist might relate it to processing load (the sentence is easier to read with the long phrase about the policeman at the end) and a discourse analyst might relate it to the writer's choice of the criminal as the topic, i.e. as what the sentence is about. The most likely answer is that all three explanations are right: considerations of style, of processing difficulty and of topicality all conspire to encourage the use of the passive. A fundamental question for future research is what happens when the pressures conflict. Does one of these different pressures always win out, and if so, which? In the meantime, sociolinguists can legitimately treat such cases as sociolinguistic variables, while bearing in mind that their account may only be a partial one, and perhaps even a subordinate one.

This completes our survey of the types of sociolinguistic variable. However, the fact remains that most of the variation that has been studied by sociolinguists has been phonetic or phonological, which we can lump together as 'pronunciation variables'. The reason for this is simple: they are the most frequent in texts. An interview which produced a handful of examples of a syntactic variable might produce several hundred examples of the most common pronunciation variables. We therefore finish this survey by looking in a little more detail at some problems that arise in the study of pronunciation variables.

One particularly serious problem has already been hinted at: the problem of deciding which words are relevant to each variable. We can use the very simple (h) variable to illustrate the problem. Imagine that some speaker S has pronounced the word *house* without [h], giving [aus]. Can we be sure that this is an example of (h): ø? It is an example if, and only if, the same word could have contained [h], but how do we decide that? Is it enough to find some speakers who (sometimes) say [haus], or do we need evidence that this particular speaker (S) sometimes says [haus]? The answer depends on what we think variables are.

If we think of them as a real part of each speaker's linguistic competence, defining genuine choice-points in their speech, then other people's behaviour is strictly irrelevant. For S, *house* may be as irrelevant as *hour* or *honour* – or even *out*. Whatever other people do, S may not see *house* as a word that starts, should start or even can start, with [h]. There is good evidence that such speakers exist: overcorrections such as [hi:t] for *eat* (for example, [h]if that 'appens, I'll [h]eat my 'at) show that their users simply do not know which words have [h] in RP, and are scattering [h] randomly among words that start with a vowel when they try to 'talk posh'. But this simple fact has dreadful consequences for practical research, if we want variables to be psychologically real. It means that we must first carry out an impossibly ambitious research project on each individual in our sample, in order to find which words they can pronounce with [h] (and likewise for every other variable we may wish to study). Armed with the individual's vocabulary list, we can then ignore any words in which they never use [h], thereby guaranteeing that our figures really do show the proportion of real choices that they make in favour of each variant. The result would be wonderfully clean data, but of course there is a fundamental flaw in this programme: it is simply impossible because the individual inventories would take too long.

For practical purposes, then, we need an alternative which produces less pure figures in a realistic amount of time. In this approach variables are simply analytical tools to help us to detect quantitative patterns. In practice variables tend to be defined by the standard, prestige accent, for the simple reason that investigators tend to know this well; so anyone studying the (h) variable would probably assume that it applies to every word that contains [h] in RP, and in particular to the word *house* regardless of who says it. The figures for some speakers will reflect psychological choices directly; these are the speakers whose personal competence has an RP-like distribution of [h] among words. For other speakers, though, the observed figures require a completely different interpretation, not in terms of choices between [h] and ø but in terms of the words which allow [h]. To take an extreme case we could have two speakers who both use 50 per cent (h): [h], but for quite different reasons. For one speaker the vocabulary is like RP, and 50 per cent of potential aitches are dropped; for the other, in contrast, far fewer words offer an opportunity for using (h), so the figure of 50 per cent could even show that only 50 per cent of words that have [h] in RP also have it in that speaker's vocabulary, but that the speaker chose to pronounce every single possible [h]. It is easy to imagine other possible interpretations. In short, when we count the same range of words as relevant for every speaker in order to make data-analysis possible, we double the uncertainty at the stage of interpretation.

Apart from problems of defining the variables themselves, there are others in listing the variants for any given variable, including the question of *discreteness*. It is hard to think of any variables which do not raise this problem to some degree, but it looms particularly large in the case of vowels. For instance, one of Trudgill's variables in the Norwich study was (aː), the vowel in words like *after*, *cart* and *path* (Trudgill 1974: 87). This vowel varies in Norwich from a back [ɑː] to a very front low vowel [aː]. Trudgill recognises one intermediate value between these two extremes, which he transcribes [ɑ̈ː~ä ː], but this is presumably a matter of convenience rather than a division determined in some way by the facts of Norwich pronunciation. We can assume that there is a continuum between [ɑ̈ː] and [a ː], any division of which is at best arbitrary, and at worst misleading if it distorts the results. For instance, if a simple two-way distinction had been made, without any intermediate stage, it would have given the impression that Norwich speakers always locate their pronunciations of this variable at one extreme or the other, without providing any way of investigating the possibility that they also use the intermediate forms. The same problem arises even with variables like (h), which appears at first to refer simply to the presence or absence of some sound-segment, whereas [h] may be present to different degrees, just as the (aː) vowel may be pronounced with different degrees of 'backness' in the mouth.

Another problem concerns *dimensions* (see especially Knowles 1978 and Milroy 1987: 122–5). The last paragraph gave the impression that the (aː) variable involved only a single phonetic dimension, namely frontness/backness, but Trudgill's transcription involves a second dimension of nasal/oral, since the front variant (though not the back and central ones) may or may not be nasalised [ãː]. Trudgill groups [aː] and [ãː] together as instances of the same variant, so there is no way of finding from his analysis whether they were used by different kinds of people or under different circumstances, and we must assume that Trudgill was sure in advance that they were not. One could fairly object that this was something of which he could not have been sure until he had made the full analysis, but the Labovian system of analysis forces one to reduce all the phonetic dimensions on which variants may differ to a single dimension, represented by a single ordered list of variants. (We shall see why this is so in 5.3.2.)

The problems become even more acute where a larger number of phonetic variables are involved, as in the Belfast (a) variable (see Milroy 1980 and Milroy 1987: 121), which is the vowel in words like *bag, back, fat, man* and *fast*. This has the following range of variants: the local prestige form associated with middle-class speakers is [a], but among working-class speakers [ɛ] (i.e. relatively raised and fronted) is used before velar consonants (*bag, back*), while other contexts show a variant further back than [a], and also sometimes raised, with or without a centring off-glide, giving for instance [ɔ·ə]. The interest of this example is not only that several different phonetic contrasts are involved (front/back, low/raised, with/without off-glide), but that it is hard to see how the variants could be reduced to a single ordered list on phonetic grounds, since there are no obvious extreme sounds to provide end-points for the lists. There are extremes, of course, but too many of them, since [a], [ɛ] and [ɔ·ə] could all justifiably be treated as extremes. The problem is that the Labovian method requires a single ordered list of variants, whereas a triangular pattern, like the one for Belfast (a), cannot be reduced to such a list.

5.3.2   *Calculating scores for texts*

The classical Labovian approach offers an attractively simple method for assigning scores to texts, as a way of showing similarities and differences between speakers' use of linguistic variables, but we shall see that it also has serious weaknesses. A score is calculated for each variable in each part of the collected data (for example, all of a particular speaker's output in one style), which we shall call a 'text'. This allows texts to be compared with respect to one variable at a time, which is the prime aim of quantitative studies of texts. To calculate the text scores for a given variable, a score is assigned to each of its variants; the score for any text is then the average of all the individual scores for the variants in that text. To take a simple example, let us say we have a variable with three variants, A, B and C, and we have calculated the score as 1 for each instance of A, 2 for each B and 3 for each C. Now assume that we have a text containing twelve A's, twenty-three B's and seventy-five C's. We calculate the text score by calculating the scores for all the A's (12 × 1 = 12), all the B's (23 × 2 = 46), and all the C's (75 × 3 = 225), then adding all these together (12 + 46 + 225 = 283) and dividing the answer by the total number of variants found (12 + 23 + 75 = 110), giving 283 ÷ 110 = 2.57. This is the score for this variable for the text concerned, and it will of course be easy to compare directly with scores for this same variable for other texts.

This method has two weaknesses when applied to variables that have more than two variants. The first is to do with the RANKING of variants, on which we touched in 5.3.2. Assigning separate scores to individual variants (1 for an A, 2 for a B and so on) has to be based on some kind of principle, otherwise the results may be nonsense. Scoring is not simply arbitrary, since the apparent relations among texts could be completely changed by using a different scoring system. The problem arises where there are three or more variants, since the scoring system reflects a particular *ordering* of the variants, with two variants picked out as maximally different and the others arranged between them as intermediate values. This means that whenever three or more variants are recognised on a single variable, the analyst has to be able to pick out two of them as the extremes and to arrange the remainder between them. This can be done on the basis of the phonetic relations among the variants if the variants can be arranged on some phonetic dimension such as vowel height. However, we have seen that this is by no means always the case – there may be more than one such dimension involved – so the phonetic facts do not tell the researcher how to order the variants. Another basis for ordering is the social prestige of the variants, which allows the most standard and the least standard variant to be picked out as the extremes and the others ranked in between according to relative 'standardness'. The problem with this approach is that it assumes in advance that society is organised in a single hierarchy reflected by linguistic variables, whereas this often turns out not to be true, so the method biasses the research towards incorrect conclusions.

A more serious weakness of the Labovian scoring system is connected with the balance among the variants, since the final figure for a text gives no idea of the relative contributions made by individual variants. A score of 2 for a text in our hypothetical case could reflect the use of nothing but B (scoring 2 each time it occurs), or of nothing but A and C, in equal numbers, with no instances of B at all. Let us take an actual example, using data from a study of the (r) variable in Edinburgh by Suzanne Romaine (1978). This study is unusual in providing separate figures for individual variants, rather than aggregate scores for the whole variable. The variable (r), like the one which Labov studied in New York, applies to words containing an *r* (in the written form) not followed by a vowel in the same word. However, these particular figures apply only to (r) occurring at the end of a word, and show the influence of the linguistic context: whether the word is followed by a pause, or by another word beginning either with a consonant or a vowel. The variants are not quite the same as those distinguished by Labov, since there are two possible types of consonantal constriction for (r) in Edinburgh, a frictionless continuant, as in RP and most American accents [ɹ], and a flapped [r]. Table 5.3 shows how these two variants, plus the zero variant (ø), were distributed among the three contexts, with some quite complex patterns of influence. A following vowel greatly favours the flapped [r] in comparison with either of the other variants, but other contexts favour both consonantal variants about equally, though the zero variant is more popular before a pause than before a consonant. If the figures in this table were reduced to text scores in the usual way, most of this information would be lost. Say we score 1 for [r], 2 for [ɹ] and 3 for ø, the average score would be 1.34 for (r) before a vowel, 1.72 before a consonant and 1.94 before a pause. From this we might guess that [r] is more common before a vowel than before a pause, and perhaps that ø is more common before a pause than before a vowel, but this would be just a guess, and there are many other ways of interpreting the figures, including of course the complex interpretation they in fact demand.

It therefore seems preferably not to reduce figures to a single score for each variable, but to keep those for each variant separate, as percentages of the total cases where the variable occurred, so making it unnecessary to assign separate scores to variants, and also solving the problem of ranking.

5.3.3 Calculating scores for individuals and groups

In a sociolinguistic study of texts, the investigator has material produced by different individuals, and often more than one text from each, produced in different circumstances (as in the case of Trudgill's tape-recordings, where each interview comprised four different texts, one for each style). A typical research project might involve the study of ten variables in the speech of sixty people under four types of circumstances, producing 10 × 60 × 4 = 2,400 separate scores for texts if the classical Labovian method were used, and a much larger figure if the alternative of quoting separate scores

Table 5.3 *Edinburgh (r): three variants as percentages of (r) in three linguistic contexts (based on Romaine 1978: 149).*

	Before vowel	Before consonant	Before pause
[r]	70	40	34
[ɹ]	26	48	38
ø	4	12	28

for individual variants were adopted. The problem is how to handle such a large amount of data without being swamped.

One strategy is to reduce the number of figures by producing averages for groups of individuals. For instance, if we can reduce sixty speakers to eight groups defined, say, by sex and socio-economic class, we immediately reduce the total number of figures from the 2,400 given above to 320, i.e. just thirty-two figures for each variable taken on its own. Moreover, the number of cases covered by each of the figures is increased, since each score for a variable will represent a whole group of speakers instead of a single one. This has the advantage of increasing the statistical significance of any differences between scores, since this depends not only on the size of the difference but also on the number of cases involved. There are thus great gains from merging separate figures into averages. All the actual figures quoted so far (Figures 5.1–5.3, Table 5.3) have been group averages and not scores for individual speakers. This is typical of the literature, where it is in fact rare to find figures for individual speakers. However, the practice of reducing individual figures to group scores has two regrettable consequences, rather similar to those that stem from reducing variant scores to variable scores.

A reliance on group scores alone conceals the amount of variation within each group. A group score of, say, 2 for some variable ranging from 1 to 3 could be produced either by all the members of the group having scores very close to 2, or by some scoring 1 and others 3. In the former case, the group average of 2 represents a norm round which the speech of the group members clusters, whereas it is completely meaningless or misleading in the second case. There is no way of knowing whether any given group average is meaningful or not without some indication of the amount of variation within the group. This variation can be measured accurately as the 'standard deviation', which is low when there is little variation and rapidly increases in size with increasing variability in the group of figures. The kind of pattern which may be found where variation is small within groups is shown in Table 5.4, demonstrating that predefined groups of speakers may turn out to be remarkably homogeneous as far as their speech patterns are concerned (in contrast with the case illustrated in Table 5.5).

The figures in Table 5.4 were collected by Labovian interviews with forty speakers of Persian in Teheran (see Jahangiri 1980). The variable is concerned with the assimilation of one vowel to another in the following syllable in words like /bekon/ 'Do!', whose first vowel varies between [e] (unassimilated) and [o] (assimilated). Each figure represents the percentage of assimilated vowels in the speech of one speaker, and the speakers are arranged in eight columns, each representing a separate group. The groups are defined on the basis of

Table 5.4   *Teheran Persian vowel-assimilation: percentage of vowels assimilated in the casual speech of forty speakers in eight groups based on education and sex.*

Sex:	Male				Female			
Education:	univ.	second.	prim.	none	univ.	second.	prim.	none
Scores:	7	24	46	71	5	21	33	55
	12	28	48	77	5	22	38	60
	13	32	53	81	6	23	39	67
	14	36	56	81	6	28	43	68
	18	41	57	82	6	29	48	73
Average:	13	32	52	78	6	24	40	65
Standard deviation:	3	6	4	4	0	3	5	6

education (university, secondary, only primary or none at all) and sex. The pattern in Table 5.4 is unusually clear, which makes it helpfully simple as an introductory example. (The next example will compensate by showing a more typically messy pattern.) The low standard deviations, in the bottom row, show how homogeneous the groups are; indeed the group of university-educated females has virtually no deviation at all, which is remarkable considering how tiny even 1 per cent deviation is in human behaviour. Another notable fact about these figures is how distinct the groups are; in fact, if we take each sex separately, the scores for different groups do not overlap *at all*, suggesting that this variable is a very important signal of educational level, on which men and women set different 'thresholds'. For example, a female with only primary education sounds different from females with either secondary education or no education at all, but similar to a male with secondary education.

Table 5.5 reveals a very different pattern. It is based on a study of the pronunciation of sixteen eleven-year old boys from three different schools in Edinburgh (Reid 1978). The children wore radio microphones while playing in the playground, and the data collected were thus expected to be close to the kind of speech the children used naturally. The three schools were chosen so that each would cover a different range of social backgrounds, but it can be seen that grouping boys according to their school produced very heterogeneous results from the point of view of the (t) variable, with a great deal of overlap between groups. Information about the occupation of the boys' fathers, was also available but even this supposedly more accurate measure of social status

Table 5.5   *Edinburgh (t): percentage of (t) realised as [ʔ] or [ʔt] by sixteen children in 'playground style' (based on Reid 1978: 160).*

School 1	School 2	School 3
30	60	65
69†	80†	71
69†	85	80
100	85	88
100	89	
100	90†	

did not produce much more homogeneous groupings. All the boys from school 1 had fathers classified as 'foremen, skilled manual workers and own account workers other than professionals', with the exception of the two marked with daggers, whose fathers were 'semi-skilled or unskilled manual workers or personal service workers'. The two boys marked with a dagger in the column for school 2 also had fathers in the 'foremen, etc.' class, whereas all the rest were in the class of 'professionals, managers and employers'. Whether we base groups on school, or on father's occupation, or on both, it seems clear that group averages for the use of (t):[ʔ] would be rather meaningless.

The other problem which arises from group scores is related to the first, and in fact arises out of it. If grouping speakers or texts is simply a matter of convenience for the analyst faced by an otherwise unmanageable mass of data, there is probably no problem. No doubt the grouping reveals broad trends in the data which might otherwise be missed. But there is a danger of moving from this position to a very different one, where one believes that society is actually organised in terms of predefined social groupings where everyone belongs clearly to one group and everyone in each group belongs to it to the same extent. One weakness of this view is that it ignores social networks of individuals with more or less strong links to each other, of the kind which the Milroys explored in Belfast (5.2.4). A network analysis cannot be translated into a division into groups, any more than a piece of fishing net can be divided into its constituent parts. Eckert's work in Belten High revealed a different kind of weakness (5.2.6), which is that the social divisions that are relevant (in her case, the division into Jocks, Burnouts and In-betweens) may not be the predefined ones based on social class. And a third weakness, to which we shall return in 5.4.2, is that where social groups are relevant speakers may belong to them to different degrees. Many of the Belten High In-betweens said they were nearer to the Jocks than to the Burnouts (or vice versa), and any classification based on variable measures (such as income or occupation) inevitably involves arbitrary cuts in continuous gradations. One interpretation of this fact is that some of us hover between two groups, but another is that the groups themselves are simply arbitrary cuts in a continuous scale – or worse still, an attempt to reduce a number of different continuous scales to a single discontinuous one.

To summarise this section, we have criticised the Labovian method of identifying variants and calculating scores because it loses too much information which may be important. Information about the use of individual variants is lost when these are merged into variable scores, and information about the speech of individuals is also lost if these are included in group averages. At each stage the method imposes a structure on the data which may be more rigid than was inherent in the data, and to that extent distorts the results – discrete boundaries are imposed on non-discrete phonetic parameters, artificial orderings are used for variants which are related in more than one way, and speakers are assigned to discrete groups when they are actually related to each other in more complex ways.

5.4   Influences on linguistic variables

5.4.1   Linguistic context

This section reviews the kinds of factors which have been found to influence the choice of variants on linguistic variables, starting with the effects of linguistic context. Strictly speaking this is not a matter for sociolinguistics at all, but for a purely 'internal' study of language structure without reference to society. However, linguists interested in relations internal to language have tended not to study texts, but to use introspective methods, so that the quantitative study of the influence of one item on contiguous ones has been left to sociolinguists.

Once again, William Labov was the first to make a detailed study of such patterns, in his study of sentences like *We on tape* and *But everybody not black*, which have nothing at all where we might expect *is* or *are*, and which are often used by black Americans (Labov 1969). Let's call this variable (is), with the variants (is):ø and (is):is (standing for *am* or *are* as well as *is*). He showed that (is):ø is much more likely after a pronoun than after a full noun-phrase, and also much more likely before an ing-form verb (especially *going to*) than before a full noun-phrase (with intermediate frequencies for locative phrases and adjectives). Interestingly, it is also more likely before a consonant than before a vowel, which suggests that it is itself a purely phonological variation (which in turn means that the syntactic structures for these sentences must contain a verb which is not pronounced). Either variant of (is) is possible (and grammatical) whatever comes before and after, but some patterns are much more common than others. These quantitative differences are linguistic facts, but a purely qualitative analysis (in terms of rules that either apply or don't apply) overlooks them completely. We saw another example of the same thing in Table 5.3, which showed that the variants of (r) in Edinburgh were used to different extents in different linguistic contexts. Facts like these pose a serious challenge to all our current theories of syntax and phonology, none of which allow us to say that some patterns are more likely than others. We shall return to this challenge in the last chapter, but for the time being we shall just survey the data that has been gathered.

Probably the most interesting aspect of the study of the linguistic context is the question of *lexical* differences between contexts. It is becoming clear that the probability of a particular variant occurring in a word may depend on what that word is, and not on general phonological or syntactic properties of the word. For example, in Belfast one of the variables is the vowel in words like *pull, put, took* and *could*, which we can call the (ʌ) variable. This varies between [ʌ] (as in RP *cut*) and [ʉ] (similar to RP *put*, but somewhat closer). As part of the analysis of data collected by the Milroys, a list of individual words containing this variable vowel was drawn up, and a score calculated for each word (Maclaren 1976, J. Milroy 1978). The occurrences of words containing (ʌ):[ʌ] (Table 5.6) illustrate the general point that gross differences in the probability of a variant may occur from one word to another which cannot be accounted for in terms of general phonological differences between the words.

The reason why figures such as these are interesting is that they provide support for the theory of LEXICAL DIFFUSION – the theory that a diachronic sound-change may spread gradually through the lexicon of a language, rather

Table 5.6 *Belfast (ʌ): percentage of [ʌ] in eight words (based on Maclaren 1976).*

	Percentage of [ʌ]	Total no. of occurrences
pull	74	69
full	47	32
put	39	309
took	33	148
could	31	266
look	27	191
would	16	541
should	8	59

than affecting all the relevant words at the same time and to the same extent (Labov 1994: ch. 15). There is evidence that the [ʌ] pronunciation of words like *pull* in Belfast is an innovation, so Table 5.6 shows that this innovation has affected different lexical items to different extents. According to J. Milroy (1978), the overall differences in Table 5.6 reflect the fact that some words are given the [ʌ] pronunciation (more or less consistently) by different proportions of the population – three-quarters of their sample of speakers say [pʌl] for *pull*, but less than one in ten says [ʃʌd] for *should*. In other words, for any given speaker each word is in one or the other of two lexical classes, the [ʉ] class and the [ʌ] class, and the change from [ʉ] to [ʌ] involves the gradual transfer of words from the [ʉ] class to the [ʌ] class.

How does the theory of lexical diffusion relate to the wave theory discussed in 2.3.2? According to the latter, changes spread gradually through the population, just as, according to the former, they diffuse through the lexicon, so we might expect a connection between them. A reasonable hypothesis is that changes spread cumulatively through the lexicon at the same time as they spread through the population, so that the words which were affected first by the change will be the first to be adopted in the new pronunciation by other speakers. From Table 5.6 we cannot tell whether this is actually the case – it could be, for example, that the few people who use the new pronunciation of *should* still use the old pronunciation of *pull*, and vice versa, whereas our hypothesis predicts that the new form of *should* will be used by people who use the new form for all the other words in the list as well.

A small amount of evidence in favour of this hypothesis comes from Table 5.7, which relates again to the phenomenon of vowel-assimilation in Teheran Persian. It gives two separate sets of data for six words which are capable of undergoing the process. The figures on the right show how often each word was assimilated in the free speech of all the speakers studied, revealing a gross difference between words like /bekon/ which assimilate nearly every time they are used, and /bebor/ which hardly ever assimilate. The plus signs on the left show which of these words were assimilated by seven selected speakers who were asked to read a list of words which could assimilate. It can be seen that speaker A used assimilated forms for all the words, in contrast with G who assimilated none of them, and that any word assimilated by one speaker would also be assimilated by all those to the left in the hierarchy. (This kind of pattern is known as an 'implicational hierarchy'.) As far as the selected words and speakers are concerned, then, Table 5.7 shows that the innovation of vowel-assimilation is diffusing cumulatively through the lexicon and the population, as predicted by our hypothesis.

Table 5.7   *Teheran Persian vowel-assimilation: use of assimilated forms of six words by seven speakers reading word list, and by all speakers in free speech (based on Jahangiri 1980).*

	Assimilation by seven speakers reading word list							Assimilation in free speech by all speakers	
	A	B	C	D	E	F	G	% assimilated	Total
/bekon/ 'Do!'	+	+	+	+	+	+		91	331
/bedo/ 'Run!'	+	+	+	+	+			78	23
/bexan/ 'Read!'	+	+	+	+				40	139
/begu/ 'Tell!'	+	+	+					22	132
/bekub/ 'Hit!'	+	+						4	122
/bebor/ 'Cut!'	+							3	124

However, it has to be admitted that the words and speakers were specially selected in order to illustrate this point as clearly as possible, and that the pattern for the research as a whole, which used ten speakers who were asked to read sixty words in all, is much messier, suggesting either that the hypothesis is too simple, or that the data are too crude to test it. Labov quotes other data which give a similar picture (1994: 427).

5.4.2   The speaker's group membership

The most obvious source of influence on linguistic variables are the speakers themselves, i.e. the kinds of person they are and the experiences they have had. Various kinds of difference between speakers have been widely and exhaustively studied by sociolinguists, including region of origin or of present home, socio-economic status, sex, race and age. According to the theory of acts of identity, such factors will influence people's speech only to the extent that they represent social groups with which speakers can identify themselves – in other words, what counts is not so much your exposure to a particular variety of speech, but rather your willingness to identify yourself with the kind of person who uses it.

We have already quoted examples of differences due to socio-economic status (pp. 156, 161), age (p. 158) and sex (p. 179), and there is no need to multiply such examples, but two factors have not yet been illustrated and are worth discussing here since they will be relevant to 5.4.3. They are the influence of place and race.

The influence of the *place* where a person lives has been studied by Trudgill (1975/1983), who studied a linguistic variable in southern Norway, the vowel (æ), which varies between [ɛ] and a slightly raised and backed [a]. The latter is an innovation which is currently spreading from the local town, Larvik, to the surrounding region. Larvik is connected by road to a village called Nevlunghamn which is on the opposite side of a peninsula (which is in fact the southern tip of Norway). Trudgill and a Norwegian colleague interviewed people living in selected houses at regular intervals along two lines between Larvik and Nevlunghamn, as well as others living in these towns themselves. Figures for (æ) in the speech of the people interviewed are shown in figure 5.5, in which the horizontal axis represents distance between the towns, the vertical axis represents the proportional use of (æ):[a], and the two lines represent the two routes between the towns. The curves in Figure 5.5 are exactly as we should expect them to be according to the wave theory (2.3.2). The highest scores are in Larvik, where the innovation started, the next highest in Nevlunghamn with its easy road link and regular commercial and other contacts, and the lowest scores are in the homesteads furthest away from either of these centres of influence. We can see how the linguistic influence of Larvik is proportional to the amount of social contact with people in Larvik.

The factor of *race* has been shown to be relevant by Labov and his associates in a study of New York, working on distinctive features of the speech of black adolescents (Labov 1972b: ch. 7). The speech of black, rather than white or other, speakers in the northern states of the United States is distinguished by various patterns of which the most distinctive is (is):ø, discussed in 5.4.1 (for example, *John tired*, 'John is tired'). It appears that whites in the northern states virtually never use (is):ø, whatever their socio-economic status, but whether blacks use it or not, and how often, depends on how close they feel to the black subculture. Evidence for this comes from Labov's study of one particular gang of black teenagers in Harlem, called the Jets. Having established regular contact with this group, he was able to study its internal structure and relations to the other black adolescents in the neighbourhood. By asking who associated with whom, he identified four separate groups: core members of the Jets, secondary members, peripheral members and non-members or 'lames'. When Labov calculated for each of the four groups their (is):ø percentage, he found a steady decline from the core to the edge of the gang. Core Jets scored 45 per cent, secondary Jets 42 per cent, peripheral Jets 26 per cent and lames 21 per cent. (The totals of (is) were respectively 340, 223, 82 and 127, i.e. large enough

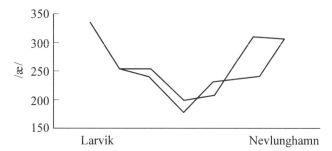

Figure 5.5 Southern Norway (æ): scores for selected households in and between two centres of influence. High score = high incidence of (æ):[a] (based on Trudgill 1975/1983)

samples for the differences to be taken seriously.) This illustrates the way in which linguistic variables may be exploited by speakers as subtle symbols of the extent to which they identify with some group, in this case one based on race. Even the lames identified themselves as black by their occasional use of (is):ø, since whites never use the zero copula, but distanced themselves from the central core of the black community by using it less often than core members.

We have already discussed examples of *socio-economic status* affecting speakers' scores, but now it is necessary to ask some fundamental questions about the concept of 'socio-economic status' itself. First, is it a unitary concept? That is, is there a *single* hierarchy for each society which has a hierarchical structure, to which various factors such as wealth, education and occupation contribute as defining characteristics, or is it just a loose term for a range of different hierarchical structures which are more or less independent of each other – one for wealth, another for education and so on? Most work in sociolinguistics has tended to accept the first position, and has used a single scoring system for speakers based on a variety of factors. For instance, Trudgill took account of occupation, income, education, housing, locality and father's occupation, reducing these factors to a single scale. On the other hand, it is rightly considered an empirical question whether such a procedure is correct, and sociolinguists feel that they have unusually clear data for answering the question, since it reduces to a matter of statistics. Given the scores for speakers in any body of texts and background information about speakers' income, education and so on, which social factors, alone or in combination, provide the best basis for predicting the scores?

Interestingly, Labov himself provided an indication of the answer, namely that different factors are relevant to different variables, which is perhaps what we might expect if society is viewed as a multi-dimensional space in which we locate ourselves. In Labov's main interview-based survey in New York, the best basis for predicting scores for some variables, for example (r), was a combination of occupation, income and education whereas, for others, it was a combination of just education and occupation (Labov 1972a: 115). An instance of the latter kind of variable is (th), pronounced as either [t^h] or [θ] in words like *thing*. Other sociolinguists have produced social hierarchies that correlate remarkably well with the scores for linguistic variables on the basis of just one factor, such as education (Table 5.4). Sociolinguistic data seem therefore to suggest that factors such as occupation and education ought to be recorded separately but allowed to interact with one another, in just the same way that they can interact with factors such as age and sex. In other words, the data give relatively little support to the notion of social status as a unitary phenomenon.

A second fundamental question is whether society can be allocated neatly into separate groups defined on the basis of social status, which we might call 'social classes'. In view of the answer to the first question, it seems unlikely that this is how societies are organised, since the different possible bases for defining the classes are likely to conflict, which means in effect that each criterion defines a different set of classes. Moreover, there is increasing evidence that the notion of discrete groups in society is generally less illuminating than the view that society is organised round a number of distinct focal points, each defining a separate norm for behaviour, and attracting, to varying degrees, allegiance from members of the society. There is no a priori reason why socio-economic classes should constitute an exception to this principle, so the notion of such classes should probably be reinterpreted in terms of focal points rather than discrete entities.

Interesting questions can then be asked in a meaningful way on the basis of sociolinguistic data. In particular, where a variable is sensitive to 'social-status' factors such as education or occupation, do the scores always suggest that the norm-setters are at the extremes of the scale, i.e. are those with the highest or lowest status? This is clearly the case, for instance, with vowel-assimilation in Teheran Persian, where the highest and lowest incidences of assimilation are among the lowest- and highest-status speakers respectively (Table 5.4). Similarly, (ng) polarises society in Norwich into the 'middle-class' norm of (ng):[ŋ] and the 'working-class' norm of (ng):[n] (Figure 5.3). Figures 5.1 and 5.2 suggest a similar interpretation for New York (r).

On the other hand, there are cases in the literature where a norm seems to be defined by a group in the *middle* of the hierachy, supporting the idea that society is not necessarily polarised between 'top' and 'bottom' as far as speech is concerned (Fasold 1990: 233). An example is the variable (e) reported by Trudgill

(1974: 104), which occurs in a rather small class of words like *tell* and *better*, where /ɛ/ is either followed by /l/, or is preceded by a bilabial consonant and followed by /t/ (which must be glottalised) in a stressed penultimate sylla-ble – a nice example of the possible complexity of linguistic variables! The vari-able (e) varies between close [e] and open [ɐ], and the highest incidence of the open variant (which, incidentally, is an innovation in Norwich) is among the *upper*-working-class speakers (Figure 5.6). Middle-class speakers seem to be relatively unaffected by this variant, but both middle- and lower-working-class speakers aspire to it. Interestingly, the middle-working-class speakers actually increased their use of the open variant in formal interview style compared with casual style, although this meant moving *away* from the norm defined by the middle class, whereas the upper-working-class speakers in formal style were moving away from their own norms in the direction of the middle-class one. To make matters even more complex, all speakers from all classes moved towards the middle-class norm when they were reading, abandoning the other norms altogether.

To make sense of these patterns, it seems that we must postulate no fewer than three norms: a middle-class norm (e):[e], a lower-working-class norm, which is phonetically the same as the middle-class one, and an upper-working-class norm (e):[ɐ]. Different norms applied in different circumstances (Figure 5.7). All three norms applied in casual speech, and their influence is shown by the arrows. In formal style, the scope of the influence of the norms changed,

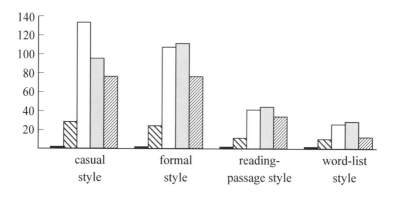

Figure 5.6 Norwich (e): scores for five socio-economic classes and four styles. High score = high incidence of (e):[ɐ]. Classes: middle-middle (solid), lower-middle (hatched), upper-working (white), middle-working (dotted), lower-working (vertical stripes) (based on Trudgill 1974: 105)

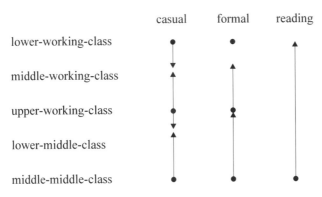

Figure 5.7 Norwich (e). Scope of influence of three norms in three styles

with the middle-class norm now reaching as far as upper-working-class speakers, whereas the lower-working-class norm did not influence any other class. In the reading-styles, only the middle-class norm is operative at all.

To conclude, we have surveyed a number of social factors on the basis of which people may associate themselves with one another – place of origin or home, age, sex, race, various factors involved in socio-economic status, such as education and occupation, and local groupings such as the Jocks and Burnouts of Belten High. Each of these factors may influence people's use of linguistic variables, either directly or in combination with other factors. This is not to say that any one of the factors may be relevant to speech in every society – for instance, in the whole of Australia there appears to be amazingly little variation due to place of origin or of present home (see, for example, Mitchell and Delbridge 1965, Horvath 1985). Nor are these the only factors which can influence speech – they are just those which most sociolinguists have studied, and many other factors, such as politics and religion, are also potential sources of influence. Indeed, it would be unwise at this stage to rule out any social factor at all as a possible source of influence. Why one set of factors is relevant in one community and a different set in another is as yet unexplained. We might guess that the relevant factors are those that, for the community concerned, were the most important from a social point of view, but it is hard to see much support for this hypothesis from the available facts. For instance, religion might be expected to be a source of influence in Northern Ireland, given the importance of religious divisions in that community, yet the Milroys' data do not appear to show significant differences between the Protestant and Catholic areas they studied which could not be explained in other terms. It would be interesting to have explanations for these (and many other) facts which the quantitative study of texts has revealed.

5.4.3   *The speaker's degree of group membership*

This section develops the notion that an individual's use of a linguistic variable depends on the *degree* to which they are influenced by one or more norms in society. We have already looked at some research which gives strong general support to this idea, such as Trudgill's data on the gradual spread of (æ):[a] in Norway and that of Labov on the use of (is):ø by black adolescents in Harlem, in addition to the many examples we have cited of the influence of differences in social status. Lesley Milroy has specifically investigated this aspect of variation, and we shall outline her theoretical interpretation, which fits very easily into the general model of language that has been developing through the previous chapters.

Milroy selected her speakers through personal introductions within a network of contacts, the structures of which allowed her to explore in detail the speakers' social relations (see 5.2.4). The three communities studied were all typical poor working-class areas, and many of the families involved were typically working-class in being part of a 'closed network', i.e. a network of people who have more contacts with other members of the same network than with people outside of it. This affects the *kinds* of relations they have, for, in a traditional working-class area, ties of friendship, work, neighbourhood and kinship all reinforce one another. One effect of belonging to such a closed network is that people are very closely constrained by its behavioural norms and there is consequently little variation between members in their behaviour (or at least in the norms which they accept). This being so, we might expect to find a relatively high degree of conformity in speech, which is one type of behaviour governed by norms. Conversely, people who do not belong to a closed network, or who belong to a network united by fewer types of bond, might be expected to show a relatively low degree of conformity to the speech norms of any closed network. This hypothesis was tested by Milroy against her data, and her findings are reported in Milroy (1980).

Briefly, the hypothesis was confirmed. Some of the people recorded were from extremely closed networks, but others had looser relations to the community. Each speaker was therefore scored for the 'strength' of the network connecting them to the other members – a 'network strength score' (NSS), which was calculated by taking account of five factors, for example, whether or not the person concerned had substantial ties of kinship in the neighbourhood, and whether they worked at the same place as at least two other people from the area. It was then possible to make statistical tests on the scores for linguistic variables to see whether any of them correlated with the speaker's NSS. Many of the variables did so, supporting the hypothesis, but the findings went beyond this.

Five of the eight linguistic variables studied showed an overall correlation with NSS, i.e. were influenced by NSS in all subsections of the communities studied – whereas the other three were influenced by network strength in some subsections, though not in all. This is an impressive finding, especially in view of the fact that the variables studied were not chosen in advance with a view to their relevance to network strength.

Secondly, following from the first point, different sections of the community recognised different ranges of linguistic variables as 'membership badges' of their core network. For instance, one variable, (ai), is only used in this way by people in Ballymacarrett and another, (I), only in the Hammer. Similarly, a third variable (called (Λ^1)) is used only by older people as an index of membership strength. This is not to say that other sections of the community avoid using the variants which are associated with core membership of the network, but only that they do not use the variable as a way of showing their group membership. To illustrate this point we can refer to differences between men and women. On two of the variables , (a) and (th), men used a higher proportion of the 'core' variants overall than women, but men's scores for these variables were less closely correlated with their NSS than women's. There is thus some tendency for men (but not women) to use the core variants often irrespective of how close they are to the core of the community. For a woman, however, a high frequency of core variants is a more reliable indicator that she is near to the core, as measured by the NSS.

Thirdly, it is possible to use the NSS to connect scores on some linguistic variables with known facts about social structure. For instance, there are clear differences between males and females for most of the variables in Belfast (just as there are in many other communities – compare, for instance, the figures for Teheran in Table 5.4), and equally there are differences in NSS, where men generally score higher than women. Since the sex differences on linguistic variables show that men use more of the core variants than women (with one exception to which we shall return), sex differences on the linguistic variables can be *explained* as an automatic consequence of differences on the network-strength variable, and consequently we need no longer postulate sex as an independent social factor influencing this linguistic variable. The question is, then, why men score higher on network strength than women. The theory of networks provides an easy answer: assuming that men go out to work more than women do, and that they work with men from their own neighbourhood, men form more work bonds than women, but have roughly the same number of other bonds.

Overall, therefore, their networks have more bonds and their NSS will thus be higher. The differences in speech can therefore be explained, more or less directly, with reference to differences in employment patterns.

However, if the employment patterns are not like this, and men do not go out to work with others from their neighbourhood any more than women do, speech differences seem to disappear, to judge by the Belfast data. Of the three areas studied, the Clonard has lost its traditional source of male employment, the linen industry, but has stayed relatively undisturbed by the large-scale movement of population which occurred in the other area affected by the decline of the linen industry (the Hammer). The third area, Ballymacarrett, still has a ship-yard to employ its men. Consequently we should expect to find the traditional differences between men and women only in the Ballymacarrett community, while at the other extreme the difference will have been neutralised by the men's loss of local employment. The NSS for the Clonard area confirmed this prediction. Indeed, on the whole women had higher NSS than men in this area, reversing the usual pattern. (It is not clear why the difference should have been reversed, rather than simply neutralised.) The scores for some linguistic variables in the Clonard area also showed that women often used the core variants as often as men (compare, for instance, the figures for the variable (Λ) in Milroy (1980)). Many facts about the Belfast pattern remain to be explained, but at least the use of network strength as a social variable seems to take us a useful step nearer to understanding them.

The three Belfast communities studied by the Milroys were all low-prestige and relatively tightly knit, but of course not everybody belongs to such a community, especially in modern urban society. What norms govern the speech of these others? They may have access to a standard dialect, in which case they are likely to use it because of its prestige. The only thing which might restrain them in accepting this norm is the knowledge that there are other local, less prestigious, ones and that, by accepting the standard, they would be rejecting the others which, for various reasons, may have some value for them. Those who are influenced totally and whole-heartedly by the standard (in Britain, those who speak standard English with an RP accent) may be just as similar to each other in their speech as members of one of the closely knit communities in Belfast, but for quite a different reason: not because they have a dense network of social contacts with each other, but because the norm to which they adhere has been standardised, with all that this implies in terms of codification in grammar books and dictionaries, teaching in schools, use in the media, and so on (see 2.2.2).

People whose norms are provided neither by a closely knit community nor by a standard dialect must, presumably, be able to choose from a wide variety of models, and will themselves contribute yet more models to the world for others to take account of. The community in which they live can therefore be expected to show a relatively high degree of diversity, or *diffusion*, in its linguistic patterns compared with the two other types of community, whose linguistic norms are relatively *focussed* (Le Page and Tabouret-Keller 1985: 115). Linguists have tended to select relatively focussed communities for their studies, and have consequently constructed theories of language which have relatively little room for variability. Even in the small, closely knit communities studied by Milroy, there was a considerable amount of variation in detail, so we may expect relatively gross variation in more diffuse communities. Indeed, it may be fundamentally misguided to look for such a simple link between social cohesion and linguistic homogeneity. This sobering conclusion is suggested by a report on variation in three small Gaelic-speaking villages in East Sutherland, in the north of Scotland (Dorian 1994). It would be hard to imagine communities that were socially more homogeneous, and yet Dorian reports a great deal of apparently random linguistic variation from individual to individual (which we shall discuss again in 7.2.2). One problem in interpreting Dorian's data is that we do not have comparable figures for other in-depth explorations of small communities to give us some standard against which to measure her variation. However, if these communities really are unusually 'diffuse' in their language, the theoretical framework described in this section needs some attention. Maybe, for example, close networks produce focussed language only when part of a larger community offering alternative models?

5.4.4 The speaker's sex

Most quantitative studies have included both male and female speakers and have included their sex among the social attributes by which they are classified. Moreover most studies have also been applied to languages that have a distinction between non-standard and standard forms (linked to some kind of social-status hierarchy). One remarkable pattern has emerged repeatedly in these studies: for virtually every variable, in virtually every community, females (of every age) use high-prestige standard variants more often than males do. (We shall return below to the exceptions.) Let us call this the 'Sex/Prestige Pattern'.

A very clear and simple example of this pattern is in the data in Table 5.4, where figures show the percentage of words in which the Persian speakers used the non-standard (assimilated) form of the prefix *be-*. The only point to understand about these figures is that the higher the score, the less standard is the speech. The table classifies speakers according to their sex and length of education so the differences between males and females cannot be due to differences in education. Each sex/education group contains five speakers. When we compare male and female speakers who have received the same amount of education, we find that the figures for male speakers are nearly all higher (less standard) than those for the corresponding females: university-educated males score between 7 and 18, compared with 5 or 6 for university-educated females; of those without any education at all, males score 71–82 but females scored 55–73 and so on. Only four of the twenty females have scores that overlap those of the equally-educated males, and the group averages for females are all between 7 and 13 percentage points lower than those for the equivalent males.

This example is perhaps unusual in its clarity, but the Sex/Prestige Pattern has been found in so many other studies, conducted in so many different societies, that we must take it as one of the most robust findings of sociolinguistics (or, indeed, of the whole of linguistics). The most convenient survey is Labov 1990, which discusses examples from English, Canadian French, Spanish and Mandarin, to which we can add Persian (discussed above) and Arabic (Abd-el-Jawad 1987, Abu-Haidar 1989, Haeri 1987, 1991, Jassem 1994; the evidence on Arabic is conveniently summarised in Chambers 1995: 139ff.). As stated, this generalisation is too general, but when we make it more precise we shall be able to dispose of virtually every known exception.

The first refinement takes account of the fact that in some countries women receive less education than men. If the society is diglossic (2.4.2), then the prestige form is taught at school and girls have less chance to learn it than boys. In such cases it is hardly surprising that women lag behind men in their use of prestige variants. As Labov says: 'The principle must be qualified by the observation that for women to use standard norms that differ from everyday speech, they must have access to those norms' (1990: 213). Another refinement is that women generally adopt new linguistic forms more enthusiastically than men do, so if an innovation conflicts with the current standard, there may be a time when the normal pattern is reversed. To allow for this complication, Labov limits the generalisation to *stable* variables.

And thirdly, the variable must be genuinely 'stratified', i.e. sensitive to social class, with higher classes using the standard variants more than the lower classes. The reason for this rider is the existence of some variables which are stratified for one sex but not for the other. Rather conveniently we can illustrate this once again from Teheran Persian (Jahangiri 1980). A glottal stop may be deleted; for example, the word 'mine' may be either /maʔdan/ or /madan/. Table 5.8 shows the group means for the percentage of deleted glottal stops. What is striking about these figures is the difference between the sexes. Males show the stratification which we should expect on the assumption that glottal-stop deletion is non-standard, but females show no such stratification (with the

Table 5.8   *Percentage of glottal stops deleted in free speech by eight groups defined by education and sex in Teheran.*

group	males	females
no education	71	69
primary education	65	69
secondary education	56	58
college education	47	67

rather puzzling exception of those with secondary education). It can be seen that virtually all the female groups use the non-standard variant more often than their male counterparts, contrary to the Sex/Prestige Pattern, but this does not count as an exception because the variable is not stratified for females. Females of (almost) all social classes delete glottal stops to the same extent, which happens (perhaps by chance) to be as high as the percentage for the lowest class of males.

To sum up, the research so far seems to support the following generalisation without exception:

> The Sex/Prestige Pattern
> In any society where males and females have equal access to the standard form, females use standard variants of any stable variable which is socially stratified for both sexes more often than males do.

Not surprisingly, the Sex/Prestige Pattern has attracted a great deal of attention and there have been a number of attempts at explaining it (for example, Trudgill 1983: ch. 9, Trudgill 1974/1983: ch. 4, Graddol and Swann 1989: ch. 3, Holmes 1992: ch. 7, Milroy 1992, Chambers 1995: ch. 3, James forthcoming). It is a very complicated issue, and as yet no single explanation has been overwhelmingly successful, but several are promising. It may be of course that the observed trend is the result of a number of different pressures which reinforce one another, so the explanations are not necessarily in competition with one another. All the explanations involve prototypes – generalisations which are typically true of women or of men, but which allow exceptions. The following paragraphs outline the three approaches which seem the most promising. They are based on status, on networks and on what I shall call 'sophistication'.

(1) The 'status' explanation is based on the link between prestigious language and social status – the position we claim (or are forced to accept) in the wider society in which we live. Men typically live and work outside the house, and

derive their social status from this work, i.e. from whatever contribution they may make to the running of the local community, including their profession. These contributions necessarily involve a man in power relationships with other people, as a subordinate, a superior or an equal, and these power relationships collectively define his social status. A woman, on the other hand, typically spends her life inside the family and has less opportunity to 'earn' a social status through work. Instead, she has to assert her status with the help of symbols which are (arbitrarily) related to the male statuses – such as linguistic variables. Prestigious language, then, is the female substitute for a prestigious job as a way of establishing a position in society, and the reason why a linguistic form is prestigious is because it is used by high-status men.

The status explanation has three weaknesses.

- It presents high-status men as the models for prestige language, when we know that among high-status speakers, it is women, not men, whose language is the most prestigious. As we saw in the Persian example, women use more prestigious language than socially equivalent men in ALL status-classes.

- It fails to explain a rather intriguing fact which Trudgill discovered when he asked his Norwich speakers about their own speech (Trudgill 1974/1983: 89ff.). For example, he played them two recorded pronunciations of *tune*, the RP one with a 'y' glide before the vowel and the local non-standard one without it, and asked them which pronunciation they themselves used. When he compared their answers with the pronunciations they had actually used during the rest of the interview, he found that if anything males 'under-reported', i.e. claimed to use a non-standard variant when they actually used a standard one, but virtually never over-reported, whereas females tended to be more accurate or even to over-report. Why should males think they use a less prestigious form than they actually do use? One plausible answer is that they would rather like to think of themselves as having LESS status than they actually have – an answer which is hard to reconcile with the status explanation, which rests on the assumption that everyone wants as high a status as possible.

- The status explanation is hard to reconcile with another very general tendency which Labov has noticed, and which we mentioned briefly above, namely the tendency for young women to be in the lead in language change (1990, 1994: 156). If prestige forms are defined by high-status men, and if women in general depend on these forms for their own status, why should women take the risky step of introducing alternative forms? (It is true, as Labov points out (1990), that young women's role in child-rearing means that their innovations are more likely to be adopted by the next generation than those made by men, but it is still odd that women innovate at all.)

(2) The 'network' explanation builds on Milroy's work on social networks, which showed that the least prestigious forms were used by the people who were most tightly integrated into the local working-class social networks. According to this view, high-status forms get their high status from their wide geographical distribution; they are the currency of the nation, or at least of the region, whereas low-status forms belong to the local community, whose norms are defined by the core members of the local networks. The extent to which a person uses a low-status form therefore reflects the strength of their ties to the local networks, and sex differences are relevant because men generally have stronger ties than women. This is (again) because men tend to work outside the house, so they build strong links to the other men with whom they work; and at least in some communities their colleagues are also their neighbours, their friends and even their relatives. In contrast, women who have no colleagues have correspondingly fewer network links.

The network explanation has the attraction of recognising the positive value of low-status forms for low-status people, in contrast with the status explanation which only recognises value in the high-status forms. It also allows clear predictions for Milroy's own work, in which the normal tendency for male networks to be stronger than female ones was confirmed in two areas but overturned in the Clonard because of the local employment situation (1980: 146). (In the Clonard, unlike the other two Belfast areas, young women all worked locally whereas men had to go elsewhere for work.) Under these circumstances, we should also expect young females in the Clonard to use low-status variants more than the local males. Unfortunately, Milroy's data do not confirm this prediction clearly, if at all. For one variable, (a), the figures were as predicted (page 124), and it is indeed interesting that this variable is the one which correlates most closely with network-strength (page 158). However, this seems to be the only variable that does fit the predictions, although the social background of the speakers is obviously the same for all variables. It seems, then, that on most variables the young Clonard men and women are behaving like men and women in all the other studies, in spite of the reverse in their network links.

(3) The 'sophistication' explanation is based on the idea that the modern urban societies to which our generalisation applies are organised hierarchically between two crude social stereotypes, the 'rough' and the 'sophisticated'. Rough people do physical work, in which they interact directly with 'nature', whereas sophisticated people deal with artefacts, people and ideas at a great distance from 'nature'. The 'rough' stereotype is the clearer of the two, as the 'sophisticated' one seems to be defined negatively as 'not rough'. The stereotypes are extremely crude, but suppose we accept that they do in fact guide our thinking about the social world. Now consider four other social stereotypes defined by social class and sex: a middle-class man and woman, and a working-class man and woman. Do these stereotypes have anything at all to do with the contrast between 'rough' and 'sophisticated'? Clearly they do. Physical work is for lower-class people – hence the name 'working' class, where the work in question is physical, unlike the more abstract work done by middle-class people. But equally, in all those societies (like Britain) where manual labourers tend to be men there is a clear link between roughness and being male; moreover, male sports are relatively rough and (literally) down to earth compared with female sports. The typical 'rough' person, then, is a working-class male. If sophistication is defined negatively as being different from the rough stereotype, we might expect it to be at its peak among upper-class females; and indeed this seems right, so long as we are talking in terms of stereotypes rather than in terms of the complexities of the real world.

According to this view of society, social behaviour should be expected to be polarised between two models defined by the 'rough' working-class male and the 'sophisticated' middle-class (or upper-class) female. Seen in these terms, low-status linguistic forms are 'rough', and high-status, standard, ones are 'sophisticated'; and the tendency for females to use high-status forms more than males is exactly as predicted. Females are attracted to the 'sophisticated', which is also middle-class, and males are attracted to the 'rough', which is also working-class. The model for sophisticated usage is defined by women, not by men (as in the status model), so we expect women to speak more standardly at all levels of society. But we also have an explanation for Trudgill's finding; Norwich men tend to 'under-report' their own usage because they are attracted by the 'rough' model, for which the clearest models are working-class men. We may even have an explanation here for a very curious experimental finding reported by Byrd (1994), who found evidence that females speak more slowly and 'distinctively' than men; maybe this too is an aspect of being sophisticated.

According to the 'sophistication' explanation, then, the original question is misleading. If we ask why females speak more standardly than males, we are assuming, on the one hand, that the oddity lies in the behaviour of females, rather than in that of males, and on the other hand, that standardness is defined primarily in terms of social class and only incidentally related to sex. If the suggested explanation is right, though, both these assumptions are wrong. Females and males are different because they are both pursuing different and conflicting models, so neither is more normal than the other. Furthermore, standardness is really defined not in terms of social class, but in terms of 'sophistication', which is determined as much by sex as by social class. As Lesley Milroy has pointed out (1992), instead of asking why females tend to use middle-class forms we might just as well ask why middle-class people tend to use female forms.

Whatever the true explanation (or explanations) may be, it is hard to see how we can fail to learn a great deal about both language and social structure in the search. This is undoubtedly one of the most important and fruitful areas of research in current sociolinguistics.

5.4.5   *The situation and 'style'*

Many of the studies that we have reported have considered the effects on speech of changes in the situation. Labov found that shop assistants were more likely to pronounce the /r/ in *fourth floor* when he asked them to repeat it (5.2.2), and he also found that people spoke differently in his interviews according to what they were talking about, and according to who they were talking to – their speech became less standard when they were talking about situations where they had been in danger of dying than when talking about humdrum routine matters, and it was less standard when talking to other members of their family than when talking to him. Differences of this kind have generally been called *style* differences, and a standard terminology has developed for naming styles. At one extreme is 'casual' speech, which is the kind of speech we use to our family and friends in everyday interaction. The other extreme is called 'formal', though there is less agreement about this end, and indeed about the very basis of these style distinctions.

According to Labov (for example, 1994: 157) the main factor responsible for changes in style is the amount of attention that the speaker pays to the speech-forms used. In normal everyday speech we pay very little attention to it, as we are more concerned with its content. According to Labov, this is where we use our least standard speech, and as attention increases, so does standardness too. In contrast an interview is a fairly formal situation, and knowing that our interviewer is interested in language is likely to direct our attention to the sounds and words we use. This is likely to be even more so if we are asked to read a prepared passage, and more so still if the passage consists of a list of selected words whose only relevance is their pronunciation. The standard Labovian interview (such as Trudgill used in the Norwich survey described in 5.2.3) is organised in such a way as to provide examples of all these different styles, and when the results are reported they generally confirm Labov's predictions: speech is least standard in parts of the interview where the speech is casual (to family or friends, or about emotionally gripping topics), more standard in the body of the interview, more standard still in the reading passage and most standard of all in the word-lists.

There is no doubt that people do speak differently in different situations. However, there has been some debate about how best to analyse and explain these differences (Milroy 1987: ch. 8). We have already seen one other explanation for some of this variation, which is speech accommodation (as illustrated by the ways in which Sue, the Cardiff travel agent, varied her pronunciation from customer to customer – see 5.2.5). This immediately raises the possibility that the differences between casual and formal style in Labov's interviews are also a matter of accommodation, with the interviewee accommodating to the (middle-class) speech of the interviewer. Bell (1984, 1991: ch. 6) has suggested that the most important element in style-shifting may be this kind of accommodation to one's audience, which he calls 'audience-design', rather than the amount of attention paid to speech. One of his main pieces of evidence for this view is that newscasters on New Zealand radio change their pronunciations in a consistent way as they move between stations; this change is easy to understand as they accommodate to different (imaginary) audiences, but makes no sense if the relevant factor is the amount of attention that they pay to their reading.

On the other hand, it is hard to see how audience design applies to the difference between spontaneous speech and reading, and in this case it may be that some different explanation is needed for whatever differences emerge – indeed, one of the facts that emerged from Milroy's Belfast work was that speakers did not use more standard pronunciations when reading (Milroy 1987: 173ff.), as Trudgill's Norwich speakers and Labov's New Yorkers had done. The way in which reading style differs from spontaneous speech seems to vary in many fundamental ways, according to how literate the speakers are, how well standard features are encoded in the spelling, and so on. We have to understand these things well before we can interpret figures based on material that has been read out loud.

The study of style is part of a much more general area of activity, the study of 'registers' (see 2.4.1), and needs to be seen in this more general context. Another contrast which is clearly relevant is that between speaking and writing, which has also been studied in great quantitative detail, especially in some careful statistical analyses of large corpora which have tried to discover the main dimensions on which registers differ (Biber 1988, 1989). A very simple example (Edwards 1994) will show the clarity of some findings that emerge from this kind of work. As I mentioned briefly in 5.3.1, English has a series of 'compound pronouns' which end in *-body*: *somebody, anybody, nobody, every-body*. Each of these is matched by another pronoun ending in *-one*: *someone*, etc. So far as we know these pairs are exact synonyms (i.e. their meanings as such are the same), so how do we choose between them? One possibility is that our choice is completely random and unaffected by anything else, in which case they should be equally frequent. This explanation may seem attractive at first, as it is very hard to find any difference between them by introspecting. But the facts are otherwise. The *-body* series are much more common than the *-one* series in ordinary informal speech (with ratios of between 3:1 and 9:1), while the relationship is reversed in written texts (ratios from 2:1 to 4:1) – in other words, the *-one* series is mainly for formal writing and the *-body* series for informal speech. These differences apply not only when we lump all the pronouns in each series together, but also when we take each pair separately.

The conclusion seems to be that our choice of linguistic items is indeed affected crucially by the situation in which we are using them, and that if we wish to compare different users we must make sure to control the situation so that we are comparing like with like – to take an extreme example, there is no point in comparing one speaker chatting to their family with another who is reading a list of words! Unfortunately we do not yet fully understand the various parameters on which situations can vary, but we can hope for some progress as quantitative work develops.

5.5 Summary

This chapter has surveyed what has probably been the main growth-point in sociolinguistics, which is called 'quantitative sociolinguistics'. The central notion is the sociolinguistic variable, a list of alternative forms which are alternative ways of expressing the same content and which are (therefore) chosen according to how well they fit the sociolinguistic context rather than how well they fit the intended meaning. Sociolinguistic variables allow objective and quantitative comparisons between texts, and when combined with the technical possibilities of tape-recorders they make an excellent method for studying ordinary speech. We have looked at some of the ways that have been used for collecting usable samples of data, and seen how important it is to plan the data-collection so that it fits the aims of the research. Although we have also considered some problems of method, and especially problems of analysis and interpretation, the methods that we have surveyed here are well-tested, straightforward and generally productive.

We have also looked at some of the main discoveries that have emerged from this kind of research. Many of these discoveries are so robust and clear that we can call them 'facts'. Here is a selection of them:

- Sociolinguistic variables are sensitive not only to 'macro' social variables for speakers: sex, age, social class, race and place, but also to 'micro' variables such as the contrast between Jocks and Burnouts in Belten High School.

- Sociolinguistic variables are also sensitive to the degree to which the speaker belongs to particular social networks or groups, the degree to which the speaker wishes to accommodate to the speech of the person addressed and the formality of the situation.

- They are also sensitive to variations in the purely linguistic context (though such variations tend to be independent of social variations, which means they can be ignored in a study of the latter).

- The links between linguistic variables and other variables, whether linguistic or social, are probabilistic (more/less) rather than categorical (present/absent).

- A single linguistic variable is likely to be sensitive to a number of other variables, each exerting a different degree of influence on it.

- Different linguistic variables are usually sensitive to other variables in different ways, i.e. each linguistic variable is socially unique.

- The Sex/Prestige Pattern is universal.

What I have not tried to do in this chapter is to discuss the various theoretical explanations that could be offered for this variation. How do sociolinguistic variables fit into a general theory of language structure, and how do the facts of variability mesh with the general ideas of face, politeness and so on that we developed during the previous chapters? We shall return to these questions in the final chapter, where I shall try to show how these ideas might be integrated into a more general theory of language structure and social behaviour.

6
Linguistic and social inequality

6.1 Linguistic inequality
6.1.1 Introduction

One of the most solid achievements of linguistics in the twentieth century has been to eliminate the idea (at least among professional linguists) that some languages or dialects are inherently 'better' than others. Linguists recognise that some varieties of language are considered by lay people to be better than others, but they point out that each variety displays characteristics common to all human language, such as being complex and rule-governed, and that even the least prestigious language varieties reveal an impressively rich set of structural patterns. Linguists would claim that if they were simply shown the grammars of two different varieties of a completely unfamiliar language, one with high and the other with low prestige, they could not tell which was which.

Moreover, most linguists would probably say the same about linguistic differences between *individual* speakers: if there are differences between the grammars of two people, there is no way of knowing which has the higher prestige in society simply by studying the grammars. Admittedly there are individuals who clearly have *inherently* incomplete grammars, such as small children, foreigners and people with mental disabilities, but these deviations are easy to explain and predict, and leave intact the claim that *all normal people are equal with regard to their grammars*. Of course, there is no shortage of differences between grammars, whether of individuals or whole communities, but there are no purely linguistic grounds for ranking any of the grammars higher than others.

This position is summed up in the well-known slogan, 'Linguistics should be descriptive, not prescriptive.' It is less widely acknowledged that this slogan raises problems. It is harder than many linguists realise to avoid prescriptivism, since the historical development of linguistic theory has been so closely linked to the description of prestigious varieties such as standard languages. Labov pointed out that the normal method of obtaining information about a person's language is to ask them for judgments on sentences, a method which is virtually useless with speakers of a non-standard variety who also know the standard one, since judgments will almost always relate to the latter rather than to normal speech (Labov 1972a: 214). Moreover, it is simply a matter of fact that linguists have studied standard varieties far more than non-standard varieties, so we know vast amounts about the details of standard English (as witness the 1,700 pages of Quirk et al. 1985), but very much less about even the best-studied non-standard varieties of English. The reasons for this are not hard to see – linguists are academics and therefore know a standard language, they work in a long tradition in which standard languages were studied so that they could be taught, and the foreign-language teaching market needs good studies of standard varieties, but not of non-standard varieties. Milroy and Milroy 1985 is a good analysis of prescriptivism, while Milroy 1987 develops linguistic methods which minimise its effects.

Another problem is that the doctrine of linguistic equality deflects attention from language as a possible source of social inequality. If language were something which automatically developed at the same pace and to the same extent in all normal people, then those of the same age or degree of maturity should automatically be at the same linguistic level. This comfortable view leaves only two problem areas, one concerned with abnormal speakers (such as foreigners and people with mental disabilities), and the other with the effects of prejudice. Prejudice does of course exist (see 6.2), but the doctrine of linguistic equality leads to the conclusion that eliminating prejudice (should that be possible) would leave abnormal speakers as the only people with linguistic problems. Evidence is given in 6.3 and 6.4 that this is not the case; there are identifiable differences between people of the same age in aspects of language such as vocabulary, certain areas of syntax, skill at using speech for certain tasks and the arts of reading and writing, which can only be described as examples of *inequality* between the individuals concerned – and these are precisely the areas of language which are taught in schools. If linguistic equality were taken literally, there would presumably be no need for schools to include any aspects of the mother-tongue in their curricula, since it could be left to look after itself!

The reason for the conflict between what linguists appear to claim about language and what every lay person knows about the need to *teach* the mother-tongue must be that the two groups have very different concepts of 'language'. When linguists make claims about linguistic equality, they are referring to the basic core of language structure, which is the area with which linguistic theory has been most concerned. However, lay people take this basic core completely for granted, and are more concerned with more 'peripheral' aspects such as vocabulary (especially academic vocabulary) and register-specific constructions. Non-linguists may overstate their case (as often happens), claiming that certain children have 'no language' at all, in which case it may be helpful for the linguist to point out the error, but linguists in turn must be careful not to overstate their own case by implying that 'linguistic equality' applies to the whole of language and its use.

6.1.2   Three types of linguistic inequality

The remainder of this chapter is divided into three main sections, each dealing with a different type of linguistic inequality and relating it to social inequality. In each case, linguistic inequality can be seen as a *cause* (along with many other factors, of course) of social inequality, but also as a *consequence* of it, because language is one of the most important means by which social inequality is perpetuated from generation to generation. The present section introduces these three types of linguistic inequality.

The first might be called SUBJECTIVE INEQUALITY, since it concerns what people *think* about each other's speech (i.e. the area of linguistic prejudice, referred to above). In some societies people are credited with different amounts of intelligence, friendliness and other such virtues according to the way they speak, although such a judgment based entirely on speech may be quite wrong. Consequently, whatever virtues are highly valued, some speakers are thought to have more of them than they really have, simply because they have the 'right' way of speaking, and others are thought to have less because their speech conveys the wrong impression. Thus language, in the form of variety differences, contributes to social inequality by being used as a yard-stick for evaluating people, and by being a highly unreliable yard-stick.

The second type can be called STRICTLY LINGUISTIC INEQUALITY, to distinguish it from the general concept of 'linguistic inequality' running through the whole chapter. Strictly linguistic inequality relates to the linguistic items that a person knows (in the very broad sense of 'linguistic item' used in 2.1.2). It is scarcely open to doubt that the items one knows reflect the experience one has had, and that people with different experiences know different ranges of items. This is particularly obvious in the case of vocabulary, where some individuals have a rich set of technical terminology for a particular field – such as fishing, pop culture or linguistics – whereas others have virtually no vocabulary for those fields. However, differences can also be found in other areas of language, where items that are familiar to some are unfamiliar to others – familiar vocabulary with unfamiliar meanings (for example, *addressing an issue*) or pronunciations, and unfamiliar syntactic constructions (for example, literary patterns like *Hard though this may be to accept* or football-commentary patterns like *Smith to Jones*). In each case, some people know the item, and others do not – or more subtly, some people are more confident in using the item, though most people know it at least passively – and of course those who do know it fare better in those social situations where it is needed. In one sense, social inequality arises on each such occasion, but some occasions are more important than others in terms of their effects on overall life-chances – performance in examinations or job interviews, for instance, has more far-reaching consequences than how one copes in a discussion on fishing. Accordingly, the interest of sociolinguists has centred on differences relevant to the more significant areas of life, notably the performance of children at school.

The significance of strictly linguistic inequality is easy to exaggerate, but there is a third type of linguistic inequality whose social importance can scarcely be overstated. We shall call this COMMUNICATIVE INEQUALITY, to emphasise that it is concerned with knowledge of how to use linguistic items to communicate successfully, rather than simply with knowledge of the linguistic items themselves. Communicative inequality refers, for instance, to the kind of knowledge or skill that is needed when using speech to interact with other people (see chapter 4). It also includes inequalities in the ways in which speakers select variants of linguistic variables in order to present a favourable image (chapter 5), which means that communicative inequality subsumes subjective inequality. Communicative inequality also concerns the themes discussed in chapter 3 on the relations of language, culture and thought, since it involves differences at the levels of conceptualisation and culture. In other words, communicative inequality brings together all the major themes running through this book, and relates them to important social questions such as equality of opportunity and educational policy.

6.2 Subjective inequality

6.2.1 *Language-based prejudice*

The first kind of inequality involves prejudices about particular ways of speaking. One person can draw conclusions about another person's character and abilities simply on the basis of how that person speaks, regardless of the content of what they say. We shall review experimental evidence for this claim below, but for the time being it can probably stand as a statement of the obvious. The reason why it is socially problematic is that the conclusions drawn may be wrong, and may either underestimate or overestimate the extent to which the speaker has various social desirable qualities. For example, if you hear me talking you may think I am smarter than I really am if my accent is an upper-class one, and conversely if it is a lower-class one. Why do we jump to conclusions in this way, when we know how easy it is to be wrong?

This is really a question for psychologists rather than for sociolinguists, but we already have the basis for a plausible answer. In a nutshell, we do it because we need the information, and we have no better source. We need information about another person's personality because it affects our own behaviour. We ask questions about them like the following: Do we trust them? Do we like them? How clever are they? How rich are they? Are their values like ours? Are they 'one of us'? Our answers determine how we treat them: When they come to our door do we let them in? When they apply to work for us do we offer them a job? Do we invite them to have a drink? Do we lend them our books? Do we believe what they say to us? All these decisions depend on what we know about them – or more precisely, on what we think we know about them, because we only have solidly reliable information about a small number of other people.

How then do we find out what other people are like? For a few people we have reliable first-hand experience of their behaviour; for example, we know that they are always late for appointments, that they always cope well with difficult situations or that they have a good sense of humour. However, most of the people who we have to deal with are relative strangers, so we have to rely either on what we hear about them from others (gossip, to be treated with great care!), or on intelligent guesswork. This is where language becomes relevant. We already know that the way in which we speak (or write) conveys a lot of socially important information because speakers use their linguistic choices in order to locate themselves socially in a multi-dimensional space, as an 'act of identity'. We saw in the last chapter that some of the linguistic means for doing this are quantitative, and extremely subtle. In other words, speakers are transmitting information about 'the kind of people they are' all the time while speaking, so it would be extremely surprising if hearers did not use this information. Putting it the other way round, there would be no point in transmitting the information if it were not used. Let's assume, then, that we do derive information about social classification from the way other people speak.

This assumption takes us part of the way to an explanation for language-based prejudices, but we still have a gap to bridge, between the social classification and the prejudices. How can we get from categories such as 'middle class' or 'female' to value judgments like 'friendly', 'reliable' or 'intelligent'? At this point we should really hand over to sociologists and social psychologists, but once again it is quite easy to construct a plausible explanation. This time we can hark back to the notion of 'prototype' which we have invoked so many times. A prototype is a concept which is typically associated with a collection of characteristics but which has no 'definition', no set of characteristics that are so important that they are indispensable. The concept is a way of recording that these characteristics tend to be associated with each other, so one of them allows us to predict the remainder. The concept 'bird' normally involves flying, laying eggs, having wings and so on, so if you know that something is flying it is a good bet that it also has feathers. The problem is that this is just a guess, and not a certainty, because the flying thing could be a bat, a very large butterfly or a model aeroplane.

Similarly for social types, i.e. 'kinds of people' – 'middle-class person', 'woman', 'middle-class woman', 'sociolinguist', 'Jock' (see p. 166), 'person who lives in Ballymacarrett' (see p. 163), 'member of my family' and so on. Each of these is a prototype which associates a number of characteristics, including characteristics such as intelligence and attractiveness which we evaluate positively or negatively. If a social prototype is shared by many people in society it is called a 'SOCIAL STEREOTYPE' (Tajfel 1981). It is easy to see the benefits of social stereotypes; after all, without them we should have to judge every stranger as a completely unknown quantity, which would make life in modern societies virtually impossible. The trouble is that they are often unreliable for the simple reason that some of the characteristics which they combine are only loosely associated with each other, and many people have one characteristic but not the others. Indeed, some social stereotypes include characteristics which have no factual basis at all but which were developed as part of a mythology about the people concerned (for example, English people tell jokes about an Englishman, an Irishman and a Scotsman in which the Irishman is stupid and the Scotsman is mean). A PREJUDICE is a characteristic of a social stereotype which is only weakly predictable from the other characteristics (or even not predictable at all).

Figure 6.1 illustrates the links from language, through an 'objective' social type, to a 'subjective' and evaluative one. The hearer's chain of thought is as follows (with S as the speaker): S has just said 'x x x x'; people who talk like that are type-T people; type-T people are nice (have halos); therefore S is nice.

In short, a language prejudice is a characteristic which we expect people to have because of the way they speak, and the link between the speech and this characteristic lies through the type of person that (we think) speaks like that. An ideal world would presumably be free of all prejudice, whatever its basis, but it is important to remember that prejudices are a negative by-product of a much more positive mental process, the ability to form concepts by associating characteristics even where the associations have exceptions. We shall return to the notion of prototypes in the last chapter.

Figure 6.1

6.2.2   *Evaluation of language*

The way a person speaks is simply a clue to social information, and is in itself neutral, neither good nor bad. Unfortunately we all know that this is not the end of the story, because the language itself can also be evaluated. Common-sense explains how this arises. Suppose a society recognises some social stereotype S, which is valued negatively – for example, people think that members of S are rough. Now it is easy to see that behaviour which is characteristic of S will attract the same evaluation – for example, if members of S smoke pipes, then people will think that smoking pipes is also rough. The link to language is obvious: people also think that the way members of S talk is rough. We all know that this happens, but we must remember that when we evaluate speech as rough, posh, effeminate, affected and so on, this evaluation is based on the evaluation of the speakers, and not on the speech forms themselves. This must be so because it is easy to find examples where the same speech pattern is evaluated quite differently in different communities – for example, we compared the (r) variable in New York and in England, and saw that an audible / r/ is prestigious in New York but low-status in England. In short, the speech characteristics of a social stereotype inherit the stereotype's evaluation; and it is worth noting, incidentally, that this in itself has the effect of reinforcing the evaluation of the stereotype itself by arguments like the following: 'They must be rough – just listen to how they speak!'.

The most important question is how people evaluate the dialect or language that they speak themselves, because this is so closely linked to their self-evaluation. It seems obvious that a society functions best when all its members are proud to be what they are, so they should all value their own speech because they value the community to which they belong. In some societies this seems to be the case; for example, Gillian Sankoff reports (1976) that each Buang-speaking village in New Guinea believes that its dialect of Buang is the best. But more familiar Western societies seem to be much less healthy, to judge by the findings of a series of sociolinguistic studies which have found rampant 'LINGUISTIC INSECURITY', a term introduced by Labov (1972a: 133). At least in the United States and Britain some people who are socially subordinate think that they speak badly. This is a judgment on the forms they use (where these contrast with the locally recognised standard dialect), and not on matters of fluency, effectiveness and so on. Why should anyone think that they speak badly, when they are speaking exactly as everyone else in their local community speaks? And if they do think this, why don't they simply swap their dialect or accent for a better one?

Members of a complex society belong to groups at many different levels – the household, the peer-group, the region or city, the 'socio-economic class' and the nation, to mention but a few of the groupings involved (which may cut across each other as well as being arranged in a part–whole relationship). If there is a conflict between the values of two groupings (for example, if the values of the nation conflict with those of regionally and socially based groups), the values of the nation may triumph at the expense of those of the less powerful group. Thus, William Labov reports that New Yorkers in general accept the values of a wider American community which leads them to devalue many of the linguistic forms characteristic of New York. He goes as far as to describe the New York speech community as 'a sink of negative prestige' (1972a: 136), and a similar lack of self-confidence has been reported from other communities, such as Glasgow (Macaulay 1975). In these communities people believe that they 'ought' to use different forms from those they in fact do use, because the former are highly valued and the later are rejected by the wider community.

This explanation disposes of the problem of linguistic insecurity, but raises another question: 'Why don't all people speak in the way that they obviously believe they should?' (Labov 1972a: 249). If all New Yorkers or Glaswegians were to give up talking like residents of those areas and started to talk like Americans or Britons instead, they would be able to congratulate themselves on speaking 'properly'. We can suggest an answer to this question, though it leaves many loose ends. To reach the answer, we must first consider the mechanism by which values get established, and recognise that on the whole the values accepted by the wider community will be those of the most powerful group within it, since this will be the one that controls such channels of influence as the schools and the media. If enough school-teachers tell enough New York or Glasgow children often enough that their speech is 'slovenly', 'ungrammatical', 'ugly' or just 'wrong', and tell them what they ought to say, then the children will presumably believe them, especially if they hear no contradictory opinions from their parents.

Secondly, we must consider the problems of actually doing what the teachers recommend. The most highly valued speech-forms are those of one particular group in a society (the most powerful), although they are accepted beyond that group as a result of the influence of schools, etc. Children who give up the forms of the local group in order to adopt those that are widely accepted in the nation would in fact be adopting forms that are the identifying symbols of a different group. The option is not a real one. On the one hand, the children may recognise that they are likely to lose more than they gain in the process, since they will almost certainly lose the respect and affection of friends and possibly family, and may in any case not succeed in adopting the prestige forms sufficiently well to pass themselves off as members of the other group – not to mention the problems of reconciling all the other aspects of their behaviour and background with membership of that group. On the other hand, they may have a negative image of at least some aspects of the personality of a prototypical member of the other group, and a correspondingly positive image of their own group. For instance, people who sound 'upper class' in their speech are commonly seen as cold, unfriendly and unreliable (Giles and Powesland 1975: chs 4 and 5), and members of other classes may prefer to stay as they are, emphasising the positive virtues of their own group, while nevertheless recognising the upper-class forms as in some absolute sense 'right'. This kind of contrast is often referred to in terms of OVERT PRESTIGE (the prestige of the high-status group representing, symbolically, the whole community) and COVERT PRESTIGE (that of the local, non–prestige group) (Trudgill 1974/1983: 96).

6.2.3   Stereotypes and how to study them

People thus use the speech of others as a clue to non-linguistic information about them, such as their social background and even personality traits like toughness or intelligence. This is an example of the way in which people use information stored in terms of prototypes: if characteristics A and B are typically ('prototypically') associated with each other, we *assume* the presence of B whenever we *observe* the presence of A, or vice versa. If A is some characteristic of speech and B is some characteristic of personality, speech will be used as a clue to personality, which is generally harder to observe directly than speech. Similarly, if some speech characteristic is linked in a prototype with a social characteristic, such as some particular type of education, the former will be used as a clue to the latter. As noted earlier, the widely shared prototypes underlying such judgments are called '(social) stereotypes', so we shall use this terminology here.

How then is it possible to study these subjective connections objectively, and to analyse the stereotypes which people use? Most people are not consciously aware of the connections between specific linguistic and non-linguistic variables, so there is little point in asking people directly about these connections ('What kind of person do you think uses such-and-such a form?'), but there are nevertheless ways of tapping people's knowledge more or less indirectly.

The most straightforward and widely used method is called the SUBJECTIVE REACTION TEST, first developed by social psychologists (Lambert 1967, Giles and Powesland 1975, Giles and Bradac 1994). However, the method has been adopted by Labov as part of his methodology for investigating linguistic variability. The investigator prepares a tape-recording of a series of people talking, usually keeping the content of what they say constant by having them read a passage of prose, or count from one to twenty, for example. The tape might typically contain a dozen voices, each speaking for a minute or so. The 'subjects', i.e. the people whose stereotypes are being investigated, are then asked to listen to these voices, one at a time, and answer a questionnaire about each. A subject might be asked to make ten to twenty judgments about the owner of each voice, and these judgments can then be compared from one voice to another. Some would be 'objective' (for example, 'Where do you think this speaker comes from?' or 'Which of the following places do you think the speaker comes from: . . . ?'), but many of them would probably be evaluative, and the subject would be asked to locate the speaker somewhere on a particular scale, such as 'toughness', 'intelligence' or 'friendliness'. The standard way to obtain such evaluations is to define each scale in terms of two contrasting adjectives, such as 'tough' and 'gentle', 'intelligent' and 'unintelligent' or 'friendly' and 'unfriendly', and then to allow seven points on the scale ranging from, say, 'very tough' through 'tough', 'somewhat tough', 'neutral', 'somewhat gentle' and 'gentle', to 'very gentle'. Subjects have to pick one of these points for each voice, but the wide range of alternatives allows quite subtle distinctions. On the other hand, the fact that the choice is restricted to the seven points on each scale, which can be numbered 1–7, makes it possible to use quantitative methods in comparing judgments, both across voices and across subjects. Needless to say, many variations on this type of questionnaire have been used by researchers. To take just one example, Labov asked subjects 'Which of the following jobs do you think the speaker might hold: . . . ?' (Labov 1972a: 128).

The results of subjective reaction tests typically show clear differences both between voices and between subjects. In other words, different voices evoke different stereotypes in the mind of the same person, whilst the same voice may suggest different stereotypes to different people. For instance, in a study of attitudes among pupils in a secondary school in Newham, in the poor East End of London, Greg Smith (1979) found quite consistent differences between the ways in which Cockney and standard-accented voices were evaluated, with Cockney voices receiving *negative* evaluations for virtually every scale, and standard-accented voices *positive* ones. This finding may surprise readers who know that in areas of London like Newham virtually everyone has a more or less 'Cockney' accent, so the subjects in this research were in fact giving negative evaluations to the stereotype evoked by their *own* accent. It is even more surprising to see that the list of characteristics on which Cockney voices were evaluated negatively include friendliness, intelligence, kindness, 'hard-workingness', good looks, cleanliness and honesty. These results appear to suggest that the values of the most powerful section of society may have spread throughout the rest of society to the extent that other sections not only devalue their own speech (as the subjects in the Newham research did on the scale of 'well-spokenness'), but also most other aspects of their self-image. This research also showed many other differences between voices and subjects. For example, voices recognisable as those of male West Indian immigrants were rated more positively by white girls than by white boys on most of the scales, suggesting that white girls were attracted by West Indian boys.

The subjective reaction method can be made more sophisticated in two ways. The pioneer of this field of study, Wallace Lambert, introduced what is called the MATCHED GUISE TECHNIQUE in order to reduce the effects of differences in voice quality between speakers. The problem is obvious: if we wanted to compare, say, attitudes of people bilingual in Welsh and English to each of these languages, it would be silly to choose as our speakers a Welshman with a booming voice and an Englishman with a squeaky one, since these voice-quality differences might well override all those due to the languages themselves. The matched guise technique aims to avoid this kind of problem by recording the *same* speaker using more than one 'voice'. In this type of experiment there might, typically, be three speakers, each producing speech in two languages or dialects, and the six voices would be ordered randomly so that hearers would not notice similarities in voice quality. Equally typically, hearers do not realise that different voices belong to the same person, and give quite different answers to the questions about status and personality for the two voices belonging to the same speaker (Lambert 1967). It seems, however, that there is little difference between results produced by the matched guise technique and those where the voices were each produced by a different speaker.

Another way in which the subjective reaction method may be made more sophisticated is by controlling the speech used in such a way as to make it possible to identify the particular linguistic features to which hearers were reacting. This is a method developed by Labov (1972a: 128, 146), who compiled a list of twenty-two tape-recorded sentences produced by five different female speakers for a different purpose, selecting the sentences so that each illustrated either just one or no sensitive phonological variable. Hearers were told to guess the job of the person speaking each sentence in the list, without, however, being told that only five different people were speaking. It was therefore possible to compare the job-rating for a given speaker on different sentences, and it could be assumed that any differences in ratings were due to differences in the variables represented. For instance, one speaker was rated as a receptionist on one sentence, but as a switchboard operator on another, although the sentences were in fact just different utterances of the same sentence ('He darted out about four feet before a car, and he got hit hard'), with a single difference in pronunciation: in the second utterance, one out of the five postvocalic *r*'s was not pronounced as /r/, whereas in the first utterance they were all pronounced. It will be recalled from 5.2.2 that this is an important sociolinguistic variable in New York City (where this experiment was carried out), but these results show how remarkably sensitive hearers are to the occurrence of individual non-standard features in the speech of others.

The subjective reaction test has drawbacks as a way of discovering people's attitudes to speech-forms, not least that it requires people to fall back upon their stereotypes, since they have no other way of answering the questions put before them. It is possible that people actually use stereotypes less in real-life situations than in these experimental situations. In order to test this hypothesis, it is necessary to find an alternative test of attitudes, where the focus is not on the experimental task as such and the situation is more normal. Several such alternatives have been devised, some remarkably ingenious. We shall describe one such experiment here (from Giles and Powesland 1975: 102), but another will be described in 6.2.5.

A researcher who could use either RP or a Birmingham accent arranged to talk to two groups of seventeen-year olds in a school, having already established that school children rate RP high and Birmingham accent low. To each group he gave a short talk about psychology, explaining that he was a university lecturer in psychology and that his department wished to find out what school students who expected to go to university knew about that subject. He asked them to write down all they knew about psychology, then went out, leaving his assistant behind with the group. She collected their writings, then explained that there was a second part to their research since they would like to know whether the lecturer who had just spoken would be a suitable person to give lectures on psychology at schools. The students were asked to write down what they thought of the lecturer, and to evaluate his intelligence on a scale. The pattern of the experiment was the same for each group of students except that the lecturer used his RP accent to one, and his Birmingham accent to the other. The differences in the responses of each group were significant. The direct question about intelligence got answers showing that the lecturer was rated higher in his RP 'guise' than in his Birmingham one – in spite of the fact that he gave precisely the same talk, introduced himself as a university lecturer, and in every other way behaved in the same way to each group. Moreover, the students wrote far more both *to* him and *about* him in his RP than in his Birmingham guise (24 per cent more to him and 82 per cent more about him). Assuming that the groups of students who heard the two guises were reasonably similar in their composition (and there is no reason to think otherwise), the explanation for these differences in *behaviour* between the groups must have something to do with their attitudes to the two accents used. One explanation is that they liked the speaker more in his RP guise, and there is some independent evidence that people will write more both to and about people they like than those they dislike. Thus it can be seen that people's actual *behaviour* can be influenced by their prejudices, and that these are not confined to what they *say* about each other.

Before leaving the general question of the experimental study of how speech is used as a clue to stereotypes, it is worth mentioning another experiment which shows that speech is not the only clue. Indeed the deductive chain may go in the reverse direction, from some other observable feature to the relevant stereotype and thence to the speech type, even when the speech itself is observable. Frederick Williams (1973) devised an ingenious experiment in which videotapes were made of three children viewed from behind, so that it was clear to the viewer that they were radically different (white, black and Mexican–American respectively), and that they were talking, though their mouths and faces were not visible. This made it possible to dub the *same* sound-track on the film of each child without the viewer realising that the speech did not fit the movements of the mouth. Student teachers acted as judges, and three matched groups were each asked to evaluate the speech of one of the children on the scales of standardness and fluency. When the ratings of the groups were compared, there was a clear difference between those for the different children, in spite of the fact that exactly the same speech was heard in each case. The speech of the black and Mexican–American children was rated less standard than that of the white child, and the speech of the Mexican–American child was rated as less confident than that of either of the others. These differences corresponded exactly to the stereotypes established in other experiments for these three racial types, and the results may be interpreted as showing that the student teachers had used visual clues to identify a stereotype and had then assumed that the speech they heard was as predicted by that stereotype. It is hardly necessary to point out that if this strategy is typical of those used by teachers in assessing pupils' speech, it could be a waste of time for pupils to try to 'improve' their speech, even if they wanted to do so.

6.2.4   *Prejudice of teachers*

This section and the next focus on the practical social problems connected with education. A great deal of sociolinguistic research has had this particular bias, and it is specially important not only because the education system itself is probably one of the main vehicles by which the upper-class prejudices are disseminated through society (see 6.2.1), but because educators should understand more clearly the potential role of prejudice. School teachers and their pupils both have fixed speech stereotypes, and both sets of stereotypes are potentially the source of serious problems. On the other hand, it is perhaps necessary to remind ourselves that there are many sorts of teacher and pupil, and not all teachers may be influenced by the speech of pupils to the extent implied by what follows (see Taylor 1973, Edwards 1994).

There is some evidence that teachers base their first impressions of pupils on speech-forms in preference to other sources of information which might appear to be more relevant. However, it is important to remember that much of the evidence is based on reactions of *student* teachers, rather than experienced ones, who may evaluate pupils in quite a different way. A few student teachers, for example, were asked to assess eight hypothetical school children on the scales of intelligence, being a good student, being privileged, enthusiastic, self-confident and gentle (Giles and Powesland 1975: 3). The eight hypothetical pupils were each defined by three types of information: a photograph, a tape-recorded sample of speech and a sample of school-work (consisting of an essay and a drawing). The individual pieces of information were based on real children, but had been recombined to provide equal numbers of instances of each type of information which would be judged favourably and unfavourably. The question to be answered by this experiment was: what would happen if information from one source gave a favourable impression but that from another source gave an unfavourable one? The very clear answer was that information from the speech sample always took priority over that from the photograph or the school-work: the impression based on the speech sample overrode impressions from the other sources.

It would be wrong to give the impression that all teachers evaluate children according to how 'standard' their speech is. Leaving aside the possibility that some teachers avoid making any evaluations at all on the basis of speech, it has been shown (Giles and Powesland 1975: 42) that teachers are of at least two kinds: those who evaluate on the basis of standardness, and those who pay more attention to fluency, which leads to judgments of confidence and eagerness. It would seem, a priori, that the fluency-oriented teachers are likely to make judgments that are more relevant to the needs of the classroom than those who are oriented to standardness.

Assuming that teachers do form first impressions of pupils on the basis of their speech (among other factors), there are problems for the child whose speech leads to an unfavourable first impression. There is the fact that first impressions are resistant to change, so that the child will have to perform that much better in class compared to a child who makes a favourable impression from the start. There is also the problem of the self-fulfilling prophecy: if a teacher expects children to perform poorly, her behaviour towards them may be such as to encourage them to do just that. There is research evidence (Rosenthal and Jacobson 1968) that the converse is true (if the teacher has high expectations, she will behave in such a way as to produce correspondingly good performance in the child), and it seems likely that negative expectations by the teacher will similarly lead to negative performance by the pupils.

An additional way in which teachers' prejudices may act against the interests of their pupils is by reinforcing any negative prejudices which the pupils may already have against their own speech, of the kind we discussed in connection with the research in the East End of London. It would be wrong to assume that all teachers fall into this trap, but it would be just as wrong to ignore the large number of teachers who believe that one of their main roles is to point out to children speaking non-standard dialects or accents that their speech is imperfect, in the hope that they will mend their ways. On the whole the only effect of this kind of criticism is either to make the children's self-image more negative or to strengthen their determination not to conform (or both!).

6.2.5   Prejudice of pupils

The first thing to establish in discussing the linguistic prejudices of school children is that the prejudices exist. According to Giles and Bradac (1994: 4261–2) the adult set of stereotypes and prejudices 'although not fully established until adolescence, begins to take hold around 9 years of age (and in some cases earlier)'. Indeed, there is even evidence that suggests an even earlier onset, perhaps even as young as age three! Rosenthal (1974) devised a method for investigating the attitudes of children to speech-types, and arrived at conclusions which were confirmed for children in Tyneside, England, by Local (1978). Rosenthal's aim was to compare the reactions of 136 American pre-school children, aged between three and six, to two types of voice, one using Standard English and the other using pronunciation, vocabulary and syntax recognisable as non-standard Black speech. Ninety of the subjects were themselves middle-class white children, but forty-six of them were lower-class and black, so it was possible to compare the reactions of these groups to the two voices. The experiment centred on two identical cardboard boxes, with faces painted on them (using the same colours, blue and red, in both cases), and each containing a cassette tape-recorder and a present which the child could not see. The children listened to the taped voices purporting to be those of the two 'heads'. Each voice described the present inside the box and made precisely the same claims about its attractions but used different speech-patterns (Standard versus Black non-standard). The children were then asked to choose one of the boxes and take the present out (the presents in the two boxes were in fact identical), then the researcher asked the children a number of questions about their reactions to the heads.

Considering how young the children in this experiment were, the results reflect the adult prejudices remarkably closer. No fewer than 79 per cent of the children said that the 'Standard' head spoke better, and about 73 per cent said they expected a nicer present from this box. Virtually *all* (92 per cent) of the white children recognised that the voice in the non-standard box belonged to a black person, and 72 per cent of them thought the 'Standard' voice was that of a white person. On the other hand, the corresponding figures for black children were only 73 per cent and 59 per cent, confirming a tendency (established by others – for example, Shuy 1970) for higher-ranking speakers to be more accurate judges than lower-ranking speakers. The black children, conversely, liked the head with the non-standard voice better, and almost half (46 per cent) took the present from this one, although most of them thought that the other one probably had the nicer present. This trend seems to follow the commonly found pattern among non-standard adult speakers, who see standard speakers as wealthy and generally successful but not particularly likeable or trustworthy (see e.g. Giles and Powesland 1975: 67). Finally, the white children, like their parents, appeared to have 'highly pejorative' attitudes towards the owner of the non-standard Black voice, which they were apparently quite willing to express to the investigator. (Another experiment, conducted in Canada on French-speaking school children, showed that five-year olds already had quite clear attitudes to French as opposed to English – see Schneiderman 1976.)

It seems, then, that we have to assume that at least some children already have quite well-developed linguistic prejudices by the time they go to primary school, and these approach adult sophistication in secondary school. Do such prejudices present problems for pupils during their school careers? It is not clearly established that they do, and we certainly should not assume that what is true of some children is necessarily true of all; but the results of two pieces of research suggest that the teacher's accent (to say nothing of other aspects of speech style) may affect the children's willingness to be influenced by what she says, and even their ability to remember it.

Edward Cairns and Barbara Duriez (1976), in Coleraine, Northern Ireland, compared thirty Catholic school children with thirty Protestant ones of the same age (around ten-to-eleven-year olds) with respect to their ability to remember the content of a story read (by the same speaker) using one of three accents: RP, middle-class Belfast (Northern Ireland) and middle-class Dublin (Eire). The choice of these three accents was determined by the connection between Catholicism and Eire and between Protestantism and Britain (represented by RP), with the Belfast accent to some extent neutral for religion. Each child heard the story read with only one of the accents, but the children were divided into groups so that all six combinations of three voices and two religions were represented. The results showed that Catholic children who heard the RP voice remembered significantly less about the story than the corresponding Protestant children – presumably because the latter were more favourably disposed towards the stereotype evoked by RP. Similarly, Catholic children who heard the RP version remembered less than the Catholics who heard the (relatively neutral) Belfast accent, and the latter also remembered more than Protestant children who heard the Dublin accent, with its Catholic associations. To confirm that Catholic and Protestant children did in fact have different attitudes to Britain and Eire, they were asked a number of questions such as 'What is the capital city of your country?', to which 3 per cent of Protestants and 70 per cent of Catholics replied 'Dublin'. In other words, all the children agreed that an RP accent was part of a 'British' stereotype, and the Dublin one reflected a 'Republican Irish' stereotype, but they disagreed sharply on their assessment of these stereotypes, according to which commanded their loyalty. The general prediction which these results seem to allow is that children will pay more attention to things said in an accent which arouses their group loyalty than in one which does not, and will consequently remember more of the former. The implications for schools seem obvious.

The second relevant piece of research was conducted by Howard Giles in South Wales and Somerset (see Giles and Powesland (1975: 93–8) for this and related pieces of research) to test the effects of different accents on the extent to which children were influenced in their opinions by the content of a message. This time the pupils concerned were seventeen-years old, selected from an initial sample of 500 so that there were five matched groups. They were all asked their opinions on capital punishment via a questionnaire, then a week later each of the matched groups was visited by Giles, posing as a criminologist interested in the opinions of school children on capital punishment. He asked the groups to consider an argument against capital punishment which, he claimed, had been produced by a friend of his. Each group received the argument worded in exactly the same way, but in a different form – one group received a duplicated sheet and the other groups heard the argument read in, respectively, RP, South Welsh, Somerset and Birmingham accents. After reading or hearing the argument, the pupils were asked to evaluate the argument as such, and then to state their views for or against capital punishment. Since they had given their views on this question the week before, it was possible to compare the answers given on the two occasions and to measure any change which had, presumably, been brought about by the argument which had just been presented to them. Ratings on the quality of the argument correlated fairly closely with the prestige of the accent used, with the highest rating for RP. However, for all their lack of prestige, it was the regional accents which had the greatest effect. This result can be interpreted in a number of ways – perhaps the children paid more attention to the message when it was in 'their' accent (as with the experiment in Northern Ireland reported above), or perhaps they were more inclined to trust the opinion of someone who sounded like one of themselves. Presumably several different factors could be at work, but whatever the explanation, there are again clear implications for teachers, if we assume that one of their aims is to influence the opinions of their pupils. (For similar findings relative to bilingual adults hearing messages in different languages, see Cooper et al.. 1977.)

It thus seems that the linguistic prejudices of both teachers and pupils are potential sources of serious problems in the education process. It is by no means clear what can or should be done to minimise these problems, but it is hard to see how anything can be achieved unless teachers themselves have a very clear understanding of the nature of linguistic prejudice, and are sensitive to their own prejudices as well as to those of their pupils.

6.3 Linguistic incompetence: strictly linguistic inequality

The title of this section makes a deliberate reference to Chomsky's notion of 'linguistic competence', by which he means a person's *specifically linguistic* knowledge – roughly, knowledge about words and word combinations. At several points in this book we have raised serious doubts about the validity of any distinction between 'specifically linguistic' and other knowledge, but for the sake of the present discussion we shall assume that some such distinction is possible. The notion of 'linguistic incompetence' concerns the *lack* of the kind of knowledge that is covered by Chomsky's 'competence'. Clearly such a lack is a reality in babies and in others who for one reason or another do not speak some particular language: with respect to that language, they are incompetent. Moreover, someone who is only part of the way towards learning some language as a second one (or towards forgetting a language which was their first language) is to that extent incompetent in the language concerned.

There is no disagreement about the existence of strictly linguistic incompetence. Nor is there any controversy about the existence of educational underachievement: the tendency of education to help least the people who needed it most, members of lower social classes. For example, in Britain children from different social-class backgrounds have very different success-rates in learning to read. Compared with a professional worker's child, an unskilled worker's child is six times as likely by age seven to be a poor reader and fifteen times as likely to be a non-reader (Romaine 1984: 168). The question is how these two facts are related. Is there any support for the idea that some children of school age (or even adults) are incompetent in their first language, compared with others of the same age? This claim has been made with reference to children from lower-class homes, and is known as the DEFICIT THEORY. Some believe that this partially explains the poor performance of such children at school: a child needs certain tools, notably language, in order to benefit from schooling, and the linguistic tools of some lower-class children are just not up to the demands made by the school. Some writers even go so far as to claim that such children come to school with hardly any language at all, unable either to ask questions or to make statements of any kind (Bereiter et al.. 1966, quoted in Labov 1972b: 205). Linguists and sociolinguists who have seriously studied these issues agree in rejecting this view as dangerous nonsense – nonsense because it is simply not true that any normal children are so short of language, and dangerous because it can distract attention from the real shortcomings of many school systems by putting the blame for educational failure on inadequacies of the child. (For a review of the controversy see John Edwards 1994.)

The influence of the extreme version of the deficit theory might be explained by the fact that many children use very little speech when they are in their classrooms 'working' (as opposed to 'messing about'), and that this is especially true of children from lower-class homes. Some children rarely give anything more than a single word in answer to a teacher's questions, and some teachers conclude that this is because they do not know the rules for putting words together into longer sequences, and that, in any case, their vocabulary is limited. A much more plausible conclusion is that the fault is in the situation, and not in the child's linguistic knowledge or lack of it. Because the children are either unwilling to cooperate, or unsure what the teacher expects of them, they keep silent at the very times when the teacher wants them to talk, in spite of using a large amount of language in more familiar situtions such as when dealing with family or friends. Thus some children's lack of speech may be more apparent than real, but this is not to say that children who are underestimated in this way in the classroom do not face a problem. A child who is unwilling or unable to interact verbally with the teacher will gain little benefit from school. However, it is important to diagnose such problems correctly before trying to solve them.

Having said all this, however, we must remember that no two speakers know precisely the same range of vocabulary and syntactic constructions, so we cannot rule out the possibility that some such differences are relevant to success at school. Even if overall children all know roughly the same amount of language, maybe they are unequal in their knowledge of particular linguistic items that are important at school? This possibility was first raised by Basil Bernstein, whose work in the 1960s led him to distinguish two very general linguistic 'codes' which he called 'restricted' and 'elaborated' (Bernstein 1973). According to his theory, the latter is what is needed at school, where it is important to be able to be explicit and clear, but children are unequal in their knowledge of it because of their different home backgrounds. This particular theory is now discredited among sociolinguists for lack of empirical evidence for either of its key assumptions: that explicitness is essential at school, and that some children are incapable of talking explicitly (Lawton 1968, Wells 1981a, 1981b, John Edwards 1994, MacLure 1994).

The most directly relevant evidence comes from a large-scale longitudinal survey of children in Bristol which was led in the 1970s by Gordon Wells (Wells 1979a, 1979b, 1981a, 1981b). In this research young children were equipped from time to time with a radio microphone which picked up not only their own speech but also that of their parents and other people who spoke to them. This allowed Wells and his team to look for connections between the children's developing competence (as measured by their output) and the type of speech which they experienced. They analysed the structures used by the children and by their carers, and found great differences among the children in the maturity of their language when measured by various 'global' criteria such as syntactic complexity. They asked how far these differences could be related either to social-class differences or to differences in the speech of their carers. In brief, social class turned out to be irrelevant (except for differences of vocabulary, which were only revealed in a test), but the carers' speech had a clear influence. Carers seemed to be able to help the children to develop linguistically by 'incorporating and extending matter previously contributed by the child or designed to focus and direct ongoing activity' (Wells 1981a: 115). This 'parental speech style' affects the child's linguistic development, which in turn affects the child's progress at school, so this is clearly an important discovery.

Wells' work confirmed that children *are* unequal from a strictly linguistic point of view, and that at least some of the inequality is due to their experiences (i.e. to nurture rather than nature). But unfortunately it does not seem to help with the fundamental social problem of educational failure because the linguistic inequalities that Wells discovered were only indirectly related to social class. It seems, then, that we cannot use global linguistic inequalities to explain why lower-class children do less well at school than upper-class children.

Another approach to the question of linguistic inequality is to focus much more specifically on 'academic language', the vocabulary and structures that teachers use when teaching and which children are expected to understand and learn – words like *identify*, *position* or *moreover*. It seems likely that, although some children learn such words at home, others may not, which leaves them at a disadvantage when they first meet the words at school, and the fact that some children do understand the words may blind the teacher to the need to explain them. We have very little research evidence for such differences, but we do have an interesting practical programme for addressing their consequences directly, called 'Illuminating English', a course of explicit instruction in academic language which appeared to have dramatic effects on the children's performance across all subjects (Mason et al., 1992). Direct targeting of specific 'deficit' areas seems much more promising than the earlier global approaches.

Other specific deficits which affect educational performance are more obvious. At one extreme are children who are fully competent in a language, but not in the language of instruction. Typically such children are members of minority groups, who have to learn the majority language before they can benefit from schooling. Even after learning enough of the school language to cope, their lack of home support in this language must put them at a disadvantage compared with children who speak it natively, a disadvantage which may be partly offset by the social benefits of being bilingual. At the other extreme are children who speak a non-standard dialect of the school's language of instruction, but who are expected to learn the standard dialect for purposes of reading and writing, and possibly also for speaking. Even if the strictly linguistic differences between the standard and non-standard varieties are trivial (as they are for most people in Britain), it is no trivial task for children to learn to use a variety whose speakers they distrust (as we saw in 6.2.4), so the change needs to be handled sensitively. Needless to say (in a book on sociolinguistics), the teacher should definitely NOT aim at the total eradication of the children's non-standard speech! If this is clear to all concerned, children can learn to switch between standard and non-standard according to the circumstances, as in any diglossic community (2.4.2).

6.4   Communicative incompetence: inequality in communication

The term 'communicative incompetence' is in contrast with the term 'communicative competence' established by Dell Hymes (1971b; cf. also Campbell and Wales (1970), who use the same term in the same sense). Communicative competence is knowledge needed by a speaker or hearer, but is much more broadly based than the 'linguistic competence' of Chomskyan linguistics. Instead of referring only to the knowledge of linguistic forms, it includes our knowledge – perhaps 'ability' would be a better term – of how to use linguistic forms appropriately. According to Hymes, the goal of a student of language should be:

> to account for the fact that a normal child acquires knowledge of sentences, not only as grammatical, but also as appropriate. He or she acquires competence as to when to speak, when not, and as to what to talk about with whom, when, where, in what manner. In short, a child becomes able to accomplish a repertoire of speech acts, to take part in speech events, and to evaluate their accomplishment by others. This competence, moreover, is integral with attitudes, values and motivations concerning language, its features and uses, and integral with competence for, and attitudes toward, the interrelation of language with the other code of communicative conduct. (Hymes 1971b)

If communicative competence is to cover all these types of ability underlying successful speech, it must include at least the whole of 'linguistic competence' plus the whole of the amorphous range of facts included under 'pragmatics' (knowledge applied in using linguistic items in context); and it must also make close contact with 'attitudes, values and motivations', with which linguistics generally has had little to do even in discussions of pragmatics.

Some parts of communicative competence may be due to universal pragmatic principles of human interaction of the kind that are discussed in pragmatics (for example, Levinson 1983, Sperber and Wilson 1986), but there are certainly other parts that vary from community to community and which have to be learned. To take a simple, and perhaps extreme, example, different communities have different conventions for answering the telephone; in English you say 'Hello', in Italian you say 'Pronto' (ready), in Spanish 'Diga!' (say!) and so on. These parts of our language behaviour are obviously controlled by rather arbitrary conventions, for which it is very easy to multiply examples under topics like 'how to . . . ' or 'what to say when . . . '. Such conventions are certainly included in the notion of communicative competence, and have become much more widely recognised since Hymes drew attention to them. They include not only greetings, farewells and all the other conventions used in structuring speech (see 4.3), but a wide range of other knowledge about when to speak, how to speak, what to speak about and so on. In some cases it could perhaps be argued that the information concerned belongs firmly in the grammar, as part of what we know about specific items (for example, one of the things we know about the word *hello* is that we use it to answer the telephone). However, there are some cases where this is clearly not so, the most obvious being the conventions for staying silent, which vary markedly from culture to culture. For example, should you speak or stay silent at meal-times? Should you avoid silence when in the presence of acquaintances? How long can a silence last before it becomes embarrassing? British culture avoids silences much more than some others that have been described (for example, the Apache use of silence mentioned in 4.3.1).

It is easy to see how inequalities can arise in communicative competence to the (considerable) extent that this is learned through experience. Once again, however, the inequalities will be specific rather than global (except in the case of young children who clearly start from zero). There is no suggestion that some people have more communicative competence overall than others, but there clearly are differences relative to specific types of situation. Some people are good at light chit-chat, others at presenting lectures or after-dinner speeches; some people know the conventions for ordering beer in a pub, or for ordering wine in a restaurant (which needs a different convention), and others don't. All these skills require knowledge; indeed, no clear line can be drawn between 'knowledge' (knowing what to do) and 'skill' (being able to put it into practice) in any kind of behaviour, from tying knots through driving a car to speaking (arguably the most complicated of all behaviour).

A particularly obvious kind of inequality in communicative competence distinguishes native speakers of a language from non-native learners. The same is of course even more obviously true of strictly linguistic competence, which has traditionally defined the syllabus for second-language teaching, but communicative competence has been recognised much more explicitly as an important part of such teaching in the last few decades. The new approach to second-language teaching, which is generally called the 'communicative' approach, has been much more successful in some respects than traditional grammar-based approaches (Howatt 1994, Littlewood 1994), but regardless of its achievements it has at least defined much more realistic (and ambitious!) goals for language-teaching in recognising that native-like fluency involves far more than a perfect command of grammar and vocabulary.

Another practical problem to which communicative competence may be relevant is the fact that working-class children tend to underachieve at school, as we noted in the last section. Does coping with school require items of communicative competence which are more familiar to middle-class children than to lower-class children? A good deal of recent work suggests that this is indeed so. We shall first consider some relevant features of 'classroom language' and then we shall look at social-class differences in the use of these features at home.

Several recent research projects have studied the ways in which language is used in typical lessons at school (Mercer 1994), so we now know far more about the realities of what children need to know in order to cope with that part of school. As mentioned in the last section, it was thought at one time that school-work required language that was specially explicit, but it is now generally agreed that it is just as important to be able to 'read between the lines' at school as it is in any other kind of language use (MacLure 1994). Indeed one of the problems that children face is precisely that teachers are not explicit about what they want children to do; the children have to read the teacher's mind (Romaine 1984: 171). A very clear (and common) example of this is the situation that arises when the teacher asks a question with a specific 'correct' answer in mind; for example, here is an extract from a lesson on pendulums, where T is the teacher and P is a pupil (Edwards and Westgate 1994: 4327):

> T: So the shorter the string – what? What happens when you shorten the string?
>
> P: The faster it gets.
>
> T: The shorter the string, the faster the swing. Right.

This pupil knew about teachers' questions – that the teacher usually already has one particular target answer, that the teacher wants the pupils to supply this answer, that this may involve completing an unfinished sentence, and that the teacher will accept a close approximation to the target but will still say the target even if a pupil has just said it. This elaborate interplay is controlled by rules, and is successful only when both parties share the rules (and accept the point of the game). The same can be said of various other parts of classroom talk, but teacher-questions are the clearest and most studied examples.

Turning now to the children's experiences of questioning at home, there is some evidence of inequality in this area of communicative competence (Romaine 1984: 173ff.). The most important research bearing on this question is a study of a community in South Carolina by Shirley Brice Heath (1984). She studied the ways in which questions were used by the local school-teachers both in the classroom and in their own homes, and also by the families of the children who attended the school, who were mainly working-class. As usual, teachers asked pupils a lot of questions to which the teacher already knew the answers, and they did the same with their own children at home. It seems reasonable to take them as typical of middle-class parents in general because other studies have found the same in middle-class families, so their behaviour in the classroom was simply an extension of what they did at home. Similarly, when their own children reached school age, they would find little difference (in this respect) between school and home. In contrast, the working-class parents did not ask questions of this kind, so children had to learn the rules of the game when they reached school. However easy or difficult this may be, it is a task which they face but the middle-class children do not so it is a source of inequality and may be part of a much more general explanation for why working-class children underachieve at school.

7
Theoretical summary

7.1 Introduction

This final chapter is an attempt to tie together some of the general ideas that have emerged in the earlier chapters. The strength of sociolinguistics is its firm foundation in concrete facts – facts about language use in particular communities, figures for linguistic variables and so on. This concreteness is one of its main appeals, but also a serious weakness because we badly need a general framework of ideas to integrate the facts into a whole that makes some kind of intellectual sense. We have mentioned a number of subtheories about particular areas, all of which are well supported by evidence:

> the 'family-tree' and 'wave' theories of change,
> variety-based and item-based models of language,
> the 'classical' and 'prototype' theories of thought,
> the Sapir–Whorf hypothesis about language and thought,
> the 'face' theory of interaction,
> the 'accommodation', 'network' and 'acts of identity' theories of linguistic
>   choices.

What we have not yet tried to do is to show how they all fit together. This is our rather ambitious aim for the next section.

Nor have we asked what all these facts imply for a general theory of language structure. Over the past decades linguists have been busy inventing theories about how language is organised internally – theories of syntax, of semantics, of phonology and of morphology. Most theories assume a clear distinction between 'language', consisting only of phonology, morphology, syntax and semantics, and everything else, which leaves most of the data of sociolinguistics outside language. According to this widely held view of language, a language is a self-contained system of words, sounds and meanings linked to each other in various complex ways. Everybody accepts that these linguistic 'items' are also linked to social 'items', as we have seen repeatedly throughout this book, but most linguists think that these other links are outside language 'proper'.

Section 3 will argue against this view on the grounds that there is no evidence for the assumed boundary around language, and that any theory of language structure should cover the links that have been explored so intensively by sociolinguists. It will spell out some general characteristics that a successful theory of language structure should have.

Before we start on this theory-building it is important to remind ourselves of the difference between individuals and communities as the focus of attention. A book on 'language in relation to society' might be expected to say a great deal about 'languages' and 'societies', but since the first chapter we have in fact broken both of these rather 'macro' and abstract notions into their smallest parts: linguistic items and individual people. One reason for this decision is simply that the macro relationships are handled by a different discipline, the sociology of language. But a more important reason is that it is impossible to understand the relationships that really matter to a sociolinguist except at the micro level of the individual person and the individual linguistic item. The macro 'varieties of language' that we considered in chapter 2 turned out to be too fluid and ill-defined to be seriously studied in their own right – languages, dialects and registers all seem to lack the clear boundaries that are needed for an objective study, even if they play a part in the individual's subjective classification of linguistic items. The same was true of 'speech communities', the macro objects on the social side to which we might wish to relate these macro linguistic objects. All the productive work in sociolinguistics has been about particular linguistic items as used (or understood) by particular people.

This stress on individuals is important for theorising about social functions of language, as we shall be doing in the next section, because it will allow us to integrate theories about how individuals interact directly – especially the theory of accommodation – with the theories about networks (still based on individuals) and acts of identity (performed by individuals), in which we are concerned with individual people's place in the larger society. We shall also be able to suggest a partial explanation for statistical variability in terms of decisions made by individuals. Seen from this perspective, differences between individuals are to be expected, and what requires explanation are the similarities; in contrast, the alternative view of language as somehow 'located' in the community makes similarity the norm, with differences, especially idiosyncratic ones, as the puzzle.

The individual focus also helps in theorising about language structure because it makes sociolinguistics directly relevant to most modern theories of language structure. One of the main contributions of Noam Chomsky to modern linguistics has been his view of language as a form of individual knowledge, or 'competence', and most alternatives to his theory of language structure are based on the same assumption. The questions these theories are trying to ask concern the knowledge that people use in producing and understanding utterances. An individualist approach to sociolinguistics focusses on one specific part of this knowledge, the part which involves 'society' – i.e. other people; we can call this knowledge 'sociolinguistic competence', in contrast with 'structural competence' in matters of syntax, phonology, morphology and semantics. If these two competences are both types of knowledge, we can raise serious research questions about the relationship between them: apart from the differences in actual content, are they so different in organisation that we have to recognise them as two separate areas of knowledge? Do they interact in any way? At what points do they meet? The discussion in section 3 will suggest that they are in fact integrated into a single system, and should be studied together.

7.2. The social functions of language

The social functions of language are the ways in which we use language to give our view of our relationships to other people. We can do this directly, for example, by saying things like 'Listen, I'm boss here!' or 'You can be my best friend' or 'She's my daughter.' Or we can do it indirectly, by our choice of words when talking about other things: 'Hi Bob, what's up?' or 'He's well fit, i'nit?' The direct method involves the meanings of words like BOSS, FRIEND and DAUGHTER, which are all relevant to the interests of some sociolinguists (as we saw in chapter 3 on language, culture and thought). In the indirect method, on the other hand, we are concerned with word-forms, not word-meanings: with the choice of HI (as opposed to alternatives such as HELLO), BOB (versus ROBERT or MR SMITH), UP (versus HAPPENING, etc.), 's (versus *is*) and so on. Using the direct method we can make our social message extremely precise, and the use of language to talk about social structures is clearly vital. Nevertheless it is not at the centre of sociolinguistics, for the simple reason that it is at the centre of lexical semantics (Hudson 1995). Sociolinguistics is the sole discipline responsible for the indirect method of communicating information about social relationships. For convenience we shall call the information which is conveyed in this way 'social information'.

7.2.1 Face

Not surprisingly, the social information is always information about the speaker, though its relevance may be only indirect. The various kinds of information comprise what we have been calling the speaker's 'face', the public image that the speaker presents to the rest of the world. Figure 7.1 shows this function diagrammatically, with an abstract 'face' resulting from

Figure 7.1

the speech coming from the speaker's mouth. (In previous diagrams the speech has been indicated by a row of *z*'s, which we could have shown as the immediate source of the face in this diagram; however the diagram is gradually going to grow so we need to reduce complexity to the minimum.) Of course even at this level of generality the diagram is an oversimplification because it implies that speech is the only source of face. As we know, other parts of our observable behaviour contribute as well – the way we walk and stand, the clothes we (choose to) wear, the way we organise other bits of our body (for example, our hair) and so on and on. We discussed the connections of speech to gestures, body language and other kinds of non-verbal behaviour in 4.4. All these extra influences should be borne in mind when looking at these diagrams.

Your face (in this sense) is a complex cluster of characteristics (unlike the diagram, where it is just sunnily happy). On the one hand, it is linked to your observable behaviour, as just described; so if you behave differently, the face you project may change. On the other hand, it is linked to various personal and social characteristics which may not in themselves be directly observable. In this respect your face is just like a word, which combines an observable form with an unobservable meaning; and just like a word, it is a prototype – defined by typical cases, with exceptions allowed. If most of your behaviour points to a particular set of unobservables, we may overlook the parts that conflict – for example, if you pronounce almost every word like an English person, but have an American pronunciation for just a few words, our classification does not simply collapse, but we classify you as English and wonder why you have that odd pronunciation. Similarly for face: if your words and your gestures express one kind of face but your clothes suggest a different one, the rest of us look for some way to reconcile the conflict rather than leaving you completely unclassified. The result of combining observable and unobservable characteristics in a prototype is that the way you speak tells

231

the rest of us about your face, i.e. about the kind of person you want us to think you are.

7.2.2   Solidarity and accommodation

We can now expand our diagram by adding some of these unobservable social characteristics. In Figure 7.1 the arrow pointed from the mouth to the 'face', showing the direction in which information flows for the hearer. We can now have arrows pointing out from the face towards the unobservables. We start by adding a second person, the person being addressed. The first piece of social information shown is the solidarity relationship between the speaker and this person. We have seen a host of ways in which solidarity is expressed – through choice of language, subtle 'accommodation' on quantitative variables (predicted by accommodation theory) and use of purpose-built solidarity-expressers such as names and pronouns. Figure 7.2 is intended to cover all these things, but we shall consider some of them more carefully below.

The solidarity relationship is the first to be introduced here because it is probably the most important of all social relationships, at least as far as language is concerned. This is because it is the relationship that reflects shared experience, which is necessarily tied to linguistic similarity. People who have spent all their life together, sharing the same experiences of language, are bound to be very similar in their language; and conversely, similarity of language is a good (though not infallible) basis for guessing similar experiences.

However the link between language and solidarity is more than a mechanical consequence of shared experience. It is noticeable in children's acquisition of language that they end up acquiring the language of their models down to the finest detail, with a precision that goes far beyond the requirements of mere comprehension. This conclusion emerges dramatically from a series of studies of Philadelphia (Payne 1980, Labov 1989) which focussed on the details of the pronunciation of the vowel in words like *bad* and *dad* (which are pronounced differently by adult Philadelphians). Apparently children can only learn all the mass of lexical detail needed to grow into true Philadelphians if their own parents were themselves born and bred in Philadelphia. Another curiosity of child language acquisition (which was mentioned in 2.4.2) is that they slavishly adopt all the pointless irregularities of the adult system, in spite of having regularised them at an earlier stage in their learning; for example, having recognised the general rule for forming past tenses, and having applied it incorrectly to give *goed* as the past tense of GO, they fall into line with the irregular adult form *went*. More dramatically still, they accept adult structural gaps like the one which ought to be filled by **I aren't your friend* (compare *Aren't I your friend?* and *He isn't your friend*) (* indicates an ungrammatical

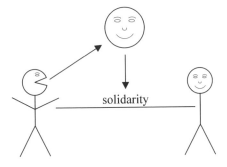

solidarity

Figure 7.2

example). The only possible conclusion is that children are driven by an urge to make their speech identical to that of their models and the most plausible explanation for this is accommodation theory – the desire to reduce differences in behaviour in order to stress solidarity.

One recent piece of work may seem to challenge this claim, but equally it may support it, according to how the data are interpreted. We mentioned in 5.4.3 the detailed investigation of a few villages in the north-east of Scotland which has been carried out over two decades by Nancy Dorian (1994). In these villages the basic language is Gaelic, a language which is on the verge of extinction in Scotland, and the main point of the research is that there is far more diversity in the linguistic details of the Gaelic spoken by different individuals than we might expect if everyone is striving to be the same as everyone else in their community. This diversity cannot be explained as the linguistic reflection of social diversity, because there is virtually no social diversity – the three small villages studied are socially extremely homogeneous. Everybody knows everybody else as individuals, and most people are related to each other by blood or by marriage. One conclusion is that accommodation has been overplayed, but another is that accommodation only applies when there are contrasting alternatives – i.e. when people with high solidarity need to be contrasted with people with low solidarity. When solidarity is universally high, linguistic accommodation is irrelevant, and the usual pressures to conform do not apply. At present we can only speculate about the explanation, and Dorian's data remain as a challenge for accommodation-based theories.

The ideas behind accommodation theory are important for theory because they contradict a theoretical claim which is widely held among linguists, called 'functionalism'. This is the idea that the structure of language can be explained by the communicative functions that it has to perform – the conveying of information in the most efficient way possible. Structural gaps like the lack of *I aren't* and irregular morphology such as *went* are completely dysfunctional, and should have been eliminated by functional pressures if functionalism was right. Labov himself has presented strong evidence against functionalism (1994: ch. 19).

The debate between sociolinguists and functionalists is particularly important because functionalism is often presented as the only alternative to 'formalism', the view that the formal structures of language are independent of the way language is used (Thompson 1992). According to this view there are only two possibilities: either language is moulded by its communicative functions, or its structure is determined by a genetic quirk for which communicative function is irrelevant (the Chomskyan view). The sociolinguistic perspective offers a third possibility: that language is adapted to its functions, but that one of its functions is to communicate social information (for example, solidarity). On this view, the various kinds of function can conflict with each other, so languages are unstable compromises which are liable to change at any time.

7.2.3 *Networks and multiple models*

It seems, then, that it is the need to show solidarity that is responsible for all this precision in language acquisition, with countless acts of accommodation as the driving force. Every time the child talks to a 'significant other' (parent at first, then peer), the desire to accommodate pushes its output a little nearer to that of the other. However, the child is not equally close to every other person whom it meets or hears. From the child's point of view the social world may well be organised in networks. It recognises a lot of individuals, and it recognises solidarity differences among them; so it accommodates more to some people than to others. In a sense this means that it is building a mental 'community', but it is only a very abstract sense; there is no reason to think that in the child's mind there is a notion 'my community' with clear members and non-members. It is much more likely that the child's mental model of the social world is like the social structures that Lesley Milroy studied in Belfast, based on social networks of individual people. Figure 7.3 adds a small network to our growing picture of the speaker's social world. Each of the straight lines indicates a solidarity relationship of some strength, with strengths differing from pair to pair. The varying thicknesses of the lines are intended to reflect this variation. It is easy to see how a close-knit network of people can become almost identical in speech as a result of thousands, or even millions, of acts of mutual accommodation.

Let's review progress so far. We started from a concrete example of face-to-face interaction between two people, in which one person's speech presents a 'face' which, among other things, defines a particular degree of solidarity

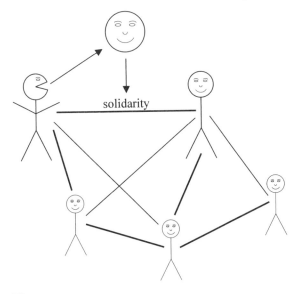

solidarity

Figure 7.3

between them. The higher the intended solidarity, the more closely the current speaker's speech matches that of the person addressed, as predicted by accommodation theory. The word *intended* is important here because we are concerned with the speaker's subjective view of the world, rather than with objective facts. According to accommodation theory, the degree of accommodation depends on how much the speaker wants the other person to like them, which is a matter of personal values and personality. Two different people could be in the same objective relationship to a third, as defined in terms of kinship, working together, being neighbours and so on; and yet they may feel very different degrees of solidarity to that person. This means, of course, that solidarity may not be reciprocal – I may like you much more than you like me, in which case I may try to make my speech more similar to yours while you for your part have the opposite aim. Strictly speaking, then, our diagram should have two solidarity lines for each pair of people, each showing one person's view of the relationship. The subjective nature of solidarity is why it is so central to our social face, and why languages provide so many subtle ways of expressing solidarity, none of which would be needed if solidarity followed automatically from objective givens.

The same applies to any speaker's relationships with everyone else they meet, which has interesting and important consequences. In a society like Milroy's working-class Belfast relationships tend to cluster in closed networks – A

235

knows B and C, who also know each other and so on. If they are all accommodating to each other, the result is a very homogeneous core community, with a few stragglers who know fewer people and are less influenced by the core linguistic models (though we have to bear in mind the challenge of Dorian's Scottish villages discussed above). But what if the networks are more open – A knows B and C, but B and C do not know each other? In that case we can also expect much less linguistic similarity (unless this is imposed in the ways which we shall discuss below). In Le Page's terms (Le Page and Tabouret-Keller 1985), the first situation is 'focussed' and the second is 'diffuse'.

A third possibility is that an individual may be linked to several distinct networks, each with its own linguistic norms. In that case we can predict that accommodation will make that person fluent in each of the norms, and able to switch among them according to the situation. This is of course very common, and possibly the most common of the three cases from a world perspective. The result is multi-lingualism, 'multi-dialectism' and 'multi-registerism'. The literature is full of case-studies of communities where most people have vast 'linguistic repertoires' from which they choose with great skill and speed.

The complex world in which we all live presents us all with multiple and conflicting models. These complex links help to explain how one person's speech affects another person's, and ultimately how changes spread through larger portions of society (as described in the wave theory of change), so we are gradually coming to understand how these patterns compete with each other. It is even possible to model the competition mathematically, as Peter Trudgill did (1975/1983) in the paper from which the data on changes in southern Norway (5.4.2) were taken. In that paper he also reports a method for calculating the strength of influence between large groups such as towns and cities on the basis of the geographical distance between them and their relative sizes. His formula makes impressively accurate predictions for the linguistic influences on Norwich. No doubt similar formulae could in principle be developed for predicting how individuals influence one another.

The network model allows us to look again at the status of notions like 'language', 'dialect' and 'register', which we have rejected as analytical concepts. The reason for rejecting them was that they did not seem to correspond to any objective reality, in particular as far as their boundaries were concerned. It is meaningless to ask how many dialects there are in England (or in any other country), or to ask precisely where London (or Norwich) English ends, simply because the only relevant objective facts concern individual linguistic items, and different linguistic items always have different social distributions (2.1.3). Similarly, for some language boundaries (2.2.3), which means that we cannot take any language boundaries for granted.

236

However, there is another perspective on these large-scale 'varieties of language', the subjective view of the individual speaker. From the individual's point of view, at least languages and dialects are probably subjectively real. Someone who is linked to one network of people who speak in one way, and to another where they speak in a different way, is bound to recognise these differences and to conceptualise them in terms of large-scale groupings which could be called 'languages' or 'dialects'. These concepts are part of their knowledge of language – for example, a Spanish–English bilingual who can speak pure English or pure Spanish as the occasion demands must know which words and constructions belong to which language. To the extent that we can explore this part of linguistic knowledge by psychological tests, observation and so on, our discoveries are objective facts; but it is important to remember that they are objective facts about individual minds, and not about the linguistic world. Consequently it is no surprise to find that different people recognise different varieties – for instance, that some English people have a single global category for 'American English' which no American would recognise, and vice versa.

7.2.4   Social types and acts of identity

This discussion has brought us to our next theoretical advance, the recognition of general social 'types'. The network model involves the relationships among individual people who know each other and talk to each other. Linguistic influence is the result of accommodation by one individual to another individual. In some simple societies this may be the end of the story, but it certainly is not the end for the modern urban societies in which we all live. As we saw in 6.2.1, we tend to organise our knowledge of society in terms of social stereotypes, which for simplicity we can call simply 'types' – general types of people such as 'coal-miner', 'yuppy', 'Londoner', 'rough', 'Burnout' or 'male'. Each of these abstractions allows us to generalise across a range of people, including people we have never met. One of the main benefits is in dealing with strangers, when the social type acts as a collecting point for observable and unobservable information. A person's observable behaviour, including their speech, gives us a clue as to their social type, which in turn gives us unobservable characteristics which we need to know in planning our own behaviour and attitudes towards them: Do we warm to them as a fellow-whatever, or do we avoid them? Do we trust them, admire them, fear them? Another benefit of thinking in terms of social types is to help us to build a mental model of society in which we personally have a clear place, and without which we can feel lost. As we saw in 6.2.1 this way of viewing people also leads to prejudice, so we pay a price for the benefits.

Figure 7.4 includes a single social type as a token of this aspect of social structure, but of course we must remember that reality is much richer, with a multiplicity of intersecting types available for classifying people. In the diagram the type is a little figure drawn in dotted lines in order to remind us that it is actually a figment of the speaker's imagination (unlike all the other figures, who are real people). It is a prototype which the speaker has extracted from experience of people who combine particular social characteristics, including (in some cases) particular ways of speaking. All the individuals who are connected to the social type are examples of it, a relationship which is represented in the diagram by the triangle whose base lies on the general category and whose apex points is linked to the particular cases. (This is the first bit of notation from Word Grammar, which will be mentioned again in 7.3.5.)

The diagram shows a situation in which the speaker belongs to the same social type as the person addressed, which implies relatively high solidarity; but of course this does not have to be so as speakers can talk to people who are

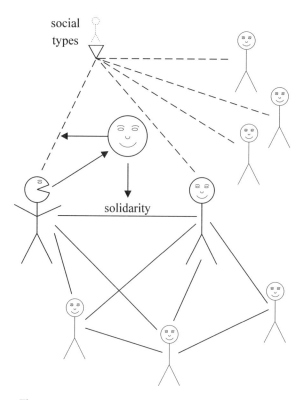

Figure 7.4

238

socially very different from them. Furthermore, a more realistic diagram would have included a range of different social types, of which some are shared by the speaker and addressee and others are not. Each of the links between the speaker and a social type is part of the speaker's face, as shown by the arrow linking the smiling face to the dotted line on the left. It is in this sense that speaking can be seen as an 'act of identity' which locates the speaker in a 'multi-dimensional social space'. It is an act of identity because it provides observable clues which other people can use in order to work out how the speaker sees their place among the various social types that are relevant to speech. The social space is multi-dimensional because it contains a (large) number of different social types, each of which provides a separate 'dimension' of classification – not only namable dimensions like age, sex and social class, but also others like 'English-ness', 'Londoner-ness' or 'linguist-ness'.

It is important to recognise the difference between the two parts of 'face' that we have just distinguished. One part is concerned with the interpersonal relationship between the speaker and the person addressed, while the other part is concerned with the social classification of the speaker alone. They are linked, of course, because people who are socially similar (classification) are more likely to feel socially close to each other (interpersonal), and conversely, accommodation theory says that the more you like a person (interpersonal), the more you want to be like them (classification). This means that the same person can present different self-classifications on different occasions according to the company they are in. We know that this is normal sociolinguistic behaviour (as witness code-switching in multilingual societies, and style-shifting in monolingual ones), so we might ask whether shifts in self-classification are always driven by the desire to accommodate to the person addressed.

A clear answer comes from an interesting study by Trudgill of pop songs recorded by British groups (1983a: 141–60). Not surprisingly, he found that many groups adopted a pseudo-American accent which must be an act of identity (wanting to sound like an American singer) not motivated by accommodation since the targeted audience are British, not American. The pop groups were simply pretending to be American, for the sake of the status this would give their performance. The same kind of pretence lies behind the very common activity of 'putting on' an accent (as one might put on clothes when dressing up). A Londoner can put on a Scottish accent, a white teenager can put on Creole and so on, without intending to deceive anyone. Rampton 1995 is a careful in-depth study of what he calls 'code-crossing' by Afro-Caribbean, Anglo and Asian youths in an English town, in which Anglo or Asian teenagers put on Creole; and Punjabi speakers put on 'stylised Asian English' (a stereotype which nobody speaks). This is usually meant to be funny, and can be either negative or positive; it probably plays an important social role, but, whatever the reasons for it, it is clearly not explained by accommodation theory, but is explained well as a 'metaphorical' application of the theory of acts of identity.

7.2.5   Power

The last element to be added to our picture is the other inter-personal relationship, power. This is shown in Figure 7.5 by the angled line, as in earlier diagrams. However important power may be in life and society at large, in a sociolinguistic model it is less important than solidarity because it has fewer consequences for language. We have seen various ways in which our choice of words can show whether we see the person addressed as a superior, an inferior or an equal (4.2.3), which justify the power link between the speaker and the person addressed in our diagram; but in most languages, most of the time, power is irrelevant to speech. The same is certainly not true of self-classification – every single word gives some information about our social classification – and as we have seen, classification is closely related to solidarity. Nor does it seem to be generally true that linguistic trend-setters tend to be more powerful people; on the contrary, in fact, most innovations seem to be launched in lower social classes, by the young and by females, all of whom tend to be relatively powerless (Fasold 1992: 218, Labov 1994: 156). These facts suggest that power is irrelevant to network relationships as far as their linguistic consequences are concerned.

On the other hand, power clearly is important for the basic organisation of society in terms of social classes, with the rich and powerful at the top and the poor and powerless at the bottom. Social class is an important influence on language in most (perhaps all) urban societies, however egalitarian they may claim to be, and it is social class that is responsible for the difference between 'overt' and 'covert' prestige (6.2.2). Some linguistic forms have overt prestige because of the high social status of their speakers in the social-class hierarchy. Furthermore, these same forms may have extra prestige from their association with professions that have official power – doctors, teachers, publishers, managers, judges and so on. Among all the alternatives of which a person is aware these forms have special status, and may be officially recognised by the title 'standard language'. In recognition of this further part played by power, the diagram has a power-link attached to its one token social type so that we could, if necessary, show this type as a subordinate or superior of some other type to which the speaker does not belong.

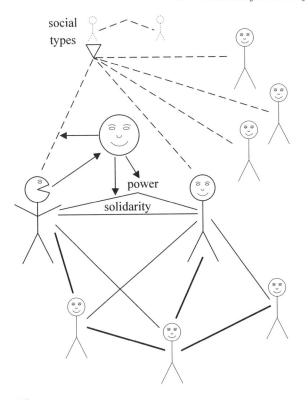

social
types

power
solidarity

Figure 7.5

7.2.6   *Analogue relationships and variability*

Although the picture is complete, we have barely mentioned what may be the most important fact about it: all the relationships that we have discussed are a matter of degree. Solidarity varies from minimum (total stranger) to maximum (most intimate), so links in the social network vary in 'strength'; power varies from most superior, through equal, to most subordinate; and a person belongs to a particular social type to some degree, from total (for a really typical member) to marginal. In other words, our social relationships are all 'analogue' (more/less) rather than 'digital' (present/absent). This is a consequence of the general idea that the relevant concepts are prototypes, organised around clear cases but allowing members that depart from the typical to varying degrees.

Analogue social relationships (in our minds) are a true reflection of the complexity of social life, full of uncertainties and ambiguities. As readers who are themselves university students may have noticed, the life of a typical university student is particularly full of uncertainty and ambiguity: Am I an independent adult or a dependent child? Where do I fit in the social-class hierarchy? Where do I 'live'? Where and when do I 'work'? What is the balance of power between me and my teachers? Are all students really equal? Am I socially closer to members of my own sex? These uncertainties make university life a good place to think objectively about social relationships, and to see how important it is to be able to leave some decisions in a state of uncertainty.

Why is this analogue view of social relationships so important? Because the linguistic signals are not analogue, but digital. Take the very simple example of names. Your solidarity with John Smith is analogue and may vary from zero to maximum, but in naming him you only have two options: *John* or *Mr Smith*. Even if you add *John Smith*, which seems to be becoming popular as a social compromise, there are only three possibilities. There are no linguistic compromises, for example, something which is linguistically half-way between *John* and *John Smith* such as *John Smi*! The problem is to find a way to convert the analogue social 'meaning' into a digital linguistic form. As we all know, this is a tricky social problem, but one way to solve it is to balance the choice of names against other linguistic choices; if *John* is really more intimate than the relationship justifies, you can compensate by using a greeting that is rather too formal. Another possibility, though, is to alternate between the two names – to call him *Mr Smith* most of the time, but to add a touch of intimacy by throwing in the odd *John*, or vice versa. The statistical balance between the alternatives gives you an opportunity to match the analogue, quantitative, nature of the social choice; and the result is a naming pattern which is variable, ripe for treatment as a sociolinguistic variable.

What we have just said about solidarity and power also applies to classification in terms of social types. As we have seen, the face that you present locates you in a multi-dimensional social space whose dimensions are defined not only by age, sex and so on, but also by 'types' such as 'Londoner' or 'American'. These are prototypes, which means that their members may be more or less 'good'. Now imagine an American who has lived in London for forty years. What is she? This is not a question about her formal status but about her feelings – does she feel herself to be an American or a Londoner? And the answer is likely to be unclear: to some extent American and to some extent a Londoner. The degree to which she accepts both of these group- memberships is how she locates herself on the dimensions of 'American-ness' and 'Londoner-ness'.

But how do these partial classifications translate into the digital code of language? Once again the items that distinguish Londoners from Americans generally allow no linguistic compromises: you say either *sidewalk* or *pavement*, you pronounce the consonant of *at* either as a glottal stop or as a / t /, you pronounce *fourth* either with or without the / r /. But what our American Londoner can do is to alternate between American and London forms, pronouncing / r / in 40 per cent of words where it could be pronounced, and so on. In short, she could treat these choices as sociolinguistic variables.

By allowing social classification to be quantitatively variable we now have a partial explanation for linguistic variability: a speaker who feels less than 100 per cent committed as a member of some social type can show this by using the linguistic forms that are associated with that type with less than 100 per cent consistency. The explanation is only partial because we know that scores on different variables are rarely the same even when they seem to be linked to the same social types. We shall be able to fill this explanatory gap in 7.4.3, but for present purposes it is important to see that if membership of a social type is a matter of degree, inconsistency in speech is virtually inevitable.

7.3.   The structure of language

7.3.1   *Background*

Language, then, has social functions; even if this conclusion did not leap out at us from everyday experience, it would have been proved conclusively by research in sociolinguistics. But does this make any difference at all to our ideas about the structure of language? One fashionable answer is that it does not. For example, the following comment appeared in a discussion of Labov's quantitative work (Smith 1989: 180):

> To be of interest to a linguistic theorist it is not sufficient that the talk be of words and such like, rather the talk has to have implications of some kind for the theory concerned, by supporting or contradicting one of the claims derivable from it . . . Any social parameter whatsoever may be the locus for some linguistic difference. Unfortunately nothing of interest to linguistic theory follows from this, so quantifying the difference is irrelevant to linguistics even though it may be of interest to the sociologist if it gives him or her a recognition criterion for some socially relevant variable.

The logic is absurd, because the writer assumes the conclusion as a premise: variability is irrelevant to linguistic theory because it is irrelevant to linguistic theory. However this passage does at least raise a fundamental question which is generally ignored by sociolinguists as well as by those who would call themselves simply 'theoretical linguists' – people who specialise in theorising about the structure of language.

By and large theoretical linguists have decided that sociolinguistics and its subject-matter, the social functions of language, have no relevance for them.

Are they right? The rest of this chapter will be an attempt to show that they are wrong. We shall first ask why linguists have come to this conclusion. Then we shall consider some evidence against it; and finally we shall consider the kind of theory of language structure that the evidence seems to support.

7.3.2 The history of the isolation of language

Why should so many linguists take it for granted that the social functions of language are irrelevant to its internal workings? This is a question about the history of linguistics which deserves much more space than we can spare here, but at one level the answer is that modern linguists have inherited this assumption from their intellectual ancestors going back at least to the early years of this century, along with the foundations of their theorising about language structure as part of a larger package of ideas called 'structuralism' (Lepschy 1992). The package, first formulated explicitly by Ferdinand de Saussure, contained some very positive ideas, in particular the idea that linguistic items must be studied in relation to the rest of the language – hence the general view of a language as a 'structure', rather than a mere heap. For example, to understand the glottal stop in English it is important to know that it is an alternative to [t], whereas in some other languages it is a phoneme in its own right. Structuralists take a further step, however: the 'external' facts about how glottal stops are produced are not part of any language because they do not involve links to other parts of the language; and social functions of linguistic items are excluded for the same reason.

Once again the logic is flawed: a language is indeed a structure in which some linguistic items are related to other linguistic items, but we cannot conclude from this that these internal links are the whole of language. This assumption is rarely recognised as an issue worth debating, and is widely reproduced by introductory textbooks which tell students that a word is a sign with either two parts (sound and meaning) or three (sound, meaning and grammatical classification), but without any mention of social function.

It is interesting and encouraging to know that linguists have not always seen language as circumscribed in this way. For example, the ancient Indian grammarian Panini (who lived about 500 BC) wrote a grammar based on a clear and explicit theory of language structure which allowed linguistic rules to be sensitive to sociolinguistic facts (Kiparsky 1994). Moreover, modern dictionaries and descriptive grammars combine sociolinguistic information quite freely with more conventional grammatical information – for example, any grammar of French will say that the 'past simple' form is only used in writing. In short, the supposed boundary around language does not leap out at us from the mere facts of language, and it is only the logic of structuralism that makes linguists think otherwise.

7.3.3   Evidence against the isolation of language

Against this intellectual background it is hardly surprising that linguists generally take it for granted that social functions are irrelevant to language structure. Why is this assumption wrong? Let's consider a particular example: the word SIDEWALK. Many speakers of English know (unconsciously) at least four facts about this word:

(1)   It is pronounced /saidwɔːk/.
(2)   It refers to the same thing as (British) *pavement*, i.e. a raised footpath on the edge of a road.
(3)   It is a common noun.
(4)   It is used by Americans but not by Brits.

These facts form a little network of relationships around SIDEWALK which link it to other concepts: its pronunciation, the concept which we can call 'pavement', the concept 'noun', and the concept 'American'. We can diagram the network as in Figure 7.6, in which the little triangles again link (large) general concepts to their (smaller) examples or members. If facts (1) to (3) belong to linguistic competence ('knowledge of language'), why shouldn't fact (4) belong to it as well? The following are reasons why it should.

- If linguistic competence is defined simply as what we know about linguistic items, fact (4) clearly does belong to it. It is possible to make the definition more complicated so as to exclude it, but why should we? No evidence has been offered, so there is no case to be answered.

- The question rests on an extremely controversial assumption: that linguistic competence is unique within our total knowledge, i.e. in current terminology that there is a 'language module' (contrast, for example, Chomsky 1986 and Hudson 1990: ch. 4). If this assumption is wrong, then there is no boundary around language, so the question about fact (4) does not arise and Figure 7.6 is right.

- None of the boundaries that are assumed to exist between language and the rest of knowledge has ever been supported by firm evidence, and all are the subject of dispute (Hudson 1989). This is true of the boundaries between phonology (linguistic) and phonetics (non-

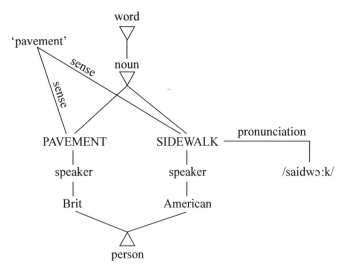

Figure 7.6

linguistic) and between semantics (linguistic) and encyclopedic knowledge (non-linguistic). There is even disagreement about whether or not vocabulary is part of the supposedly unique 'language module' (Curtiss 1988). If the language module turns out to be just a 'grammar module', where does this leave the notion of linguistic competence? The gross uncertainties in the debate make it hard to take a narrow definition of linguistic competence at all seriously.

- All the social functions that sociolinguists study belong to individual linguistic items. (This is not to deny that whole languages have social functions, but studying such things would probably be called sociology of language rather than sociolinguistics.) As far as fact (4) is concerned, it belongs to the item SIDEWALK, which is exactly the same mental object that facts (1) to (3) apply to. What, then, does it mean to say that fact (4) belongs to a different mental compartment if it is linked to the same concept as the other facts? This has never been made clear, and until we have a clear explanation there can be no debate.

- The grammatical structures to which social information attaches are very similar to the ones to which ordinary semantic information relates. The clearest example of this is the special status of the 'root' verb, i.e. the main verb of the sentence's main clause, which we discussed in 4.2.3. In both Japanese and Basque, we saw that power and solidarity relationships can be signalled by the choice of verb in the main clause, but not in subordinate clauses. The same restriction applies in most, perhaps all, languages to at least some constructions that are restricted to certain speech acts or other 'special' meanings – for example, imperatives, exclamations and 'presentatives' (for example, *Here comes our bus*) are all restricted in this way in English. No one would suggest that these patterns are outside the scope of grammatical theory, so the same should be true of the Japanese and Basque power–solidarity markers if they are to be covered by the same generalisation.

- Some linguistic items have no function except a social one. Obvious examples are greetings, farewells, politeness signals (*sorry, please, thank you*), cheers (*hurray!*) and toasts (*your health!*). Surely the very fundamental idea that a word is a sign which combines a form with a meaning or function demands that any word must have at least some function as part of its linguistic definition.

- The social types such as 'American' which are typically involved in social functions often have names in the language concerned; for example, 'American' is the meaning of the word AMERICAN. If word-meanings are part of language, then this is also true of 'American', as the meaning of AMERICAN; so it is very odd to say that the same concept is outside language when it is mentioned in fact (4).

- Most social functions of language involve facts about the speaker – about some social type to which the speaker belongs (for example, SIDEWALK versus PAVEMENT), about the solidarity and/or power of the speaker in relation to the addressee (JOHN versus MR SMITH), and so on. These facts are linked to the item concerned by the 'speaker' link. But this link is not restricted to social functions: it is also involved in definitions of words whose meaning is 'deictic', i.e. based on the immediate situation of speaking. The obvious example is the word ME, which can easily be defined as referring to the speaker (Hudson 1990: 128). This analysis is shown in Figure 7.7. It is a matter of debate whether

247

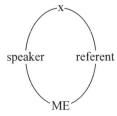

Figure 7.7

the definition of a word's meaning is inside language or outside (a good example of uncertainty over boundaries!), but if it is, the 'speaker' link must be inside language when it is part of the definition of ME – so why not also when it is part of fact (4)?

7.3.4   *Two further sources of variability*

We can now return to the partial explanation of quantitative variability introduced in 7.2.6. We saw there that inconsistency in speech is a good way to use the digital means of language to achieve the analogue ends of signalling social information. Someone who feels partly American, but not totally so, can reflect this fact in their speech by sometimes choosing American forms and sometimes choosing their alternatives. The general point was that quantitative differences between speakers was an automatic consequence of their different degrees of allegiance to the social types linked to each variant. We can call this variation '*social-type allegiance*'. However, we also saw that this only went part of the way to explaining variability in speech, because we still need an explanation for the differences between variables that sociolinguists have found. In this section we shall introduce two other sources of variation, and then we shall bring all three sources together by applying this view of variability to some actual data.

The fact that needs to be explained is that a given speaker, or group of speakers, uses a range of different variants which all seem to be associated with the same social type but uses them to different extents. For example, Trudgill found in Norwich (Trudgill 1974) that lower working class (LWC) speakers used the non-standard variant for 100 per cent of (ou)'s (the vowel in words like *know* and *old*) but only for 90 per cent of (t)'s. Why should the figures be different? (Unfortunately we cannot apply statistical tests for significance to Trudgill's data, but we shall see below that the difference is part of a larger pattern, so we must take it seriously.) One possibility is that, in the minds of LWC Norwich speakers, the non-standard variant is more closely linked to the social type with which they identify in the case of (ou) than for (t). This is exactly as expected from what we know about prototypes; we know that a given prototype may be associated to different degrees with different characteristics, so it would be surprising if the same were not true of the links between social types and speech characteristics. This, then, gives us our second source of variation: the strength of the link in the speaker's mind between the social type and the variant. We can call this '*social distinctiveness*'. In our example, the social distinctiveness of (ou) is different from that of (t).

The third source arises from the fact that social distinctiveness reflects the individual's experience, so different speakers may come to different conclusions about the social distinctiveness of the same range of variables. In general, the more similar the experiences the more similar the views of social distinctiveness, but people from opposite ends of the social spectrum, whose experiences are very different, may well have different views. In fact it would again be strange if this was not the case. We shall call this third source of variation '*distinctiveness view*', meaning the speaker's view of how closely the variants concerned are linked to the relevant social types.

The theory that we have just developed allows three influences on the choice by any individual I among the variants of some variable: for any variant V, the chances of I using V depend on (1) I's distinctiveness view, i.e. I's personal beliefs about the social distinctiveness of V and (2) I's social-type allegiance. We shall now introduce some typical data, from Trudgill's survey of Norwich, and show how this theory throws light on the figures. Table 7.1 shows scores for four variables as used in casual speech. (Trudgill's figures for (t) are actually twice those shown, as he scored 2 for a simple glottal stop and 1 for a glottalised [t]. The lower scores could therefore show a large number of glottalised [t]'s rather than a small number of glottal stops. This uncertainty illustrates the objection to global scores which was raised in 5.3.2.)

A glance at Table 7.1 shows that the figures all show the same broad pattern of a gradual decrease with social class, but the interest lies in the slight differences from column to column. In the first three columns the numbers cover a range of about 50 per cent, though the maximum varies from 100 per cent to 61 per cent; for (ing), in contrast, the range is over 70 per cent (and would have been 100 per cent if we had shown the 0 per cent for MMC females – Trudgill 1974: 94). Furthermore, each column contains one especially large jump between adjacent classes, but the jump is of different sizes and in different places for different columns: a 35 per cent jump above MMC for (ou), a 25 per cent jump above LMC for (t) and (h) and an enormous jump of 45 per cent above LMC for (ing). All the last three jumps divide all the Working Class groups from the Middle Class groups, but the jump for (ou) groups the LMC with all

Table 7.1 *Four variables in the casual speech of Norwich speakers from five
social classes (Lower, Middle and Upper Working Class and Lower and
Middle Middle Class). (Trudgill 1974: 92, 96, 116, 131)*

social class	(ou):[ɒu]	(t):[ʔ]	(h):∅	(ing):[ɪn]
LWC	100	90	61	100
MWC	100	90	59	95
UWC	95	85	40	87
LMC	85	60	14	42
MMC	50	40	9	28

the Working Class groups. The challenge for us is to use the three-source view
of variation to explain these details. What follows is just one guess, which
seems to fit the data considered here but which may not work when confronted
with other data.

We start with three assumptions.

(1)   The variable (ing) seems to be different from all the other vari-
      ables – the scores cover a much wider span, there is an enormous
      gap between the Middle Class and Working Class scores, and we
      know that it applies everywhere that English is spoken so it is un-
      likely to have local associations. Let us call the social type to which
      it is linked simply '*rough*', as suggested in the discussion of male–
      female differences in 5.4.4. It seems reasonable to assume that the
      link between (ing): [ɪn] and this type has maximum strength, which
      we can show as 100 per cent.

(2)   In contrast all the other variables are more or less local, so we can
      associate them with a different social type which we can call simply
      'Norwich'.

(3)   Of these other variables only (ou) shows 100 per cent for any class,
      so we can assume that (ou) has 100 per cent linkage for all classes.

The last assumption allows us to take the observed figures for (ou) as a measure
of the speaker's allegiance to the 'Norwich' type, so we can then use this figure
in order to calculate the social distinctiveness figures for the other variables.
For example, the UWC speakers used 95 per cent (ou): [ɒu], so their social-
type allegiance is 95 per cent; but they used only 85 per cent (t): [ʔ], so their distinctiveness view for (t) must be about 90 per cent (because 85 per cent = 90 per
cent of 95 per cent). As mentioned earlier, there is no reason to assume that
any of the figures are the same across all social classes, and the method just

outlined allows us to deal with each class separately. When we compare the calculated figures we shall see some interesting shifts between classes.

Table 7.2 gives the calculated figures for the two kinds of mental links that we are assuming: the link between the speaker and the social type ('social-type allegiance') and the perceived link between this social type and the non-standard variants ('distinctiveness view'). For example, the LWC speakers have 100 per cent   allegiance to both the 'Norwich' and 'Rough' social types, and see links between 'Norwich' (N) and the first three non-standard variants of 100 per cent, 90 per cent and 60 per cent, and a 100 per cent link between 'Rough' (R) and non-   standard (ing). The ditto marks are used in order to highlight the outstanding fact about this table: most of the distinctiveness values are the same. The only shifts with social class are for (h) and (t), which includes a shift of social type: for working-class Norwich, dropped aitches are a Norwich feature, but for middle-class Norwich they are a 'rough' feature. (This change is easy to understand given that aitches are dropped by working-class people only inside Norwich, and not in the local villages; Trudgill 1974: 131).

Most of the variation, then, is due to changes in social-type allegiance rather than in distinctiveness, but social-type allegiance is quite complex because two distinct social types are at stake. The main social split for the 'Rough' type is between Working Class and Middle Class, but for 'Norwich' it is between the two Middle Classes.

This interpretation can be checked against the figures that Trudgill observed, since it is based only indirectly on them. We can calculate for each social class what proportion of each variable should be non-standard; for example, the MMC speakers, with their 50 per cent allegiance to the 'Norwich' type and their perceived 75 per cent link between this type and (t): [?], should use this variant on 50 per cent of 75 per cent of all occasions, i.e. on 37.5 per cent. The calculated figures should be close to the ones that Trudgill actually observed,

Table 7.2   *Social-type allegiances and distinctiveness view of five social classes in Norwich*

SEC	Social-type allegiance		distinctiveness view							
	Norwich	Rough	(ou):[ʊu]		(t):[?]		(h):Ø		(ing): [ɪn]	
LWC	100	100	N	100	N	90	N	60	R	100
MWC	"	95	"	"	"	"	"	"	"	"
UWC	95	85	"	"	"	"	N	45	"	"
LMC	85	40	"	"	"	75	R	30	"	"
MMC	50	30	"	"	"	"	"	"	"	"

Table 7.3   *Percentage of non-standard variants for four variables spoken by five social classes: predicted (observed)*

class	(ou):[ɒu]	(t):[ʔ]	(h):Ø	(ing):[ɪn]
LWC	100 (100)	90 (90)	60 (61)	100 (100)
MWC	100 (100)	90 (90)	60 (59)	95 (95)
UWC	95 (95)	85 (85)	43 (40)	85 (87)
LMC	85 (85)	64 (60)	12 (14)	40 (42)
MMC	50 (50)	38 (40)	9 (9)	30 (28)

which in this case is 40 per cent, an acceptably close fit. The next table shows the figures predicted by our interpretation compared with the figures Trudgill observed. The match between the two sets of figures is reassuring.

The conclusion of this discussion is that our choice of variants on sociolinguistic variables is determined by at least two independent mental variables: our social-type allegiance, which links us to some social type, and our distinctiveness view, which links that social type to the use of some variant. Different experiences lead to different mental 'settings' in both respects, but the crude categories of social class are sufficiently real for us to calculate the settings of a typical member of each class. We did not assume from the start that variables had the same social significance throughout Norwich society, so we were able to find important differences which confirm the view that grammars and social constraints belong to individual speakers and not to whole communities (2.1.4). On the other hand, variation across Norwich society is clearly very systematic, which shows how deeply the individual's behaviour is influenced by the rest of their community.

7.3.5   *Implications for theories of language structure*

The findings of sociolinguistics are not simply neutral with regard to theories of language structure, a kind of optional add-on which is compatible with any and every theory. If the above discussion is right, any theory of language structure must satisfy the following specifications in order to accommodate these findings:

(1)   It must be a theory about the linguistic competence (i.e. knowledge) of individual people, not of whole communities.

(2)   It must be part of a larger theory of knowledge which also applies to social structure (as seen from the point of view of an individual member).

(3) It must be possible to include facts about particular linguistic items regarding their typical speakers, addressees and situations of use.

(4) It must allow differences in the 'strength' of competence relationships of all kinds, including relationships between individual cases and the general concepts to which they belong, which must therefore be prototypes.

These four criteria eliminate most of the theories of language structure which are currently available, and no single theory is so well developed in these areas that we can proclaim it the champion. However there are some more or less plausible candidates.

Generative Phonology and Transformational Grammar. Labov's early work used the then popular theory of generative phonology to express phonological variables (Labov 1972b: ch. 8). The assumption was that each variable corresponded to a rule (a 'variable rule') which either deleted or changed some phonological segment, and which (unlike standard rules) had a probability of applying which varied according to the context, the type of speaker and so on. Variation in syntax was handled by means of transformations which similarly deleted, moved or changed whole words or phrases with varying probabilities. Variable rules suffer various weaknesses (not least being the general abandonment of generative phonology and of construction-specific transformations by other linguists), and 'in current work in variation analysis, the variable rule as a part of linguistic theory has been quietly abandoned' (Fasold 1990: 256).

Lexical Phonology. More recently Labov and some of his followers have adopted lexical phonology, which is one of the current descendants of generative phonology. Lexical phonology has inherited the 'destructive' rules of generative phonology, which take one structure and change it into a different one, but its special characteristic is that these rules have to apply in a small number of cycles, first within the word (as 'lexical' rules) and then across word-boundaries (as 'post-lexical' rules). The idea of variable rules lives on in these rules which have a variable probability of applying.

A particularly interesting and impressive application of variable lexical phonology is presented in a series of papers by Guy (1991a, 1991b, 1994), which all deal with the same phenomenon: the loss of the final /t/ or /d/ where it follows another consonant in words like *fist* and *walked*. Guy's rich collection of data on this variable allows him to make a fascinating generalisation: the probability of t/d loss in a monomorphemic word like *fist* is always the cube of its probability when the t/d is a separate morpheme as in *walked*. For example, if the t/d has a probability of 0.8 (= an 80 per cent chance) of being lost in *walked*, the likelihood that it will be lost in *fist* is $0.8^3 = 0.512$, i.e. 51.2 per cent. Words like the past-tense *left* lie in between the two cases because the /t/ is added to an irregular root which also shows the past tense, and in such cases the chances of t-loss are the square of what they would be in *walked* ($0.8^2 = 0.64$). Guy explains these facts in terms of lexical phonology, by assuming that the same rule applies, with the same probability, on one, two or three cycles, depending on the word's morphological structure. If the probability is p, then the probability of applying on three cycles is p^3, which is what is needed for *fist*; application on two cycles fits past-tense *left*, and gives p^2; and the rule applies just once to *walked*, giving just p.

Unfortunately this explanation has some serious weaknesses (Hudson 1996). It shares the fundamental weakness of variable rules, which is that the explanation does not generalise to any variation which is not due to the application of rules (notably variation between lexical items). But it also rests on some theoretical assumptions which are quite controversial in lexical-phonology circles (such as allowing a rule to apply on every cycle), and on some doubtful factual assumptions (for example, that *left* is stored as /li:v/ + Past, rather than as /left/).

Principles-and-Parameters Theory. Some people have tried to apply the theory which Chomsky developed in the 1980s to sociolinguistic data. The most distinguished advocate of this approach is Kroch (for example, 1994), whose main interest is in syntactic change. According to a now standard Principles-and-Parameters analysis, there is a single 'parameter' (called 'verb-raising') which explains several differences between modern English and some other European languages such as French and German, such as the fact that the other languages allow any verb to change places with the subject, whereas in modern English this is possible only for 'auxiliary' verbs:

	A	B
(1)	He has finished.	He finished.
(2)	Has he finished?	*Finished he?
(3)	*Does he have finished?	Did he finish?

In other languages the equivalent of (2)B is grammatical, but neither (3)A nor (3)B is. The same was true in Old English, and Kroch's aim is to trace the way in which this 'parameter' shifted during late Middle English, using statistical data about the gradual increase of the modern pattern during the fifteenth and sixteenth centuries. The most interesting point of these figures is the way the change spread gradually through several different constructions starting with negative and transitive questions.

However persuasive one may find the idea of parameters, including the head-raising parameter, Kroch's analysis hardly comes to terms with the variable data (Hudson 1996. He assumes that the change reflected the shifting balance between two completely different grammars, with and without head-raising, and makes very few suggestions about why the different constructions were affected at different times. It would certainly be interesting if Chomsky's strictly asocial theory of language structure turned out to be suitable for explaining variable data, but at present this seems unlikely.

Head-Driven Phrase Structure Grammar. HPSG is a widely used theory of language structure. Its inventors (Ivan Sag and Carl Pollard) have concentrated on developing an account of syntactic and semantic structure whose clarity and detail have made it popular with computer scientists and more mathematically-minded linguists rather than with sociolinguists, but it is also related to a theory of semantics called 'situational semantics' which brings it within the realm of sociolinguistics. This theory allows the semantic structures to refer to the parameters of situations in which language is used, including the speaker, the addressee and the relations between them. The most relevant consequence of this link is an interesting discussion in the main published account of the theory of how a formal grammar should incorporate the information about power and solidarity which is conveyed by verb-forms and pronouns (Pollard and Sag 1994: 27, 91, 92–5).

Cognitive Grammar. This is a theory of linguistic structure within a general theory of cognition (i.e. thought) – hence its name. Its creator is Ronald Langacker, whose main interests are in semantics and grammar rather than in sociolinguistics (Langacker 1994 is a convenient summary). However the theory seems to satisfy our four criteria:

(1)   Individual competence: it is a theory of individual knowledge.

(2)   Applicable to social structure: one of Langacker's most basic assumptions is that language is closely integrated with the rest of cognition, rather than separated from it as a distinct module. What is distinctive about language is that the units are 'signs', pairings of sound and meaning; otherwise it builds on the same mental apparatus as the rest of cognition. There is no reason to exclude social structure, though it is rarely discussed.

(3)   Speakers: some of the most productive work in this theory has been concerned with semantics, where the speaker's viewpoint is central – as, for example, in explaining the difference between *half empty* and *half full*, which describe the same objective state of affairs from very different viewpoints. If the speaker can be included in these analyses, then the same is presumably possible for social functions.

(4) Strength differences and prototypes: the theory also allows information to have different degrees of 'entrenchment', which is the same as our idea that relationships have different strengths. Concepts are prototypes whose members may be more or less deviant.

One application of Cognitive Grammar to sociolinguistics is Kemmer and Israel 1994, an interesting but rather programmatic discussion of Guy's t/d loss data.

Word Grammar. I end with Word Grammar because it is my own favourite (Hudson 1984, 1990). The most relevant fact about Word Grammar is that, like Cognitive Grammar, it denies any boundary around linguistic competence. Cognition is a (vast) network of prototypes, in which language forms a (fairly vast) subnetwork which is linked at numerous points to concepts which are not strictly linguistic. The diagrams in this chapter have used some of the Word Grammar conventions for showing networks of interconnected concepts. Not surprisingly, perhaps, Word Grammar satisfies all our criteria:

(1) Individual competence: it is a theory of individual knowledge.

(2) Applicable to social structures: our diagrams have shown that social structures are as easy as linguistic structures to analyse in terms of Word Grammar.

(3) Speakers: the notion 'speaker of X' is just as easily defined as (say) 'subject of X', and similarly for 'addressee of X'. The situation (needed, for example, for 'style' differences – see 5.4.5) is harder to define, so this is an area of weakness. Defining these relationships is made all the easier because words are taken to be examples of communicative actions, so 'speaker' is actually just the local name for the more general relationship 'actor' inherited from actions, and words have addressees because communicative actions do (Hudson 1986, 1990: 63).

(4) Strength differences and prototypes: the idea that a relationship has a strength or degree of entrenchment has not been developed as seriously in Word Grammar as in Cognitive Grammar. Hudson 1996 is an attempt to fill this gap as an alternative to the proposals by Guy and Kroch which were outlined above. The idea that concepts are prototypes is fundamental to Word Grammar, as I explained above.

There was a time when sociolinguists probably deserved the following criticism made by John Rickford, himself a distinguished sociolinguist (1988).

[Sociolinguists have] a tendency to be satisfied with observation and description, and [are] insufficiently imbued with the thirst for theoretical explanation and prediction which drives science onward.

There was also a time when 'theoretical linguists' could generally be criticised for ignoring the work of sociolinguists. Both of these criticisms still apply, but there may be light at the end of the tunnel.

BIBLIOGRAPHY

KEY:

ELL: Asher, R. (1994) *Encyclopedia of Language and Linguistics*. Oxford: Pergamon Press.

IEL n: Bright, W. (1992) *International Encyclopedia of LInguistics*, volume n. (4 volumes). Oxford: Oxford University Press.

Abd-el- Jawad, H. (1987) 'Cross-Dialectal Variation in Arabic: Competing Prestigious Forms'. *Language in Society* 16: 359–68.

Abercrombie, D. (1968) 'Paralanguage'. *British Journal of Disorders of Communication* 3: 55–9.

Abu-Haidar, F. (1989) 'Are Iraqi Women More Prestige Conscious than Men? Sex Differentiation in Baghdad Arabic'. *Language in Society* 18: 471–81.

Aitchison, J. (1987) *Words in the Mind: An Introduction to the Mental Lexicon*. Oxford: Blackwell.

(1994) 'Pidgins, Creoles and Change'. *ELL*: 3181–6.

Allan, K. and Burridge, K. (1991) *Euphemism and Dysphemism*. Oxford: Oxford University Press.

Allan, W. S. (1994) 'Wave Theory'. *ELL*: 4965–6.

Andersen, E. (1990) *Speaking with Style: The Sociolinguistic Skills of Children*. London: Routledge.

Anderson, L. and Trudgill, P. (1990) *Bad Language*. Oxford: Blackwell.

Apte, M. L. (1994) 'Taboo Words'. *ELL*: 4512–15.

Ardehali, J. (1994) 'Persian'. *ELL*: 3003–4.

Argyle, M. (1973) *Social Encounters: Readings in Social Interaction*. Harmondsworth: Penguin.

Argyle, M. and Dean, J. (1965) 'Eye Contact, Distance and Affiliation'. *Sociometry* 28: 289–304.

Argyle, M. and Kendon, A. (1967) 'The Experimental Analysis of Social Performance'. In L. Berkowitz, ed. *Advances in Experimental Social Psychology*. New York: Academic Press, 55–98.

Austin, J. (1962) *How to Do Things with Words*. Cambridge, MA: Harvard University Press.

Bainbridge, E. (1994) 'Sex Differences'. *ELL*: 3864–8.

Ball, C. (1993) 'A Diachronic Study of Relative Markers in Spoken and Written English'. Mimeo.

Barrett, M. (1994) 'Language Acquisition: Vocabulary'. *ELL*: 1927–31.

Basso, K. (1970) '"To Give up on Words": Silence in Western Apache Culture'. *Southwestern Journal of Anthropology* 26: 213–30.

Bauman, R. and Sherzer, J., eds. (1974) *Explorations in the Ethnography of Speaking*. Cambridge: Cambridge University Press.

Belazi, H. M., Rubin, E. J. and Toribio, A. J. (1994) 'Code Switching and X-bar Theory: the Functional-Head Constraint'. *Linguistic Inquiry* 25: 221–37.

Bell, A. (1984) 'Language Style as Audience Design'. *Language in Society* 13: 145–204.

(1991) *The Language of News Media*. Oxford: Blackwell.

Bereiter, C., Engelman, S., Osborn, J. and Reidford, P. (1966) 'An Academically Oriented Pre-School Program for Culturally Deprived Children'. In F. Hechinger, ed. *Pre-School Education Today*. New York: Doubleday.

Berko Gleason, J. (1973) 'Code Switching in Children's Language'. In T. Moore, ed. *Cognitive Development and the Acquisition of Language*. London: Academic Press, 159–67.

Bernstein, B., ed. (1973) *Class, Codes and Control*, volume II: *Empirical Studies*. London: Routledge & Kegan Paul.

Besnier, N. (1989) 'Information Withholding as a Manipulative and Collusive Strategy in Nukulaelae Gossip'. *Language in Society* 18: 315–41.

(1994) 'Conversation: Quantity'. *ELL*: 747–9.

Biber, D. (1988) *Variation Across Speech and Writing*. Cambridge: Cambridge University Press.

(1989) 'A Typology of English Texts'. *Linguistics* 27: 3–43.

Bickerton, D. (1975) *The Dynamics of a Creole System*. Cambridge: Cambridge University Press.

(1981) *The Roots of Language*. Ann Arbor: Karoma.

(1988) 'Creole Languages and the Bioprogram'. In F. Newmeyer, ed. *Linguistics: The Cambridge Survey*, volume II, 268–84.

Blake, R. (1987) 'Is *to/a* the Head of S? I Don't Want to Decidir la Cuestión, but I'm Going to'. In Denning, K., Inkelas, S., McNair-Knox, F. and Rickford, J. (1987) *Variation in Language*. NWAV-XV at Stanford. Stanford: Linguistics Department, Stanford University, 22–34.

Blom, J.-P. and Gumperz, J. (1971) 'Social Meaning in Linguistic Structure: Code-Switching in Norway'. In J. Gumperz, ed. *Language in Social Groups*. Stanford: Stanford University Press, 274–310.

Bloomfield, L. (1933) *Language*. New York: Holt, Rinehart & Winston.

Bolinger, D. (1975) *Aspects of Language*, 2nd edition. New York: Harcourt Brace Jovanovich.

Bourdieu, P. and Boltansky, L. (1975) 'Le fétichisme de la langue'. *Actes de la Recherche en Sciences Sociales* 4: 2–32.

Brown, P. and Levinson, S. (1978/1987) *Politeness. Some Universals in Language Usage.* 2nd edition. Cambridge: Cambridge University Press.

Brown, R. (1958a) 'How Shall a Thing be Called?' *Psychological Review* 65: 14–21.

(1958b) *Words and Things.* Glencoe, IL: Free Press.

Brown, R. and Ford, M. (1961) 'Address in American English'. *Journal of Abnormal and Social Psychology* 62: 375–85.

Brown, R. and Gilman, A. (1960) 'The Pronouns of Power and Solidarity'. In T. Sebeok, ed. *Style in Language.* Cambridge, MA: MIT Press, 253–76.

Burling, R. (1959) 'Language Development of a Garo- and English-Speaking Child'. *Word* 15: 45–68.

(1970) *Man's Many Voices: Language in its Cultural Context.* New York: Holt, Rinehart & Winston.

Butler, C. (1985) *Statistics in Linguistics.* Oxford: Blackwell.

Bynon, T. (1977) *Historical Linguistics.* Cambridge: Cambridge University Press.

Byrd, D. (1994) 'Relations of Sex and Dialect to Reduction'. *Speech Communication* 15: 39–54.

Cairns, E. and Duriez, B. (1976) 'The Influence of Speaker's Accent on Recall by Catholic and Protestant School Children in Northern Ireland'. *British Journal of Social and Clinical Psychology* 15: 441–2.

Campbell, R. and Wales, R. (1970) 'The Study of Language Acquisition'. In J. Lyons, ed. *New Horizons in Linguistics.* Harmondsworth: Penguin, 242–60.

Carroll, J., ed. (1956) *Language and Thought: Selected Writings of Benjamin Lee Whorf.* Cambridge, MA: MIT Press.

Carroll, J. and Casagrande, J. (1958) 'The Function of Language Classification in Behavior'. In E. Mccoby, T. Newcomb and E. Hartley, eds. *Readings in Social Psychology.* New York: Holt, Rinehart & Winston.

Casad, E. and Langacker, R. (1985) '"Inside" and "Outside" in Cora Grammar'. *International Journal of American Linguistics*, 51: 247–81. Also reprinted in Langacker 1990: 35–58.

Casagrande, J. (1948) 'Comanche Baby Talk'. *International Journal of American Linguistics* 14: 11–14.

Cazden, C. (1994) 'Socialization'. *ELL*: 4004–5.

Chambers, J. (1995) *Sociolinguistic Theory: Linguistic Variation and its Social Significance.* Oxford: Blackwell.

Chambers, J. and Trudgill, P. (1980) *Dialectology.* Cambridge: Cambridge University Press.

Cheshire, J. (1992) 'Register and Style'. *IEL* 3: 324–6.

Choi, J. (1991) 'Korean-English Code-Switching: Switch-Alpha and Linguistic Constraints'. *Linguistics* 29: 877–902.

Chomsky, N. (1986) *Knowledge of Language. Its Nature, Origin and Use.* New York: Praeger.

Clark, H. and Clark, E. (1977) *Psychology and Language: An Introduction to Psycholinguistics.* New York: Harcourt Brace Jovanovich.

Clyne, M. (1987) 'Constraints on Code-Switching: How Universal are They?' *Linguistics* 25: 739–64.

Cooper, R., Fishman, J., Lown, L., Scheier, B. and Seckbach, F. (1977) 'Language, Technology and Persuasion in the Middle East: Three Experimental Studies'. In Giles, H., ed. *Language, Ethnicity and Intergroup Relations*. London: Academic Press, 83–98.

Coulthard, R. M. (1977) *An Introduction to Discourse Analysis*. London: Longman.

Coupland, N. (1980) 'Style-Shifting in a Cardiff Work-Setting'. *Language in Society* 9: 1–12.

(1984) 'Accommodation at Work'. *International Journal of the Sociology of Language* 46: 49–70.

(1988) *Dialect in Use*. Cardiff: University of Wales Press.

Crystal, D. (1987) *The Cambridge Encyclopedia of Language*. Cambridge: Cambridge University Press.

Curtiss, S. (1988) 'Abnormal Language Acquisition and the Modularity of Language'. In F. Newmeyer, ed. *Linguistics: The Cambridge Survey*, volume II: *Linguistic Theory: Extensions and Implications*. Cambridge: Cambridge University Press, 96–116.

de Léon, L. (1994) 'Explorations in the Acquisition of Geocentric Location by Tzotzil Children'. *Linguistics* 32: 857–84.

Denison, N. (1971) 'Some Observations on Language Variety and Plurilingualism'. In E. Ardner, ed. *Social Anthropology and Language*. London: Tavistock; also in Pride and Holmes (1972), 65–77.

Dillard, J. L. (1976) 'The Creolist and the Study of Negro Non-Standard Dialects in the Continental United States'. In Hymes (1971a), 393–408.

di Sciullo, A., Muysken, P. and Singh, R. (1986) 'Government and Code-Mixing'. *Journal of Linguistics* 22: 1–24.

Dixon, R. (1991) *A New Approach to English Grammar, on Semantic Principles*. Oxford: Oxford University Press.

Dorian, N. (1994) 'Varieties of Variation in a Very Small Place: Social Homogeneity, Prestige Norms and Linguistic Variation'. *Language* 70, 631–96.

Downes, W. (1994) 'Register in Literature'. *ELL*: 3509–11.

Eibl-Eibesfeld, I. (1973) 'The Expressive Behaviour of the Deaf -and-Blind Born'. In M. von Cranach and I. Vine, eds. *Social Communication and Movement*. New York: Academic Press.

Eckert, P. (1988) 'Adolescent Social Structure and the Spread of Linguistic Change'. *Language in Society* 17: 183–207.

(1989) *Jocks and Burnouts: Social Identity in the High School*. New York: Teachers College Press.

(1991) 'Social Polarization and the Choice of Linguistic Variants'. In P. Eckert, ed. *New Ways of Analyzing Sound Change*. London: Academic Press, 213–32.

(1994) '(ay) Goes to the City: Exploring the Expressive Use of Variation'. Mimeo.

Edwards, A. and Westgate, D. (1994) 'Spoken Language in the Classroom: Observation and Analysis'. *ELL*: 4324–9.

Edwards, Jane (1994) 'Corpus Analysis of -BODY/-ONE'. Message 5.1196 broadcast on linguist@tamsun, tamu, edu, 29 October 1994.

Edwards, John (1994) 'Educational failure'. *ELL*: 1094–100.

Ekman, P. and Friesen, W. (1971) 'Constants Across Culture in the Face and Emotion'. *Journal of Personality and Social Psychology* 17.

Fasold, R. (1984) *The Sociolinguistics of Society*. Oxford: Blackwell.

(1990) *The Sociolinguistics of Language*. Oxford: Blackwell.

(1992) 'Variation Analysis'. *IEL* 4: 217–20.

Ferguson, C. (1959) 'Diglossia'. *Word* 15: 325–40.

(1971) 'Absence of Copula and the Notion of Simplicity: A Study of Normal Speech, Baby Talk, Foreigner Talk and Pidgins'. In Hymes (1971a: 141–50).

(1976) 'The Structure and use of Politeness Formulas'. *Language in Society* 5: 137–51.

Fischer, J. (1958) 'Social Influences on the Choice of a Linguistic Variant'. *Word* 14: 47–56.

Fishman, J. (1971) *Sociolinguistics: A Brief Introduction*. Rowley: Newbury House.

Fox, J. (1974) '"Our Ancestors Spoke in Pairs": Rotinese Views of Language, Dialect and Code'. In Bauman and Sherzer (1974: 65–85).

Gardener, P. (1966) 'Symmetric Respect and Memorate Knowledge: The Structure and Ecology of Individualistic Culture'. *Southwestern Journal of Anthropology* 22: 389–415.

Garvin, P. (1959) 'The Standard Language Problem: Concepts and Methods'. *Anthropological Linguistics* 1: 28–31.

Garvin, P. and Mathiot, M. (1956) 'The Urbanization of the Guaraní language: A Problem in Language and Culture'. In A. Wallace, ed. *Men and Cultures*. Philadelphia: University of Philadelphia Press, 783–90.

Gauchat, L. (1905) 'L'unité phonétique dans le patois d'une commune'. In *Aus Romanischen Sprachen und Literaturen: Festschrift Heinrich Morf*. Halle: Max Niemeyer, 175–232.

Geertz, C. (1960) *The Religion of Java*. Glencoe: The Free Press.

Giddens, A. (1989/1993) *Sociology*, 2nd edition. Oxford: Blackwell.

Giles, H. (1994) 'Accommodation in Communication'. *ELL*: 12–15.

Giles, H. and Bradac, J. (1994) 'Speech Styles: Attitudes and Inferences'. *ELL*: 4260–4.

Giles, H. and Powesland, P. (1975) *Speech Style and Social Evaluation*. London: Academic Press.

Goffman, E. (1955) 'On Face-Work: An Analysis of Ritual Elements in Social Interaction'. *Psychiatry* 18: 213–31.

(1957) 'Alienation from Interaction'. *Human Relations* 10: 47–60.

(1967) *Interaction Rituals: Essays on Face to Face Behavior*. Garden City, New York: Doubleday.

(1969) *The Presentation of Self in Everyday Life*. Harmondsworth: Penguin.

Goodenough, W. (1957) 'Cultural Anthropology and Linguistics'. In P. Garvin, ed. *Report of the 7th Round Table Meeting on Linguistics and Language Study*. Washington: Georgetown University Press, 167–73.

Goodman, M. (1971) 'The Strange Case of Mbugu'. In Hymes (1971a: 243–54).

Graddol, D. and Swann, J. (1989) *Gender Voices*. Oxford: Blackwell.

Grice, P. (1975) 'Logic and Conversation'. In P. Cole and J. Morgan, eds. *Syntax and Semantics*, volume III: *Speech Acts*. London: Academic Press, 41–58.

Gumperz, J. (1962) 'Types of Linguistic Community'. *Anthropological Linguistics* 4: 28–40.

(1968) 'The Speech Community'. In *International Encyclopedia of the Social Sciences*. London: Macmillan, 381–6.

Gumperz, J. and Hymes, D., eds. (1972) *Directions in Sociolinguistics: the Ethnography of Communication*. New York: Holt, Rinehart & Winston.

Gumperz, J. and Wilson, R. (1971) 'Convergence and Creolization: A Case From the Indo-Aryan/Dravidian Border in India'. In Hymes (1971a), 151–67.

Guy, G. (1980) 'Variation in the Group and the Individual: The Case of Final Stop Deletion'. In W. Labov, ed. *Locating Language in Time and Space*. London: Academic Press, 1–36.

(1991a) 'Contextual Conditioning in Variable Lexical Phonology'. *Language Variation and Change* 3: 223–39.

(1991b) 'Explanation in Variable Phonology: An Exponential Model of Morphological Constraints'. *Language Variation and Change* 3: 1–22.

(1994) 'The Phonology of Variation'. *Proceedings of the Chicago Linguistics Society* 30, *Parasession on Variation in Linguistic Theory*: 133–49.

Haeri, N. (1987) 'Male/Female Differences in Speech: An Alternative Interpretation'. In K. Denning et al., eds. *Variation in Language*: NWAV-XV. Stanford: Department of Linguistics, Stanford University, 173–82.

(1991) 'Sociolinguistic Variation in Cairene Arabic: Palatalization and the Qaf in the Speech of Men and Women'. University of Pennsylvania dissertation.

Halliday, M. (1972) 'Sociological Aspects of Semantic Change'. In *Proceedings of the 11th International Congress of Linguists*. Bologna: il Mulino, 853–88.

(1975) *Learning How to Mean: Explorations in the Development of Language*. London: Arnold.

(1978) *Language as Social Semiotic*. London: Arnold.

Harris, J. (1993) 'The Grammar of Irish English'. In J. Milroy and L. Milroy, *Real English: The Grammar of English Dialects in the British Isles*. London: Longman, 139–86.

Haugen, E. (1966) 'Dialect, Language, Nation'. *American Anthropologist* 68: 922–35.

(1994) 'Standardization'. *ELL*: 4340–2.

Hawkins, J. (1986) *A Comparative Typology of English and German: Unifying the Contrast*. London: Croom Helm.

Heath, J. (1994) 'Borrowing'. *ELL*: 383–94.

263

Heath, S. B. (1984) *Ways with Words: Language, Life and Work in Communities and Classrooms*. Cambridge: Cambridge University Press.

Hill, J. (1988) 'Language, Culture and World View'. In Newmeyer, F., ed. *Linguistics: The Cambridge Survey*, volume IV. Cambridge: Cambridge University Press, 14–36.

Hirschman, L. (1994) 'Female–Male Conversational Differences'. *Language in Society* 23: 427–42.

Hockett, C. (1950) 'Age-Grading and Linguistic Continuity'. *Language* 26: 449–59.

(1958) *A Course in Modern Linguistics*. New York: Macmillan.

Holm, J. (1988, 1989) *Pidgins and Creoles*, 2 volumes. Cambridge: Cambridge University Press.

Holmes, J. (1992) *An Introduction to Sociolinguistics*. London: Longman.

Horvath, B. (1985) *Variation in Australian English: The Sociolects of Sydney*. Cambridge: Cambridge University Press.

Howatt, A. (1994) 'Language Teaching: History'. *ELL*: 2020–7.

Hudson, A. (1994) 'Diglossia'. *ELL*: 926–30.

Hudson, R. (1984) *Word Grammar*. Oxford: Blackwell.

(1986) 'Sociolinguistics and the Theory of Grammar'. *Linguistics* 24: 1053–78.

(1989) 'Review of F. Newmeyer, ed. *Linguistics: The Cambridge Survey*'. *Language* 65: 812–9.

(1990) *English Word Grammar*. Oxford: Blackwell.

(1995) *Word Meaning*. London: Routledge.

(1996) 'Inherent Variability and Linguistic Theory'. *Cognitive Linguistics*.

(forthcoming) 'Syntax and Sociolinguistics'. In Jacobs et al., eds. *Syntax. An International Handbook of Contemporary Research*, volume II. Berlin: De Gruyter, 1514–28.

Hymes, D. (1971a) *Pidginization and Creolization of Language*. Cambridge: Cambridge University Press.

(1971b) 'Competence and Performance in Linguistic Theory'. In R. Huxley and E. Ingram, eds. *Language Acquisition: Models and Methods*. London: Academic Press, 3–28.

(1972) 'Models of the Interaction of Language and Social Life'. In Gumperz and Hymes (1972: 35–71).

(1974) *Foundation of Sociolinguistics: An Ethnographic Approach*. Philadelphia: University of Pennsylvania Press.

Irvine, J. (1974) 'Strategies of Status Manipulation in the Wolof Greeting'. In Bauman and Sherzer (1974: 167–91).

Jackendoff, R. (1983) *Semantics and Cognition*. Cambridge, MA: MIT Press.

Jackson, J. (1974) 'Language Identity of the Colombian Vaupés Indians'. In Bauman and Sherzer (1974: 50–64).

Jahangiri, N. (1980) 'A Sociolinguistic Study of Persian in Teheran'. London University PhD dissertation.

Jahangiri, N. and Hudson, R. (1982) 'Patterns of Variation in Teherani Persian'. In S. Romaine, ed. *Sociolinguistic Variation in Speech Communities*. London: Arnold, 49–63.

James, D. (forthcoming) 'When do Women use More Prestige Speech and Why? A Critical Review'. In A. Freed et al., eds. *Language and Gender Research: Theory and Methods*. London: Longman.

Jassem, Z. (1994) *Lectures in English and Arabic Sociolinguistics*, 2 volumes. Kuala Lumpur: Pustaka Antara.

Keenan, E. (1977) 'The Universality of Conversational Implicatures'. In R. Fasold and R. Shuy, eds. *Language Attitudes: Current Trends and Prospects*. Washington: Georgetown University Press, 255–68.

Kemmer, S. and Israel, M. (1994) 'Variation and the Usage-Based Model'. *Proceedings of the Chicago Linguistic Society* 30, *Parasession on Variation in Linguistic Theory*: 165–79.

Kempson, R. (1977) *Semantic Theory*. Cambridge: Cambridge University Press.

Kendon, A. (1967) 'Some Functions of Gaze-Direction in Social Interaction'. *Acta Psychologica* 26: 22–47.

Key, M. (1992) 'Nonverbal Communication'. *IEL* 3: 107–10.

Kindaichi, H. (1942) *Ga-gyō bionron*. Reprinted in Kindaichi, H. (1967) *Kokugo on'inron*. Tokyo: Tōkyōdō.

Kiparsky, P. (1994) 'Paninian Linguistics'. *ELL*: 2918–23.

Knowles, G. (1978) 'The Nature of Phonological Variables in Scouse'. In Trudgill (1978: 80–90).

Kroch, A. (1994) 'Morphosyntactic Variation'. *Proceedings of the Chicago Linguistics Society* 30, *Parasession on Variation in Linguistic Theory*: 180–211.

Labov, W. (1963) 'The Social Motivation of a Sound Change'. *Word* 19: 273–309; = Labov (1972a: ch. 1).

(1966) *The Social Stratification of English in New York City*. Washington DC: Center for Applied Linguistics.

(1969) 'Contraction, Deletion and Inherent Variability of the English Copula'. *Language* 45: 715–62; = Labov (1972b: ch. 3).

(1971) 'The Notion of System in Creole Studies'. In Hymes (1971a: 447–72).

(1972a) *Sociolinguistic Patterns*. Oxford: Blackwell.

(1972b) *Language in the Inner City*. Oxford: Blackwell.

(1973) 'The Boundaries of Words and Their Meanings'. In C-J. Bailey and R. Shuy, eds. *New Ways of Analyzing Variation in English*. Washington: Georgetown University Press.

(1975) *What is a Linguistic Fact?* Lisse: The Peter de Ridder Press.

(1978) 'Denotational structure'. *Proceedings of the Chicago Linguistic Society Parasession on the Lexicon*: 220–60.

(1989) 'Exact Description of the Speech Community: Short A in Philadelphia'. In R. Fasold and D. Schiffrin, eds. (1989). *Language Change and Variation*. Amsterdam: Benjamins, 1–57.

(1990) 'The Intersection of Sex and Social Class in the Course of Linguistic Change'. *Language Variation and Change* 2: 205–54.

(1994) *Principles of Linguistic Change*, volume I: *Internal Factors*. Oxford: Blackwell.

Lakoff, G. (1977) 'Linguistic Gestalts'. *Proceedings of the 13th Annual Regional Meeting of the Chicago Linguistic Society* 13: 236–87.

(1987) *Women, Fire and Dangerous Things: What Categories Reveal About the Mind*. Chicago: University of Chicago Press.

Lambert, W. (1967) 'A Social Psychology of Bilingualism'. *Journal of Social Issues* 23: 91–108.

Langacker, R. (1990) *Concept, Image and Symbol: The Cognitive Basis of Grammar*. Berlin: Mouton de Gruyter.

(1994) 'Cognitive Grammar'. *ELL*: 590–3.

Lawton, D. (1968) *Social Class, Language and Education*. London: Routledge & Kegan Paul.

Le Page, R. (1968a) 'Problems of Description in Multilingual Communities'. *Transactions of the Philological Society*: 189–212.

(1977) 'Processes of Pidginization and Creolization'. In A. Valdman, ed. *Pidgin and Creole Linguistics*. Bloomington: Indiana Press, 222–55.

Le Page, R. and Tabouret-Keller, A. (1985) *Acts of Identity: Creole-Based Approaches to Language and Ethnicity*. Cambridge: Cambridge University Press.

Lepschy, G. (1992) 'History of Linguistics: Early Structuralism'. *IEL* 2: 163–6.

Levine, L. and Crockett, H. (1966) 'Speech Variation in a Piedmont Community: Postvocalic'. *Sociological Inquiry* 36 (2): 76–98.

Levinson, S. (1983) *Pragmatics*. Cambridge: Cambridge University Press.

Linde, C. and Labov, W. (1975) 'Spatial Networks as a Site for the Study of Language and Thought'. *Language* 51: 924–39.

Littlewood, W. (1994) 'Language Teaching Methods'. *ELL*: 2027–35.

Local, J. (1978) 'Studies Towards a Description of the Development and Functioning of Linguistic Variability in Young Children'. University of Newcastle upon Tyne PhD dissertation.

Lounsbury, F. (1969) 'Language and Culture'. In S. Hook, ed. *Language and Philosophy*. New York: New York University Press, 3–29.

Lucy, J. (1992a) *Language Diversity and Thought: A Reformulation of the Linguistic Relativity Hypothesis*. Cambridge: Cambridge University Press.

(1992b) *Grammatical Categories and Cognition: A Case-Study of the Linguistic Relativity Hypothesis*. Cambridge: Cambridge University Press.

Lyons, J. (1977) *Semantics*, 2 volumes. Cambridge: Cambridge University Press.

(1981) *Language, Meaning and Context*. London: Fontana.

Lyons, J. ed. (1970) *New Horizons in LInguistics*. Harmondsworth: Penguin.

Macaulay, R. (1973) 'Double Standards'. *American Anthropologist* 75: 1324–37.

(1975) 'Negative Prestige, Linguistic Insecurity and Linguistic Self-Hatred'. *Lingua* 36: 147–61.

McGivney, J. (1993) '"Is She a Wife or a Mother?" Social Order, Respect and Address in Mijikenda'. *Language in Society* 22: 19–39.

McCormick, K. (1994a) 'Code-Switching and Mixing'. *ELL*: 581–7.

(1994b) 'Gender and Language'. *ELL*: 1353–60.

Maclaren, R. (1976) 'The Variable (ʌ), A Relic Form with Social Correlates'. *Belfast Working Papers in Language and Linguistics* 1: 45–68.

MacLure, M. (1994) 'Home Language and School Language'. *ELL*: 1593–5.

McNeill, D. (1992) *Hand and Mind: What Gestures Reveal about Thought*. Chicago: University of Chicago Press.

Malinowski, B. (1923) 'The Problem of Meaning in Primitive Languages'. In C. K. Ogden and I. A. Richards. *The Meaning of Meaning*. London: Routledge & Kegan Paul.

Mandelbaum, D., ed. (1949) *Selected Writings of Edward Sapir in Language, Culture and Personality*. Cambridge: Cambridge University Press.

Mason, M., Mason R., and Quayle, A. (1992) 'Illuminating English: How Explicit Language Teaching Improved Public Examination Results in a Comprehensive School'. *Educational Studies* 18: 341–53.

Matthews, P. (1979) *Generative Grammar and Linguistic Competence*. London: Allen & Unwin.

Mercer, N. (1994) 'Spoken Language in the Classroom'. *ELL*: 4320–4.

Milroy, J. (1978) 'Lexical Alternation and Diffusion in Vernacular Speech'. *Belfast Working Papers in Language and Linguistics* 3: 101–14.

Milroy, J. and Milroy, L. (1978) 'Belfast: Change and Variation in an Urban Vernacular'. In Trudgill (1978: 19–36).

(1985) *Authority in Language. Investigating Language Prescription and Standardisation*. London: Routledge.

Milroy, L. (1980) *Language and Social Networks*. Oxford: Blackwell.

(1987) *Observing and Analysing Natural Language*. Oxford: Blackwell.

Mitchell, A. and Delbridge, A. (1965) *The Speech of Australian Adolescents*. Sydney: Angus & Robertson.

Mitchell, T. (1975) *Principles of Firthian Linguistics*. London: Longman.

Omondi, L. (1976) 'Paralinguistics: A Survey of Non-Verbal Communication'. Mimeo.

Opie, I. and Opie, P. (1959) *The Lore and Language of School-Children*. London: Oxford University Press.

Payne, A. (1980) 'Factors Controlling the Acquisition of the Phildelphia Dialect by Out-of-State Children'. In W. Labov, ed. *Locating Language in Time and Space*. London: Academic Press, 143–78.

Pedersen, E. (1995) 'Language as Context, Language as Means: Spatial Cognition and Habitual Language Use'. *Cognitive Linguistics* 6: 33–62.

Pocheptsov, G. (1994) 'Proxemics'. *ELL*: 3389–90.

Pollard, C. and Sag, I. (1994) *Head-Driven Phrase Structure Grammar*. Stanford: Center for the Study of Language and Information; Chicago: University of Chicago Press.

Pride, J. and Holmes, J., eds. (1972) *Sociolinguistics*. Harmondsworth: Penguin.

Bibliography

Quirk, R., Greenbaum, S., Leech, G. and Svartvik, J. (1985) *A Comprehensive Grammar of the English Language*. London: Longman.

Rampton, B. (1995) *Crossing, Language and Ethnicity Among Adolescents*. London: Longman.

Reid, E. (1978) 'Social and Stylistic Variation in the Speech of Children: Some Evidence from Edinburgh'. In Trudgill (1978: 158–71).

Reisman, K. (1974) 'Contrapuntal Conversations in an Antiguan Village'. In Bauman and Sherzer (1974: 110–24).

Rickford, J. (1988) 'Connections between Sociolinguistics and Pidgin-Creole Studies'. *International Journal of the Sociology of Language* 71: 51–57.

Romaine, S. (1978) 'Postvocalic /r/ in Scottish English: Sound Change in Progress?' In Trudgill (1978: 144–57).

(1980) 'The Relative Clause Marker in Scots English: Diffusion, Complexity and Style as Dimensions of Syntactic Change'. *Language in Society* 9: 221–47.

(1982) *Socio-Historical Linguistics*. Cambridge: Cambridge University Press.

(1984) *The Language of Children and Adolescents: The Acquisition of Communicative Competence*. Oxford: Blackwell.

(1988) *Pidgin and Creole Language*. London: Longman.

(1989) *Bilingualism*. Oxford: Blackwell.

Rosch, E. (1976) 'Classification of Real-World Objects: Origins and Representations in Cognition'. In S. Ehrlich and E. Tulving, eds. *Le Mémoire Sémantique*. Paris: Bulletin de Psychologie; reprinted in P. Johnson-Laird and P. Wason, eds. *Thinking: Readings in Cognitive Science*. Cambridge: Cambridge University Press, 212–22.

Rosenthal, M. (1974) 'The Magic Boxes: Pre-School Children's Attitudes Towards Black and Standard English'. *Florida F. L. Reporter*: 55–93.

Rosenthal, R. and Jacobson, L. (1968) *Pygmalion in the Classroom: Teacher Expectations and Pupils' Intellectual Development*. New York: Holt, Rinehart & Winston.

Sachs, J. and Devin, J. (1976) 'Young Children's use of Age-Appropriate Speech Styles in Social Interaction and Role-Playing'. *Journal of Child Language* 3: 81–98.

Sankoff, G. (1971) 'Quantitative Analysis of Sharing and Variability in a Cognitive Model'. *Ethnology* 10: 389–408.

(1972) 'Language Use in Multilingual Societies: Some Alternative Approaches'. In Pride and Holmes (1972: 33–51).

(1973) 'Dialectology'. *Annual Reviews of Anthropology* 2: 165–77.

(1976) 'Political Power and Linguistic Inequality in Papua New Guinea'. In W. and J. O'Barr, eds. *Language and Politics*. The Hague: Mouton, 283–310.

Sankoff, G. and Brown, P. (1976) 'The Origins of Syntax in Discourse'. *Language* 52: 631–66.

Sapir, E. (1915) 'Abnormal Types of Speech in Nootka'. *Canada Geological Survey Memoir* 62, *Anthropological Series* 5. Ottawa: Government Printing Bureau. Also in Mandelbaum (1949: 179–96).

(1929) 'Male and Female Forms of Speech in Yana'. In S. Teeuwen, ed. *Donum Natalicum Schrijnen*. Nijmegen: Dekker & Van de Vegt, 79–85.

Saussure, F. de (1916/1959) *Course in General Linguistics*. New York: McGraw-Hill.

Schiffrin, D. (1994) *Approaches to Discourse*. Oxford: Blackwell.

Schneiderman, E. (1976) 'An Examination of the Ethnic and Linguistic Attitudes of Bilingual Children'. *ITL Review of Applied Linguistics* 33: 59–72.

Schusky, E. (1994) 'Kinship Terminology'. *ELL*: 1848–52.

Sherzer, J. (1992) 'Ethnography of Speaking'. *IEL* 1: 419–20.

Shibatani, M. (1990) *The Languages of Japan*. Cambridge: Cambridge University Press.

Shuy, R. (1970) 'The Sociolinguists and Urban Language Problems'. In F. Williams, ed. *Language and Poverty: Perspectives on a Theme*. Chicago: Markham, 335–50.

Simpson, S. (1994a) 'Mutual intelligibility'. *ELL*: 2659–60.

(1994b) 'Areal linguistics'. *ELL*: 206–12.

Sinclair, J. and Coulthard, R. M. (1975) *Towards an Analysis of Discourse: The English Used by Teachers and Pupils*. Oxford: Oxford University Press.

Smith, G. (1989) 'Attitudes to Language in a Multilingual Community in East London'. London University dissertation.

Sorensen, A. P. Jr. (1971) 'Multilingualism in the Northwest Amazon'. *American Anthropologist* 69: 670–84; also in Pride and Holmes (1972: 78–94).

Sperber, D. and Wilson, D. (1986) *Relevance: Communication and Cognition*. Oxford: Blackwell.

Stross, B. (1974) 'Speaking of Speaking: Tenejapa Tzeltal Metalinguistics'. In Bauman and Sherzer (1974: 213–39).

Tajfel, H. (1981) 'Social Stereotypes and Social Groups'. In J. Turner and H. Giles, eds. *Intergroup Behaviour*. Oxford: Blackwell, 144–67.

Tannen, D. (1986) *That's not What I Meant! How Conversational Style Makes or Breaks Your Relations with Others*. London: Virago Press.

(1990) *You Just Don't Understand. Women and Men in Conversation*. Virago Press.

Taylor, D. (1951) *The Black Carib of British Honduras*. New York: Wenner-Gren Foundation for Anthropological Research.

Taylor, J. (1989) *Linguistic Categorisation: An Essay in Cognitive Linguistics*. Oxford: Oxford University Press.

Taylor, O. (1973) 'Teachers' Attitudes Toward Black and Nonstandard English as Measured by the Language Attitude Scale'. In Shuy, R. and Fasold, W., eds. *Language Attitudes: Current Trends and Prospects*. Washington: Georgetown University Press, 174–201.

Thompson, S. (1992) 'Functional Grammar'. *IEL* 2: 37–40.

Todd, L. (1994) 'Pidgins and Creoles'. *ELL*: 3177–81.

Trask, L. (1995) 'Basque'. Tutorial at the Spring meeting of the Linguistics Association of Great Britain.

Trudgill, P. (1974) *The Social Differentiation of English in Norwich*. Cambridge: Cambridge University Press.

(1974/1983) *Sociolinguistics*, 2nd edition. Harmondsworth: Penguin.

(1975/1983) 'Linguistic Change and Diffusion: Description and Explanation in Sociolinguistic Dialect Geography'. *Language in Society* 2: 215–46; reprinted in Trudgill (1983a: 52–87).

(1978) *Sociolingustic Patterns in British English*. London: Arnold.

(1983a) *On Dialect*. Oxford: Blackwell.

(1983b) 'Sociolinguistics and Linguistic Theory'. In Trudgill (1983a: 8–30).

(1983c) 'Acts of Conflicting Identity'. In Trudgill (1983a: 141–60).

(1990) *The Dialects of England*. Oxford: Blackwell.

Wakelin, M. (1972) *English Dialects: An introduction*. London: Athlone.

(1978) *Discovering English Dialects*. Aylesbury: Shire.

Wardhaugh, R. (1986) *An Introduction to Sociolinguistics*. Oxford: Blackwell.

Watson, O. and Graves, T. (1966) 'Quantitative research on proxemic behavior'. *American Anthropologist* 68: 971–85.

Weeks, T. (1971) 'Speech Registers in Young Children'. *Child Development* 42: 1119–31.

Weischedel, R. (1994) 'Knowledge Representation for Natural Language Processing'. *ELL*: 1856–62.

Wells, G. (1979a) 'Variation in Child Language'. In P. Fletcher and M. Garman, eds. *Studies in Language Acquisition*. Cambridge: Cambridge University Press: also in V. Lee, ed. *Language Development*. London: Croom Helm, 382–409.

(1979b) 'Language Development in Pre-School Children'. Final report to Social Sciences Research Council, unpublished.

(1981a) *Learning through Interaction. The Study of Language Development*. Cambridge: Cambridge University Press.

(1981b) 'Some Antecedents of Early Educational Attainment'. *British Journal of Sociology of Education* 2: 181–200.

Wells, J. (1982) *English Accents*, 3 volumes. Cambridge: Cambridge University Press.

Wetzel, P. (1994) 'Contemporary Japanese Attitudes towards Honorifics (*keigo*)'. *Language Variation and Change* 6: 113–47.

Whiten, A. (1994) 'Primate Communication'. *ELL*: 3327–32.

Whorf, B. (1940) 'Science and Linguistics'. *Technological Review* 42: 229–31. Reprinted in Carroll (1956: 207–19).

Wierzbicka, A. (1980) *Lingua Mentalis. The Semantics of Natural Language*. London: Academic Press.

Williams, F. (1973) 'Some Research Notes on Dialect Attitudes and Stereotypes'. In Shuy, R. and Fasold, W., eds. *Language Attitudes: Current Trends and Prospects*. Washington: Georgetown University Press, 113–28.

Williams, S., Savage-Rumbaugh, S. and Rumbaugh, D. (1994) 'Apes and Language'. *ELL*: 139–46.

Zimmerman, D. and West, C. (1975) 'Sex Roles, Interruptions and Silences in Conversation'. In B. Thorne et al., eds. *Language, Gender and Society*. Rowley: Newbury House.

INDEX

(a), Belfast, 175, 197
(a:), Norwich, 166, 174
Abd-el-Jawad, 194
abercrombie, 137
Abipon, 120
Abu-Haidar, 194
academic language, 223–4
accent, 42–3, 219; *see also*
    pronunciation
accommodation, 68, 164–6, 200, 232–4,
    239–40
acrolect, 64
act of communication, 46–7
act of identity, 12, 40, 43, 46, 68, 120,
    184, 207, 239–40; *see also* space,
    multidimensional
address terms, 114
addressee, 253, 255–6; *see also*
    classification of addressee
adjacency-pair, 134
adolescents, 14–6
age-differences; *see also* generation
    differences
age-grading, 15
Aitchison, 60, 64, 66
Allan, 40
Amazon, 7–9
America
    see United States of America
analogue/digital, 241
Andersen, 17
Anderson, 14
anthropology, 70–2, 76, 79, 85–8, 97,
    108, 167
Antigua, 117–19, 141
Apache, 133–4, 225
Apte, 14
Arab, 137
Arabic, 49–50, 194

Ardehali, 104
areal feature, 44, 58
Argentina, 120
Argyle, 108, 112, 134, 139
artificial auxiliary languages, 59
artificial intelligence, 108
attention
    see formal/informal
attitudes 224; *see also* evaluation of
    language; face; prestige;
    stereotypes; self-evaluation
audience-design, 200
Austin, 109
Australia, 87, 93, 189

baby-talk, 14
Bainbridge, 121
Balkans, 44
Ball, 172
Bantu, 58–9
Barrett, 80
basic-level concepts, 88–90, 92
basilect, 64–5
Basque, 131
Basso, 133
Belazi, 55
Belfast, 13, 163–4, 182–3, 197, 234–5
Bell, 200
'Belten High', 166–9
Bereiter, 221
Berko Gleason, 17
Berlin, 89
Bernstein, 222
Besnier, 117–18
Biber, 45, 201
Bickerton, 65–6
bilingualism
    see multilingualism

Black American English, 15, 64, 181–2, 185–6, 215, 218
Blake, 55
Bloomfield, 24, 38, 58
Blom, 53
Bolinger, 26, 39
Boltanski, 16
borrowing, 55–9, 63
Bourdieu, 16
Bradac, 212
Brazil, 7
Bristol, 222
Brown, 67, 88, 122, 124, 126–7
Buang, 54, 62, 67, 210
Burling, 16, 85, 87
Burnouts, 166–9, 180
Burridge, 115
Bynon, 37, 39, 58, 156
Byrd, 198

Cairns, 219
calque
    see loan translation
Campbell, 224
Canada, 121–2, 218
Cardiff, 164–6
Carroll, 95, 98
Casad, 83
Casagrande, 98
caste, 44, 52
casual speech, 163; *see also* formal/ informal
categorical
    see probabilistic/categorical links
Cazden, 92
Chambers, 14–16, 38, 194–5
change
    see language change
channel cues, 160
Cheshire, 45
children, language of, 5, 12, 14–17, 76–7, 92–5, 98–9, 141, 232–4; *see also* incompetence, linguistic
children, prejudices of, 217–20
chimpanzee
    see primate
Chinese, 35, 126, 129, 194
Choi, 55
Chomsky, 3, 66, 145–6, 220, 224, 229, 234, 245, 254–5
circumstances
    see situation

Clark, 74, 76, 80, 88, 89, 90, 92
classical theory of concepts, 74–5
classification of addressee, 120–34, 232
classification of speaker, 120–34, 184–99, 231–4; *see also* acts of identity; speaker
classification of speech, 109–11
classroom language, 226–7
Clyne, 55
code-crossing, 239–40
code-mixing, 44, 53–5, 58
code-switching, 51–3, 239
Cognitive Grammar, 255–6
cognitive linguistics, 70, 104
Colombia, 7
common-sense knowledge, 21–2, 72
communicative approaches to language teaching, 225
communicative competence/ incompetence, 224–7
communicative inequality
    see inequality, communicative
community
    see speech community
community grammar, 28, 229
competence, communicative
    see communicative competence/ incompetence
competence, linguistic, 220, 245
component, semantic, 82
compound pronoun, 171, 201
concept, 9, 72–105
conformity, 12–14, 190–3, 232–3; *see also* accommodation
construction, 21–2, 44, 54, 65, 83; *see also* syntax
conversation analysis, 134
Cooper, 220
Cora, 84–4, 97
corpus linguistics, 201
Coulthard, 117, 135
Coupland, 164–6
covert prestige
    see overt/covert prestige
creativity, 77, 88
creole, 15, 18, 63–8, 239
creolisation, 63–4
Crockett, 150
Crystal, 37, 59
culture, 6, 9, 31, 70–2, 79–91, 105
Curtiss, 246

de Saussure, 12, 106, 116, 119, 244
Dean, 139
decreolisation, 64–6
deficit theory, 221–2
degree of group-members
  see group-membership, degree of
degree of relationship 241–3, 249–52,
  256; *see also* entrenchment; group-
  membership, degree of
dietic meaning, 107, 247–8
Delbridge, 189
Denison, 52
Denmark, 117
descriptive/prescriptive, 203–5
determinism, linguistic, 91–105
Detroit, 166–9
Devin, 17
di Sciullo, 55
dialect, 23, 30–4, 37–45, 236; *see also*
  variety of language
dialect geography, 38
dialectology, 38–9, 146–7
diffusion, 39–41, 63
diffusion/focussing
  see focusing
digital
  see analogue/digital
diglossia, 49–51, 53, 56, 194, 224
Dillard, 15
discourse, 7, 134–6, 172
distinctiveness view, 249–52
distribution, social, 22, 147, 236
Dixon, 110
domain, 77–8, 81
Dorian, 193, 233, 236
Downes, 45
Duriez, 219
Dutch, 61

(e), 187–8
Eckert, 166–9
Edinburgh, 176–7
education as a social variable
  see social class
educational problems
  see schools
Edwards, 171, 201, 216, 221–2, 226
Eibl-Eibesfeld, 138
emotion, expression of, 13
encyclopedic knowledge, 136
entrenchment, 256; *see also* degree of
  relationship

equality
  see inequality
equivalence rule, 86
Ekman, 138
elaborated
  see restricted/elaborated codes
Esperanto, 59
ethnography of speaking or
  communication, 108, 167–9
ethology, 108
euphemism, 115
evaluation of language, 209–11
experience, 11, 36, 73–4
eye-contact, 115, 134, 138–9

face, 113–16, 124, 132, 230, 239
face-to-face interaction, 106, 234
face-work
  see face
family tree model, 36–8, 58–9
farewells
  see greetings/farewells
Farsi, 104, 129, 178–9, 183–4, 187,
  193–6
Fasold, 4, 77, 171, 187, 240, 253
Ferguson, 49–50, 133
Firth, 3
Fischer, 150
Fishman, 50, 77
fluency, 217
focusing, 13, 193, 236
Ford, 122, 126
formal/informal, 6, 47, 160, 199–201
formalism, 234
Fowler, 158–9
Fox, 117
French, 31, 34, 56, 58, 60, 81–2, 107,
  123, 194, 218, 254
frequency, 144–202
Friesen, 138
functionalism, 233–4

Gaelic, 193, 233
Gardener, 116
Garo, 16
Garvin, 32
Gauchat, 149
Geertz, 131
generation differences, 125, 156–7, 184,
  191
generative phonology, 253
genetics

genetics (*continued*)
    see innateness
German, 42, 58, 60, 82, 90, 119, 254
Gibbons, 4
Giddens, 114–5, 138
Giles, 17, 164, 211–12, 214, 216–20
Gilman, 122, 124
Glasgow, 210
Goffman, 113, 116, 132–3
Goodenough, 71, 79
Goodman, 58
Graddol, 102, 104, 121, 195
grammar 21–22, 129–30; *see also*
    Cognitive Grammar; Head-driven
    Phrase-Structure Grammar;
    Principles-and-Parameters Theory;
    Transformational Grammar; Word
    Grammar
grammar, community *see* community
    grammar
grammar, transformational
    see Transformational Grammar
Greek, 31–2, 49, 56
greetings/farewells, 6, 114, 132–4, 138–
    9, 170, 247
Grice, 118
group-membership, degree of 185–6,
    190–3, 241–3; *see also* Burnouts;
    networks, social
Guaraní, 50
Gumperz, 25, 44–5, 50, 53
Guy 29, 253–4, 256
Guyana, 65

(h), 145, 148, 151, 173–4, 249–52
Haeri, 194
Haiti, 49
Halliday, 3, 17, 25, 46
Harris, 83
Haugen, 31–4
Hawkins, 90
Head-driven Phrase Structure
    Grammar, 255
Heath, 55, 226
Hebrew, 33
Hill, 97
Hirschman, 142
Hockett, 24, 38
Holm, 60
Holmes, 195
honorific form, 128, 130
Horvath, 189

Howatt, 225
Hudson, 49, 76, 79, 91, 127, 129, 171,
    230, 245, 247, 254–7
Hymes, 25, 46, 108, 116, 120, 224
hypercorrection
    see overcorrection

Iban, 126
idiolect
    see individuals
illocutionary force, 111
implicational hierarchy, 183
incompetence, communicative, 224–7
incompetence, linguistic, 220–4
India, 16, 44–5, 52, 93, 116, 126, 139,
    244
individualism, 12–14, 106
indirectness, 124
individuals, 10–14, 29–30, 38–9, 71–2,
    173, 193, 228–30, 237
Indo-European, 37, 44
Indonesia, 117
inequality, communicative, 206
inequality, social, 48, 50, 102–4, 112,
    203–27; *see also* sex differences;
    sexism in language; socio-economic
    status
inequality, strictly linguistic 205–6; *see
    also* incompetence, linguistic
inequality, subjective, 205–20
inference, 72, 80–1
(ing), 150, 161–2, 165, 187, 249–52
innateness, 66–7, 73–4, 78, 115, 138
intelligibility, mutual, 34–6, 50
interruptions, 118
interviews
    see structured interviews
Iran
    see Farsi
Ireland, 219
Irish English, 83, 97, 189; *see also*
    Belfast
Irvine, 139
(is), 181–2, 185–6
Island Carib, 121
isogloss, 38–9, 147
Israel, 256
Italy, 52, 224
item, linguistic
    see linguistic item
item of vocabulary
    see lexical item

Jackendoff, 76
Jackson, 6
Jacobson, 217
Jahangiri, 129, 178–9, 184, 194–5
James, 195
Japanese, 121, 126, 128–31, 149–50, 247
Jassem, 194
Javanese, 131–2
Jocks
  see Burnouts

Keenan, 118
Kemmer, 256
Kempson, 82
Kendon, 112, 139
Kenya, 124–5
Key, 115, 119
Kindaichi, 149
kinship terms, 85–8
Kiparsky, 244
knowledge 71–2, 79, 105; *see also*
  common-sense knowledge;
  competence, linguistic;
  competence, communicative;
  encyclopedic knowledge; networks,
  cognitive; thought
Knowles, 152, 174
Koasati, 121
Kroch, 254–6

Labov, 3, 25, 27, 28–30, 54, 75, 104, 136,
  145–6, 149–50, 155–9, 172, 181–7,
  194, 199, 204, 210, 212, 214, 221,
  232, 234, 240, 253
Lakoff, 70, 76, 80
Lambert, 212–13
Langacker, 70, 83, 255–6
language change, 5, 36–41, 64–5, 124,
  145, 156, 194, 254–5; *see also* family
  tree model; lexical diffusion; wave
  theory
language, definition, 1, 22, 107, 228–9
languages, 23, 30–8, 61–2, 95, 236; *see*
  also variety of language
Larvik, 185
Latin, 37, 56, 124
Lawton, 222
Le Page, 12, 13, 26, 68, 193, 236
Lepschy, 244
levels of language, 70
Levine, 150
Levinson, 80, 124, 126–7, 224

lexeme
  see lexical item
lexical gap, 92
lexical item, 20–2, 38–9, 182–3; *see also*
  vocabulary
lexical diffusion, 182–4
lexical phonology, 253–4
lexical variable, 171
lexicon, 21
Linde, 136
Linggi, 126
Lingua Franca
  see trade language
linguistic community
  see speech community
linguistic context, influence of, 181–4
linguistic inequality
  see inequality, strictly linguistic
linguistic insecurity, 210–1
linguistic item, 21, 43–5, 48–9, 65–6,
  79–80, 205–6, 228–30, 236
linguistic variable
  see variable, linguistic
linguistics, definition, 3–4, 18, 243
linguistics, structural, 3
literature, 31, 33
Littlewood, 225
loan translation, 58
loan-word
  see borrowing
Local, 218
London, 213
Lounsbury, 85
Lucy, 95, 98–9
Lyons, 24, 82

Macaulay, 33, 210
McCormick, 51, 102, 121, 141–2
McGivney, 124
Maclaren, 182
Maclure, 222, 226
McNeil, 140
Madagascar, 118–19
Malaysia, 126
male/female differences
  see sex differences
Malinowski, 109
Mandelbaum, 95
map, mental
  see space, multidimensional
Martha's Vineyard, 150, 155
matched-guise technique, 213

Index

Mason, 223
Mathiot, 32
Matthews, 36
Mayan, 93, 99, 111
Mbugu, 58
meaning, 6, 9, 80, 93, 104–5, 230
memory, 72
mental model
see space, multidimensional
Mercer, 226
mesolect, 64–6
metaphorical code-switching, 53, 81
methods of research, 71–2, 74, 76, 94,
    97–101, 108, 146–8, 150–69, 203–4,
    212–30
Mexico, 83, 93, 99–101, 111
Mijikenda, 124–5
Milroy, 33, 83, 146, 150, 163–4, 171,
    174–5, 182–3, 189–93, 195, 197,
    200, 204, 234–5
Mitchell, 126, 189
modularity, 245
moiety, 87
morphological variables, 170–1
morphology, 12, 43, 56, 58, 61, 120–1,
    253–4
mother tongue, 7, 66
motivation, 35–6, 113–16, 119–20
multilingualism, 4, 8–9, 16, 24–5, 44–5,
    48, 51–5, 77–8, 223, 236
names, 107, 114, 122–3, 126–7, 129, 242
Navajo, 98–9
negation, variation in
see (no/any)
negative face
see power-face
Neo-Melanesian Pidgin
see Tok Pisin
network strength, 190–2
networks, cognitive, 79, 256
networks, social, 29, 163–4, 168–9, 180,
    190–3, 197, 234–7; see also group-
    membership, degree of
New Guinea
see Papual New Guinea
New York City, 28, 41, 54, 126, 155–9,
    185–7, 209–10, 214
Nigeria, 18, 65
Njamal, 87
(no/any), 145, 148–9
non-standard language
see standard language

non-verbal communication, 115, 119,
    137–40, 231; see also eye-contact;
    proxemics
Nootka, 121
norms of speech
see speech, rules/norms of
North Africa, 126
Norway, 33, 35, 53
Norwich, 28, 149, 159–62, 166, 170, 174,
    187, 196, 236, 248–52
notation, 148, 238
NSS
see network strength
number, 99–101, 140
observation
see rapid anonymous observation;
    participant observation
Omondi, 140
Opie, 15
(ou), 248–52
overcorrection, 173
overt prestige, 211, 240

Panini, 244
Papua New Guinea, 54, 61–2, 138, 210
Paraguay, 50
passive, 172
Payne, 232
Pedersen, 93–4
peer-group, 15, 185
percept, 79
performative utterance, 109
perlocutionary force, 110–11
Persian
see Farsi
Phatic communion, 109
Philadelphia, 30, 232–3
philosophy, 108
phonetic variables, 170
phonological variables, 170
phonology
see lexical phonology; generative
    phonology
phratry, 7
pidgin, 59–63, 67–8
Pidgin, Nigerian, 18, 65
place, 184–5; see also dialect geography
Pocheptsov, 137
Polish, 126
politeness, 114–16, 247
Pollard, 255
pop songs 239

Portuguese, 61–2
positive face
    see solidarity-face
post-creole continuum, 64–5
power, 46, 122–33, 137–8, 141, 196,
    240–1, 255
power-face, 114–16
power-politeness, 114–16
Powesland, 17, 211–12, 214, 216–19
pragmatics, 80–1, 118, 224
prejudice, 16–17, 204, 206–20
prescriptive
    see descriptive/prescriptive
prestige, 32, 64; *see also* overt/covert
    prestige; social class
Principles-and-Parameters Theory,
    254–5
primates, 115, 138, 140
probabilistic/categorical links 202; *see*
    also degree of relationship
pronoun, 121, 123, 129, 255; *see also*
    compound pronoun; sex-neutral
    pronoun
pronunciation, 21, 33, 45, 156, 173; *see*
    also accent; phonetic variable;
    phonological variable
proper noun
    see name
proposition, 72–105
prototype, 26, 75–8, 85–9, 103–5, 122,
    125, 195, 207–8, 231, 238, 256; *see*
    also social stereotype
proxemics, 137
psycholinguistics, 172
psychology, 72–8, 97–101, 108, 207; *see*
    also prototype
Puliya, 116
putting on an accent, 239–40

Quirk, 204
question, 226–7

(r), 150, 155–9, 169, 176, 187, 209, 214
race, 184–7
Rampton, 239–40
rapid anonymous observation, 155–9
reading, 161–2, 200; *see also* reading;
    style
Received Pronunciation, 39, 42, 156,
    161, 214
referring, 126–9
region of origin

    see place
register, 23, 45–51, 56, 67, 171, 200; *see*
    also style; writing
Reisman, 117
relative clause, 67, 172
relativity, 81–91, 139; *see also* universals
replication, 158–9
restricted/elaborated codes, 222
Rickford, 257
Romaine, 16, 51, 172, 176, 221, 226
Romany, 13
root verb, 247; *see also* verb form
Rosch, 75–6, 88, 90
Rosenthal, 217
Roti, 117
RP
    see Received Pronunciation
rules of speech
    see speech, rules/norms of

Sachs, 17
Sag, 255
Saks, 136
Sankoff, 39, 54, 67, 72, 146, 210
Sapir, 95, 120–2
Sapir-Whorf Hypothesis, 91, 95–105
Scandinavia, 35
Schiffrin, 108–9, 134
Schneiderman, 218
schools, 64, 204–5, 211, 215–27; *see also*
    classroom language
Schusky, 85
scores for speakers, 177–81
scores for texts, 175–7
Scotland, 193, 233; *see also* Edinburgh,
    Glasgow
second-language teaching, 225
self-evaluation, 209–10
self-report, 196
semantic relativity
    see relativity
semantics
    see meaning; situation semantics
Senegal, 139
sex differences, 15, 120–1, 140–3, 149–
    50, 178–9, 184, 191; *see also* sex-
    prestige pattern
sex-neutral pronoun, 91, 103–4
sex-prestige pattern, 193–9
sexism in language, 102–5
Shakespeare, 104
Sherzer, 108

Shibatani, 121, 129–30, 149
Shuy, 218
silence, 225
Simpson, 34, 40, 44
Sinclair, 135
situation, 6, 45, 52–3, 77–8, 160, 177–8, 199–201, 221–2, 256; *see also* register; speech-event
situation semantics, 255
slang, teenage, 15
slaves, 62
Smith, 213, 243
social class, 42, 149–50, 156–8, 161, 165, 168–9, 178–9, 184, 240, 248–52; *see also* inequality, social
social constraints on speech
see speech, rules/norms of
social dialect, 42, 51
social distinctiveness, 249–52
social distribution
see distribution, social
social functions of language, 230–57
social inequality
see inequality, social
social information, 230
social interaction, 108, 115
social stereotype, 208, 211–16; *see also* social type
social structures, 166–9; *see also* networks, social
social type, 168–9, 237–40, 242–3, 248–52; *see also* social stereotype
social type allegiance, 248–52
socialisation, 92–5, 106–7, 120
socio-economic status, 186–9; *see also* inequality, social; social class
sociolect
see social dialect
sociolinguistic competence, 230
sociolinguistics, definition, 1–4, 18, 48
sociology, 113–14
sociology of language, 4, 32–4, 78
solidarity, 46–7, 122–33, 137–8, 141, 232–40, 255
solidarity-face, 114–16, 137–8, 165–6
solidarity-politeness, 114–16
sophistication, 198–9, 250–2
Sorensen, 6
sounds
see pronunciation

space, multidimensional, 11–12, 26, 81, 147, 187, 239–40; *see also* acts of identity
Spanish, 50, 54, 99, 126, 194, 224
speaker, 48, 77–8, 84, 253, 255–6; *see also* classification of speaker; scores for speakers
speech, 1, 106–43
speech community, 24–30, 151, 229
speech-act, 109–11, 224
speech-event, 107, 224; *see also* situation
speech, rules/norms of, 107–9, 112–20, 225
speed of speech, 198
spelling, 56
Sperber, 80, 118, 224
standard deviation, 178–9
standard language, 13, 16, 32–4, 43, 47–51, 67, 151, 161, 203–5, 215, 217, 223, 240; *see also* prestige; sex-prestige pattern
statistical significance, 153–4
status
see prestige; social class
stereotype, 198; *see also* prototype; social stereotype
Stross, 111
structural competence, 230
Structuralism, 244
structured interviews, 159–63
student, 241–2
style, 23, 131, 172, 199–201, 256; *see also* formal/informal
subjective inequality
see inequality, subjective
subjective reaction test, 212–16; *see also* self-evaluation
subject-verb agreement, 170
Swann, 102, 104, 121
swearing, 13–14, 115
Switzerland, 49, 149
symbolic value of language, 52–3, 55
synonyms, 171, 201
syntactic pattern
see construction
syntactic variable, 171–2
syntax, 43–5, 54–5, 58, 61, 247, 254–5; *see also* grammar

(t), 162, 166, 170, 179–80, 248–52
Tabouret Keller, 12, 13, 26, 68, 236
Tajfel, 208

Tamil, 93
Tannen, 141–2
Tanzania, 58
tape-recorder, 150, 152
Taylor, 70, 121, 216
t/d loss, 253–4, 256
teaching
　see schools
Teheran
　see Farsi
text-scores
　see scores for texts
(th), 187
theories, 228–57
Thompson, 234
thought, 72–81; *see also* knowledge
Todd, 18, 61, 63, 65
topic, 134–6
Tok Pisin, 54, 61–2, 66–8
Tokyo, 149
trade language, 7, 60, 62
Transformational Grammar, 3, 253
Trask, 131
Trudgill, 4, 14, 28, 38–9, 40, 43, 121, 144,
　149, 159–62, 166, 170, 174, 185,
　187–8, 195–6, 211, 236, 239, 248–52
Tukano, 7–9, 60
turn-taking, 134
type, social
　see social type
typology, sociolinguistic, 51
Tzeltal, 111
Tzotzil, 93–4

United States of America, 42–3, 117,
　119, 137, 150, 226–7; *see also* black
　American English; Detroit; New
　York City; Philadelphia
universals, 124–7, 132, 138, 140; *see also*
　relativity; sex-prestige pattern

value-judgements, 207–8

variability
　see variation
variable, linguistic, 146–202
variable rule, 253
variant, 146–202
variation, 12–14, 18–19, 242; *see also*
　variable, linguistic
variety of language, 22–4, 38–9, 68–9,
　229, 236–7
verb-form, 255; *see also* root verb
vernacular, 49
vocabulary, 43, 45, 131, 246; *see also*
　lexical item
vocative, 127–9

Wakelin, 22, 39
Wales, 219; *see also* Cardiff
Wales, R., 224
Watson, 137
wave theory, 38, 39–41, 183–5, 236
Weeks, 17
Weischedel, 79
Wells, 42, 222–3
West, 142
West Indian English, 64
Westgate, 226
Wetzel, 130
Whiten, 115, 138
Whorf, 139
Wierzbicka, 82
Williams, 115, 215
Wilson, 44–5, 80, 118, 224
Wolof, 139
women
　see sex differences
word-formation, 88
Word Grammar, 238, 256–7
writing, 32, 200–1

Yana, 120

Zimmerman, 142